Studies in European Economic Law and Regulation

Volume 23

The series "Studies in European Economic Law and Regulation" is devoted to the analysis of European Economic Law. The series' scope covers a broad range of topics within economics law including, but not limited to, the relationship between EU law and WTO law; free movement under EU law and its impact on fundamental rights; antitrust law; trade law; unfair competition law; financial market law; consumer law; food law; and health law. These subjects are approached both from doctrinal and interdisciplinary perspectives.

The series accepts monographs focusing on a specific topic, as well as edited collections of articles covering a specific theme or collections of articles. All contributions are subject to rigorous double-blind peer-review.

Pamela Finckenberg-Broman

Weaponizing EU State Aid Law to Impact the Future of EU Investment Policy in the Global Context

Springer

Pamela Finckenberg-Broman
Griffith University' LFC
Gold Coast, QLD, Australia

ISSN 2214-2037 ISSN 2214-2045 (electronic)
Studies in European Economic Law and Regulation
ISBN 978-3-031-10107-6 ISBN 978-3-031-10108-3 (eBook)
https://doi.org/10.1007/978-3-031-10108-3

This Springer imprint is published by the registered company Springer Nature Switzerland AG
The registered company address is: Gewerbestrasse 11, 6330 Cham, Switzerland

Foreword

EU State Aid Law as a Policy Tool for Tame Investment Protection

Investment protection has been a hotly debated topic in international economic law. For some it is perceived as a condicio sine qua non to facilitate investments in trade, and for harvesting the benefits connected to it. For others, investment protection is a vehicle of capitalism which deprives vulnerable groups of their rights and privileges and needs to be tamed. This work can be localised in the middle of these two camps, probably leaning a bit more to the latter side. If investment protection needs taming, why not by the rules of EU state aid law? And if so, how does this relate to the specific rationale to the legal system of EU state aids?

The author starts in Chap. 1 with providing the reader with an overview of investment protection schemes from the perspective of EU law. Investor State Dispute Settlement (ISDS) systems, which are at the heart of global investment protection regimes, sit uneasy with EU state aid law. Likewise, she investigates whether Bilateral Investment Treaties (BITs) as a major substantive regulative tool shall be replaced by Free Trade Agreements. She hence covers an assessment of the two major regulative tools of investment protection regimes: ISDS and BITs. Thereby, she sets the general framework for the assessment to come. In Chap. 2, the author investigates the parallel development of FDI and WTO and EU competition policy, substantiating the major argument that state aid law can be used as a tool to control investment protection policy from a theoretical perspective. In Chap. 3, she builds upon these insights, providing an in-depth analysis of EU state aid laws through the lens of assessing its suitability as a policy tool to tame investment protection. She devotes Chap. 5 to exemplifying these insights looking on the example of the Court proceedings concerning the Micula Award. She does not stop at a mere analysis of the decision, but rather excellently puts it into the bigger context by using the thorny dilemma as an analytical framework. Chapters 6 and 7 concern the illustration of the dilemma identified before, presenting likewise potential solutions to solve the conflict between the two regimes which seem to have divergent rationales. She summarises this book by presenting three clear arguments concerning the future of BITs and ISDS under the scrutiny of EU state aid law.

The book covers an area which has so far not been subject to intensive research on the borderline of EU competition law, external relations, and international economic law. The author took on this difficult task and presented a book covering the question from many angles, starting from a broad introduction to specific application soundly embedded in economic theory.

I am happy to have the opportunity to welcome this new addition to our series.

University of Bayreuth, Bayreuth,
Germany
May 2022

Kai P. Purnhagen

Foreword

This monograph, derived from the Ph.D. thesis of Dr Pamela Finckenberg-Broman, constitutes an original contribution to this topical issue of the effects of state aid law on the future of EU investment policy in a global context. I was very glad to act as an examiner of this Ph.D. thesis, which was submitted to Griffith University, Queensland, Australia. The main research question, 'How does EU state aid law affect the future of EU investment policy in a global context?' is certainly an original one. This monograph provides a comprehensive and in-depth analysis of this topic by articulating and underpinning some original arguments and proposals. It is of great interest because it covers a very topical and evolving area of EU law and international investment law. The detailed examination of how the policy of EU state aid practice collaborates with the EU investment regime within the internal market, and from there reflects on the external trade relations of the Member States and the EU through this practice, constitutes the original contribution of this monograph. More specifically, its originality lies in the exhaustive examination of the interplay of state aid rules and EU investment policy internally and externally, either within the EU or on a global level. This dual approach—that is, within the EU and on a global level—is a distinctive characteristic of this monograph. The analysis of both the internal and external dimension is probably its biggest advantage. This cumulative research on both the internal and external dimension widens the scope of this research and results in some very interesting overarching conclusions. Dr Finckenberg-Broman demonstrates impressive critical thinking, expresses her personal view on the matter, and analyses and judges the previous bibliographical materials. Her critical comments are very interesting. Her in-depth knowledge of the international bibliography assists her in commenting successfully on various issues of the effects of state aid law on the future of EU investment policy in a global context.

Apart from the general research question, the originality of this monograph is proved by the more specialised research questions answered by each chapter. Chapter 2 answers the questions 'What drives and shapes international subsidy control and investment law?' and 'How do these interact and what are the inherent tensions?' Chapter 3 responds to the question 'What are the dimensions of law, policy, and institutions of state aid?' Chapter 4 identifies and scrutinises the problems deriving from the *Micula Award* and intra-EU BITs. Chapter 5 answers the question of 'How and why do the EU's procedural and substantial rules collide with ISDS?' I stress that Chap. 4 on the *Micula Award* and Chap. 5 are particularly remarkable. Chapter 6 answers the question 'How is EU law going (from regional) international (to global)?' by examining the EU's multilateral agreements, plurilateral agreements, and bilateral agreements. Chapter 7 analyses the dilemma of extra-EU BITs 'adjusting to a new reality or being phased out'. It asks, 'Is there really a problem? And if yes, can this problem be solved?' Chapters 6 and 7 indisputably contain some original thoughts. All these more specialised questions answered by individual chapters are characterised by coherency and evolve from the main research question, 'How does the EU state aid law affect the future of EU investment policy in a global context?' Actually, all these more specialised research questions facilitate the answer to the main research question, making it easy for the reader to follow her original arguments and contribute to the overall coherency, clarity, and succinctness of this monograph.

This monograph constitutes a contribution to the scientific research of the issue in question. It considers a topical issue of EU and international law. It is a contribution to the ongoing debate on the effects of state aid law on the future of EU investment policy in a global context. It should be stressed that this monograph is absolutely important. Dr Finckenberg-Broman develops this topic comprehensively and discovers new intricacies of this area of law. This monograph would definitely attract the interest of academics, practitioners, and policy makers at the EU and global level.

Dr Finckenberg-Broman covers all issues of this complex topic. She manages to identify and develop sufficiently all the crucial problems of this topic and, on the basis of this, to express some original thoughts. At the end, she reaches some excellent conclusions. She takes into account views expressed in the relevant international bibliography and identifies the crucial problems arising from the interplay of state aid rules and EU investment policy internally and externally. Her comprehensive analysis covers all aspects of the effects of state aid law on the future of EU investment policy in a global context. The categories of literature with emphasis on legal literature, which have been used for the analysis of the subject of this monograph, are more than satisfactory and sufficient.

After a detailed literature review, Dr Finckenberg-Broman proceeds to an original and detailed analysis of her answer to the research question by reaching three main arguments. Her arguments are presented in a clear, succinct, and precise way. She underpins successfully and convincingly these three main arguments analysing how EU state aid law is affecting the future of EU investment policy in a global context. First, Dr Finckenberg-Broman argues that state aid law applies to the EU's incorporation of clauses promoting fair competition and state aid policy in international trade agreements. Second, she argues that state aid law and policy has contributed to recent EU internal development, which led the EU Member States to terminate their bilateral agreements with each other (intra-EU BITs) by the end of 2019. Third, she argues that the EU has been working towards replacing the existing BITs between the EU's Member States and third countries (extra-EU BITs) with the EU's own trade agreements, which are aligned with EU legislation. This argumentation is based on solid and satisfactory justification. The debate on who gets to decide on the scope of state aid law now and in the future is one of the most remarkable parts of this monograph. This debate on competence is one of the most interesting parts of this monograph as it sheds light on a question with great potential and, more specifically, on which body delineates the scope of state aid law and policy with regard to investment protection. I am sure that this detailed analysis of this competence issue is crucial for future developments and will be taken into account by future similar discussions in bibliography, case law, and policy documents. The analysis of case law and the various analogies and conclusions inferred from it constitute a strength of this monograph.

Every chapter develops its primary theme clearly and in depth by exhaustive reference to the relevant bibliography and by the expression of original arguments and ideas. Chapter 1 is an introductory one setting the scene of this research. Chapter 2 examines the development and rationale of trade agreements, subsidies control, and investment law and discusses their parallels, interlinkage, and conflicts. Chapter 3 has a legal, policy, and institutional analysis of what state aid is. Chapter 4 focuses on a case study of giving power to EU and various intricacies deriving from this issue. Chapter 5 examines the procedural differences between International Investment Law and EU law through a state aid lens and scrutinises how elements in BITs eventually threaten to erode EU's procedural autonomy and the right to regulate. It also discusses EU's sui generis nature and how this translates to the legal aspects behind investment protection and state aid. Chapter 6 analyses how EU translates into international dimensions by using trade instruments to structure and to confirm that argument. Chapter 7 examines the clash between bilateral agreements in international conflict tribunal and EU law (going outside the EU for enforcement). Chapter 8 provides a summary, an overview of the previous analysis, and some very interesting and challenging concluding remarks about the central topic of this monograph on the effect of EU state aid law on EU investment policy.

Although Dr Finckenberg-Broman touches many different aspects of EU state aid law, the cohesion of the book remains solid, as all these aspects are evolving around the subject matter of the interplay of state aid rules and EU investment policy internally and externally, either within the EU or on a global level. She scrutinises succinctly the crucial elements of these areas of state aid law without expanding into superfluous issues and without deviating from its goal, which is the analysis of the effects of state aid law on the future of EU investment policy in a global context. The cohesion of this monograph is strengthened by the fact that the three main arguments mentioned above are intertwined on such a common basis.

The application of a doctrinal approach by Dr Finckenberg-Broman is excellent. This doctrinal approach is based on an analysis and discussion of legal provisions, texts of international agreements, opinio juris, case law, and literature on the subject where relevant. She also takes into account practical implications of law by scrutinising the combination of concepts, considerations, and actions of states and their institutions, and their interaction with international institutions, such as the EU. It is remarkable that this monograph scrutinises this topic in the light of EU law and international law through an analysis of the interaction of the EU's trade, state aid, and investment policy. This combined analysis of two different areas of law, EU law and international law, results in some very interesting conclusions. She extensively scrutinises various EU and international law materials. This doctrinal approach affects also the audience that could be interested in this monograph, which is addressed to a wider audience at the global level because of its focus on EU's interactions with other international organisations. This doctrinal approach is excellent and assists Dr Finckenberg-Broman in structuring and underpinning her arguments in a concrete manner. This doctrinal approach is certainly one of the major advantages of this monograph. Moreover, this doctrinal approach scrutinises thoroughly the roles and the interaction of the legislative (European Parliament and Council), judicial (CJEU), and enforcement (Commission) organs of the EU in this content. The approach that she follows towards the analysis of the *Micula Award* by adapting to any situation, including an extra-EU BIT and BITs or by drawing analogies to FTAs concluded between the EU and a third country is really impressive.

This is undoubtedly a well-documented monograph. The thorough study of bibliographical materials sharpened Dr Finckenberg-Broman's critical ability and resulted in some original and remarkable arguments. Additionally, this thorough study of international bibliography made her capable of scrutinising carefully these topical issues and of commenting extensively on them. At the end of each chapter, there is an impressive bibliography of EU and international case law and of EU, international and domestic legislative and policy documents, which Dr Finckenberg-Broman considered carefully. There are also four Appendixes at the end of the monograph: Appendix 1: The EU's BITs, TIPs, and IPAs with countries (state of play, October 2018), Appendix 2: EU's BITs, TIPs, and IPAs with trading blocs (state of play in October 2018), Appendix 3: Micula case timeline, and Appendix 4: Map of EU's free trade agreements in 2018.

This monograph offers a wide scope by examining both EU investment policy internally and externally in the context of EU state aid rules, but Dr Finckenberg-Broman manages to scrutinise comprehensively all available EU and international bibliographical materials and to justify her arguments. The need to discuss the topic internally and externally was a quite challenging task, which she fulfilled successfully. Dr Finckenberg-Broman considers carefully all relevant EU and international legislative, jurisprudential, and policy materials. This latter issue is quite important as EU and international legislative, jurisprudential, and policy materials play a crucial role in this area of law and were taken into account to a great extent in her work.

I was delighted to examine the Ph.D. thesis, which evolved into this excellent and original monograph, and to write this foreword. I strongly recommend this remarkable and distinguished monograph to readers.

Department of Law, University of Cyprus, Nicosia, Cyprus
September 2020

Thomas Papadopoulos

Preface[1]

On July 2017, the Commission of the European Union (Commission) officially rejected investor state dispute settlement (ISDS). Apart from the fundamental public distrust of ISDS, its rejection by the European Union (EU) is a symptom of several underlying causes, the foremost of which is the need to protect the autonomy of the EU legal order and its right to regulate public policy objectives, as well as to avoid jurisdictional conflicts. With this backdrop, EU state aid law, which enjoys public policy status, has emerged as a major example of the conflict between investor protection and the right to regulate. As state aid law imposes measures on the EU Member States that conflict with these states' international obligations to foreign investors under bilateral investment treaties (BITs), they have become subject to claims and substantial liabilities. This dilemma can arise in any setting that involves the EU or one or more of its Member States. It also includes relations with non-EU countries, as the web of international investment agreements (IIAs) operates, in different forms, on an international scale.

Therefore, this dilemma and the EU's responses to it is analysed through different forms in which EU state aid law appears, dependent on the EU investment policy aspect utilised as a platform for analysis. Utilising a doctrinal analysis by studying, discussing, and analysing the impact of EU state aid law on the EU Member States' BITs and EU Trade Agreements, this monograph provides an insight into the function and logic behind international treaties involving the EU's competition and investment policy. This is done by utilising the research question: *How does the European Union (EU) state aid law affect the future of EU investment policy in a global context?* Further, this thesis puts forward three arguments in which EU state aid law is affecting the future of EU investment policy in a global context.

[1] Parts of the abstract of this thesis were introduced at the ANZIL 2018 HDR workshop at the Victoria University of Wellington, New Zealand and hence were published by the Australian and New Zealand Society of International Law Postgraduate Workshop information booklet, available at https://www.anzsil.org.au/resources/Documents/ANZSIL%20Postgraduate%20Workshop%202018%20Booklet.pdf.

First, state aid law applies in the EU's incorporation of clauses promoting fair competition and state aid policy in international trade agreements. Second, state aid law and policy has contributed to recent EU internal development, which led the EU Member States to terminate their bilateral agreements with each other (intra-EU BITs) by the end of 2019. Third, the EU has been working towards replacing the existing BITs between the EU's Member States and third countries (extra-EU BITs) with the EU's own trade agreements, which are aligned with EU legislation.

Essentially, this book's golden thread is a debate on who gets to decide on the scope of state aid law now and in the future. In other words, is it the EU that sets the borders and the status of state aid law and policy law regarding investment protection or the international investment tribunals by their legal practice? Hence, this monograph offers a glimpse of a conceivable future of EU investment policy in a global context.

An analysis of the relevant literature, and observation of recent policy changes on its subject matter, as reflected in the Commission's policy documents, the EU's international agreements and declarations by the Member States, leads to the findings of this dissertation. A conflict situation that originated from legal conflicts within the EU, the EU experience of investment protection and state aid regarding intra-EU BITs, provided some lessons to learn for the EU organs. These lessons learned have found expression on a global scale. By incorporating fair competition and state aid policy in international trade, the EU is reasserting that it is the EU that decides on state aid law and policy law regarding investment protection. Indeed, the EU is attempting to tame investment protection in such a way that fair competition and investment protection can peacefully coexist in international trade. Ultimately, the interplay of state aid and the EU's investment policy within the internal market reflects on the external trade relations of both the Member States and the EU through this practice. Thus, state aid law affects and will continue to affect the future of EU investment policy in a global context.

Gold Coast, QLD, Australia Pamela Finckenberg-Broman

Acknowledgements

This book is derived from my Ph.D. thesis for Griffith University Law School and has also benefited from the support of Charles Darwin University and Griffith Law School as a whole, as well as several individuals. I wish to express my heartfelt gratitude and sincere thanks to them all. I wish to specially mention Sue Harris Rimmer, Charles Lawson from Griffith University, Kieran Tranter from the Queensland of Technology, and Jörgen Hettne from Lund University in Sweden who have greatly supported me through this process. Also, I would like to sincerely acknowledge Susan Jarvis for her great editing. My book looked beautiful after her work. A special thank you also goes to Thomas Papadopoulos for encouraging and supporting me to publish this book with Springer Nature.

Also, this book would have never came to be without my family. You are my strength and inspiration. My husband Morgan Broman, you are my rock, my greatest support, and you never fail to listen and give great advice. My children Chany, Charlie, and Cassie, I am eternally grateful for all your patience and understanding through these years when you have had to share me with my love for researching law.

Contents

Abbreviations

EU Specific

Acquis/acquis communautaire	The body of EU legislation
AFFGN	The non-paper tabled by Austria, Finland, France, Germany, and the Netherlands
CETA	EU–Canada Comprehensive Economic and Trade Agreement
CIL	Customary International Law
CJEU	Court of Justice of the European Union, which constitutes the ECJ and the GC
Commission	European Commission
DCFTA	Deep and Comprehensive Free Trade Area
DG	Directorate General (a department in the European Commission)
EC	European Community
ECHR	European Convention for the Protection of Human Rights and Fundamental Freedoms
ECI	European Citizens' Initiative
ECJ	European Court of Justice
ECLI	European Case Law Identifier
ECR	European Court Reports
ECSC	European Coal and Steel Community (1951)
EEC	European Economic Community (1957)
EP	European Parliament
EU	European Union
EUSFTA	EU–Singapore Free Trade Agreement and Investment Protection Agreement
EVFTA	EU–Vietnam Free Trade Agreement and Investment Protection Agreement

Extra-EU	External EU
GC	General Court (of the Court of Justice of the European Union)
GPEUL	General Principles of EU Law
Internal market	The internal market of the EU is one market in which goods, services, capital, and persons enjoy free movement
Intra-EU	Internal EU
JEEPA	Japan–EU Economic Partnership Agreement
Member States	Member State of the EU
MoU	Understanding Concerning Certain U.S. Bilateral Investment Treaties, signed by the United States, the European Commission, and acceding and candidate countries for accession to the European Union
O.J.	Official Journal of the European Union (previously of the EC)
SAAs	Stabilisation and Association Agreement(s)
TEU	Treaty on the European Union
TFEU	Treaty on the Functioning of the European Union
The Charter	The Charter of Fundamental Rights in the European Union
Third countries	Countries not part of the EU
Third-country nationals	Individuals and legal entities that are not EU nationals

International

BIT	Bilateral Investment Treaty
CCP	Common Commercial Policy
CPSNR	UN Commission on Permanent Sovereignty over Natural Resources
ECOWAS	Economic Community of West African States
ECT	Energy Charter Treaty
EPA	Economic Partnership Agreement
FDI	Foreign Direct Investment
FTA	Free Trade Agreement
GATT	General Agreement on Tariffs and Trade
ICC	International Chamber of Commerce
ICCPR	International Covenant on Civil and Political Rights 1966
ICSID Convention	Convention on the Settlement of Investment Disputes Between States of Investment Disputes
ICSID	International Centre for Settlement of Investment Disputes
IIA	International Investment Agreement

IIL	International Investment Law
IPA	Investment Protection Agreements
ISA	Investor State Arbitration
ISDS	Investor State Dispute Settlement
ITA	Investment Treaty Arbitration
MERCOSUR	A South American trade bloc formed by Argentina, Brazil, Paraguay, and Uruguay
MFN	Most-Favoured-Nation
NAFTA	North American Free Trade Agreement
New York Convention	United Nations Convention on the Recognition and Enforcement of Foreign Arbitral Awards of 10 June 1958
NGO	Non-governmental organisation
OECD	Organisation for Economic Co-Operation and Development
PTA	Preferential Trade Agreement
PTIA	Preferential Trade and Investment Agreement
Subsidies agreement	Agreement on Subsidies and Countervailing Measures
TIP	Trade and Investment Partnership
TPP	Trans-Pacific Partnership
TTIP	Transatlantic Trade and Investment Partnership
UN	United Nations
UNCITRAL	The United Nations Commission on International Trade Law
UNCTAD	United Nations Conference on Trade and Development
UNGA	The United Nations General Assembly
VCLT	Vienna Convention on the Law of Treaties 1969
WTO	World Trade Organization

List of Figures

List of Table

Chapter 1
Introduction

1.1 Structure

For a smooth and comprehensive reading, this book is divided into eight chapters, each with themes and sub-questions.

The present chapter provides an introduction to the subject of the book, describing the legal framework used for the subject matter of the book, providing an insight into the relevant legal situation. It specifies and explains EU Law and the EU's investment regime, as well as international law relevant to investment treaty arbitration. This chapter also clarifies the focus of this book.

Chapter 2 offers a historical and comparative perspective, focusing on the parallel development of norms governing FDI and competition policy through international legal instruments. It links these two central concepts to trade, providing the reader with an insight into how, despite being supportive of each other, these concepts can also diverge and contradict. It shows that, besides the common economic objective of enhanced global wealth, current competition policy (particularly in the EU) also has other objectives, which create tensions when these policies are implemented and applied nationally and supranationally. Finally, it explains how, in an EU context, competition rules cover all type of anti-competitive practices, thus infusing the control of anti-competitive behaviour by both private enterprises and state interventions under the same law. Furthermore, state aid rules apply similarly to goods, services and capital alike, while other public international norms, such as those of the World Trade Organization (WTO) treat goods, services and capital movements differently.

Chapter 3 focuses on the examination of EU state aid law and policy to give the reader an insight into how EU state aid law affects the future of EU investment policy in a global context. It clarifies the law and its evolution through the EU Courts and Commission's practice of it, and examines how it has developed into such a complex legal framework and potent policy tool. It explains how state aid law

P. Finckenberg-Broman, *Weaponizing EU State Aid Law to Impact the Future of EU Investment Policy in the Global Context*, Studies in European Economic Law and Regulation 23, https://doi.org/10.1007/978-3-031-10108-3_1

enables the EU to influence the behaviour of its Member States' policy choices and how countries outside of the EU are not necessarily immune to the effect of EU state aid rules. This chapter also explains the reason for the unique features of state aid control, which puts the State aid norms in context with the global subsidies control by the WTO. Further, some essential procedural aspects of state aid control—such as the notification obligation and enforcement—are introduced.

Chapter 4 demonstrates the issues arising from situations when a Member State's investment policy is not in line with EU State aid law, and an international investment treaty is entered into between EU Member States that challenges the EU judicial system. It particularly asks what problems follow where the international investment regime, as applied and interpreted by international investment tribunals, necessitates that the Member States act against EU state aid law. Using a case study of the *Micula Award*, and the substantial and procedural legal complications that followed, as an example of how this situation can play out in practice. Besides causing substantial legal uncertainty to all parties, a sovereign state of the EU is faced with two conflicting obligations: one to follow the terms of the BIT and the other to abide by EU state aid law.

In Chap. 5, investment law in respect of intra-EU BITs vs EU law is examined from a procedural perspective (through a state aid lens), as it is these elements in BITs that eventually threaten to erode the EU's procedural autonomy and right to regulate. It explains the EU's unique status of *sui generis* and how this status translates to the legal aspects behind investment protection and state aid. It further examines how a critical common denominator behind the current treaty collision is that both regimes have gradually expanded their scope through their jurisprudence until these have overlapped, leading to a collision which is both legal procedural and substantial, which stems from their procedural (principle of legitimate expectations) nature. This discussion is developed from an internal aspect to cover the spill-over effect on the EU's external relations. The link between FDI and competition policy is elaborated upon—particularly where they diverge and collide within the sphere of state aid law and investment protection.

Chapter 6 provides the global perspective. This chapter provides an insight into how the EU uses trade instruments for regulatory export of state aid law and how this practice interacts with the EU's IAAs (including both bilateral investment agreements and investment chapters in trade agreements). It shows how EU state aid law translates into the international dimensions by observing and analysing the EU's trade instruments. Hence, this chapter explicitly discusses how the EU incorporates provisions of fair competition and state aid policy in international trade agreements to guarantee that these agreements in general, and investment chapters in particular, will not conflict with EU state aid law. Further, the EU's current actions to hinder future conflicts from claims arising of government measures that are not compatible with EU state aid law are explained to provide an insight into whether arbitration Awards that are incompatible with EU state aid law are enforceable.

With the aim of providing some legal certainty, Chap. 7 adds another global perspective by looking at how the situation of intra-EU BITs has affected/will affect the extra-EU BITs of the EU's Member States and third countries. In particular, the reform of Member States' model BITs will be analysed by studying and assessing ongoing reform on the subject matter. Furthermore, the enforceability of extra EU-BIT claims/Awards stemming from illegal state aid will be focused upon to identify which judicial forum would be optimal for disputes between investors and states in claims of which the EU or an EU Member State is part.

Chapter 8, the final chapter of this book, summarises the discussion around, and analysis of the materials presented, and based on this analysis presents its conclusion.

1.2 'For the EU: ISDS Is Dead'

On 1 July 2017, the Commission announced that investor state dispute settlement (ISDS)[1] was dead in a fact sheet on the Agreement between Japan and the European Union (EU) for an Economic Partnership Agreement (JEEPA).[2] Within a few days, the EU confirmed that this decision, starting a new chapter in its new investment policy, was permanent.[3] It was a bold standpoint, as the other party to the treaty, Japan, had systematically included ISDS, in the form of traditional investor state arbitration, in all its investment and economic partnership agreements.[4] Within the global arbitrations circles reactions ranged from unconvinced to rejection.[5] Yet the final text of the JEEPA does not include an investment chapter, as the parties did not reach consensus on ISDS and investment protection.[6] It does, however, contain an extensive subsidies chapter.

While ISDS features in headlines and on billboards carried by protesting crowds, the civil society or conventional academia rarely recognises the existence of state aid, which is present in our everyday lives in various forms of subsidies from public resources. It takes place as energy subsidies where countries support coal mining or renewables in line with national energy policies. It is also present when an undertaking[7] benefits from government action. In relation to cross-border investments—

[1] ISDS is an international arbitration procedure to resolve conflicts, with substantial and procedural provisions. It enables investors, through a specific dispute-resolution procedure, to sue states on grounds of breach of investment protection obligations bypassing national courts by bringing a case directly before an international tribunal.

[2] EC (2017c), p. 6. See also the Commission's 6 July 2017 media release on the importance of JEEPA (EC 2017f).

[3] Key elements of the EU–Japan Economic Partnership Agreement (EC 2017b), pp. 5–6.

[4] Adascalitei (2017).

[5] Allen (2017); Fietta (2017); Trehearne (2017).

[6] See the Commission's media release of 8 December 2017 (EC 2018c).

[7] An undertaking in EU competition law context means 'any entity engaged in an economic activity, that is an activity consisting in offering goods or services on a given market, regardless of its legal status and the way in which it is financed'. See *Cassa di Risparmio di Firenze and Others* (2006), paras 107–108.

especially foreign direct investment (FDI)—subsidies are often in the form of grants based on a bilateral agreement between the public authority of an EU Member State and the foreign investor anywhere on the globe within a long-term investment support program.[8] These types of state aid/subsidies, often used as an investment policy instrument, are also called investment incentives.[9] In other words, subsidies/ state aids are a built-in feature of investment policy.

In contrast to worldwide practice and norms, where this type of arrangement would rarely run afoul of rules on subsidies control,[10] the stringent control over state aid within the EU can lead to a different outcome, with consequences. Since all international agreements entered by the EU, its Member States or both must be compatible with EU primary law, these must not breach state aid law. Therefore, the investment policy of both the EU and its Member States, including investment incentives, must be consistent with the state aid provisions of the Treaty of the Functioning of the European Union (TFEU).

State aid rules in Articles 107–109 of the TFEU address actions of states.[11] Intervention under EU state aid law happens to an investment when public support, through resources imputable[12] by the Member State, is selectively granted for the benefit of certain entities in such a way that it can distort the competition on the internal market.[13] State aid law prohibits the Member States from offering state aid under other than specified exemptions that are codified by state aid law.[14] If a Member State implements state aid measures in breach of these laws, it must apply remedies, as stated in the same law. These remedies require the Member State to discontinue the unlawful measure and possibly to retroactively recover paid aid from its recipient.[15] Hence, the most visible manifestation of the impact of state aid rules for the investors is being cut off from economic enticements they have been receiving from the host Member State due to a discontinuation of an unlawful scheme or even being obliged to repay the money to the granting state.[16]

---

[8] Most of the disputes on intra EU BITs have the discontinuation of these type of arrangements at their core. For a definition of investment incentives, see Sect. 2.1.

[9] UNCTAD (2004), p. 1. For more on investment incentives, see Sect. 2.4.3 in Chap. 2.

[10] Because subsidies control on a multilateral level is limited to actionable subsidies affecting trade in goods in the WTO and lack of transparency obligations. See Sect. 2.4.1 in Chap. 2 and Sect. 3.3 in Chap. 3.

[11] See Chap. 3 for details on the EU state aid regime.

[12] This means the state must have granted the benefit independently. See Sect. 3.2.2 in Chap. 3 for more details.

[13] 'The internal market of the European Union (EU) is a single market in which the free movement of goods, services, capital and persons is assured, and in which citizens are free to live, work, study and do business' (EUR-Lex n.d.).

[14] There are some exceptions to this general prohibition: see Chap. 3.

[15] *Alcan Deutschland* (1997), para 25, and *BUG-Alutechnik* (1990), para 16.

[16] The remedy for state aid illegally granted is the restoration of the competition neutrality on the internal market through a clawback procedure.

The EU also has the strictest state aid/subsidies control in the world. Bound by the general prohibition of state aid, Member States have limited means of supporting European firms and investors. Consequently, the EU is not competing on the same terms or level for FDI as the rest of the world. Uneven management of state aid norms internationally, therefore, becomes a significant dilemma for international businesses operating within the EU,[17] nation-states, supranational organisations and national courts/arbitration tribunals. The EU is therefore driven to export its state aid rules through trade instruments.[18] According to a 2015 International Centre for Trade and Sustainable Development E15 Expert Group on Competition Policy, competition law and policy have never before figured so prominently in the international trade system.[19] Within the EU, the implications of this belief catch a wide variety of public and private actors as the EU's competition policy and law consist of two main branches—those applicable to enterprises and those applicable to state aid.

Given that the EU is aware that state aid rules need to be recognised and also respected in the international field for comprehensive competition policy, the EU is an active proponent of multilateral subsidies control in line with its Common Commercial Policy (CCP) Articles 206 and 207 TFEU.[20] EU also imposes stringent state aid-related obligations derived from EU law on their accession and neighbouring countries.[21] The disrespect of these rules by investment tribunals when in conflict with international investment agreements (IIAs), embodied in the case *Micula*,[22] is one more reason why the EU has rejected ISDS in its trade agreements.

Rejection of ISDS in bilateral trade agreements is a relatively new trend, whereas regulatory transfer of state aid is not.[23] Yet the time for the denunciation of traditional investor state arbitration by the EU was ripe. By unilaterally declaring the ISDS dead just months before the intended signing of the JEEPA, the EU broadcast a reform of the only ten-year-old investment policy of the European Union. No longer would the EU tolerate the traditional investor state arbitration, the legal regime of which has been reproached by many. Instead, the EU's

---

[17] Businesseurope (2015).

[18] These rules also benefit other countries. See Blomström and Kokko (2003), p. 20. For specific concerns relating to substantial subsidies to foreign investors, see also EC (2017e), p. 11.

[19] Laprévote et al. (2015).

[20] EU (2008). Accordingly, the EU shall contribute towards harmonisation of global trade, especially in removing trade barriers on *inter alia* foreign direct investment Article 206 and protection of distortion of trade by dumping or subsidies. See also Rubini (2004), p. 1.

[21] See EEA agreement and association agreements with Turkey and Albania. See also bilateral agreements with Switzerland and Israel (EC 2015c). See also Cremona (2003); Rydelski (2004).

[22] The Commission refers to the *Micula Award* (2013) as one of the factors that it no longer trusts in investor state arbitration (EC 2015a).

[23] Japan, like other nations, is aware of the EU's protagonist role on promotion of global subsidies policy and would have expected the Commission to insist on subsidies regulation being included in the Economic Partnership Agreement (EPA) between the parties, even before starting negotiations with the EU in March 2013. See Italianer (2013), p. 4.

proposition for an Investment Court System (ICS)—a permanent, unbiased, and more transparent dispute settlement system designed to be compatible with EU law—would be applicable to future investment disputes.

Unsurprisingly, many do not share the EU's enthusiasm about ICS, strongly doubting its success in the face of the global tradition of old-style investor state arbitration[24] or its compatibility with EU law.[25] Nevertheless, the finalisation of the negotiations on the JEEPA, without the inclusion of investment protection,[26] signals the EU's commitment to stand firm in its position. The EU's abandoning of the ISDS system, globally seen as an essential element of investment agreement protection,[27] signals the culmination of a process that has been ongoing for many years within the EU.

This process, adopted by the Commission, due to increased, mainly state aid-related litigation on intra-EU BITs[28] and years of debate[29] within political,[30] academic[31] and legal circles,[32] on the heavily criticised legal regime of ISDS, was in the end taken out of the hands of the Commission.[33] Responding to the strong opposition of ISDS, the European Parliament rejected the use of investor state arbitration in EU's international agreements,[34] effectively rendering ISDS dead for the EU in an attempt to ease the tension and conflict caused to the EU's legal order by international investment agreements.

[24] Allen (2017); Deli and Marceddu (2015), pp. 4–5. On 6 September 2017, Belgium requested the CJEU's opinion on the compatibility of CETA's ICS with EU law (Kingdom of Belgium 2017) and *Opinion 1/17* (2019) on ICS in CETA.

[25] German Association of Judges (Schneiderhan 2016; see also Eberhardt 2016; Van Harten 2015a).

[26] See the Commission's media release dated 8 December 2017 (EC 2018c).

[27] The ISDS system has especially strong ties with European nations because it originates from a post-World War II European project, just like the Treaty of Rome ('Treaty of Rome (EEC)', 1958).

[28] See UNCTAD database for data (UNCTAD 2016a, b). See also EC (2015d), pp. 5, 6.

[29] Byström (2016); EC (2015e), Politico (2015).

[30] E.g., a compromise solution tabled by a delegation formed of Austria, Finland, France, Germany and the Netherlands (the AFFGN states) to redeem the intra-EU BITs (AFFGN 2016), pp. 6, 8. On TTIP, see Sims and Stone (2016). See also European Parliament think tanks workshop in April 2014 (EP 2014), p. 21; Bierbrauer 2014, Ch. 3.3) and European Parliament report (Cole 2014).

[31] For example: Ankersmit (2015, 2016a, b); Konttinen and Teivainen (2013); Fleming (2014); Schneiderman (2016); Van Harten (2015b); Kleinheisterkamp (2015). See also legal statement on investment protection and investor-state dispute settlement mechanisms in TTIP and CETA signed by several high-ranking academics (Albi et al. 2016). For pro-ISDS, see Happ and Tietje (2013); Tietje et al. (2012); Ortolani (2015); Struckmann et al. (2016).

[32] Statement from the European Association of Judges on the proposal from the European Commission on a new Investment Court System (EAJ) 2015); *Achmea C-284/16* (2018). See also Dimopoulos (2011); Tietje (2013), pp. 16–17; Hindelang (2012b), p. 1; Gubrynowicz and Wierzbowski 2009), p. 3; Andersen and Hindelang (2016), p. 1; Moskvan (2015), pp. 101–38.

[33] The European Parliament approval is mandatory for most international commitments of the EU, including FTAs and IIAs: see Articles 207 and 218 TFEU.

[34] Parliament (2015), paras (xiv)–(xv).

1.3 EU's Rationale for Abolishing ISDS from a State Aid Law Perspective

ISDS has been argued to favour the capital owners at the cost of the public interest,[35] so is an easy target for distrust.[36] However, besides the fundamental distrust by the public of ISDS,[37] its rejection by the EU is a symptom of several underlying reasons. Tensions caused by an uncoordinated investment policy between EU internal and external action as well as the unwillingness of EU Member States to let go of their investment agreements have played a vital role in this development.[38] Above all, as shown by Kleinsterkamp,[39] Eckes,[40] and Gallo and Nicola,[41] is the need to protect 'the autonomy of the EU legal order' and the right to regulate public policy objectives, as well as to avoid jurisdictional conflicts.[42]

To preserve the autonomy of the EU law, the Court of Justice of the European Union (CJEU) has rejected the ability of international courts to interpret the provisions of an international agreement that are binding on EU institutions if this adversely affects the autonomy of the EU legal order.[43] EU law has an autonomous position concerning national and other public international law, with primacy over national law and provisions with direct effect for EU citizens and the Member States. Thus, EU law is part of and in force in Member States' national law—and arises from an international agreement entered by those states.[44] EU autonomy serves as

---

[35] Communication from the Commission *Trade for All* (EC 2015b), p. 13.

[36] ISDS has been fiercely resisted by EU citizens (ECI 2017), who can make their voices heard by the public consultation process (EC 2017d) and the European Citizens' Initiative (ECI). See the European Parliament decision of 22 May 2012 amending Parliament's Rules of Procedure regarding the implementation of the ECI (2011/2302(REG) (EP), 2013) and (EC 2017a).

[37] Trade commissioner Cecilia Malmström official blog (Malmstom 2015). After the massive opposition to ISDS, a multilateral reform of ISDS became imminent (EC 2015e). This led to two public consultations on a multilateral reform of investment dispute resolution, initiated on 21 December 2016.

[38] Kleinheisterkamp (2012, b). For the Commission's infringement proceedings against Austria, Sweden, Belgium, Luxembourg, Portugal, Romania and Italy for not effectively removing their intra-EU BITs see https://ec.europa.eu/commission/presscorner/detail/EN/INF_21_6201.

[39] Kleinheisterkamp (2012, 2015).

[40] Eckes (2016), pp. 10 and 31.

[41] Gallo and Nicola (2015).

[42] For a detailed explanation of these issues and the structure of the EU, see Chap. 4.

[43] See *Opinion 1/91* (1991) EEA Agreement of 14 December 1991, paras 40 and 70; *'Opinion 1/09'* (2011) Agreement creating a unified patent litigation system of 8 March 2011, paras 74 and 76; *Opinion 2/13 of the Court (Full Court)* (2014) paras 182 and 183; and *Achmea C-284/16* (2018).

[44] *Case 6-64 – Costa v ENEL* (1964); *Case 26-62 van Gend & Loos* (1963); *Achmea C-284/16* (2018). This makes EU law a *sui generis* legal order. The source of the validity of EU law, being integrated and applied within the national legal orders of its Member States as a result of its supranational source, is not merely dependent on a wilful act: it belongs to the Member States. In public international law, where the application of international law usually depends upon the intent of the state (Maduro 2007), p. 4 et seq.

the base for its legitimacy.[45] EU imbuing its legal norms with a public policy dimension expansively, as part of EU's most fundamental objectives, does not fit well with the regime of international investment arbitration that has a substantially different point of view about procedural autonomy and public policy.

For investment tribunals, public policy is subject to a narrow interpretation, due to its inherent function of overriding party autonomy or circumventing/overriding the enforcement of an applicable judgment or even law.[46] ISDS enables investors, through a specific dispute-resolution procedure, to sue states on the grounds of breach of investment protection obligations, bypassing national courts by bringing a case directly before an international tribunal. It thus provides a twofold basis for these tribunals to interpret and apply EU law.

These tribunals—private forums created to protect foreign investors in the public law domain—do not feel bound to respect EU law when deciding on subject matter covered and regulated by EU *acquis*.[47] Domestic courts cannot review their decisions for conformity with EU law. Being exceptions to the legal system of the EU (not being national courts), tribunals cannot make a reference to the CJEU for a preliminary ruling according to Article 267 of the TFEU. Consequently, tribunals may undermine the autonomy of the EU legal order and compromise its specific characteristics.[48]

Protecting the right to regulate public policy objectives has been emphasised by the legislative bodies of the EU.[49] High-profile investment cases such as *Philip Morris v Australia* on tobacco regulations,[50] out-phasing nuclear energy in *Vattenfall*,[51] *Veolia* on increasing the minimum salary[52] and reinstitution of unlawful state aid in *Micula*[53] have fuelled their concerns. Against this backdrop, EU state

---

[45] *Achmea C-284/16* (2018), paras 33 and 34. See also Eckes (2016), pp. 10, 31; Bermann (2012).

[46] Bermann (2012), p. 419.

[47] European Parliament report (Cole 2014) p. 15. This is also presented in *Micula* as well as *Achmea C-284/16* (2018) previously: *Eureko* (2010); *AES v Hungary (III) Award* (2010) settled by parties: *AES v Hungary (Anullment)* (2012); *EDF v Hungary* (2014). The award was set aside by the Swiss Federal Supreme Court *(EDF International SA v Republic of Hungary, Swiss*, 2015); *Micula Award*, (2013) and *Saluka* (2006). In *Achmea C-284/16* (2018) para 34, the ECJ stresses the importance of respecting EU law.

[48] Primacy (*Case 6-64 – Costa v ENEL*, 1964), direct effect (*Van Gend en Loos*, 1963), mutual trust (Article 2 TEU) and sincere cooperation (Article 4(3)1 TEU; *Achmea C-284/16* (2018), para 58). See *Opinion 2/13 of the Court (Full Court)* (2014), para 176.

[49] European Parliament in Resolution on the future European international investment policy, para 23. Conclusions on a comprehensive European international investment policy (Council of the European Union 2010); Towards a comprehensive European international investment policy (EC 2010), p. 9; and Trade for all (EC 2015b), p. 14.

[50] *Philip Morris v Australia* (2015); *Philip Morris v Australia, UNCITRAL, PCA Case No. 2012–12* (2016).

[51] *Vattenfall 2* (pending) is about Germany ending the use of nuclear power for civilian purposes in the wake of the Fukushima disaster in Japan.

[52] *Veolia Propreté v Egypt* (2012).

[53] *Micula Award* (2013). For more on the multiple Micula case proceedings see Chap. 4.

aid law, which enjoys public policy status,[54] has emerged as a substantial example of the crossfire between investor protection and the right to regulate.[55] As state aid law imposes measures on EU Member States that conflict with those states' international obligations to foreign investors under BITs, those states become subject to claims and substantial liabilities. However, the fact that so far these collisions between state aid law and international treaty arbitration have mainly occurred in intra-EU disputes (namely intra-EU BITs and the ECT)[56] does not exclude similar disputes arising in external relations. These may occur where IIAs lack sufficient guarantees that investors cannot use investment incentives constituting state aid as grounds for initiating ISDS or ICS. This situation can arise in any setting that involves EU or one or more of its Member States, including their relations with non-EU countries as the web of IIAs in different forms, like the multilateral Energy Charter Treaty (ECT), treaties with investment provisions (TIPs) and/or relevant Bilateral Investment Agreement s (BITs)[57] that operate on an international scale.

A memorandum of understanding (MoU), signed in 2003 by the EU, the United States, and the Central and Eastern European accession states,[58] aiming to eliminate the possibility of American investors using the BITs for challenges to Member States' administrative or regulatory measures for EU law compliance.[59] It proved the Commission's foresight on the risk of cases like *Micula* occurring, with the MoU attempting to prevent it.[60] As a further precaution, the Commission started criticising the traditional investment treaty arbitration model and updated its investment policy by introducing clauses into EU's international investment agreements to temper the scope of investment protection post-*Micula*. In this context, subsidies stand out.[61]

[54] State aid policy is part of EU competition policy. The *Eco Swiss case* (*C-126/97 – Eco Swiss*, 1999, para 39) established EU competition policy as EU public policy in an arbitration setting. Later cases (*C-295/04 –Manfredi*, 2006, para 31; *T-Mobile Netherlands BV v Raad van beestuur van de Nederlandse Mededingingsautoriteit*, 2009, para. 49) affirmed this.

[55] The Commission recognises that disputes involving state aid have raised specific problems regarding ISDS (EC 2015a), p. 5.

[56] *Eastern Sugar – Final Award* (2007); *Eastern Sugar – Partial Award* (2007); *AES v Hungary (III) Award* (2010); *EDF v Hungary* (2014); *Electrabel Decision on Jurisdiction* (2012); *Electrabel Award* (2015); *Binder v Czech Republic Award* (2007); *Oostergetel v Slovak Republic* (2010); *Achmea B.V Final Award* (2012; *Achmea v Slovak Republic* (2008); *Charanne Final Award* (2016); *RREEF Infrastructure* (2016); *Isolux Award* (2016); *WNC Award* (2017); *Anglia Auto Accessories Final Award* (2017); *Eiser Award* (2017).

[57] EU Member States have signed around 1400 IIAs; of these, 190 are intra-EU BITS (Commission 2015). In 2016 the EU had 55 TIPs in force and more under negotiation (UNCTAD 2016a).

[58] Apart from Hungary and Slovenia (Matei 2015c).

[59] 'Understanding Concerning Certain US Bilateral Investment Treaties, signed by the United States, the European Commission, and acceding and candidate countries for accession to the European Union (22 September 2003)' (2003), hereafter: MoU EC & US on Certain BITs.

[60] Matei (2015c).

[61] As one of four main areas (intellectual property, increased transparency, limiting trade-distortive subsidisation and behaviour of state-owned enterprises (SOEs)) that the Commission seeks to safeguard in its bilateral or regional agreements (EC 2017h), p. 6.

The EU-Vietnam FTA (Chapter 1, Article 4(t), CETA (Article 9.2) and EUSFTA (Article 9.2) state aid carve-out provisions declare investment protection not applicable to subsidies, and a party's decision not to issue, renew or maintain subsidies, cannot be considered an expropriation.

To address the issue, there are two obvious solutions: to attain common grounds on how the issue should be solved by agreeing on shared norms on the scope and interpretation of the matter; or to eliminate threats to autonomy by unilaterally rejecting the validity of the other system attempting to expand its influence or eliminating the invasive substance from all matters in its relations. The EU has undertaken both paths in its investment policy reform.[62]

On 1 July 2017, the Commission escalated the battle against traditional investment treaty arbitrations by announcing that ISDS was 'dead'.[63] Seven months later, to preserve the specific characteristics and the autonomy of the EU legal order, the CJEU declared ISDS provisions vis-à-vis intra-EU BITs incompatible with EU law in *Achmea,*[64] which eventually led to the Member States jointly denouncing these BITs by the end of 2019.[65]

Since then, this legal topic has witnessed many changes. On 5 May 2020, 23 Member States signed the Agreement for the termination of Bilateral Investment Treaties between the Member States of the European Union (Intra-EU BIT Termination Agreement).[66] Investment protection provisions in the EU's trade agreements have also been negotiated to include ICS instead of ISDS.[67] Within the internal market, the Commission is pushing for the end of intra-EU BITs.[68] Extra-EU BITs, the existing BITs of Member States with third countries (non-EU states), are being scrutinised to eliminate incompatibilities with EU law and will ultimately be

[62] Commission Communication on Protection of intra-EU investment (EC 2018a), p. 2.

[63] EC (2017c), p. 6. See also the Commission's media release dated 6 July 2017 on the importance of JEEPA (EC 2017f).

[64] On the basis of a joint reading of Articles 267 and 344 TFEU (*Achmea C-284/16*, 2018, paras 31, 59 and 60), *Achmea* confirms and enforces CJEU's decision in *C-64/16 – Associação Sindical dos Juízes Portugueses* (2018).

[65] See Declaration of the Member States of 15 January 2019 on the legal consequences of the *Achmea* judgment and on investment protection (FISMA 2019a, b, c).

[66] Agreement for the Termination of Bilateral Investment Treaties between the Member States of the European Union, SN/4656/2019/INIT, OJ L 169, 29.5.2020, p. 1–41 (FISMA 2020). This Agreement entered into force on 29 August 2020 and was signed by Belgium, Bulgaria, Croatia, the Republic of Cyprus, the Czech Republic, Denmark, Estonia, France, Germany, Greece, Hungary, Italy, Latvia, Lithuania, Luxembourg, Malta, the Netherlands, Poland, Portugal, Romania, Slovakia, Slovenia and Spain. Ireland did not have any intra-EU BITs in force (UNCTAD 2016a).

[67] Introduced and applied in CETA (EC 2017b) and insisted by the Commission for other TIPs as shown by the JEEPA (EC 2017b, p. 6). The compatibility of investment dispute provisions of CETA was settled by the CJEU in *Opinion 1/17* (2019). See also EC (2018b).

[68] For infringement procedures against five Member States of the EU with active intra-EU BITs (EC 2015f).

replaced by EU's agreements.[69] It seems that the final legacy of *Micula* is the EU's resolution to make it clear that international investment agreements in any form cannot be used to stop the EU from enforcing its state aid laws. In this way, tension and conflict within the EU's legal order may ease.

1.4 The Current Situation of Intra-EU BITs and Extra-EU BITs

The current legal situation with the intra-EU BITs creates tension and conflict within the EU's legal order. These issues are both substantive, regarding State aid and possible discrimination, and procedural, vis-à-vis the principles of effectiveness and mutual trust.[70]

As EU legislation currently stands, they constitute an anomaly and logically should be phased out. At the time of the EU's creation by the six founding Member States, it was already clear that this type of bilateral agreement between the Member States was not aligned with the creation of the European Single Market.[71] The Lisbon Treaty[72] (or its predecessors) does not include an IIA. However, due to its *sui generis* character, the EU evokes controversy that is not present at other preferential trade agreements (PTAs). In the EU's Single Market, investment protection is already integrated, and the CJEU has exclusive jurisdiction in the matter of international market disputes within the ambit of EU law.

The extra-EU BITs, on the other hand, have historically been concluded between the individual EU Member States and third countries. This situation continued until the external competence of the EU (the external commercial policy) was extended to also include investment treaties in 2009,[73] hence creating the EU's investment policy.[74] However, with the ascension to the EU by Central and Eastern European States, some pre-existing extra-EU BITs had been turned into intra-EU BITs. Thus, extra-EU BITs are now governed by the EU's investment policy and Member States can only conclude an extra-EU BIT with special permission from the Commission,[75] indicating that this form of a bilateral agreement is only acceptable in cases where

[69] See Regulation (EU) No. 1219/2012 European Parliament (EP) & Council (2012) Art. 3 and European Commission (2017g).

[70] See Chaps. 4 and 5.

[71] The Brussels Report on the General Common Market (Spaak 1956), Title II Ch. I section 2. For an English summary, see http://aei.pitt.edu.ludwig.lub.lu.se/995/1/Spaak_report.pdf.

[72] Treaty of Lisbon amending the Treaty on European Union and the Treaty establishing the European Community.

[73] Art 207 TFEU – the EU's competence CCP includes FDI post-Lisbon (EU 2008; see also Anderer 2010; Basedow 2016).

[74] See Commission's web page at http://ec.europa.eu/trade/policy/accessing-markets/investment.

[75] European Commission (2017i) and Regulation (EU) No. 1219/2012 Articles 5 and 6(2)–(3) (2012).

the EU has no interest in concluding a similar agreement. The existing extra-EU BITs, with the potential to evoke an open conflict between EU's investment policy and EU law, as exhibited by the case law of CJEU,[76] are also part of an ongoing process of being replaced with EU trade agreements aligned with EU legislation.

While legal and political tensions on the matter intensified both internally,[77] on intra-EU BITs, and externally on EU's investment agreements, one case, *Micula,*[78] made the hypothetical conflict of State aid and international investment agreements a reality, generating strong reactions on both sides of the Atlantic Ocean. Parallel to acting as an appellant in a US Court of Appeals regarding *Micula,*[79] the Commission launched infringement procedures against five Member States to end intra-EU-BITS,[80] due to the discord those cause within the EU's internal market.[81] According to the Commission, a built-in conflict between some arbitration awards and EU State aid law is what leads to the Member State being prosecuted by the Commission for breach of the same law.[82] *Micula* also alerted the Commission to the possibility of the same situation reoccurring in an international agreement that the EU is part of, providing a boost for the renewal of the EU's investment protection regime.[83]

The conclusion, from an EU law perspective, is then that there should not exist either any intra-EU BITs nor extra-EU BITs, leaving this area within the scope of EU Investment Treaties concluded between the EU and third countries. This is far from the current situation with both intra-EU BITs and extra-EU BITs existing, with a potential for legal conflict with EU law. This includes both a conflict between legal

[76]See *C-205/06 – Commission v Austria* (2009); *C-249/06 – Commission v Sweden* (2009); *C-118/07 – Commission v Finland* (2009) on the obligation for acceding Member States to align their extra EU-BITs in accordance with Article 351 TFEU and Article 4(3) TEU. See also Lavranos (2013, pp. 6–11). However, for Awards stemming from pre-EU BITs, meaning BITs concluded by a Member State before accession to the EU with a third country, falling under and Article 351(1) TFEU, see *C-264/09 – Commission v Slovakia* (2011b) for a IIA between Slovakia and Switzerland. These types of Awards do not necessarily have to comply with EU law, but the incompatibility with EU law needs to be addressed by the Member State. However, most of the extra-EU BIT signed by the founding Member States with a set deadline under Article 351(1) of 1 January 1958, would not be protected by this provision.

[77]ECOFIN (2006), p. 7.

[78]*Micula Award* (2013). See *Micula I (EU)* (2014); *Micula II (EU)* (2014); *Micula III (EU)* (2016); *Micula IV (EU)* (2019); *Micula V (EU)* (2019) and *Micula VI (EU)* (2022).

[79]For the judicial proceedings in the United States, see *Micula I (USA)* (2015a); *Micula I (USA)* (2015b); *Micula III (USA)* (2016) and *Micula VI (USA).*

[80]EC (2015f).

[81]EC (2016a), Chapter 4.3.

[82]For example, *Electrabel* (2012); *Achmea C-284/16* (2018) previously *Eureko* (2010); *AES v Hungary (III) Award* (2010) settled by parties: *AES v Hungary (Anullment)* (2012). The *EDF v Hungary Award* (2014) was set aside by the Swiss Federal Supreme Court (*EDF International SA v Republic of Hungary, Swiss*, 2015). *US Steel v Slovakia* (2013) was withdrawn by the claimant-stipulated termination order (*Stipulated Termination Order US Steel* (2014) and *Micula Award* (2013). See also *Saluka* (2006).

[83]The Commission refers to the *Micula* case as one of the factors it no longer trusts in ITA (EC 2015a).

sources and jurisdictions—CJEU/national courts/arbitration tribunals. Therefore, this is an area of law that is topical and current as a subject for legal research.

1.5 EU Investment Policy in a Global Context

This book argues that EU state aid law is affecting the future of EU investment policy in a global context in three ways. First, it occurs via the EU's incorporation of clauses promoting fair competition and state aid policy in international trade agreements. Second, until the Member States' bilateral agreements with each other (intra-EU BITs) were officially terminated by the end of 2019, these agreements still favoured some EU investors over others in the internal market. Given that EU state aid law has often been at the heart of the crossfire between investor protection and EU law,[84] any existing and new dispute-resolution mechanism for the protection of cross border intra-EU investments must be constructed in such a way that it cannot ignore state aid law. Third, the EU is working towards replacing the existing bilateral agreements (BITs) between the Member States and third countries (extra-EU BITs) with EU trade agreements that are aligned with EU legislation.

1.5.1 Effect on the Future of EU Global Trade

Essentially, EU's incorporation of clauses promoting fair competition and state aid policy in international trade agreements[85] will ensure that these agreements in general, and investment chapters in particular, will not conflict with EU competition law. This is necessary to ensure EU bodies do not violate EU primary law in application, practice and enforcement of EU state aid policy. EU investment policy must therefore align with EU primary law,[86] to maintain the autonomy and stability of the EU and avoid three other negative effects; one static and two dynamic.[87] First,

[84] *Micula Award* (2013). *Micula Award* (2013) started a lengthy procedure of appeals and cases. See *Micula I (EU)* (2014); *Micula II (EU)* (2014); *Micula III(EU)* (2016); *Micula V (EU)* (2019); *Micula IV EU* (2022). See also *Micula I (USA)* (2015a); *Micula I (USA)* (2015b); *Micula I (USA)* (2016).

[85] For an example see CETA Articles 7. And 8.9 available at EU and Canada (2016), and EU–Singapore Free Trade Agreement (EUSFTA) Article 9.2 available at EU and Singapore (2017). For a list of all EU existing trade agreements and those under negotiation, see the Commission's web page at https://ec.europa.eu/trade/policy/countries-and-regions/negotiations-and-agreements. See also the European Commission White Paper on levelling the playing field as regards foreign subsidies (Commission's White Paper on Foreign Subsidies), Brussels, 17.6.2020 COM(2020) 253 final (EC 2020).

[86] *Case 6-64 – Costa v ENEL* (1964). See also *Opinion 2/13 of the Court (Full Court)* (2014).

[87] State aid being dynamic is argued by Chari and Cavatorta (2002); Griswold and Marine (1996) and López (2015). On evolution of state aid, see also Biondi (2013); Biondi and Rubini (2005).

as a static effect, the Commission's ability to prevent discrimination against undertakings would be impeded.[88] Second, as a dynamic effect, the capacity of the Commission to employ European governance (namely, implementing policy objectives in line with changing EU policy priorities) would be hampered. Third, a dynamic effect, the CJEUs ability to utilise state aid law as a tool for internal market integration, would also be hampered.

This book proposes, first, that future conflicts could be handled by ascertaining that any international trade agreement to which the EU is a party contain sufficient elements of state aid regulation. Second, it suggests a combination of state aid clauses with a limited scope of investment protection provisions, so any subsidies issued, renewed or maintained by the signatory party avoid constituting a breach of investment protection. The outcome would be that fair competition and investment protection would no longer be conflicting objectives. The treaty would also have to assure that any potential independent arbitration tribunal would not be in a position to ignore these provisions.[89]

1.5.2 Ending Intra-EU BITs

The Intra-EU BIT Termination Agreement which entered into force on 29 August 2020[90] was the culmination of a decade long power struggle.[91] This ongoing EU internal strife is, and has been, political between the Member States and the Commission,[92] and judicial, between the Commission and the international investment tribunals.[93] After 60 years of intra-EU BITs reigning over intra-EU foreign investment, a solution to this power struggle seemed distant. The CJEU partially

[88] *C-20/15 P – Commission v World Duty Free Group* (2016) para 86. See Commission's White Paper on Foreign Subsidies (Commission 2020) which discusses methods to address the distortions that foreign subsidies create on the internal market.

[89] This could be accomplished by all the three models put forward by Kleinheisterkamp and Poulsen (2016, p. 2) for investment protection to TTIP.

[90] FISMA (2020).

[91] The mutual termination of these BITs was announced by the Declaration of Representatives of the Governments of the Member States, of 15 January 2019 on the legal consequences of the judgment of the Court of Justice in *Achmea* and on investment protection in the European Union: see FISMA (2019b), https://ec.europa.eu/info/sites/info/files/business_economy_euro/banking_and_finance/documents/190117-bilateral-investment-treaties_en.pdf. Six Member States made separate declarations (two in total) on 16 January due to differences in opinion regarding the impact of *Achmea C-284/16* (2018) on the ECT. FISMA (2019a, c).

[92] The Commission evoked Article 258 TFEU infringement procedures to remedy the breach against EU law – in this case, Member States not terminating their intra-EU BITs. See Commission's media release (EC 2015f).

[93] See, for example, *AES v Hungary (III) Award* (2010); *Micula Award* (2013); *Electrabel Decision on Jurisdiction* (2012).

solved it by ruling in its *Achmea C-284/16* decision that these were BITs incompatible with EU law.

Until all intra-EU dispute resolution has been aligned with EU law, arbitration tribunals may keep on not respecting EU state aid law, meaning that some EU investors will still be favoured over others in the internal market. Hence, intra-EU BITs (besides not being compatible with Articles 344 and 267 TFEU) are inherently discriminatory. In this way, awards such as the *Micula Award*,[94] used as a case study for this book, will no longer emerge to create tension and conflict within the EU's legal order. In the EU's internal market, investment protection is already integrated, and the CJEU has exclusive jurisdiction in the matter of international market disputes within the ambit of EU law. Similar problems should be expected in the case of an extra-EU BIT having an anti-competitive effect on the EU's internal market. A similar answer should be expected in the case of an extra-EU BIT having an anti-competitive effect on the EU's internal market.

1.5.3 Replacing Extra-EU BITs with EU FTAs

There is an ongoing process in the EU to replace the existing extra-EU BITs with EU trade agreements that are aligned with EU legislation. The extra-EU Bilateral Investment Treaties (extra-EU BITs) have historically been concluded between the individual EU Member States and third countries (non-EU states). This situation continued until up the external competence of the EU (the external commercial policy) was extended to include investment treaties (Lisbon 2009). However, with the ascension to the EU by Central and Eastern European states, pre-existing extra-EU BITs were turned into intra-EU BITs.

This book proposes that the ongoing process in the EU to replace the existing extra-EU BITs with the EU's trade agreements that are aligned with EU legislation, particularly state aid law, should be speeded up. The current extra-EU BITs lacking provisions for competition policy and state aid, and as a counterbalance to investment protection, should be the first ones to be replaced by EU FTAs. In the meantime, by using the process of the Grandfathering Regulation, these BITs must be promptly altered to include provisions that transfer traditional ISDS to ICS as in CETA and the new Dutch BIT.

[94] *Micula Award* (2013).

1.6 Purpose, Contribution and Research Question (What This Monograph Contributes to the Research on the Subject)

While the transformation of EU investment law in the wake of the Lisbon Treaty has been addressed abundantly in the relevant literature,[95] with academic contributions covering the problems relating to investment treaty arbitration, especially regarding its conflict with state aid on intra-EU BITs,[96] legal academia and practitioners, being litigation focused, tend to refer to the intense conflicts generated by overlaps between state aid law and international investment agreements as if this concept would be limited to the internal market. This inward-looking stance on the concept of state aid law, miss the fact that the internal market is not an entity existing in isolation, apart from and immune to external evolution of the context in which it is applied. Most legal authors also fail to recognise the external effects of the application of this concept.[97] The paradox lies within the wording of Article 107 TFEU, which does not require the receiver of the subsidy to be based on the internal market, only that the effect is potentially distortive to the internal market. Explicitly, it is enough that an investor from a third country invests in a subsidiary (including non-resident holding companies) in an EU Member State or States to operate in the internal market through different corporate arrangements which then receives subsidies granted by EU Member States.[98]

In a debate over the development of EU global investment policy through a state aid law lens, the examination of the position the EU has adopted on the internal and external dimension of both state aid policy and investment policy is central. Indeed, state aid control is one of the foundation stones "of the entire European Union'[99] and part of its *acquis communautaire*, a vital tool for the ongoing constitutionalising of European values and the deepening integration of the internal market. The EU's external action is driven by its *acquis*. Article 21.1 of the Treaty on European Union

[95] To mention a few: Eilmansberger (2009); Kleinheisterkamp (2011, 2012, 2014b, 2015); Lenk (2015a, b, 2017); Pascual Vives (2014); Ankersmit (2015, 2016b); Kokott and Sobotta (2016); Van Harten (2007, 2015b); Van Harten and Malysheuski (2016); Reinisch (2013); Cole (2014); Eckes (2016); Bermann (2012); Gallo and Nicola (2015).

[96] See Dimopoulos (2011); Tietje (2013); Andersen and Hindelang (2016); Hindelang (2012a, b); Kende (2015); Gubrynowicz and Wierzbowski (2009); Gallo and Nicola (2015); Ortolani (2015); Happ and Tietje (2013); Tietje et al. (2012); Tietje and Wackernagel (2014, 2015); Matei (2015a, 2016); Matei and Ciurtin (2016); Saavedra Pinto (2016).

[97] Only few, such as Bermann (2012), Kleinheisterkamp (2014b), Matei (2015a, b, c; Matei and Ciurtin (2016), Kende (2015) and Gallo and Nicola (2015) bring up the role of state aid law in relation to development of extra-EU BITs and/or FTAs and IIAs.

[98] European Commission (2016c); see also Luja (2017). If the economic activities are actually carried out by the subsidiary itself: *Cases T-778/16 and T-892/16- Ireland and Apple v. Commission*, (2020).

[99] See McGowan and Wilks' (1995) p. 141 statement regarding EU competition policy in general.

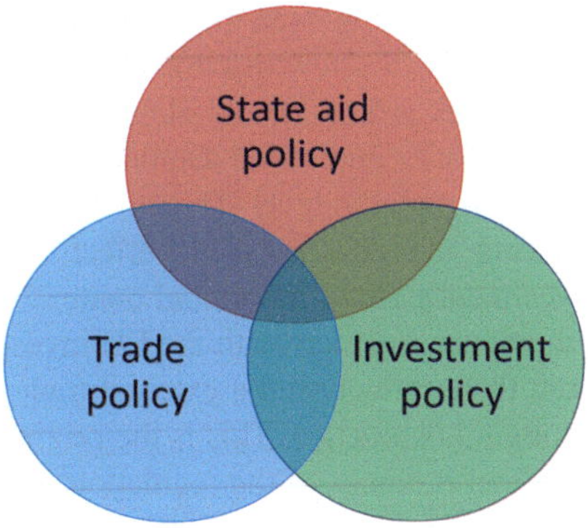

Fig. 1.1 Interaction of the EU's trade, state aid and investment policy

(TEU) forces the EU to reinforce, even externally, that this is a union with its legitimate foundation being law and democracy,[100] the repercussion being the development of an external dimension, which consists of attempts to transfer EU state aid law and policies to third countries and international organisations.

Accordingly, the policy of EU state aid practice interacts with the EU investment regime within the internal market and from there reflects on the external trade relations of both the Member States and the EU through this practice (see Fig. 1.1). Beyond the overlap with international investment agreements, the regional and extraterritorial state aid policy has a significant role in shaping the EU investment regime.

Some authors have recognised the state aid factor in a global setting. Most are from political scientists on empirical implications of European integration[101] and governance. Some from legal literature of practising academia,[102] especially practising academics associated with the European Commission.[103] Some studies

[100] The EU's Common commercial policy (CCP) promotes contributing to the harmonisation of world trade, inter alia in direct investment.

[101] See Blauberger and Krämer (2010); Botta (2013); Botta and Schwellnus (2015); Cremona (2003); Kassim and Lyons (2013). Others, such as Blauberger and Krämer (2010), Damro (2013), Damro and Guay (2016), Featherstone and Radaelli (2003), Lavenex and Schimmelfennig (2009), Schimmelfennig (2012a, b), discuss exportation of EU laws and norms beyond Europe by means of European governance.

[102] OECD (2011) assessed the global status of Competition, State Aids and Subsidies in 2010. There is also literature on the state aid regulation in specific non-EU countries: in candidate countries (Fornalczyk 2004), other countries in the EU's neighbourhood (Cremona 2003) and Switzerland (Luja, 2007; Obrist 2013) as well as, more recently, the United Kingdom after Brexit (Peretz and Bacon 2016; Peretz et al. 2017; Schonberg 2017). In a regional context see Rydelski (2004) for state aid and the EEA agreement and Geradin (2004) for state aid rules in the context of Euromed Agreements. Szepesi (2004) reviews state aid provisions in EU FTAs. Papadopoulos (2010) has published a substantial work on the EU position in all the levels of international cooperation on competition, including state aid control.

[103] Bourgeois et al. (2007); Galindo (2015); Gallo and Nicola (2015); Jarosz-Friis et al. (2010); Laprévote et al. (2015); Papadopoulos (2010); Van de Casteele (2006, 2016).

concentrate on the area of global subsidies control through multilateral trade instruments,[104] with a few discussing EU's position in the field of international bilateral agreements with state aid elements.[105] No single work examines the interplay of state aid rules and EU investment policy internally and externally, either within the EU or on a global level. This book aims to fill that gap explicitly by identifying and showing the effect/possible effect, the State aid law has on the future of EU investment policy in a global context. It will focus on how the policy of EU state aid practice interacts with the EU investment regime within the internal market and from there reflect on the external trade relations of the Member States and the EU through this practice. This is the original contribution of this book.

When it comes to the regulation of global trade in general, studying and understanding the impact of EU state aid law on the EU Member States' BITs and the EU's trade agreements in the current chaotic situation can provide an understanding that will inform the future of international treaties involving the EU. More explicitly, the EU experience of intra-EU BITs can provide some lessons to learn for glimpsing a conceivable future of EU investment policy in a global context, incorporating fair competition and state aid policy in international trade. Thus, providing an understanding of how the policy of EU state aid practice collaborates with the EU investment regime within the internal market with reflections on the external trade relations of the Member States and the EU, ultimately impacting third countries.

The golden thread for this book is about the debate on who gets to decide on the scope of state aid law now and in the future, when and where it intersects and collides with another distinct legal field, investment protection. The international agreements deliberated on are EU bilateral trade agreements with third countries, extra-EU BITs and the intra-EU BITs, with state aid elements. The special status of the Energy Charter Treaty (ECT), while a multilateral investment treaty to which the EU and its Member States are signatories,[106] forms an integral part of the EU legal order, enjoying primacy over secondary EU legislation;[107] will also be discussed briefly.

In this discussion, it is necessary to separate the motives and the means. The position that the EU has adopted on the internal and external dimension[108] of both state aid policy and investment policy is driven by the need to evolve and protect the

[104]Rubini (2010) found that many forms of government action are covered by both the EU and the World Trade Organization (WTO) rules. The relevance of WTO rules on the development of EU State Aid Control is examined by Goyette (2006) and Hoekman and Holmes (1999).

[105]Fornalczyk (2004); Geradin (2004); Luja (2007); Obrist (2013); Peretz (2016); Peretz and Bacon (2016); Peretz et al. (2017); Rydelski (2004); Szepesi (2004); Bourgeois et al. (2007) and EC (2008).

[106]The Final Act of the Energy Charter Conference was signed in Lisbon on 27 December 1994.

[107]See *C-308/06 – Intertanko and Others* (2008) paras 42 and 53 and *C-17/03 – VEMW and Others* (2005). According to the CJEU, ECT as *lex generalis* trumps the *lex specialis* EU directives.

[108]Already in 2001, the Commission in the Ninth Survey on State Aid in the European Union observed that state aid policy had to take the international context into account, especially WTO rules (EC 2001), para 23.

EU legal order and will utilise all the policy tools it has available, internally and on all levels of international cooperation. With the European internal market not existing in a vacuum, to protect state aid policy in the internal market from erosion by external distortions and actors, the export of state aid has taken place in diverse forms on both the multilateral plain—for example, *mutatis mutandis* by the introduction of the WTO Agreement on Subsidies and Countervailing Measures (Subsidies Agreement) in 1995—and the bilateral plain—through the EU's accession, associate, economic partnership and free trade agreements (FTAs). Subsequently, while state aid as part of competition law is considered unique to the EU,[109] 'there exists a large heterogeneity among systems of control of state aid and subsidies, both at the supranational and national levels'.[110]

Article 207 of the Treaty on the Functioning of the European Union (TFEU),[111] which establishes the EU's Common Commercial Policy (CCP) as an exclusive competence of the EU, particularly mentions foreign direct investment and trade defences regarding subsidies. The link between these two, provided by CCP after the Lisbon Treaty moved competence over FDI from the Member States to the EU in 2009, will be explored.

Externally, besides its CCP, the EU works on the development of international cooperation on subsidies regulation and the development of international competition norms. This book recognises and systematically reviews three types of international agreements that can be used for control of state aid and investment in the external dimension;[112] multilateral, bilateral and plurilateral agreements, with a focus on the second and third categories. The first category, multilateral agreements, will be discussed in less detail because these have been studied extensively in the past.[113]

Further, this book shows that four categories of countries are distinguishable according to the similarity of EU state aid rules and the success of local/international enforcement and control.

1. The global, with three sub-categories:

    a. megaregional bilateralism (such as CETA, JEEPA, EUSFTA)
    b. megaregional plurilateralism,[114] with regional trade blocs (such as Cariforum,
    c. Mercosur, ASEAN)

---

[109] Bacon (2017), p. 4; Goyette (2006), p. 1. The term 'state aid' is used only within a European context, while the term 'subsidies' is used on a global scale.

[110] OECD (2011), p. 9.

[111] EU (2008).

[112] For a map of the EU's free trade agreements in 2018, see Appendix 4.

[113] See, for example, Hoekman and Holmes (1999); Rubini (2004); Goyette (2006); Damro (2013); Damro and Guay (2016).

[114] *The Washington Trade Report Dictionary for Trade Policy* defines plurilateralism *as* 'a form of trade agreement that is more than bilateral, less than multilateral, and not exactly regional'. See http://www.washingtontradereport.com/dictionarym.htm.

   c. supranational subsidies control, through multilateral instruments (WTO, UNCTAD)

2. European Neighbourhood Policy, which is bilateral with two sub-categories of countries:[115]
   a. the eastern neighbourhood consists of Armenia, Azerbaijan, Belarus, Georgia, Moldova and Ukraine
   b. the southern neighbourhood consists of Algeria, Egypt, Israel, Jordan, Lebanon, Libya, Morocco, Palestine, Syria and Tunisia
3. accession and candidate countries through bilateral agreements with three sub-categories of countries:
   a. accession
   b. candidate
   c. Stabilisation and Association Agreements (SAAs) for the Western Balkans: Albania, Macedonia, Montenegro, Serbia, Kosovo and Bosnia.
4. the EEA/EFTA model—a plurilateral regional agreement:
   a. EEA, which fully implements EU state aid rules
   b. EFTA, which introduces a parallel multilateral state aid system
   c. Switzerland, which is in EFTA but not part of the EEA; it is also not part of the multilateral system but instead has introduced domestic laws on subsidies control.

For a systematic analysis of the export of EU state aid provisions, this book looks at type of control applied, and the level of success,[116] which may vary depending on the distinct category of international agreements,[117] however the type of agreement seems to correlate with the significance of trade and cooperation with the EU's third country/countries.[118]

Extra-EU BITs (due to being EU exclusive competence) and intra-EU BITs are both subject to the EU's internal control. Thus, as demonstrated by this book, these are also covered by state aid rules. For extra-EU BITs, however, this control is limited to the actions of the Member States. With regard to the actions of the third country, this is the part of the agreement that will fall under other public international law, including GATT if the actions are related to goods. In the discussion in this

[115] See Commission's website at https://ec.europa.eu/neighbourhood-enlargement/neighbourhood/countries_en.

[116] According to Lavenex and Schimmelfennig (2009), the EU's success in extending parts of the *acquis communautaire* beyond EU borders depends on the instruments used for the regulatory transfer. Blauberger and Krämer (2010) identify three major groups of countries, which consist of categories 2, 3 and 4 discussed and studied by this thesis, where this has been successful.

[117] See Papadopoulos (2010).

[118] To demonstrate the state of the EU's trade agreements in 2019, see the Commission's web page (EC 2016b).

dissertation, special attention is paid to the fact that, in a system that tries to create and develop a harmonised and nation neutral internal market with a comprehensive and coordinated investment policy between EU internal and external action, a parallel existence of another system that applies a most favoured nation (MFN) treatment intra-EU is detrimental. As some academics have pointed out, intra-EU BITs potentially include even national treatment (NT) disguised, which is prohibited by Article 18 of the TFEU as non-discrimination on the grounds of nationality[119] and constitutes a crucial element of the notion of state aid control.[120] The research question is therefore:

> How does the European Union (EU) state aid law affect the future of EU investment policy in a global context?

Furthermore, each chapter utilises an individual sub-question.

Overall, depending on importance and influence of trade with the EU and the third country, the application and effect of EU state aid law on a global scale generally occurs in a pattern similar to ripples in a pond. While the inner ripples, from the internal market to EEA and EFTA countries, are distinct, every subsequent ripple of the external dimension becomes more obscure, relating to the type and content of the international agreement regulating subsidies.

---

[119] According to the Commission (EC 2015f). Many academics echo the Commission's viewpoint: see Kokott and Sobotta (2016); Von Papp (2013); Dimopoulos (2011); Reinisch (2013); Andersen and Hindelang (2016); Hindelang (2012b). Advocate General (AG) Wathelet in *C-284/16 Achmea (AG Opinion)* (2017) held that intra EU-BITs and ISDS were compatible with EU law. According to AG Wathelet, Article 18 of the TFEU, which prohibits discrimination based on nationality, only prohibits national treatment (NT) – that is, it is not applicable to most favoured nation (MFN) provisions. Further, AG Wathelet argued that investors covered by a BIT were not in the same situation as those not included by the BIT due to the BIT itself (paras 65, 71–5). Wathelet drew analogies from double tax treatments (paras 79–82). AG Wathelet also concluded that arbitral tribunals were courts conforming to EU law, so they should be able to request preliminary rulings from the CJEU on questions concerning the interpretation of the EU treaties (paras 84–131). Similar arguments have been echoed in literature by Tietje and Wackernagel (2014), Eilmansberger (2009). His opinion has been highly criticised, and claims of lack of impartiality have even been raised—see, for example, van Harten (2017), Wessels (2017) and Carta and Ankersmit (2018), due to the fact that AG Wathelet's opinion reflects the previously published work of his legal assistant, Paschalis Paschalidis, who has had ties to the ISDS legal industry since 2009. As the CJEU Grand Chambers judgment in *Achmea C-284/16* (2018) did not answer the question regarding discrimination, the issue remains in doubt. Even responses from arbitration circles have been controversial: see Dimitrov (2017) and Lavranos (2017). For situations where NT may take place, see Burgstaller (2006), p. 857; Dimopoulos (2011), p. 83 and Lenk et al. (2016), p. 5, referring to *Factortame II* (1991).

[120] See Notion of Aid Notice, paras. 55,84, 89 118,120-122, 125; *C-20/15 P - Commission v World Duty Free Group* (2016), para 55; *C-106/09 P – Commission and Spain v Government of Gibraltar and United Kingdom* (2011) and *C-279/08 P – Commission v Netherlands* (2011), paras 88 et seq.

1.7 The Method, Material and Delimitations

In its attempt to assess and demonstrate the application and effect of state aid law on the future of EU investment policy on a global scale and the validity of the arguments put forward by the author, this research will, among other things, entail:

- a study of the tensions relating to state aid law created by the investment protection clauses in intra-EU BITs, extra-EU BITs and the EU's IIAs as interpreted by the Commission, the CJEU and international investment tribunals
- the solutions that the Member States and the EU have come up with to deal with these tensions.

This is done by utilising a doctrinal analysis—namely, by analysing and discussing legal provisions, texts of international agreements,[121] *opinio juris*, case law and literature on the subject where relevant. Special attention is also paid to reviewing the law in practice by studying the combination of concepts, considerations and actions of states and their institutions, and their interaction with international institutions,[122] such as the EU. Further, because the focus of this book is not on states, but on the EU and its interactions with other international actors, this book also discusses the EU's interactions with other international organisations.

In a debate over the development of EU global investment policy through a state aid law lens, the examination of the position the EU has adopted on the internal and external dimension of both state aid policy and investment policy is central. To examine this properly the roles and the interaction of the legislative (European Parliament and Council), judicial (CJEU) and enforcement (Commission) organs of the EU in this context will have to be analysed and explained.

Relevant case law from the CJEU on the specific subject is still sparse.[123] This book uses *Micula*[124] as a case study to exemplify the problems explored. It is about intra-EU BITs, but can well be adapted to any situation, including an extra-EU BIT

[121] For this purpose, provisions on subsidies and investment in EU trade instruments (every bilateral and plurilateral trade agreement with countries or trading blocs in force or under negotiation by the EU) have been catalogued in Appendices I and II of this thesis. Subsequently, the data collected have been observed and analysed. These data have provided an insight into how the EU systematically includes subsidies/state aid provisions in its trade instruments.

[122] See by analogy, Ibbetson (2005), p. 864. McCrudden (2006) argues that this type of research is covered by doctrinal analysis as well.

[123] Cases such as *Opinion 2/15 of the Court (Full Court)* (2017); *Achmea C-284/16* (2018); *Opinion 1/17* (2019); *Micula V (EU)* (2019) and *Micula VI (EU)* (2022). have surfaced since work on this book commenced.

[124] *Micula Award* (2013). This started a lengthy procedure of appeals and cases. See *Micula I (EU)* (2014); *Micula II (EU)* (2014); *Micula III (EU)* (2016). Micula's first appeal to the CJEU *Micula IV* (EU) was withdrawn by the appellant as of 29 February 2016 for amendment but the *Micula V (EU)* (2019) judgment emerged from the CJEU (General Court) in June 2109. This decision was successfully appealed by the Commission to the ECJ as C-638/19 P - Commission v European Food and Others, (*Micula VI (EU*). See also *Micula I (USA)* (2015a); *Micula I (USA)* (2015b); *Micula III (USA)* (2016).

and BITs or by analogy to FTAs concluded between the EU and a third country. The *Micula* case, is prominent and a prime example of a possible collision between state aid law and BITS, as it assesses a situation where an arbitration tribunal does not respect EU state aid law. Based on the EU's view of bilateral investment treaties, the EU's response is clear—under EU law jurisdiction, a BIT between two Member States cannot legally distort competition in the internal market (state aid law being part of EU competition law). The same principle should apply for extra-EU BITs, as these also have an anti-competitive effect on the EU's internal market.

One way to understand this conflict is to look at the different parties applying the hierarchy of sources of law. The international sources of law used by arbitration tribunals are, in order of precedence, (1) international treaties, (2) general customary international law and (3) general principles of law.[125] At the same time, the EU court's sources of law are, in order of precedence, (1) EU primary legislation,[126] (2) general principles of law, (3) the EU's international agreements, (4) EU secondary legislation,[127] and (5) conventions between the Member States.[128] It means that, contrary to the traditional sources of international law for EU courts, EU primary law takes precedence over other international law.

Although based on treaties (TEU & TFEU) and the Charter of Fundamental Rights (Charter), EU law is hard law, not soft law. It is integrated into and included in the Member States' national legislation and enforceable through national courts as an extension of the EU's organs. The legal instance, under EU law, that has the final word in interpreting EU law is the CJEU. In addition to literal interpretation applied in public international law, other interpretation methods are used frequently by CJEU, including contextual interpretation and teleological interpretation.

The arbitration tribunals posit that the Vienna Convention on the Law of Treaties (VCLT) supersedes the EU legislation, seen by them as *lex specialis*, while the CJEU posit that EU law is *lex superior* in relation to EU's international agreements. Thus, there is a built-in conflict in the evaluation of current intra-EU and extra-EU BITs between the two. This situation leads to increased ISDS and puts the Member States in conflict with either their BITs or EU law.

Selected material for this book consists of case law from the CJEU, EU Commission decisions and policy documents, as well as investment tribunal practices. The criteria for selection are that: they relate to the specific subject; they apply analogically to the specific subject; or they have a specific impact on how the subject should be interpreted or applied. Doctrinal work is, by necessity, not averse to

[125] According to the Statute of the International Court of Justice (ICJ), Article 38 §1 (UN), 1945.

[126] Treaty on European Union (TEU), Treaty on the Functioning of the European Union (TFEU) and the Charter of Fundamental Rights (Charter)—General Principles of Law.

[127] Legislative Acts: Regulations, Directives & Decisions; Non-legislative Acts; Delegated Acts and Implementing Acts; other Acts—that is, Recommendations and opinions, etc.

[128] Committee of Permanent Representatives in the European Union (COREPER) decisions—international agreements.

sources of inter-disciplinary engagement.[129] Therefore, to explain the development of international rules for competition and investment and forces driving these, theories such as those concerning the free market, European integration and European governance are described. By drawing and synthesising from interdisciplinary literature relevant to the subject matter, this book aims to display a coherent overview of the interplay between EU state aid law and EU investment policy, rather than ending up lonely, isolated and perhaps missing pieces of the puzzle.[130]

The following limitations are deemed inherent and coherent for the subject of this book: the notion of competition policy and the law will cover all EU competition law, anti-competitive measures by firms and states alike. Competition law outside the EU's sphere of influence is beyond the scope of this work. It covers only the core state aid provisions, as established by Title VII, Ch. 1, Rules on Competition, Section 2.[131] Further, in the context of the EU, only individual countries' trade relations for bilateral investment treaties and investment provisions in bilateral or plurilateral trade agreements are covered in depth.

Political Dialogue and Co-operation Agreements, which typically include provisions promoting investment and cooperation in competition policy, are outside of the scope of this work due to their difference in focus from the BITs and TIPs.[132] However, where no trade agreements exist between the EU and other trading blocs, Political Dialogue and Co-operation Agreements are included in the data collected to obtain more complete data on investment and subsidies provisions.

The focus of this work is the timeline from SAAP, 2005 and forward, which is reflected by the literature chosen. For reasons of consistency and overall comprehensibility, backward glimpses are provided to establish the notions behind subsidies/state aid control and the development of state aid law and international investment agreements.

---

[129] McCrudden (2006), p. 635.

[130] See Simpson (1981), p. 632.

[131] This means that that Article 106.2 of the TFEU, the legal basis for services of general economic interest (SGEI), is not included in this thesis. Basically, the author deems that inclusion of SGEIs is not relevant. Even though the full impact of state aid law is dampened for SGEI, investment protection proceedings based on revocation of an SGEI that constitutes internal market incompatible state aid would not fundamentally differ from proceeding without the SGEI element.

[132] For example, see Political Dialogue and Co-operation Agreement between the Andean community and the European Community (Andean–EC Cooperation Agreement, 2016), the Partnership and Cooperation Agreement between Azerbaijan and the EU (Azerbaijan–EC Cooperation Agreement, 1999), currently being updated to a trade agreement, and the Partnership and Cooperation agreement between the EU and Tajikistan. Each agreement includes several investment provisions and cooperation on competition policy.

This book uses the EU's terminology for its trade agreements,[133] with EU categorising its trade agreements into three main types:[134]

- Customs unions, which eliminate tariffs in bilateral trade and determine joint customs duties for other imports
- Association Agreements, Stabilisation Agreements, Free Trade Agreements (which also can be 'Deep and Comprehensive') and Economic Partnership Agreements, which either remove or reduce tariffs in bilateral trade[135]
- Partnership and Cooperation Agreements, which set the general scheme for bilateral economic relations but does not deal with tariffs.

Four main categories of literature have been used for the analysis of the subject matter of this book; the primary category consists of legal literature. Second and third, the rationale behind state aid and investment agreements shows evidence of the interaction between state aid law, politics and economics. Therefore, publications on political science and economic science are utilised to fill gaps existing in the legal literature on this book's subject matter. In the same vein, the fourth and final category of literature constitutes material on other driving forces shaping the direction of EU politics and law indirectly by lobbying or shaping public opinions, these are published by the NGOs and the press.

For cogency, other sources for this monograph include materials beyond the appropriate traditional sources of legal analysis. Due to the Commission's central role in the field of state aid policy, insights provided by unofficial sources like speeches and blogs by key EU officials (besides official documents) are included. Some relevant legal blogs written by specialists in the state aid area have also been included, as these are able to provide up-to-date insights and reflections. The literature presented, cases and other relevant information and statistics for this book originate from international and national databases.[136]

---

[133] The WTO classifies the EU as a regional trade agreement (RTA) and the EU's trade agreements as PTAs. According to the WTO, RTAs are reciprocal preferential trade agreements that 'include free trade agreements and customs unions'. See WTO homepage (WTO) at https://www.wto.org/english/tratop_e/region_e/rta_pta_e.htm.

[134] See the Commission's web page at https://ec.europa.eu/trade/policy/countries-and-regions/negotiations-and-agreements.

[135] Which is the function of PTAs. FTAs are a specific type of PTA. While both types of agreement may apply for goods, services and investment, and broadly share the same goals, the scope of FTAs is much broader.

[136] These are, among others, the EU's databases (mainly EUROPA) (EU 2016). For news on EU policy, Euractiv. Internationally from Google Scholar, ResearchGate, Wolters Kluwer, SSRN and Oxford Academic Journals. From the US, LexisNexis, Westlaw and EBSCOhost. For other data, many databases employed have free access for all. For arbitration cases, useful databases are UNCTAD's Investment Policy Hub at https://investmentpolicy.unctad.org, UNCITRAL at https://www.iisd.org/itn/tag/uncitral, the World Bank (ICSID) database at https://icsid.worldbank.org/en/Pages/resources/Bilateral-Investment-Treaties-Database.aspx, Italaw at https://www.italaw.com and the Investment Arbitration Reporter at https://www.iareporter.com. The author had access to this website for four months and wishes to express gratitude to the Griffith University library

Cases

Achmea BV (formerly known as Eureko BV) v Slovak Republic Final Award, PCA Case No. 2008-13 (UNCITRAL, 2012)
Achmea BV (formerly known as Eureko BV) v Slovak Republic Award on Jurisdiction, Arbitrability and Suspension PCA Case No 2008-13 (Permanent Court of Arbitration, 2008)
AES Summit Generation Limited and AES-Tisza Erömü Kft v The Republic of Hungary, ICSID Award, ICSID No. ARB/07/22, Italaw (International Centre for Settlement of Investment Disputes, 2010)
AES Summit Generation Limited and AES Tisza Eromu Kft v Republic of Hungary (Application for Annulment), No. ICSID Case No. ARB/07/22 (ad hoc, 2012)
Anglia Auto Accessories Limited v Czech Republic Final Award, SCC Case V 2014/181 (Stockholm Chamber of Commerce, 2017)
Associação Sindical dos Juízes Portugueses v Tribunal de Contas, case C-64/16, ECLI:EU:C:2018:117 (European Court of Justice (Grand Chamber) 2018)
Bundesgerichtshof Beschluss des I. Zivilsenats vom 31.10.2018 – I ZB 2/15 (Bundesgerichtshof, 2018)
Cassa di Risparmio di San Miniato and Cassa di Risparmio di San Miniato SpA, case C-222/04, ECLI:EU: C:2006:8 (European Court of Justice, 2006)
Charanne B.V. and Construction Investments S.à.r.l. v Kingdom of Spain Final Award, SCC Case No. 062/2012 (Stockholm Chamber of Commerce, 2016)
Commission of the European Communities v Federal Republic of Germany, case C-5/89 ECLI:EU:C:1990:320 (European Court of Justice, 1990)
Commission of the European Communities v Kingdom of Sweden, ECLI:EU: C:2009:119 (European Court of Justice (Grand Chamber), 2009)
Commission of the European Communities v Republic of Austria C-205/06, ECLI: EU:C:2009:118 (European Court of Justice (Grand Chamber), 2009)
Commission of the European Communities v Republic of Finland, ECLI:EU: C:2009:715 (European Court of Justice, 2009)
Eastern Sugar B.V. (Netherlands) v The Czech Republic, SCC Case No. 088/2004 – Final Award (UNCITRAL ad hoc arbitration tribunal, 2007)
Eastern Sugar B.V.(Netherlands) v The Czech Republic, Partial Award SCC Case No. 088/2004 – Partial Award, Italaw (Stockholm Chamber of Commerce (SCC), 2007)
Eco Swiss China Time Ltd v Benetton International NV, case C-126/97, ECLI:EU: C:1999:269 (European Court of Justice, 1999)
EDF International SA v the Republic of Hungary, Swiss, No. 4A 34/2015 (Tribunal Federal, 2015)

personnel, especially Kim Kelly, and to Luke Petersen from the IA Reporter who offered a free trial period for Griffith University.

Eiser Infrastructure Limited and Energía Solar Luxembourg S.à.r.l. v Kingdom of Spain Award, ICSID Case No ARB/13/36 (International Centre for Settlement of Investment Disputes ad hoc, 2017)

Electrabel S.A. v Hungary Award, ICSID Case No ARB/07/19 (International Centre for Settlement of Investment Disputes, 2015)

Electrabel S.A. v The Republic of Hungary, Decision on Jurisdiction, Applicable Law and Liability, ICSID Case No. ARB/07/19 Italaw (ICSID 2012).

Electricite de France (EDF) International S.A. v Republic of Hungary (PCA (Permanent Court of Arbitration), 2014)

Eureko B.V. v The Slovak Republic, Award on Jurisdiction, Arbitrability and Suspension, PCA Case No. 2008-13, Italaw (Rermanent Court of Arbitration, 2010)

European Commission and Spain v Government of Gibraltar and United Kingdom, joined Cases C-106/09 P and C-107/09 P, ECLI:EU:C:2011:732 (European Court of Justice (Grand Chamber), 2011)

European Commission v Kingdom of the Netherlands, Case C-279/08 P, ECLI:EU:C:2011:551 (European Court of Justice, 2011)

European Commission v Slovak Republic, Case C-264/09, ECLI:EU:C:2011:580 (European Court of Justice, 2011)

European Commission v Banco Santander and Santusa, joined Cases C 20/15 P and C 21/15 P, ECLI:EU:C:2016:981 (European Court of Justice (Grand Chamber), 2016)

European Commission v European Food and Others, Case C-638/19 P, ECLI:EU:C:2022:50 (European Court of Justice, 2022)

Flaminio Costa v ENEL, Case 6-64 No. 61964J0006, ECLI:EU:C:1964:66, Eurlex (European Court of Justice (ECJ), 1964)

Ioan Micula, Viorel Micula, S.C. European Food S.A, S.C. Starmill S.R.L. and S.C. Multipack S.R.L. v Romania, No. No. 1:14-cv-00600 (APM) (U.S. Dist. LEXIS 64461 (DC), 2015a)

Ioan Micula, Viorel Micula, S.C. European Food S.A, S.C. Starmill S.R.L. and S.C. Multipack S.R.L. v Romania, No. WL 4643180, at *1 No. 15 MISC. 107, 2015 (Southern District of New York, 2015b)

Ioan Micula, Viorel Micula, S.C. European Food S.A, S.C. Starmill S.R.L. and S.C. Multipack S.R.L. v Romania, ICSID Award, Case No. ARB/05/20, Italaw (ICSID ad hoc, 2013)

Ireland and Apple Sales International and Apple Operations Europe v European Commission, joined cases T-778/16 and T-892/16, No. EU:T:2020:338 (Court of Justice of the European Union (GC), 2020).

Isolux Infrastructure Netherlands B.V. v Kingdom of Spain Award, SCC Case V 2013/153 (Stockholm Chamber of Commerce, 2016).

Jan Oostergetel & Theodora Laurentius v Slovak Republic Decision on Jurisdiction (UNCITRAL ad hoc, 2010).

Land Rheinland-Pfalz v Alcan Deutschland GmbH, case C-24/95, ECLI:EU:C:1997:163 (European Court of Justice, 1997)

Manfredi et al. v Lloyd Adriatico Assicurazioni SpA et al, joined Cases C-295–98/04, ECLI:EU:C:2006:461 (European Court of Justice, 2006)
Micula and Others v Commission, case T-646/14, ECLI:EU:T:2016:135, OJ C 136 Removal from the register (Court of Justice of the European Union (GC), 2016)
Micula and Others v Commission, joined cases T-624/15, T-694/15 and T-704/15, ECLI:EU:T:2019:423, Curia (Court of Justice of the European Union (GC), 2019)
Micula v Commission, case T-694/15 (Court of Justice of the European Union, 2019)
Ministero dell'Economia e delle Finanze v Cassa di Risparmio di Firenze SpA, Fondazione Cassa di Risparmio di San Miniato and Cassa di Risparmio di San Miniato SpA, case C-222/04, ECLI:EU: C:2006:8 (European Court of Justice, 2006)
NV Algemene Transport- en Expeditie Onderneming van Gend & Loos v Netherlands Inland Revenue, Case 26-62, ECLI:EU:C:1963:1, Eur-Lex (European Court of Justice, 1963)
Opinion 1/09 of the Court (Full Court), EU:C:2011:123 (European Court of Justice, 2011)
Opinion 1/17 of the Court (Full Court), ECLI:EU:C:2019:341 (European Court of Justice (Full Court), 2019)
Opinion 1/91 of the Court, ECLI:EU:C:1991:490 (European Court of Justice, 1991)
Opinion 2/13 of the Court (Full Court), ECLI:EU:C:2014:2454 (European Court of Justice (Full Court), 2014)
Opinion delivered pursuant to the second subparagraph of Article 228 (1) of the Treaty – Draft agreement between the Community, on the one hand, and the countries of the European Free Trade Association, on the other, relating to the creation of the European Economic Area, ECLI:EU:C:1991:490 (European Court of Justice, 1991)
Philip Morris Asia Limited (Hong Kong) v The Commonwealth of Australia, 2012-12 (Permanent Court of Arbitration (PCA), 2015)
Philip Morris Asia Limited v The Commonwealth of Australia, UNCITRAL,| PCA Case No. 2012-12 (Permanent Court of Arbitration, 2016)
The Queen, on the application of International Association of Independent Tanker Owners (Intertanko) and Others v Secretary of State for Transport., case-308/06, EU:C:2008:312 (European Court of Justice (Grand Chamber), 2008)
The Queen v Secretary of State for Transport, ex parte Factortame Ltd and others (European Commission 2009), Decision on State aid granted by Austria to the company Postbus in the Lienz district C 16/07 (ex NN 55/06) (notified under document C(2008) 7034) No. 2009/845/EC
RREEF Infrastructure (G.P.) Limited and RREEF Pan-European Infrastructure Two Lux S.à.r.l. v Kingdom of Spain Decision on Jurisdiction, ICSID Case No ARB/13/30 (ICSID, 2016)
Rupert Joseph Binder v Czech Republic Award on Jurisdiction of 6 June 2007 (UNCITRAL ad hoc, 2007)

SA.38517 Micula v Romania, 2014/NN (Commission DG Comp, 2014)
Saluka Investments BV v The Czech Republic Partial Award (Permanent Court of Arbitration, 2006)
Slowakische Republik (Slovak Republic) v Achmea BV Case C-284/16, ECLI:EU:C:2018:158 (European Court of Justice (Grand Chamber), 2018)
Slowakische Republik v Achmea BV, case C-284/16 Opinion of Advocate General Wathelet, ECLI:EU:C:2017:699 (Advocate General Wathelet, 2017)
State Aid SA.38517(2014/C) Romania Implementation of Arbitral award Micula v Romania of 11 December 2013 (ex 2014/NN), No. C(2014) 6848 final, Italaw (European Commission, 2014)
T-Mobile Netherlands BV v Raad van beestuur van de Nederlandse Mededingingsautoriteit, ECLI:EU:C:2009:343 (European Court of Justice, 2009)
US Steel Global Holdings IBV v The Slovak Republic, PCA Case No. 2013-6 (Permanent Court of Arbitration, 2013)
US Steel Global Holdings IBV v The Slovak Republic, UNCITRAL Procedural Order No. 6 (Stipulated Termination Order) PCA Case No. 2013-6 (2014)
Vattenfall AB and others v Federal Republic of Germany, ICSID Case No. ARB/12/12 (ICSID Tribunal, pending)
Vattenfall AB; Vattenfall GMBH; Vattenfall Europe Nuclear Energy GMBH; Kernkraftwerk Krummel GMBH & CO. OHG; Kernkraftwerk Brunsbuttel GMBH & CO. OHG v Federal Republic of Germany (Decision on the Achmea issue), No. ICSID Case No. ARB/12/12 (ICSID ad hoc, 2018)
Veolia Propreté v Arab Republic of Egypt, ICSID Case No. ARB/12/15 (ICSID, 2012)
Vereniging voor Energie, Milieu en Water and Others v Directeur van de Dienst uitvoering en toezicht energie, case 17/03, ECLI:EU:C:2005:362 (European Court of Justice (Grand Chamber), 2005)
WNC Factoring Ltd v Czech Republic Award PCA Case No 2014-34 (Permanent Court of Arbitration, 2017)

References

Adascalitei S (2017) EU–Japan Partnership Agreement. CIArb News. http://www.ciarb.org/news/ciarb-news/news-detail/features/2017/08/31/eu-japan-partnership-agreement
AFFGN (2016) Intra-EU Investment treaties - Non-paper Austria, Finland, France, Germany and the Netherlands. http://www.s2bnetwork.org/wp-content/uploads/2016/05/Intra-EU-Bits2-18-05.pdf
Albi A, Diamond A, Antoine B (2016) Legal statement on investment protection and investor-state dispute settlement mechanisms in TTIP and CETA. https://stop-ttip.org/wp-content/uploads/2016/10/28.10.16-Updated-Legal-Statement_EN.pdf
Allen R (2017) New EU–Japan trade deal: EU declares ISDS "dead". Global Arbitration News, 17 July. https://globalarbitrationnews.com/new-eu-japan-trade-deal-eu-declares-isds-dead
Anderer CE (2010) Bilateral investment treaties and the EU legal order: implications of the Lisbon Treaty. Brook J Int Law 35:851

Andersen TT, Hindelang S (2016) The day after: Alternatives to intra-EU BITs. J World Invest Trade 17(6):984–1014

Ankersmit L (2015). Legality of investor-state dispute settlement (ISDS) under EU law. http://www.clientearth.org/health-environment/health-environment-publications/legality-of-investor-state-dispute-settlement-under-eu-law-3020

Ankersmit L (2016a) The compatibility of investment arbitration in trade agreements with the judicial system. J Eur Environ Plan Law 13(1):46–63

Ankersmit L (2016b) Is ISDS in EU trade agreements legal under EU law? Investment Treaty News, 29 February. https://www.iisd.org/itn/2016/02/29/is-isds-in-eu-trade-agreements-legal-under-eu-law-laurens-ankersmit

Bacon K (2017) European Union law of state aid, 3rd edn. Oxford University Press, Oxford

Basedow R (2016) A legal history of the EU's international investment policy. J World Invest Trade 17(5):743–772

Bermann GA (2012) Navigating EU law and the law of international arbitration. Arbitr Int 28(3): 397–446

Bierbrauer E (2014) Transatlantic Trade and Investment Partnership (TTIP) negotiations: State of play. http://www.europarl.europa.eu/RegData/etudes/BRIE/2014/536397/EXPO_BRI(2014)536397_EN.pdf

Biondi A (2013) State aid is falling down, falling down: an analysis of the case law on the notion of aid. Common Mark Law Rev 50(6):1719–1743

Biondi A, Rubini L (2005) Aims, effects and justifications: EC state aid law and its impact on national social policies. In: Dougan M, Spaventa E (eds) Social welfare and EU law. Hart, Oxford

Blomströ M, Kokko A (2003) The economics of foreign direct investment incentives. NBER Working Paper 9489. https://econpapers.repec.org/paper/nbrnberwo/9489.htm

Blauberger M, Krämer RU (2010) European competition vs global competitiveness: Transferring EU rules on state aid and public procurement beyond Europe. CCP Working Paper 10-10. https://www.uea.ac.uk/documents/107435/107587/1.168372!ccp10-10.pdf

Botta M (2013) State aid control in South-East Europe: the endless transition. Eur St Aid LQ 12(1): 85–96

Botta M, Schwellnus G (2015) Enforcing state aid rules in EU candidate countries: a qualitative comparative analysis of the direct and indirect effects of conditionality. J Eur Public Policy 22(3):335–352

Bourgeois J, Dawar K, Evenett, SJ (2007) A comparative analysis of selected provisions in free trade agreements. http://sro.sussex.ac.uk/id/eprint/59639

Burgstaller M (2006) Nationality of corporate investors and international claims against the investor's own state. J World Invest Trade 7(6):857–877

Businesseurope (2015) EU state aid control in the context of global competition. Paper presented at ERA annual conference on European state aid law 2015, TRIER. https://www.businesseurope.eu/publications/eu-state-aid-control-context-global-competition-address-morten-qvist-fog-era-annual

Byström N (2016) TTIP vs Europeans: A wake-up call for the Commission. http://www.euractiv.com/section/trade-society/opinion/ttip-vs-europeans-a-wake-up-call-for-the-commission

Carta A, Ankersmit L (2018) AG Wathelet in C-284/16 Achmea: Saving ISDS? http://europeanlawblog.eu/2018/01/08/ag-wathelet-in-c-28416-achmea-saving-isds

Chari RS, Cavatorta F (2002) Economic actors' political activity in 'overlap issues': privatisation and EU state aid control. West Eur Polit 25(4):119–142

Cole T (2014) Legal instruments and practice of arbitration in the EU. European Parliament, Brussels. http://www.europarl.europa.eu/studies

Council of the European Union (2010) Conclusions on a comprehensive European international investment policy. Publications Office of the European Union, Luxembourg

Cremona M (2003) State aid control: Substance and procedure in the Europe agreements and the stabilisation and association agreements. Eur Law J 9:265

Damro C (2013) EU State aid policy and the politics of external trade relations. J Ind Compet Trade 13(1):159–170
Damro C, Guay T (2016) European competition policy and globalization. Springer, New York
Deli MB, Marceddu ML (2015) Is the European Commission issuing a dismissal letter to arbitrators. http://arbitrationblog.kluwerarbitration.com/2015/10/19/the-investment-court-system-for-ttip-is-the-european-commission-issuing-a-death-certificate-for-arbitrators
Dimitrov I (2017) Digesting the AG Wathelet Opinion in Case C-284/16 Slowakische Republik v Achmea BV. Is it a trap? Kluwer Arbitration Blog, 7 October. http://arbitrationblog.kluwerarbitration.com/2017/10/07/digesting-ag-wathelet-opinion-case-c-28416-slowakische-republik-v-achmea-bv-trap
Dimopoulos A (2011) The validity and applicability of international investment agreements between EU Member States under EU and international law. Common Mark Law Rev 48(1):63
Eberhardt P (2016) The zombie ISDS. https://www.tni.org/files/publication-downloads/the_zombie_isds.pdf
Eckes C (2016) International rulings and the EU legal order: Autonomy as legitimacy? CLEER Papers 2:31. Centre for the Law of EU External Relations, The Hague
ECOFIN (2006) 2006 EFC Report to the Commission and the Council on the Movement of Capital and the Freedom of Payments. http://register.consilium.europa.eu/doc/srv?l=EN&f=ST%205044%202007%20INIT
Eilmansberger T (2009) Bilateral investment treaties and EU law. Common Mark Law Rev 46(2): 383–429
EUR-Lex (n.d.) Internal market. European Union, Brussels
European Association of Judges (EAJ) (2015) Statement from the European Association of Judges on the proposal from the European Commission on a new Investment Court System. European Association of Judges, Paris
European Commission (EC) (2001) Ninth survey on state aid in the European Union. European Union, Brussels
European Commission (EC) (2008) Provisions on international relations in EU competition policy: Situation as of 1 January 2008. European Union, Brussels. https://publications.europa.eu/en/publication-detail/-/publication/50fd3279-5b8b-4f81-b534-b00fbedbff85/language-en
European Commission (EC) (2010) Communication from the Commission to the Council, the European Parliament, the European Economic and Social Committee and the Committee of the Regions: Towards a comprehensive European international investment policy (Vol. COM (2010)343. European Union, Brussels
European Commission (EC) (2015a) Investment in TTIP and beyond – the path for reform. European Union, Brussels. http://trade.ec.europa.eu/doclib/docs/2015/may/tradoc_153408.PDF
European Commission (EC) (2015b) Investor to state dispute settlement (ISDS) Some facts and figures Retrieved from Brussels: http://trade.ec.europa.eu/doclib/docs/2015/january/tradoc-153046.pdf.
European Commission (EC) (2015c) Provisions on international relations in EU competition policy. http://ec.europa.eu/competition/international/legislation/legislation.html.
European Commission (EC) (2015d) Trade for all towards a more responsible trade and investment policy. European Union, Brussels
European Commission (EC) (2015e) Report on the online consultation on investment protection and investor-to-state dispute settlement in the Transatlantic Trade and Investment Partnership Agreement. Media release. http://europa.eu/rapid/press-release_MEMO-15-3202_en.htm.
European Commission (EC) (2015f) Commission asks Member States to terminate their intra-EU bilateral investment treaties. Media release. http://europa.eu/rapid/press-release_IP-15-5198_en.htm.
European Commission (EC) (2016a) Commission staff working document on the movement of capital and the freedom of payments. DG FISMA, Brussels
European Commission (EC) (2016b) Map of EU free trade agreements. http://trade.ec.europa.eu/doclib/docs/2012/june/tradoc_149622.pdf

European Commission (EC) (2016c) Aid to Apple SA.38373 $, IP/16/2923
European Commission (EC) (2017a) Agreements – trade – European Commission. http://ec.europa.eu/trade/policy/countries-and-regions/agreements
European Commission (EC) (2017b) Commission staff working document on the movement of capital and the freedom of payments. DG FISMA, Brussels
European Commission (EC) (2017c) Investment. http://ec.europa.eu/trade/policy/accessing-markets/investment
European Commission (EC) (2017d) Treaty of Lisbon enters into force: Implications for the EU's trade policy. http://trade.ec.europa.eu/doclib/press/index.cfm?id=493.
European Commission (EC) (2017e) Welcoming foreign direct investment while protecting essential interests. European Union, Brussels
European Commission (EC) (2017f) EU and Japan reach agreement in principle on Economic Partnership Agreement. Media release. http://europa.eu/rapid/press-release_IP-17-1902_en.htm
European Commission (EC) (2017g) CETA–EU–Canada Comprehensive Economic and Trade Agreement. http://ec.europa.eu/trade/policy/in-focus/ceta/index_en.htm
European Commission (EC) (2017h) Stop TTIP: European initiative against TTIP and CETA. https://stop-ttip.org
European Commission (EC) (2017i) A new EU trade agreement with Japan. http://trade.ec.europa.eu/doclib/docs/2017/july/tradoc_155684.PDF
European Commission (EC) (2018a) Communication from the Commission to the European Parliament and the Council, protection of intra-EU investment. European Union, Brussels
European Commission (EC) (2018b) #EUTrade news, the Multilateral Investment Court Project. http://trade.ec.europa.eu/doclib/press/index.cfm?id=1608
European Commission (EC) (2018c) EU and Japan finalise Economic Partnership Agreement. Media release. http://trade.ec.europa.eu/doclib/press/index.cfm?id=1767
European Commission (EC) (2020) White paper on levelling the playing field as regards foreign subsidies. European Union, Brussels
European Parliament (2015) European Parliament resolution of 8 July 2015 containing the European Parliament's recommendations to the European Commission on the negotiations for the Transatlantic Trade and Investment Partnership (TTIP)
European Parliament (EP) (2014) Investor-state dispute settlement (ISDS), Provisions in the EU's International Investment Agreements. European Union, Brussels. http://www.europarl.europa.eu/thinktank/en/document.html?reference=EXPO_STU(2014)534979
European Parliament (EP) and Council (2012) Regulation 1219/2012 establishing transitional arrangements for bilateral investment agreements between Member States and third countries
European Union (2008) Consolidated version of the Treaty on the Functioning of the European Union. Official Journal of the European Union,Vol. C 115/47). Lisbon: European Union
European Union (2016). EUROPA – reports, studies and booklets. http://europa.eu/european-union/documents-publications/reports-booklets_en
European Union and Canada (2016) EU–Canada Comprehensive Economic and Trade Agreement. European Union, Brussels
European Union and Singapore (2017) EU–Singapore Free Trade Agreement. European Union, Brussels
Featherstone K, Radaelli CM (2003) The politics of Europeanization. Oxford University Press, Oxford
Fietta V (2017) The king is dead, long live the king: The EU and the future of investor-state dispute settlement. http://isds.bilaterals.org/?the-king-is-dead-long-live-the
FISMA (2019a) Declaration of the representative of the Goverment of Hungary of 16 January 2019 on the legal consequences of the judgment of the Court of Justice in Achmea and on investment protection in the European Union. European Union, Brussels
FISMA (2019b) Declaration of the representative of the goverments of the Member States of 15 January 2019 on the legal consequences of the judgment of the Court of Justice in Achmea and on investment protection in the European Union. European Union, Brussels

FISMA (2019c) Declaration of the representative of the governments of the Member States of 16 January 2019 on the legal consequences of the judgment of the Court of Justice in Achmea and on investment protection in the European Union: The representatives of Goverments of Finland, Luxembourgh, Malta, Slovenia and Sweden. European Union, Brussels
FISMA (2020) Agreement for the termination of bilateral investment treaties between the Member States of the European Union. European Union, Brussels
Fleming J (2014) ISDS clause: A gateway to future trade deals. http://www.euractiv.com/section/trade-society/news/isds-clause-a-gateway-to-future-trade-deals
Fornalczyk A (2004) State aid regulation in candidate countries: the case of Poland. In: Biondi A, Eeckhout P, Flynn J (eds) The law of state aid in the European Union. Oxford University Press, Oxford
Galindo BR (2015) State aid control in the context of globalisation. European Commission, Brussels
Gallo D, Nicola FG (2015) The external dimension of EU investment law: Jurisdictional clashes and transformative adjudication. Fordham Int Law J 39:1081–1152
Geradin D (2004) Competition law and regional economic integration: An analysis of the southern Mediterranean countries. World Bank, Washington, DC
Goyette C-D (2006) The interface between EU state aid control and the WTO disciplines on subsidies. Eur State Aid Law Q 4:695–718
Griswold CP, Marine GM (1996) Political influences on state policy: higher-tuition, higher-aid, and the real world. Rev Higher Edu 19(4):361
Gubrynowicz A, Wierzbowski M (2009) Conflict of norms stemming from intra-EU BITs and EU legal obligations: some remarks on possible solutions. Oxford University Press, Oxford
Happ R, Tietje C (2013) EU, investment treaties, and investment treaty arbitration: Current developments and challenges. Transnatl Disp Manag 10(2) https://www.transnational-dispute-management.com/article.asp?key=1937
Hindelang S (2012a) Circumventing primacy of EU law and the CJEU's judicial monopoly by resorting to dispute resolution mechanisms provided for in inter-se treaties: the xase of intra-EU investment arbitration. Legal Iss Econ Integr 39:179
Hindelang S (2012b) Member State BITs: there's still (some) life in the old dog yet: Incompatibility of eexisting Member State BITs with EU law and possible remedies. In: Coleman J, Sachs L, Johnson L (eds) Yearbook on international investment law & policy. Oxford University Press, Oxford
Hoekman B, Holmes P (1999) Competition policy, developing countries and the WTO. World Econ 22(6):875–893
Ibbetson D (2005) Historical research in law. In: Cane P, Tushnet M (eds) The Oxford handbook of legal studies. Oxford University Press, Oxford
Is ISDS dead? No, multi-million lawsuits still on the horizon (2016). http://www.euractiv.com/section/trade-society/opinion/is-isds-dead-no-multi-million-lawsuits-still-on-the-horizon
Italianer A (2013) European competition policy and Japan KEIDANREN (Japan Business Federation). Japan Business Federation, Tokyo
Jarosz-Friis A, Pesaresi N, Kerle C (2010) EU–Korea FTA: A stepping stone towards better subsidies control at the international level. Competition Policy Newsletter 1. http://ec.europa.eu/competition/publications/cpn/2010_1_19.pdf
Kassim H, Lyons B (2013) The new political economy of EU state aid policy. J Ind Compet Trade 13(1):1–21
Kende T (2015) Arbitral awards classified as state aid under European Union law. ELTE LJ 37. https://eltelawjournal.hu/arbitral-awards-classified-state-aid-european-union-law
Kingdom of Belgium (2017) Minister Reynders submits request for opinion on CETA. Media release. https://diplomatie.belgium.be/en/newsroom/news/2017/minister_reynders_submits_request_opinion_ceta
Kleinheisterkamp J (2011) The next 10-year ECT investment arbitration: a vision for the future – from a European law perspective. London School of Economics and Political Science, London

Kleinheisterkamp J (2012) European policy space in international investment law. ICSID Rev Foreign Invest Law J 27(2):416–431

Kleinheisterkamp J (2014a) Who is afraid of investor-state arbitration? Or comparative law? LSE Law: Policy Briefing Paper No. 4. https://ssrn.com/abstract=2483775

Kleinheisterkamp J (2014b) Who is afraid of investor-state arbitration? Unpacking the riddle of 'no greater rights' in the TTIP. http://www.iisd.org/itn/2014/11/18/who-is-afraid-of-investor-state-arbitration-unpacking-the-riddle-of-no-greater-rights-in-the-ttip

Kleinheisterkamp J (2015) Investment treaty law and the fear for sovereignty: transnational challenges and solutions. Mod Law Rev 78(5):793–782

Kleinheisterkamp J, Poulsen LNS (2016) Investment protection in TTIP: three feasible proposals. European Yearbook of International Economic Law. Springer, Cham

Kokott J, Sobotta C (2016) Investment arbitration and EU law. In: Armstrong K (ed) Cambridge yearbook of European legal studies. Cambridge University Press, Cambridge

Konttinen J, Teivainen A (2013) Professor: Finland's legislative power may be in jeopardy. Helsinki Times, 16 Dec. http://www.helsinkitimes.fi/finland/finland-news/domestic/8717-professor-finland-s-legislative-power-may-be-in-jeopardy.html

Laprévote F-C, Frisch S, Can B (2015) Competition policy within the context of free trade agreements. The E15 Initiative, September. http://e15initiative.org/publications/competition-policy-within-the-context-of-free-trade-agreements

Lavenex S, Schimmelfennig F (2009) EU rules beyond EU borders: theorizing external governance in European politics. J Eur Public Policy 16(6):791–812

Lavranos N (2013) In defence of Member States' BITs gold standard: The Regulation 1219/2012 establishing a transitional regime for existing extra-EU BITs – a Member State's perspective. Transnatl Disp Manage (TDM) 10(2) https://papers.ssrn.com/sol3/papers.cfm?abstract_id=2226979

Lavranos N (2017) The poison pill for maintaining intra-EU BITs arbitration. http://arbitrationblog.practicallaw.com/the-poison-pill-for-maintaining-intra-eu-bits-arbitration

Law no. 18/2017 on approving the termination of agreements regarding the promotion and mutual protection of the investments concluded by Romania with the Member States of the European Union. Vol. Part I, no. 198. Bukarest: Official Journal of Romania

Lenk H (2015a) Challenging the notion of coherence in EU foreign investment policy. Eur J Legal Stud 2:6–20

Lenk H (2015b) Investor-state arbitration under TTIP: Resolving investment disputes in an (autonomous) EU legal order. SIEPS, Stockholm

Lenk H (2017) Investment arbitration under EU investment agreements: is there a role for an autonomous EU legal order? Eur Bus Law Rev 28(2):135–162

Lenk H, Rönnelid L, Dahlquist J (2016) The infringement proceedings over intra-EU investment treaties: An analysis of the case against Sweden. SIEPS, Stockholm

López JJP (2015) The concept of state aid under EU law: From internal market to competition and beyond. Oxford University Press, Oxford

Luja R (2007) Should fiscal state aid go global? EC Tax Rev 16(5):231–235

Luja R (2017) State aid recovery & investor protection for non-EU taxpayers. https://cris.maastrichtuniversity.nl/en/publications/state-aid-recovery-amp-investor-protection-for-non-eu-taxpayers-h

Maduro M (2007) Interpreting European law: judicial adjudication in a context of constitutional pluralism. Eur J Legal Stud 1:137

Malmstom C (2015). Proposing an investment court system. https://ec.europa.eu/commission/commissioners/2014-2019/malmstrom/blog/proposing-investment-court-system_en

Matei E (2015a) The chamber of secrets: the repudiation of the ISDS. RRDE 83. https://heinonline.org/HOL/LandingPage?handle=hein.journals/rianrwioe13&div=46&id=&page=

Matei E (2015b) An European approach to BITs, MITs and ISDS. https://www.slideshare.net/EmanuelaMatei/eu-approach-to-bit-autosaved

Matei E (2015c) Putting the cart before the horse: A doomed constitutional strategy for negotiating the T-TIP. http://eulawanalysis.blogspot.com/2015/08/putting-cart-before-horse-doomed.html
Matei E (2016) SA.38517 – Commission Decision of 30 March 2015 on state aid granted by Romania to Micula. Eur State Aid Law Q 15(1):134
Matei E, Ciurtin H (2016) Turning enemies into adversaries: TTIP negotiations and the quest for a new Westphalia momentum. Turkish Commer Law Rev 2(1):27–76
McCrudden C (2006) Legal research and the social sciences. Law Quart Rev 122. https://www.researchgate.net/publication/228183697_Legal_Research_and_the_Social_Sciences
McGowan L, Wilks S (1995) The first supranational policy in the European Union: Competition policy. Eur J Polit Res 28(2):141–169
Moskvan D (2015) Clash of intra-EU bilateral investment treaties with EU law: a bitter pill to swallow. Colum J Eur Law 22:101
Obrist T (2013) The end of Switzerland's cantonal tax regimes is near: what's next? Tax Notes Int 71(7):647
OECD (2011) Roundtable on Competition, State Aids and Subsisdies. Retrieved from Paris: http://www.oecd.org/competition/sectors/48070736.pdf
Ortolani P (2015) Intra-EU Arbitral Awards vis-à-vis Article 107 TFEU: state aid law as a limit to compliance. J Int Disp Settlement 6(1):118–135
Papadopoulos AS (2010) The international dimension of EU competition law and Policy. Cambridge University Press, Cambridge
Partnership and Cooperation Agreement between the European Communities and their Member States, of the one part, and the Republic of Azerbaijan, of the other par. (1999). European Communities, Brussels
Pascual Vives FJ (2014) Shaping the EU investment regime: Choice of forum and applicable law in international investment agreements. Cuadernos De Derecho Transnacional 6(1):269–294
Peretz G (2016) A star is torn: Brexit and state aid. Eur State Aid Law Quart 15(3):334–337
Peretz G, Bacon K (2016) Post-Brexit options for state aid. http://uksala.org/paper-on-post-brexit-options-for-state-aid
Peretz G, Bacon K, Taylor I (2017) Bringing state aid home: Could an effective domestic state aid regime be devised for the UK? http://uksala.org/bringing-state-aid-home-could-an-effective-domestic-state-aid-regime-be-devised-for-the-uk/#_ftn1
Pinto CS (2016) The 'narrow' meaning of the legitimate expectation principle in state aid law versus the foreign investor's legitimage expectations. Eur St Aid LQ 15(2):270–285
Political dialogue and co-operation agreement between the European Community and its Member States, of the one part, and the Andean Community and its Member States, Bolivia, Colombia, Ecuador, Peru and Venezuela, of the other part (2016). European Union, Brussels
Politico (2015) ISDS: The most toxic acronym in Europe. http://www.politico.eu/article/isds-the-most-toxic-acronym-in-europe
Reinisch A (2013) EU on the investment path, Quo Vadis Europe: the future of EU BITs and other investment agreements. Santa Clara J Int Law 12:111
Rubini L (2004) The international context of EC state aid law and policy: the regulation of subsidies in the WTO. In: Biondi A, Eeckhout P, Flynn J (eds) The law of state aid in the European Union. Oxford University Press, Oxford
Rubini L (2010) The definition of subsidy and state aid: WTO and EC law in comparative perspective. Oxford University Press, New York
Rydelski MS (2004) The EEA state aid regime. In: Biondi A, Eeckhout P, Flynn J (eds) The law of state aid in the European Union. Oxford University Press, Oxford
Schimmelfennig F (2012a) EU external governance and Europeanization beyond the EU. In: Levi-Faur D (ed) The Oxford handbook of governance. Oxford University Press, Oxford
Schimmelfennig F (2012b) Europeanization beyond Europe. Living Reviews in European Governance 7. https://doi.org/10.12942/lreg-2012-1
Schneiderhan P (2016) Stellungnahme zur Errichtung eines Investitionsgerichts für TTIP. Vorschlag der Europäischen Kommission 4(16):4

Schneiderman D (2016) On suffering and societal constitutionalism: at the border of international investment arbitration and human rights. In: Kahana T, Scolnicov A (eds) Boundaries of state, boundaries of rights: human rights, private actors, and positive obligations. Cambridge University Press, Cambridge

Schonberg M (2017) Continuity or change? State aid control in a post-Brexit United Kingdom. Compet Law J 1:47–57

Simpson AB (1981) The rise and fall of the legal treatise: legal principles and the forms of legal literature. Univ Chicago Law Rev 48(3):632–679

Sims A, Stone J (2016) TTIP has officially failed – but no one is admitting it, says German Vice-Chancellor Sigmar Gabriel. News, Europe, 28 Aug. http://www.independent.co.uk/news/world/europe/ttip-trade-deal-agreement-failed-brexit-latest-news-eu-us-germany-vice-chancellor-a7213876.html

Spaak C (1956) The Brussels Report on the General Common Market. http://aei.pitt.edu.ludwig.lub.lu.se/995/1/Spaak_report.pdf

Struckmann K, Forwood G, Kadri A (2016) Investor-state arbitrations and EU state aid rules: conflict or co-existence. Eur St Aid LQ 15(2):258–269

Szepesi S (2004) Comparing EU free trade agreements competition policy state aid. ECDPM, Maastricht

Tietje C (2013) Bilateral investment treaties between EU Member States (intra-EU-BITs): Challenges in the multilevel system of law. Transnational Dispute Management (TDM) 10(2) https://www.transnational-dispute-management.com/article.asp?key=1945

Tietje C, Wackernagel C (2014) Outlawing compliance? The rnforcement of intra-EU investment awards and EU state aid law. Transnational Dispute Management (TDM) 3. https://www.transnational-dispute-management.com/article.asp?key=2116

Tietje C, Wackernagel C (2015) Enforcement of Intra-EU ICSID awards. J World Invest Trade 16(2):205–247

Tietje C, Sipiorski E, Töpfer G (2012) Responsibility in investor-state-arbitration in the EU: managing financial responsibility linked to investor-state dispute settlement tribunals established by EU's International Investment Agreements. European Union, Brussels

Trehearne C (2017) Will 2018 mark a tipping point for binding investor-state arbitration? http://arbitrationblog.kluwerarbitration.com/2017/10/31/will-2018-mark-tipping-point-binding-investor-state-arbitration

UNCTAD (2004) Series on Issues in International Investment Agreements, series 1 INCENTIVES (UNCTAD/ITE/IIT/2003/5) 09 Feb 2004

UNCTAD (2016a) International Investment Agreements Navigator. http://investmentpolicyhub.unctad.org/IIA

UNCTAD (2016b) Investor-state dispute settlement: Review of developments in 2015. UNCTAD, Geneva. http://unctad.org/en/PublicationsLibrary/webdiaepcb2016d4_en.pdf

Understanding Concerning Certain U.S. Bilateral Investment Treaties, signed by the U.S., the European Commission, and acceding and candidate countries for accession to the European Unio, 22 September 2003

Van de Casteele K (2006) The international dimension of state aid. In: Rydelski MS (ed) The EC state aid regime: distortive effects of state aid on competition and trade. Cameron May, London

Van de Casteele K (2016) Changes and what drives them: evolution of state aid control. In: Rubini L, Hawkins J (eds) What shapes the law? Reflections on the history, law, politics and economics of international and European subsidy disciplines. European University Institute, Florence

Van Harten G (2007) Investment treaty arbitration and public law. Oxford University Press, Oxford

Van Harten G (2015a) Key flaws in the European Commission's proposals for foreign investor protection in TTIP. Osgoode Legal Studies Research Paper, No. 16/2016

Van Harten G (2015b) A Parade of Reforms: The European Commission's Latest Proposal for ISDS. https://ssrn.com/abstract=2603077 or https://doi.org/10.2139/ssrn.2603077

Van Harten G (2017) The ISDS legal industry and the European Court of Justice. https://gusvanharten.wordpress.com/all-posts

Van Harten G, Malysheuski P (2016). Who has benefited financially from investment treaty arbitration? An evaluation of the size and wealth of claimants. https://doi.org/10.2139/ssrn.2713876

Von Papp K (2013) Clash of autonomous legal orders: Can EU Member State courts bridge the jurisdictional divide between investment tribunals and the ECJ? A plea for direct referral from investment tribunals to the ECJ. Common Mark Law Rev 50(4):1039–1082

Wessels A (2017) An ISDS lobbyist in the EU Court of Justice? https://blog.ffii.org/an-isds-lobbyist-in-the-eu-court-of-justice

Chapter 2
The Parallel Development of FDI and Competition Policy

2.1 Introduction

The EU has rejected traditional ISDS in its international investment agreements and intra-EU BITs to protect the autonomy of the EU legal order and the right to regulate on public policy objectives, as well as to avoid jurisdictional conflicts. The Member States of the EU have also declared the intra-EU BITs obsolete. Only a few years ago, not many would have expected such a development; nevertheless, even though this major overhaul of the treatment of foreign direct investment has happened within the last few years, looking back reveals that it has been decades in the making.[1]

The basis for the modern global economic system was set in at the end of World War II by two parallel projects: the United Nations Monetary and Financial Conference (the Bretton Woods conference) in 1944 and the negotiations of the General Agreement on Tariffs and Trade (GATT), which was signed on 30 October 1947. This established a new world economic order that promoted regulation of fiscal and monetary policies and free trade. Inspired by economists such as John Maynard Keynes and James Meade,[2] some world leaders believed that free trade, based on a rule-based system with procedures, would ensure international economic growth and peace.[3]

In today's world order of free trade and flow of capital, the elimination, or at least control measures, are logical. Therefore, the drivers to adopt subsidy and investment

[1] Eckes (2016); Gallo and Nicola (2015); Kleinheisterkamp (2012a, b, 2015).

[2] Meade (2013) saw a rule-based international order for trade to combat unnecessary economic conflicts.

[3] Such as President Franklin D. Roosevelt and Secretary of State Cordell Hull of the United States (US Department of State Archive 2001). Later research shows that trading nations are less likely to declare war on each other (Jackson and Nei 2015).

P. Finckenberg-Broman, *Weaponizing EU State Aid Law to Impact the Future of EU Investment Policy in the Global Context*, Studies in European Economic Law and Regulation 23, https://doi.org/10.1007/978-3-031-10108-3_2

policies as international norms are inherently linked to trade/trading policies and the free-market economy theories that speak for these policies. Liberal trade policies aim to either eliminate or lower barriers to trade, which come in the form of tariffs and non-tariff measures.[4] Thus, foreign firms gain market access and can compete with domestic enterprises on similar grounds. In theory, the impact on a domestic market and competition leads to enhanced innovation, more efficient allocation of resources and increased choice for consumers.[5]

However, regardless of the shared goals and objectives of trade, investment policies and subsidies control have points of contradiction and divergence.[6] The pursuit for foreign investment is connected to competition policy by an entangled skein.[7] While 'FDI liberalisation is a means of promoting competition among firms', Government use of 'market-power inducements' to attract FDI has been perceived as particularly harmful to competition and consumer welfare in the 'host country markets'.[8]

International trade needs national rules to protect domestic enterprises and international rules to protect foreign enterprises from public authorities facilitating anti-competitive practices by private actors in the same markets. Similarly, Governments, by using subsidies to provide advantages to certain firms, may distort competition in multiple ways.[9] In a global market, subsidisation in one domestic market may spill over to affect other domestic markets.

Awareness of these issues has led to the adoption of national and international norms on subsidies control and trade remedy, such as anti-dumping and countervailing measures,[10] and competition laws dealing with restrictive trade practices, such as agreements, decisions and concerted practices or different types of misuse of market power which distort or potentially distort competition including merger control.[11] Further international norms were also adopted to promote and protect FDI.

---

[4]World Trade Organization (WTO) World Trade Report (2011), p. 61.

[5]Kennedy (2000), p. 588.

[6]Kennedy (2000), p. 585.

[7]WTO (1998a); UNCTAD (1997), pp. xv, 183; Miroudot and Bartók (2008); Simmons (2014).

[8]UNCTAD (1997), p. xxviii. Authors such as Kenneth P. Thomas (2016), Blomström and Kokko (2003), p. 20 and Tavares-Lehmann et al. (2016), p. 2 support this view. These authors hold that the competition between host government trying to attract FDI mostly benefit multinational corporations (Tavares-Lehmann et al. 2016) at the cost of general welfare in the host countries (Blomström and Kokko 2003) and that 'investment incentives have substantial potential drawbacks (Thomas 2016, p. 253).

[9]For example, specific firms therefore that receive subsidies receive an artificial competitive advantage compared with other firms, domestic or foreign, that are not receiving subsidies but compete in the same market. See WTO homepage, Anti-dumping, subsidies, safeguards: contingencies, etc. at https://www.wto.org/english/thewto_e/whatis_e/tif_e/agrm8_e.htm#subsidies.

[10]The main international legal framework regulating these types of measures is WTO. See Sect. 2.3.1 below.

[11]For multilateral global norms, see UNCTAD, The United Nations Set of Principles on Competition (The UN Set) at https://unctad.org/en/Pages/DITC/CompetitionLaw/The-United-Nations-Set-

Given this backdrop, efforts to develop international legal instruments to cover subsidies control and investment policy have taken the shape of bilateral, plurilateral and multilateral trade agreements with subsidies and investment provisions, international enforcement agreements and self-standing international investment agreements.[12] Globally, it is the GATT/WTO that is the multilateral core regulating trade. The WTO rules cover subsidising practices relating to goods and prohibit dumping in two separate legal instruments.

In Europe, the EU's predecessor, the European Coal and Steel Community, created a common economic area in 1951, which also aspired to peace and an increase in the standard of living for the peoples of Europe.[13] Thereafter, the EU started developing its unique legal system. By adopting the following treaties interpreted by the Court of Justice, it continuously evolved. The utmost expression of evolution came in the form of treaty changes, such as the Treaty of Rome,[14] The Treaty of Amsterdam[15] and the Treaty of Lisbon.[16] The Treaty of Rome established competition law to apply to both enterprises and state aid as an exclusive competence of the EEC[17] and introduced the notion of market integration. It was the Treaty of Amsterdam that sowed the seeds for the notion of European governance. Finally, the Treaty of Lisbon provided the last element of change to the EU's investment policy by shifting exclusive competence over foreign direct investment to the EU.

Unlike other entities in public international law, when an EU Member State or the EU itself is involved in these proceedings, there are multiple layers of hard law to be considered; this affects the outcome and enforcement for other nations. Indeed, the EU has evolved from other public international law to become a *sui generis*, an autonomous legal order, with its own values and specific characteristic.[18] These features include subsidy control and laws governing the movement of capital and FDI.

From there, the EU's state aid policy has developed its branch of global subsidies control to cover a wide range of government measures and policies. Regulating

---

of-Principles-on-Competition.aspx. For examples of national and regional competition laws, see EU Articles 101 and 102 TFEU, for the United States, Sherman Anti-Trust Act (1890), Clayton Act, Celler-Kefauver Act in 1950.

[12] Like EU Law, WTO and the worldwide web of BITs. Both GATT, on trade of goods, and GATS, on trade of services, include both rules on competition and investment (Working Group on the Relationship between Trade and Investment 1998). See also Clarke (2003), pp. 18–20.

[13] The Preamble of the Treaty Establishing the European Coal and Steel Community (Paris, 18 April 1951) (1951).

[14] Treaty of Rome establishing the European Economic Community (Rome, 25 May 1957).

[15] Treaty of Amsterdam amending the Treaty on European Union, the Treaties establishing the European Communities and certain related acts – Final Act OJ C 340, 10 Nov. 1997, p. 115.

[16] Treaty of Lisbon amending the Treaty on European Union and the Treaty establishing the European Community.

[17] This means that the Member States shifted state sovereignty over state aid to the EU.

[18] The EU's *sui generis* characteristics were established by the CJEU in *C-26/62 van Gend & Loos* (1963) and *C-6/64 Costa v ENEL* (1964).

foreign direct investment within the EU has, however, developed starkly different from the centrally controlled state aid policy. Until the entry of the Treaty of Lisbon, the EU's international investment was mostly governed by general international investment law through a web of BITs.

As this chapter deals with subsidies, foreign direct investment and investment incentives, these notions will be defined as follows:

- *Subsidies* take place when public revenue is transferred to private actors—for example, when a firm benefits from government support in various forms such as tax cuts and lowered fees. The WTO's Subsidies Agreement Articles 1 and 2 define 'subsidies' as measures that (1) involve a financial contribution derived from the state; (2) confer a benefit upon recipients; and (3) are specific to a company, an industry or a group of industries.
- *Foreign investment*, namely FDI, takes effect via a joint venture (with a foreign company already operating in the industry) or by merger. FDI may be outbound (OFDI) or inbound, or a combination of these two—so-called 'roundtripping'. Some OFDI is made only for re-import, to enjoy preferential FDI treatment and other advantages in the country of origin or even in both countries, thus enabling doubled benefits.[19] These types of transactions enable the investor to enjoy 'doubled state aid'.
- *Investment incentives* are, according to UNCTAD, 'frequently used as a policy instrument to attract foreign direct investment (FDI) and to benefit more from it.'[20] UNCTAD sorts incentives into three categories: fiscal, financial or other; these also include regulatory incentives.[21] In other words, any designation of investment incentives affecting the choice of investor location by economic or other inducements constitutes subsidies for FDI.[22]

This chapter is presented in five parts. It begins by providing an overview of this chapter and key definitions. It then describes the three relevant theories of liberal trade, European integration and European governance, which have been essential to the process of creation and development of international rules for competition and investment. The next part examines the development of international regulation of foreign direct investment and subsidies since World War II. The chapter then examines how the EU's own rules have developed in parallel. The chapter concludes by summarising the analysis.

---

[19] See, for example, Rosen and Hanemann (2009), p. 3 on Chinese companies utilising this method by investing in Hong Kong only to export the capital back to China for access to preferential treatment benefits. China also offers foreign tax credits to income generated from abroad.

[20] UNCTAD (2004), p. 1.

[21] UNCTAD (2004), p. 1.

[22] Thomas (2007), p. 1.

2.2 Three Theories on Free Trade and European Integration

2.2.1 Theories Behind Free Trade

The concepts of free capital flows and free competition, part of the theories of a free market economy, have their origins in the work of late nineteenth and early twentieth century economists. Mercantilism, the predominant thinking of the previous century's mercantilism endorsing beggar-thy-neighbour policies,[23] had motivated the rise of barriers to trade and the public fostering of exports by numerous nation-states.[24]

Economists such as Adam Smith[25] and Ricardo[26] have, since the turn of the eighteenth century, argued that trade policies were encouraging nation-states to reinforce their power through state intervention in the economy,[27] leading to economic inefficiencies. Accordingly, these policies perhaps looked individually beneficial but were multilaterally destructive.[28] Smith and Ricardo held that any base for a relevant comparison of cost advantage between trading nations was in the labour-productivity and questioned bounties,[29] today known as subsidy practices.[30] However, these early theories were narrow as the measurements used were limited. In the mid-twentieth century, the notion of liberal markets was developed and promoted by the Austrian, Chicago and Stockholm School economists.[31] Speaking against government market intervention were well-known economic theorists such as Ludwig von Mises,[32] James Edward Meade,[33] Milton Friedman[34] and George Stigler,[35] who considered subsidies to be extremely inefficient.[36]

---

[23] López (2015), Ch 2, p. 2 referring to Comín et al. (2010), pp. 98, 148. 'Beggar-thy-neighbour' refers to policies that seek benefits for one country at the expense of others.

[24] Such as subsidies in different forms by France and Spain (López 2015), Ch. 2, pp. 2–3.

[25] *The Wealth of Nations* (1776), together with industrialisation, that profoundly changed the nature of competition: see World Trade Organization (WTO) World Trade Report (2011); Gerber (2000), p. 22; Papadopoulos (2010), p. 8.

[26] *Principles of Political Economy and Taxation* (Ricardo 1891).

[27] In Britain, Corn Laws were used to maintain high import barriers on corn in the 1840s (Brown 2009).

[28] World Trade Organization (WTO) World Trade Report (2011).

[29] World Trade Organization (WTO) World Trade Report (2011); Gerber (2000), p. 22; Papadopoulos (2010), p. 8. Smith (1776), Ch V. Smith used the term 'bounties' instead of 'subsidies'.

[30] World Trade Organization (WTO) World Trade Report (2011); Gerber (2000), p. 22; Papadopoulos (2010), p. 8.

[31] For example, Ludwig von Mises from the Austrian School, Milton Friedman and George Stigler from the Chicago School and Heckscher and Ohlin from the Stockholm School.

[32] von Mises (1949).

[33] Meade (1951).

[34] Friedman (1951, 1956).

[35] Samuelson and Stigler (1963); Stigler (1971).

[36] Stigler (1971).

Ricardo's theory of comparative advantage was also further developed by Heckscher and Ohlin.[37] The Heckscher-Ohlin Theory of International Trade studies patterns of international trade by describing how the price differences of commodities in different countries provide comparative advantages to the trading countries. The Heckscher-Ohlin theory provided the foundation for the structure of the modern theory of international trade. From it stems *inter alia* the New Trade Theory[38] from the late nineteenth century, which has led to the enactment of modern competition laws and international subsidies control (see Sect. 2.3.2). This theory adopted a consumer aspect to free trade, today reflected in current competition policies (including subsidies control), by demonstrating that it provided increased options for consumers. In other words, competition laws and subsidy policy deliver more goods and services to consumers at lower prices.

Unregulated market ideas have also met with opposition. Karl Marx (1818–83) strongly criticises the capitalist exploitation of the labour force. The 'laissez-faire' approach to busts and booms was questioned by John Maynard Keynes (1883–1946), a principal designer of the Bretton Woods Conference. While Keynes advocated free markets, he held that government interventions such as fiscal policy measures and export subsidies[39] were essential to combat economic swings.[40] According to Joseph Stiglitz (1943–), 'Macroeconomic policy can never be devoid of politics: it involves fundamental trade-offs and impacts different groups differently.'[41] As will be shown later by this book, the EU's state aid policy tries to address these aspects while promoting free trade.

Two main effects associated with PTA-driven trade policy[42] are highlighted by the economic literature: terms of trade and production relocation. The basis of different type of trade agreement is to neutralise negative cross-border effects—for example, subsidies. Trade policies are based on the logic that nations with strong economies will unilaterally use their market power to influence the trade balance, increase their national income and improve their terms of trade. Johnson,[43] however, notes the inefficiency of these trade policies as the unilateral actions cancel each other out.[44] Bagwell and Staiger refer to this as terms of trade-driven Prisoners'

[37] Bergstrand (1990); Heckscher and Ohlin (1991).

[38] Developed by economists such as Dixit and Norman (1986); Krugman (1979, 1991).

[39] Keynes (1978), p. 51.

[40] Keynes (1936), pp. 378–97.

[41] Stiglitz (2005).

[42] Which is a considerable area of the EU's external action (Kleimann 2013), p. 3.

[43] Johnson (1953).

[44] When a government launches internal supportive economic programs, other affected countries react by putting in place various types of responses in a move to balance the competitiveness of their own market.

Dilemma,[45] resulting in a reduction of aggregate welfare due to the countries' restrictive trade policies, in turn producing a contraction of trade volumes.[46]

Venables[47] referred to what he called the 'production relocation effect', which is when the trade policy tries to boost domestic production through a change in relative prices, at the cost of foreign production. This is similar to the terms of trade-driven Prisoners' Dilemma in that the unilateral actions cancel each other out. No government succeeds if all aim to attract more production through their trade policies. There is no production relocation and a reduction in trade due to the increase in restrictive trade measures—in other words, the countries are in the grip of the production relocation Prisoners' Dilemma. This logic certainly applies to subsidies, which are commonly used as trade barriers, as argued by Damro and Guay.[48] A trade agreement for cooperation between countries, rather than unilateral acts, can be used to avoid any such non-cooperative situation.

From a political perspective, looking at political motives, an FTA's or PTA's design is an indication of power relations. A stronger state can often dictate terms of an agreement in either a bilateral or regional context. Unilateral political pressure can also cause a change in national laws, even when outside of the scope of a free or preferential trade agreement.[49] Countries may be prompted to sign PTAs due to underlying global changes in trade relationships. Indeed, corresponding to the weak outcome of the WTO's Doha Round negotiations, the Global Europe strategy was adopted in 2006,[50] which geared the EU's approach to PTA negotiation towards greater reciprocity of mutual commitments with its partner countries.[51]

A model resting on a 'domino theory' of regionalism was provided by Baldwin (1993)[52] for enlargement of Europe's economic integration. A chain reaction, or contagion, is triggered when a non-member loses market share to a member, inducing the non-member to join an existing PTA. Baldwin and Jaimovich (2012)[53] state that the potential damage of preferential trade liberalisation induces exporters in non-member countries to pressure their governments into either joining

---

[45] The prisoner's dilemma describes a situation where individual rational behaviour of individual group members leads to a poor outcome for the group overall (Haucap and Schwalbe 2011), p. 4.

[46] Bagwell and Staiger (1999, 2006). (Damro (2013) and Damro and Guay (2016) raise the same issue relating to subsidies/state aid policy in trade.

[47] Venables (1987).

[48] Damro and Guay (2016).

[49] Some literature addresses 'the EU as a conflicted power' (Meunier and Nicolaïdis 2006), which by use of its market power (e.g., by offering access to the EU's internal market or customs union) pressures weaker powers, such as other trading blocs or countries, into accepting trade arrangements that are aligned with EU law (Farrell 2005; Lavenex and Schimmelfennig 2009), such as the EEA Agreement.

[50] See the Commission's Communication 'Global Europe: Competing in the world (2006) 567 final of 4 October 2006.

[51] Kleimann (2013), pp. 4, 59–73.

[52] Baldwin (1993).

[53] Baldwin and Jaimovich (2012).

existing PTAs or creating new ones. This, according to Egger and Larch (2008),[54] is a particularly useful model for understanding and predicting the EU's regional integration process. Causal mechanisms behind this domino effect are the focus of the political science literature—particularly reactions to discrimination by interest groups and decision-makers. Mattli (1999)[55] applies the argument for the competitive spread of trade agreements to the EU's enlargement. In much the same way, Dür (2010)[56] looks at the PTAs negotiated and signed in the 1990s and 2000s by the United States and EU from the perspective of competition for access to emerging markets and economies.

2.2.2 *European Integration Theories*

Theories aiming to explain European integration are by now numerous. Their purpose is to explain the EU's inception and the current situation. It is crucial to understand different theoretical approaches, explaining the concepts behind the creation of the EU, to enable hypothesising about its future. A familiarity with the assumptions behind these different approaches is also essential and must be taken into account when reflecting on them.

Of these theories, four stand out as relevant for state aid and its conflict with the investment regime. The first and oldest is *neo-functionalism*. This theory of European integration, which was founded by Karl Deutsch and Ernst Haas,[57] sees it as a self-sustaining process centred in Brussels, which culminates in a newly created polity. Accordingly, this integration process is the result of a functional and political spillover effect. While functional spillover drives integration achieved in one policy area to escalate integration in other areas, behind political spillover are supranational and subnational actors that pressure for further integration in pursuit of their interests.[58] Indeed, neo-functionalism explains well the effect of state aid control, as it is of exclusive competence of the EU.[59] Because the Member States do not have the competence to legislate in this area, the functional and political spillover effect is very substantial.

The second came out of the critique of neo-functionalism, claiming that its explanation of European integration was lacking, which led to the adoption of *intergovernmentalism*.[60] It focuses on the individual nation-state's role in the

[54] Egger and Larch (2008).

[55] Mattli (1999).

[56] Dür (2010).

[57] Sandholtz and Sweet (1997), p. 300.

[58] See, for example, Haas (1961); Haas and Dinan (1958).

[59] Meaning that the Member States have delegated their sovereign rights to regulate or decide on matters regarding state aid control to the EU. For more details on what this means, see Chap. 3.

[60] Haas (1975); Hoffmann (1966).

integration, arguing that European integration does not make it obsolete.[61] Hoffmann and Milward (1935–2010) were influential proponents of this theory.[62] Milward's book *The European Rescue of the Nation State*[63] argues that the primary actors in the European integration process were the national governments that, by delegating selected parts of their sovereignty to the EU, strengthened their position through pooling them. This theory focuses on bargaining between the national governments in the process of integration. It is also very applicable to state aid control, as this is one of the areas in which member states have delegated their sovereignty to the EU for mutual benefit.

Solemn questions about the core of intergovernmentalism, the dichotomy of low and high politics, were raised by events not fitting into this theoretical framework—in particular, the signing of the Single European Act (1986) and later the Maastricht Treaty (1991), the Treaty on the European Union (TEU). Andrew Moravcsik, when faced with this conundrum combined with a resurgence of neo-functionalism, undertook the task of adapting it to the development during the 1990s of a new European reality. It led to the third theory, *liberal intergovernmentalism.*[64]

It is a development of the intergovernmental theory presented above, emphasising national governments as key actors on integration. Unlike the neo-functionalists, this theory assigns limited importance to supranational institutions in the process. Liberal intergovernmentalism applies to the new principles introduced by the Treaty of Amsterdam (1997), which increased the power of the EU while providing more manoeuvring space for the Member States.[65] Reflecting the at the time 'underlying divergence of national interests' and needs of the Member States, the Treaty of Amsterdam encourages integration[66] while enhancing the democratic aspects of the EU, by promoting the European Parliament[67] to a co-legislator with the Council. Thereby setting up a cooperative mechanism for the Member States' to coordinate their policies. Hence the Treaty of Amsterdam foreshadows the era of governance, which was officially launched in 2001 by the Commission's White Paper on Governance.[68]

Yet Moravcsik recognises that the constitutionalisation role of the EU has enabled the Commission to perform supranational entrepreneurship and thus 'induce authoritative political decisions that would not otherwise occur'.[69] Critics of

[61] Hoffmann (1966); Milward (2000).

[62] Milward (2000).

[63] Milward (2000).

[64] Moravcsik established this theory in his book *The Choice for Europe.* See Moravcsik (1998).

[65] Moravcsik (1993); Moravcsik and Nicolaidis (1999). See also See European Commission web page, Governance, at https://ec.europa.eu/archives/governance/governance/index_en.htm.

[66] Moravcsik and Nicolaidis (1999).

[67] The European Parliament is directly elected by the EU citizens.

[68] European Governance, Commission White Paper, Brussels 25 July 2001 COM (2001) 428 final (EC 2001).

[69] Moravcsik (1993), p. 271.

intergovernmentalism also point out that the way state aid policy has developed casts doubt on this state-centred theory.[70] It stands on four points. First, EU decisions in this policy area can substantially impact the Member States and their industries.[71] Second, the ambiguous formulation of Articles 107 and 108 of the TFEU leaves room for interpretation vis-à-vis the scope of the delegation implied by the EU Treaties, hence permitting 'the Commission to act as a supranational entrepreneur'.[72] Third, the CJEU has primarily supported the Commission's decisions and policy measures, which has made it harder for the Member States to not comply with state aid rules. Fourth, diminishing the Commission's power in the field of state aid would significantly weaken the internal market.[73]

The fourth and last theory is *multi-level governance (MLG).* It is a relatively new European integration theory, and key proponents, such as Gary Marks and Liesbet Hooghe in *Multi-Level Governance and European Integration*,[74] see EU policy-making as frequently changing and uneven. They present a multi-level approach, highlighting the limitations in other, static integration theories that tend to disregard a large number of dispersed actors from different governance levels that are involved in the integration process. They argue that authority and sovereignty have moved both up to the supranational EU and down to the subnational levels—that is, local and regional authorities/assemblies. In principle, this theory is also applicable to state aid, as the legislation takes place on a supranational level and regional authorities can still apply aid that falls under block exemptions.[75] However, some scholars studying explicitly multilevel governance regarding state aid law and policy[76] show that tension remains between the EU (predominantly the Commission) and some subnational actors (Member State authorities) about the EU's (then EC's) centralised state aid regime.[77] Thus the new European integration theory is not optimal for explaining these tensions. Instead, the impact of both national and the supranational, formal and informal (say hard and soft law) diverging decision-making rules should be recognised.[78]

Initially, political theorists attempted to apply the European integration model to explain the increase in the number of trade agreements elsewhere in the world. However, the limits of these efforts soon became apparent: trade integration outside

[70] Smith (1998).

[71] See, for example, Spanish renewable energy schemes (*State aid SA.40348 (2015/NN)*, 2017) or Apple State aid (*SA.38373 $ Apple*, 2016).

[72] Blauberger (2008); Smith (1998).

[73] Smith (1998), p. 61.

[74] Hooghe et al. (2001).

[75] Block Exemption Regulations (which are defined by the Commission) and *de minimis* Regulation (EC 2013a) give automatic approval for a range of aid measures. For more see Sect. 3.2 in Chap. 3.

[76] Thielemann (1999) studied Saxony, Germany.

[77] This is a mismatch 'with the institutional logics of Germany's cooperative federalism'. Also, these actors at times have different policy objectives.

[78] Thielemann (1999), pp. 413–14.

Europe lacked concomitant political integration and proceeded under different patterns.[79]

2.2.3 European Governance

In 2001, the Commission declared that European Governance had become an EU imperative by launching its White Paper on European Governance.[80] This notion, according to the EU, 'designates the body of rules, procedures and practices that relate to the way powers are exercised in the EU'. The introduction of European Governance aimed to 'strengthen democracy at the European level and to bring citizens closer to the European institutions'.[81] This is highly suitable, as the EU and its different institutions function largely as a government,[82] which through its governance policies coordinates, steers and regulates various policy areas. Hence it should not be surprising that expressions towards the notion of governance are identifiable in the Treaty of Amsterdam (1997), which emphasised balanced and sustainable development as European Community objectives.[83] Certainly, these two objectives are among those highlighted by the White Paper on European Governance.[84]

Moreover, in pace with the development of EU governance, policy-making at the EU level has expanded massively in both scope and depth.[85] Because the EU institutions have continuously gained more powers from the Member States, the necessity for enhanced transparency in the EU's policy and decision-making process has been looming. Therefore, the EU's governance policy is regularly updated by the Commission[86] and is a topic of interest and research for many academic institutions and authors of political science.[87] Some of these authors hold that EU policy mainly consists of 'network governance' because this is perceived to be the proper way to govern the EU.[88]

---

[79] World Trade Organization (WTO) World Trade Report (2011).

[80] EC (2001).

[81] See Commission's web page, European Governance, at https://ec.europa.eu/archives/governance/governance_eu/white_paper_en.htm.

[82] Smith (1998), pp. 55–78 argues that the EU indeed functions as a government. Maduro (2007) and Sauter (1997) hold that the EU has a de facto constitution.

[83] See European Commission web page, Governance, at https://ec.europa.eu/archives/governance/governance/index_en.htm.

[84] EC (2001), p. 13.

[85] Hooghe et al. (2001), p. 1; EC (2001).

[86] See Commission's web page, European Governance, at https://ec.europa.eu/archives/governance/governance_eu/white_paper_en.htm.

[87] Kohler-Koch (2003); Kohler-Koch and Eising (2007); Kohler-Koch and Larat (2009); Kohler-Koch and Rittberger (2006).

[88] Kohler-Koch (2003), p. 275.

Certainly, the Commission has been driving a softer consensus-based type of governance approach ever since.[89] Even policy areas such as state aid, in which decision-making is of an interventionist and legalistic nature, have witnessed the introduction of block exemptions and informal rule-making by the EU and its Member States[90] to ease national authorities from implementing certain subsidy measures without having to request the Commission's approval. This soft law approach[91] has made it easier for the Member States to accept the sensitive political issues that are governed by state aid policy.[92]

European governance also has an external dimension.[93] By this method, the EU's internal policies and rules may be exported to third countries employing different types of international agreements, such as association, trade or cooperation agreements. The notion of the EU's 'external governance', which will be explained in more detail in Sect. 3.4 in Chap. 3, is meant to capture this process.

2.3 Subsidies and Foreign Investment Globally Since the 1940s

The globalisation of trade in the twentieth century brought with it a perception that FDI could boost economic development, which triggered developing countries to launch campaigns to attract FDI from developed countries. To better protect the economic assets of their citizens, calls were raised by capital-exporting countries to codify foreign investment protection, particularly under a single institutional core. One of these attempts was launched by the League of Nations in 1924, culminating in the Hague Conference for the Codification of International Law in March 1930, which ultimately failed to reach consensus.[94] This started a long-lasting dialogue that is yet to be resolved.

In its 1927 World Economic Conference (WEC), in order to reinstate vigour to the world economy,[95] the League of Nations investigated the rise in trade barriers

[89] Blauberger (2008).

[90] Snyder (1994). For example, see Boasson (2019) on renewable energy.

[91] The Commission has applied soft law instruments ever since the 1970s (Biondi and Stefan 2018), p. 3.

[92] For more on European governance regarding state aid law, see Sects. 3.2 and 3.4 in Chap. 3.

[93] EC (2001), p. 28. See also Blauberger and Krämer (2010); Cremona (2003); Damro (2013); Damro and Guay (2016); Lavenex and Schimmelfennig (2009).

[94] The capital-exporting and capital-importing countries were miles apart in their opinion of the minimum standards to be applied (Hackworth 1940), pp. 500–501; Abbott et al. (2014), p. 4.

[95] A reduction of trade barriers, including subsidies, had been accomplished by the incorporation of subsidy (anti-bounty) clauses to some early preferential trade agreements: Brown (2009); Bairoch (1989). This process was initiated by 'the Cobden-Chavalier Treaty' of 1860 between Britain and France. The first multilateral convention that regulated subsidy usage for domestic production and export concerned sugar and was entered by France, Belgium, the Netherlands and the UK in 1864.

during wartime. This conference initiated an international discussion of trade-related topics, including tariffs, MFN provisions and subsidy-based 'indirect means of protecting national trade'.[96] However, the Great Depression that began in 1929[97] initiated the reoccurrence of the adoption of 'beggar-thy-neighbour'[98] trade strategies by many nations.[99] These strategies led to increased regionalism, particularly in the form of trading blocs[100]—for instance, in Europe (north,[101] south and east),[102] the United States,[103] the Commonwealth[104] and Asia.[105] Non-tariff barriers to trade, such as subsidies, became a severe issue.[106] Efforts to end the world's economic crisis took place in different forums. In particular, the League of Nations 1933 World Economic Conference in London (the London Monetary and Economic Conference of 1933) sought to fight the Great Depression by resisting protectionism, revitalising international trade and stabilising currency exchange rates.[107] The attending nations also attempted to create a distinction between 'bad' and 'good' subsidies.[108] Even though these efforts were unsuccessful as delegations from different nations could not agree on which subsidies should be categorised as harmful,[109] the idea for identifying harmful subsidies resurfaced at the end of World War II in 1944.

[96] Irwin et al. (2008), p. 9; League of Nations (1927), p. 44.

[97] Basically, in the early 1930s.

[98] This expression describes policies that seek benefits for one country at the expense of others.

[99] Subsidising practices that were systematically employed by nations in the wake of mercantilism in the eighteenth century. These bestowed economic benefits to enterprises by use of state funds, and thus had motivated barriers to trade by public fostering of exports. For example, France implemented such practices by publicly supporting fiscal exceptions, favourable credits, low-interest loans, production subsidies and export bonuses for manufactures. See López (2015), Ch 2, pp. 2–3 referring to Comín et al. (2010), pp. 98 and 148.

[100] Irwin et al. (2008), pp. 8–10.

[101] By signing the Oslo Convention 1930, which was entered by Norway, Denmark, Sweden, Belgium/Luxemburg and the Netherlands (Olsson 2006), p. 5.

[102] Through a series of German bilateral agreements with countries located in these geographical territories from 1930: Olsson (2006), pp. 8–9; Irwin et al. (2008), p. 9.

[103] The Hawley-Smoot tariff in 1929, intended to protect domestic agriculture from tougher international trade competition, led to higher duties on agricultural imports: Irwin et al. (2008), p. 8. However, in 1934 the United States, attempted to reinitiate a more open trade policy by enacting the Reciprocal Trade Agreement Act (the RTAA), lowering tariffs in trade agreements. Such agreements were concluded in the 1930s with Britain, Canada and several countries in Latin America: Irwin et al. (2008), pp. 10–12.

[104] The 1932 Ottawa Imperial Conference introduced protectionist measures such as duty tariffs and import quotas to nations that were not part of the British Commonwealth: Irwin et al. (2008), p. 9.

[105] To extend its influence—both political and economic—in the region, the Japanese Empire created the Greater East Asian Co-prosperity Sphere (1930–45): Irwin et al. (2008), p. 9; Duus (1996), p. 60.

[106] Irwin (2016), p. 11.

[107] The conference was attended by *inter alia* delegations from United States, France, Germany, Great Britain, Switzerland, Germany, Italy, Belgium, Japan and Norway.

[108] Even today, this debate is ongoing. See Alan O. Sykes (2010).

[109] See League of Nations Report (1933), p. 34.

The London Monetary and Economic Conference of 1933 utterly failed because the United States rejected the stabilisation of currency agreement to preserve domestic interests[110] and protectionism did not ease before the end of World War II. It took about 10 years before the United States called for the Bretton Woods Conference, which revitalised the agenda for more open international trade and financial stability.[111] From this era of recovery stems the modern global economic system, including a major overhaul of the treatment of foreign investment and competition policy. The GATT 1947 was negotiated by 23 contracting parties, and the Bretton Woods Conference drafted the International Trade Organization (ITO) agreement[112] and founded international organisations such as the International Monetary Fund (IMF)[113] and the World Bank.[114]

2.3.1 *Subsidies: GATT and the WTO*

While World War II (1939–45) was still raging, the first tentative steps towards the modern global economic system were taken during the preparations for GATT and the signing of the Bretton Woods Agreement at the Bretton Woods Conference in July 1944 creating the IMF and the World Bank. The ITO, 'meant to oversee the administration of an open and non-preferential multilateral trading order',[115] including covering services, control of subsidies, anti-competitive business practices and protections of international investment, never got to be. After the Congress of the United States rejected ratifying the finalised Havana Charter for the International Trade Organization Charter (the Havana Charter)[116] in 1948 due to fears of losing sovereignty to the ITO, the ITO collapsed.[117]

The idea for an international trade organisation, however, was preserved by the GATT, and was signed on 30 October 1947 in Geneva by the United States, Great Britain, Canada, Australia, France and the Benelux Countries,[118] only a month

---

[110] President Franklin D. Roosevelt rejected this agreement on 3 July 1933: Nichols (1951), p. 316.

[111] US Department of State Archive (2001).

[112] World Trade Organization (WTO) World Trade Report (2011).

[113] The IMF, with 188 member nations, was created to keep the international monetary system stable. See IMF web page at https://www.imf.org/external/index.htm.

[114] The World Bank funds developing countries to reduce poverty, and to promote economic growth, equity and sustainable development, and has 189 member countries.

[115] World Trade Organization (WTO) World Trade Report (2011).

[116] The United Nations Conference on Trade and Employment establishing The International Trade Organization Charter, 'the Havana Charter' of 1947, was held at the Havana Conference in Havana, Cuba in March 1948: ITO (1948).

[117] See WTO (2020) home page, The GATT years: from Havana to Marrakesh, at https://www.wto.org/english/thewto_e/whatis_e/tif_e/fact4_e.htm.

[118] Belgium, the Netherlands and Luxembourg.

before the ITO's Havana Conference.[119] As a wartime brainchild of the governments of the United States and Great Britain, the GATT was similarly intended to revitalise international trade.[120] The GATT also established an international rule-based system between nations that restricted their ability to raise barriers to trade.[121] However, the GATT's scope was much narrower than the Havana Charter, as it specifically focused on the support of and encouragement of international trade in goods.[122] Within this scope, the GATT Article XVI introduced international subsidies controls.[123]

For the next 47 years, the GATT was expanded to cover more trade-related areas.[124] However, it took almost 50 years before the WTO was founded in Marrakesh after the successful completion of the Uruguay Round of 1986–94.[125] The WTO agreement, a multilateral umbrella agreement that governs most trade-related issues, incorporated the GATT into its framework and added its role to its functions.[126] While the GATT Article XVI is still part of the WTO core rules, the WTO includes a much improved and more sophisticated tool for international subsidies control, the Subsidies Agreement. It provides the globally most comprehensive established definition for subsidies—that is, a subsidy (which is still restricted to goods only) exists when a measure satisfies three cumulative criteria spelt out by Article 1 of the Subsidies Agreement (see Fig. 2.1).

Further, due to the interplay between Articles 1.2 and 2 (the preamble), a subsidy must also be 'specific' according to Article 2 of the Subsidies Agreement,[127] which lays down the parameters that this term includes (see Fig. 2.2). Specificity can take place *de jure* Article 2.1(a) or *de facto* Article 2.1(c). The function of Articles 2.1 (b) and 2.2. is to explain where specificity does not exist.

Like the GATT, the rules of the WTO are the outcome of member state negotiations, as agreements whose main function is to provide, as extensively as possible, a

---

[119] See WTO (2020) homepage, The GATT years: from Havana to Marrakesh.

[120] During the war, these two nations' government officials had been discussing how to implement international policies that would foster trade and restrict protectionist measures that was one of the reasons that had led to the war. With the pre-World War II protectionism fresh in their memory, other nations were also keen to pursue this type of system: Irwin et al. (2008) p. 109.

[121] Irwin et al. (2008), Ch. 1.

[122] What is the WTO? At WTO homepage at https://www.wto.org/english/thewto_e/whatis_e/whatis_e.htm.

[123] See Preparatory Committee of the International Conference on Trade and Employment Report (UN 1946) pp. 7–8.

[124] For example, in the mid-1960s Kennedy Round negotiations, the nations agreed to establish an Anti-Dumping Code In the 1970s Tokyo Round, a major aim was to use indirect barriers to trade, resulting in the introduction of the Subsidies Code. See WTO home page, The GATT years: from Havana to Marrakesh at https://www.wto.org/english/thewto_e/whatis_e/tif_e/fact4_e.htm.

[125] The Marrakesh Agreement Establishing the World Trade Organization.

[126] What is the WTO? At WTO homepage at https://www.wto.org/english/thewto_e/whatis_e/whatis_e.htm.

[127] DSU Appellate Body Report (n.d.)

AGREEMENT ON SUBSIDIES AND COUNTERVAILING MEASURES

Members hereby *agree* as follows:

PART I: GENERAL PROVISIONS

Article 1

Definition of a Subsidy

1.1 For the purpose of this Agreement, a subsidy shall be deemed to exist if:

(a)(1) there is a financial contribution by a government or any public body within the territory of a Member (referred to in this Agreement as "government"), i.e. where:

(i) a government practice involves a direct transfer of funds (e.g. grants, loans, and equity infusion), potential direct transfers of funds or liabilities (e.g. loan guarantees);

(ii) government revenue that is otherwise due is foregone or not collected (e.g. fiscal incentives such as tax credits) [1];

(iii) a government provides goods or services other than general infrastructure, or purchases goods;

(iv) a government makes payments to a funding mechanism, or entrusts or directs a private body to carry out one or more of the type of functions illustrated in (i) to (iii) above which would normally be vested in the government and the practice, in no real sense, differs from practices normally followed by governments;

or

(a)(2) there is any form of income or price support in the sense of Article XVI of GATT 1994;

and

(b) a benefit is thereby conferred.

1.2 A subsidy as defined in paragraph 1 shall be subject to the provisions of Part II or shall be subject to the provisions of Part III or V only if such a subsidy is specific in accordance with the provisions of Article 2.

[1] In accordance with the provisions of Article XVI of GATT 1994 (Note to Article XVI) and the provisions of Annexes I through III of this Agreement, the exemption of an exported product from duties or taxes borne by the like product when destined for domestic consumption, or the remission of such duties or taxes in amounts not in excess of those which have accrued, shall not be deemed to be a subsidy.

Fig. 2.1 Article 1 of the Subsidies Agreement

free, predictable and effortless trade flow. The WTO's rules are vertical; they bind states but do not regulate actions between individuals or provide legal remedies for individual rights. Subsidy disputes under the WTO are also complaint driven. This means that unless a WTO member state raises a complaint against other nations'

Article 2

Specificity

2.1 In order to determine whether a subsidy, as defined in paragraph 1 of Article 1, is specific to an enterprise or industry or group of enterprises or industries (referred to in this Agreement as "certain enterprises") within the jurisdiction of the granting authority, the following principles shall apply:

(a) Where the granting authority, or the legislation pursuant to which the granting authority operates, explicitly limits access to a subsidy to certain enterprises, such subsidy shall be specific.

(b) Where the granting authority, or the legislation pursuant to which the granting authority operates, establishes objective criteria or conditions[2] governing the eligibility for, and the amount of, a subsidy, specificity shall not exist, provided that the eligibility is automatic and that such criteria and conditions are strictly adhered to. The criteria or conditions must be clearly spelled out in law, regulation, or other official document, so as to be capable of verification.

(c) If, notwithstanding any appearance of non-specificity resulting from the application of the principles laid down in subparagraphs (a) and (b), there are reasons to believe that the subsidy may in fact be specific, other factors may be considered. Such factors are: use of a subsidy programme by a limited number of certain enterprises, predominant use by certain enterprises, the granting of disproportionately large amounts of subsidy to certain enterprises, and the manner in which discretion has been exercised by the granting authority in the decision to grant a subsidy.[3] In applying this subparagraph, account shall be taken of the extent of diversification of economic activities within the jurisdiction of the granting authority, as well as of the length of time during which the subsidy programme has been in operation.

2.2 A subsidy which is limited to certain enterprises located within a designated geographical region within the jurisdiction of the granting authority shall be specific. It is understood that the setting or change of generally applicable tax rates by all levels of government entitled to do so shall not be deemed to be a specific subsidy for the purposes of this Agreement.

2.3 Any subsidy falling under the provisions of Article 3 shall be deemed to be specific.

2.4 Any determination of specificity under the provisions of this Article shall be clearly substantiated on the basis of positive evidence.

Fig. 2.2 Article 2 of the Subsidies Agreement

subsidising practices, the WTO cannot act. Any breach by a member state of relevance to the agreements carries the risk of sanctions in the form of economic remedies that will impact exports. While the WTO's discipline rests upon the threat of economic sanctions, it does not have the executive power to act independently on these sanctions. Instead, it can only approve a sovereign state's implementation of sanctions as a countermeasure for other states' breach of WTO rules (i.e. trade remedies). The current Marrakesh Agreement at the heart of the WTO is a major revision of the original GATT, and is the outcome of the Uruguay Round of negotiations (1986–94). However, it does not govern international investment.[128] To address this issue, the EU has tabled a proposal to modernise the WTO, and one of the three substantive issues subject to modernisations are enhanced rules for subsidies. This would include reining in state-owned enterprises by clarifying the scope of public policy in such a manner that it would be better covered by the Subsidies Agreement.[129] Furthermore, the EU is also promoting the development and adoption of new rules to comprehensively address services and FDI within the WTO framework.[130]

2.3.2 *International Investment, IIL and the Network of IIAs*

In stark contrast to international trade being governed by the WTO multilateral treaty, the international investment regime is institutionally decentralised because states have not been able to agree on multilateral treaty provisions. BITs and other types of IIAs are agreed and signed by states or regional trade blocs. However, although parties to BITs and TIPs mostly negotiate these provisions bilaterally, these are very uniform, with modern BITs having a broad definition of investment.

International investment law, which applies to all type of IIAs, has developed into its own section of international law.[131] Unlike a conventional trade agreement, where rights and obligations are applied and enforced vertically, the IIAs cover horizontal relations. Salacuse explains that 'in ratifying a BIT, a country makes the treaty part of its legal system'. At the heart of IIAs are investment protection provisions intended to secure investors' assets against undue interferences by the host state.[132] These provisions empower investors to exercise a private right of action against states on the grounds of breach of the investment protection obligations directly before an international investment tribunal.[133] Disputes stemming from these events are regularly settled through ISDS, an international arbitration procedure that aims to provide a neutral, rapid, and effective means to resolve conflicts.[134] ISDS includes substantial and procedural provisions and often takes place in an ad hoc fashion. This could lead to such ramifications as a state becoming

[128] With the exception of prohibited subsidies that are intended for goods. See Articles 1 and 2 of the Subsidies Agreement.

[129] European Commission (2018a), pp. 3–5.

[130] European Commission (2018a), p. 5.

[131] Generally, see Salacuse and Sullivan (2005).

[132] The legal basis for ISDS is the international investment agreement, which in turn is governed by public international law.

[133] This system enables investors to bypass national courts. I.e., these tribunals are the deciding authority for ISDS. National authorities are bound to enforce their decisions by the AAI and international law.

[134] This has been questioned by many sources. See UNICTRAL's working group III (Investor-State Dispute Settlement Reform) reports at http://www.uncitral.org/uncitral/en/commission/working_

liable to compensate investors for damages or even being obliged to reinstitute the terminated legal framework.[135]

Protection of foreign investment has developed to cover the principle of state liability for damages on alien property by customary international law (CIL) to a global network of international investment agreements. CIL 'obligated host states to treat investment in accordance with an international minimum standard'.[136] Before World War II international agreements mostly focused on trade and at times even on the protection of property instead of FDI.[137] As an example of this type of agreements are the friendship, commerce and navigation treaties (FCAs) stemming from the late 1700s and favoured by the newly independent United States. These FCAs, which had established three principles, the national treatment (NT), the most-favoured nation treatment (MFN) and fair and equitable treatment (FET) are argued to be the BITs forerunners.[138]

However, the international minimum standard by CIL was vague and thus debatable. Some developing nations insisted on a minimum standard of norms that were not appreciated by the developed countries.[139] Particularly the developing countries, obliged to sign 'unequal treaties' by their former occupants during the decolonisation process in the 19th-century felt exploited.[140] As CIL offered only a diplomatic process called 'espousal' to solve enforcement of CIL, the 'espousal' the developed nations engaged in to protect the economic assets of their citizens varied from negotiations to gunboat diplomacy (the use of military threat to support a

groups/3Investor_State.html – for example, UNICTRAL (2018a, 2019). For more on this, Sect. 5.4.1 in Chap. 5.

[135] *Micula Award*, 2013) paras 1309–12.

[136] Brownlie (1990) and Vandevelde (2005), p. 159.

[137] Salacuse (2015), p. 84 and Vandevelde (2005), p. 159.

[138] World Trade Organization (WTO) World Trade Report (2011); Vandevelde (2005), pp. 162–166; Brown (2009), p. 4. According to Vandevelde (2005), following World War II 'the United States launched a new series of FCN agreements'. From 1946 to 1966, 21 FCAs were with other nations, such as Greece.

[139] For example, the Calvo Doctrine empowered Latin American countries to avoid having to grant alien investors special treatment. See (Calvo 1896), sec. 256, pp. 231–232. In 1933 the Latin American countries response to the attempts of codification of FDI protection was the Convention on the Rights and Duties of States (the Montevideo Convention), rejecting negative discrimination of national investors. Also other land reforms going on in Latin America and Eastern Europe between 1915 to 1940 led to a rise in expropriations Guzman (1997), p. 645. The Soviet Union had nationalized its whole economy in 1917–1919 by the Decree on Land 1917 and the Fundamental Law of Land Socialization of 1918, Lenin (2016).

[140] Such as the former colonies of Britain were forced open their markets without receiving sufficient reciprocity. Shafaeddin (1998), p. 23. These nations rightly perceived FDI as a form of neocolonialism because it allowed for foreign control, particularly 'over the means of production' Vandevelde (2005), p. 166. Nations that resisted entering theses treaties faced war such as the British-Chinese Opium War of 1839–1842: see Brownlie (1990), p. 509; Kirayoglu (2014), p. 5.

State's foreign policy).[141] As a consequence, many countries perceived CIL as no longer being sufficient for FDI protection.

Therefore, a new era for IIAs began at the shift from the nineteenth to the twentieth century, based on the development of the internationalisation of the world economy. Since the failed codification efforts by the League of Nations in 1924,[142] there have been several attempts to codify FDI protection under a single institutional core (see Table 2.1). All these failed to establish a binding multilateral forum that would cover both developed and developing countries in lack of consensus. According to Simmons, only two of these, the Havana Charter[143] and the Multilateral Agreement on Investment (MAI),[144] count as notable efforts to multilateralise the international investment regime.[145]

This lack of consensus reflected the profound difference of concerns and needs, regarding FDI, between the developing and developed countries. After World War II many former colonies in Asia and Africa, now independent countries nationalized their natural resources sectors and refused to accept additional foreign investment.[146] Nationalisation was repeated by the Eastern European countries after slipping behind the iron curtain. These nations were not willing to compensate for the assets of developed countries broadly. Instead, they used domestic calculus.[147] As a countermeasure, the developed countries adopted the Hull rule.[148] This rule provided a baseline for discussions of compensation standards related to foreigners' property expropriation.[149]

The United Nations General Assembly (UNGA) also provided an effective forum for the least developed and developing countries, being a majority, to get a say in the foreign property issue. In 1958, these efforts led to UNGA establishing the UN Commission on Permanent Sovereignty over Natural Resources (CPSNR). In 1962 the draft resolution by CPSNR, resolution 1803 (XVII) on the 'Permanent

[141] See International Law Commission (2000), p. 212. For the scope of protection, where a state has caused an injury by an 'internationally wrongful act' to a natural or legal person that is a national of the former state, see Dugard (2000), Chapter II.

[142] Hackworth (1940), pp. 500–501.

[143] The Havana Charter (ITO 1948).

[144] The Multilateral Agreement on Investment (MAI). The idea for MAI was to be a freestanding international treaty covering the OECD members and for the MS of the European Communities. MAI was also intended to be open to accession for non-members of the OECD through a negotiations progress (OECD 1995).

[145] Simmons (2014), p. 15.

[146] Such as Cuba led by Castro from 1959 and Vietnam, China, Algeria and Libya in 1955.

[147] Ghouri (2011), p. 3.

[148] The Hull rule bases on a 'standard of prompt, adequate and effective compensation for expropriation' which was set the United States Secretary of State Cordell Hull in 1938: see Vandevelde (2005), p. 172.

[149] Newcombe and Paradell (2009), p. 18.

Table 2.1 Attempts to codify FDI protection with most EU relevance

Year	Title	Setting	level	form	status
1948	Havana Charter for an International Trade Organisation	International Conference on Trade and Employment	Multilateral	Binding	Not ratified
1948	ILA Draft Statutes of the Arbitral Tribunal for Foreign Investments Court[a]	International Law Association (ILA)	Non-governmental	Non-binding	Not adopted
1949	International Code of Fair Treatment for Foreign Investment (ICC Code)[b]	International Chamber of Commerce	Non-governmental	Non-binding	Adopted
1957	Treaty Establishing the European Economic Community	European Economic Community	Regional	Binding	Adopted
1958	The New York Convention on the Recognition and Enforcement of Foreign Arbitral Awards[c]	United Nations	Multilateral	Binding	Adopted
1961	Code of Liberalisation of Capital Movements	OECD	Regional	Binding	Adopted
1961	1961 Harvard Draft Convention on the International Responsibility of States for Injuries to Aliens[d]	United Nations	Multilateral	Binding	Not adopted
1966	The ICSID Convention	World Bank	Multilateral	Binding	Adopted
1967	Draft Convention on the Protection of Foreign Property	OECD	Regional	Non-binding	Not signed
1976	The OECD Declaration on International Investment and Multinational Enterprises[e]	OECD	Multilateral	Non-binding	Adopted
1994	Marrakesh Agreement Establishing the World Trade Organization, The Agreement on Trade-Related Investment Measures (TRIMs) and Annex 1B: General Agreement on Trade in Services and Ministerial Decisions Relating to the General Agreement on Trade in Services (GATS)	WTO	Multilateral	Binding	Adopted
1994	Energy Charter Treaty	European Energy Charter Conference	Regional	Binding	Adopted
1995	The Multilateral Agreement on Investment (MAI)[f]	OECD	Multilateral	Binding	Not adopted

[a]Newcombe and Paradell (2009), p. 21

[b]'International Code of Fair Treatment for Foreign Investment' (ICC 1949)

[c]'The New York Convention on the Recognition and Enforcement of Foreign Arbitral Awards' (1958)

[d]Ago (1969) p. 135. The United Nations Secretariat invited the Harvard Law School to revise and bring up to date its 1929 draft on state responsibility in 1955. The first draft convention was completed by the International Law Commission in 1961

[e]'The OECD Declaration on International Investment and Multinational Enterprises' (1976)

[f]The Multilateral Agreement on Investment (MAI). The idea for MAI was to be a freestanding international treaty covering the OECD members and for the MS of the European Communities. MAI was also intended to be open to accession for non-members of the OECD through a negotiations progress (OECD 1995)

Sovereignty over Natural Resources',[150] that scrapped the Hull rule was adopted by UNGA.

One solution for FDI exporters to neutralise the risk of uncompensated expropriation came from Europe. Germany, in desperate need for capital after losing World War II, initiated a development project for a contemporary investment treaty framework with other individual European countries.[151] It resulted in the first BIT, which was signed between Germany and Pakistan in 1959.[152] Undeniably, this European project is the foundation for the modern BITs.[153] The primary reasoning behind BITs was investment protection against expropriation by states lacking developed property rights—thereby making redress through action in domestic courts uncertain and at times impossible.[154] Unlike any former commercial agreements, the BITS dealt solely with FDI and aimed to build a basic legal framework to administer investments of subjects of the capita exporting nation in the host state.

By 1958 the urge to further develop a modern investment treaty framework led to the establishment of the New York Convention,[155] which Bermann sees as the foundation stone for an increasingly durable and resilient international arbitration regime.[156] A few years later, another attempt by the developed nations to counterpoint the UN debates that led to the resolution 1803 (XVII) was the ICSID Convention by the World Bank. The World Bank provided a greater influence to the developed states than the UN[157] and it's officials convinced the participating states that such a system would benefit both parties of investment flows.[158] Concerned that its proposal for an arbitration convention would be rejected by politicians, the World Bank officials consulted lawyers instead. Therefore, individuals such as the Bank's General Counsel and the main drafter of this convention, Aron Broches who became both and ICSID's first Secretary-General (Ch 4) largely influenced the adoption of

[150]UNGA (1962a).

[151]Salacuse (2015), p. 657.

[152]Notably, this BIT favours the capital-exporting country, Germany. Article 1.2 of the BIT hinders the state's right to regulate if the German subjects are negatively affected. Values like protection of human health, environment and labour standards are totally absent. Only a public policy exemption is present in Article 1.1. Article 12 of this BIT prohibits any alteration of the agreement in case of conflict between the parties, and empowers Germany to adopt all methods permitted by IL 'to assuring supervision of investments'. Most following BITS were similar in nature.

[153]Salacuse (2015).

[154]Abbott et al. (2014), p. 5.

[155]'The New York Convention on the Recognition and Enforcement of Foreign Arbitral Awards' (1958) entered into force on 7 June 1959 (article XII), UNICTRAL.

[156]Bermann (2012), p. 400.

[157]Particularly the United States, as its largest shareholder. According to St John (2018) pp. 111, 123, the Bank operated within the political constraints determined by the US government. Therefore, concerns relating to 'investment climate' was approached from the perspective of foreign investors.

[158]In 1964, at the annual World Bank meeting in Tokyo, an investor-state mechanism resolution was approved in the face of strong opposition. The ICSID Convention entered into force on 14 October 1966.

investor-state arbitration by the ICSID Convention.[159] Developing countries were, however, not thrilled by this litigation forum.[160]

Since then, the BIT regime has developed into a substantial network of bilateral treaties. Currently, it encompasses over 173 countries, among them all Organization of Economic Cooperation and Development (OECD) members.[161] The total number in 2018 is over 3000 agreements. A perpetual disagreement between capital-exporting and capital-importing countries on the regulation of foreign investment[162] has nevertheless left a substantial mark on this area of international law. The ICSID Convention is a prime example of this discrepancy. The ICSID Convention tempers the UNGA declarations for countries' perpetual sovereignty over their resources[163] as it replaced the state-to-state dispute resolution with investor-state dispute settlement.[164] The first IIA to incorporate such an investor-state dispute settlement clause was the 1968 Indonesia–Netherland BIT.[165] ISDS has been applied extensively to BITs ever since.

In the 1980s, many developing countries began to make drastic changes to their laws and policies towards liberalisation, promotion and protection of FDI.[166] This reversal from the earlier post-war investment approach focusing on conditions for entry and establishment with restrictions and controls on FDI had its roots in the debt crisis.[167] The crisis made FDIs more desirable than the alternative, bank lending, thus changing perceptions of the FDI's role in development and growth.

One of these policies led to another major European Community initiative, the Energy Charter Treaty,[168] which has been a major source of intra-EU disputes. Its

---

[159] Lowenfeld (2009), Ch III and St John (2018), Ch 5.

[160] Lowenfeld (2009), p. 54; Paulsson (1987); Shalakany (2000); see also Lowenfeld (2009), pp. 48 and 50 et seq. Twenty-one countries voted against this resolution.

[161] See UNCTAD (2017a, 31.12.2017). Investment Dispute Settlement Navigator. Investment Policy Hub at http://investmentpolicyhub.unctad.org/ISDS/CountryCases/197?partyRole=2.

[162] For example, the US Supreme Court in *Banco Nacional de Cuba v Sabbatino* (1964) remarked on the notable division of opinions between states on a state's power to expropriate the property of aliens.

[163] Newcombe and Paradell (2009), p. 33. See UNGA Resolution 1803 (XVII) on the Permanent Sovereignty Over Natural Resources (UNGA 1962b) and Resolution 3281 (XXIX), which founded the Charter of Economic Rights and Duties of States (CERDS) (UNGA 1974).

[164] Schreuer (2001), pp. 257, 258; Newcombe and Paradell (2009), p. 44. This means that instead of a requirement for consent to arbitration through contract clause, an investor-state arbitration could occur between the parties without any formal contractual relationship under an IIA or foreign investment law.

[165] Newcombe and Paradell (2009), p. 44. See also Art 22 of the Indonesia–Netherlands BIT.

[166] The World Investment Report 1996 Overview (UNCTAD 1996), p. 18.

[167] Stemming from the collapse of the Bretton Woods system in 1971, ending the fixed exchange rate system with the consequence that interest radically increased. This led to significant economic policy changes, known as the Washington Consensus, which thrived to stabilise the world economy by liberalisation and privatisation. The World Economic and Social Survey 2017, 17 July 2017 (UN 2017), Ch III.

[168] SEC (ECT 2016)

purpose was to assist in efforts to restructure and reconstruct the energy sector in the formerly communist-ruled countries of Central and Eastern Europe (CEE countries) after 1989 by securing a market economy approach to the efforts.[169] The Energy Charter Treaty, which Kleinheisterkamp portrays as a descendant of the EU due to its origins, is the only multilateral IIA to which the EU and all its Member States are signatories.[170]

Today, several options are available for investor treaty arbitration, which administers arbitration proceedings by a variety of rules—for example, UNICTRAL.[171] Both the ICSID Convention and the New York Convention also established and developed rules and principles broader than those from the past.[172] The BITs or TIPs set the boundaries for which forum the disputing parties may choose—institutional, non-institutional or ad hoc. Besides providing robust investment protection, implementation of ISDS clauses has caused a notable increase in the use of international arbitration to resolve foreign investment disputes. Notably, governments have increasingly offered investment incentives since the mid-1980s,[173] yet states were not sued by investors on a large scale before the beginning of 2000.[174] Since then, ISDS has been initiated with increasing frequency. Between 2015 and 2016, foreign investors launched about 70 ISDS claims each year.[175]

According to the proponents of IIAs, besides the primary purpose of encouraging international investment by protecting the property rights of investors in foreign jurisdictions, the IIAs also boost investor confidence by ensuring a steadier regulatory framework in the host state. Some authors also note that BITs aim to oppose anti-competitive conduct.[176]

However, the approach adopted towards regulatory stability clearly depends on the views of the individual arbitral tribunals. Due to the diversity of the investment arbitration community, some tribunals hold that a regulatory status quo should be upheld, while other tribunals adopt a wider contextual approach in respect of broader regulatory governance matters. Further, since investment incentives are commonly used by nations to attract foreign investment,[177] these incentives may clash with the Subsidies Agreement or other laws (such as state aid law) controlling subsidies.[178]

[169] Kleinheisterkamp (2012b), p. 86.

[170] Kleinheisterkamp (2012b), p. 86. Article 1(3) ECT acknowledges that the EU has the status of Regional Economic Integration Organisation (REIO) as a contracting party to the ECT.

[171] United Nations Commission on International Trade Law (UN 1976), approved by the General Assembly of the United Nations by resolution No. 31/98 on 15 December 1976.

[172] Abbott et al. (2014), p. 5.

[173] UNCTAD (1996).

[174] UNCTAD (2015), p. 114.

[175] UNCTAD (2017b). In 1990, the New York Convention had 80 contracting states. In 2018, it had 159 parties (UNICTRAL 2018b).

[176] Niemelä (2017), p. 270.

[177] UNCTAD (2004), p. 1.

[178] Such as the EU's state aid laws.

2.3.3 *Investment Incentives: The Elephant in the Room*

Indeed, the closest multilateral definition for investment incentives comes from the Subsidies Agreement. Otherwise, there is no uniform definition of what this widely used concept 'investment incentives' entails. However, because 'subsidy' and 'incentive' are overlapping terms, Articles 1 and 2 of the Subsidies Agreement provide at least a partial definition for the concept.[179] These provisions explain that for a subsidy (as explained in Sect. 2.2.1 in this chapter) or an incentive to exist, a measure must: (1) involve a financial contribution derived from the state; (2) confer a benefit upon its recipients; and (3) be specific to a company, an industry or a group of industries. Hence it can be concluded that the designation of investment incentives, affecting the choice of investor location by an economic or other inducement, is actually designer subsidies.[180]

Thomas argues that governments use location subsidies when competing for investments for two reasons: (1) the need for investment, and (2) the simple fact that capital is mobile.[181] The result is the first part forces governments to negotiate on conditions for an investment with the capital owners, while the second part provides a potential for a given investment to be located in several jurisdictions, due to the relationship's competitive aspect. Furthermore, several sources support the positive effects of FDI for both the host and investor country.[182]

As a consequence, in order to attract FDI, the race for investment has become a global competition in which investment incentives play a major role. Investment subsidies, due to other restrictions, are one of the few remaining tools available to policy-makers to affect the outcome of their domestic economy. This situation is created by, for instance, the WTO member states' commitment to restrictions on the use of trade policy and restrictions on exchange rate manipulation in the capital market.[183]

However, as all countries, and even the territories within some countries, continue to try to bid over the others regarding incentives offered to foreign investors, some scholars[184] and reports from IGOs[185] warn that the risk of this competition ending up

---

[179] UNCTAD (2004), p. 1.

[180] Thomas (2007), p. 1.

[181] Thomas (2007), p. 3; see also Blomström and Kokko (2003); Lindblom (1977).

[182] For example by IGOs such as the OECD (OECD 1976, 1995, 2017; Miroudot and Bartók 2008), the UN (UNCTAD 1994, 1997, 2004, 2014), the WTO Secretariat, Trade and Foreign Direct Investment (WTO 1996) and the Synthesis Paper on the Relationship of Trade and Competition Policy to Development and Economic Growth (WTO 1998b).

[183] Blomström and Kokko (2003), pp. 4–5.

[184] Blomström and Kokko (2003); Lindblom (1977); Tavares-Lehmann et al. (2016); Thomas (2007).

[185] For that reason, IGOs such as UNCTAD, the WTO and the OECD have also devoted several studies on the relationship between foreign investment liberalisation and competition policy. For the WTO, see WTO (1998a). For UNTAD, see UNCTAD (1996, 2015). For the OECD, see Miroudot and Bartók (2008).

a zero-sum game is great.[186] Evidence points out that investment incentives tend to have either a neutral or outright negative effect.[187] Specifically because often cut-throat competition between different incentive schemes creates a vicious race-to-the-bottom.[188] Hence the benefit associated with FDI explicitly as a stimulus to the national economy may turn out to be redundant due to the global competition for capital and investment. In the end, the perceived benefits tend to end up mostly in the pockets of multinational enterprises instead of those of consumers and local businesses.[189] Indeed, dominant in this 'race of investment incentives' is the short time perspective for the fix of an ailing economy, causing concern about the lack of sustainability objectives.[190]

In an attempt to control investment incentives subsidy races, the OECD adopted the Decision of the Council on OECD Legal Instruments International Investment Incentives and Disincentives on 17 May 1984.[191] The Singapore Ministerial Conference also established a WTO working group on trade and investment in 1996.[192] Despite these moves, evidence that speaks against investment subsidies has not stopped governments from offering these. Instead, the use of this kind of policy has increased since the 1980s.[193] As in the age of mercantilism and the Great Depression, FDI policies perceived to be serving national interests keep attracting support, particularly from the capital-exporting governments.[194] Consequently, little progress has been achieved in controlling subsidy races for foreign investment on a global level for the last 80 years.

[186] Blomström and Kokko (2003); Lindblom (1977); Tavares-Lehmann et al. (2016); Thomas (2007).

[187] See UNCTAD home page at https://unctad.org/SearchCenter/Pages/results.aspx?k=investment%20incentives and OECD home page at https://www.oecd.org/general/searchresults/?q=International%20Investment%20Incentives&cx=012432601748511391518:xzeadub0b0a&cof=FORID:11&ie=UTF-8.

[188] Elkins et al. (2006).

[189] Tavares-Lehmann et al. (2016), p. 2. Accordingly, 80 per cent of all cross-border flows of are internal transactions of multinational firms or through supply chains supervised by them.

[190] UNCTAD (1999), p. 140; Thomas (2016), p. 253; Blomström and Kokko (2003); Gabisa (2014).

[191] OECD, Decision of the Council on International Investment Incentives and Disincentives (OECD 2019).

[192] See WTO home page at https://www.wto.org/english/tratop_e/invest_e/invest_e.htm.

[193] Thomas (2007), pp. 2–3.

[194] The similarity is by analogy, as the situation regarding capital is in fact the reverse. Instead of governments supporting exports and restricting imports of goods and services, the governments are not in favour of exports and support imports of capital.

2.4 Subsidies and Foreign Investment Development in the EU

Some regions have stricter subsidies control and wider scope for what is regarded as a prohibited subsidy. Investment incentives offered by states and aimed at foreign investors are often covered by the rules. This imposes substantial limitations on the ability of nations to engage in an investment incentive race.

Since the establishment of the European Coal and Steel Community (ECSC) in 1956, the focal rationale behind state aid control has been the integration of the internal market.[195] With memories of economic protectionism in the past—partly blamed for causing the two World Wars—still fresh in mind, the Intergovernmental Committee on European Integration responsible for preparing the EEC Treaty[196] foresaw the importance of supranational control to hinder this type of behaviour. Notably, it wished to restrict the Member States of the future European Economic Community (EEC) from subsidising their domestic firms.[197]

Therefore, state aid control for the internal market was introduced with the Treaty of Rome,[198] while the GATT (and later the WTO) rules continued to apply to trade relations of the EU's Member States with third countries.[199] State aid law, however, was of much wider scope because the Spaak Report focused on firms instead of products.[200] That is, state aid law also covered investment incentives offered by a Member State and aimed at foreign investors. Further, to regain their political and economic status, the founding nations were willing to empower the EEC with enforcement powers that were far greater than those of the GATT to uphold these rules.[201] However, none of the EU Treaties included an IIA.

---

[195] *Competition Policy is One of the Fundamental Means for Preserving the Unity of the Market.* See EC (1977); see also Grin (2003), p. 7; Sauter (1997), p. 118.

[196] The Intergovernmental Committee on European Integration, *The Brussels Report on the General Common Market* (Spaak Report), Title II Ch. I section 2.

[197] Verouden (2016), p. 129.

[198] Treaty of Rome (EEC) (1958).

[199] Over time, the EU also adopted other, different type of trade instruments to protect its internal market from external interference through the subsidising practices of third countries (Damro and Guay 2016; Blauberger and Krämer 2010; Kassim and Lyons 2013; Botta and Schwellnus 2015; Lavenex and Schimmelfennig 2009; Gallo and Nicola 2015; Papadopoulos 2010; Van de Casteele 2016; Galindo 2015; Bourgeois et al. 2007; Fornalczyk 2004; Svechkar and Glushchenko 2018). For GATT, the EU subsumed these obligations because all its Member States were party to it and it was transferred under the exclusive competence of the EU. See *Joined Cases 21 to 24–72 International Fruit Company NV and Others* (1972), para. 18. This type of transfer of competence from the Member states to the EU was reconfirmed by *C-308/06 – Intertanko and Others* (2008) para 49 and *C-379/92-Peralta* (1994), para 16.

[200] Rubini (2004), p. 149; Van de Casteele (2006), p. 789.

[201] Bacon (2017), p. 3; Rubini (2010).

2.4.1 *The Era of the Market Economy: The Treaty of Paris*

After World War II, Europe was in tatters. Not only were trade relations broken, but all industry and production sectors were struggling and mostly under-delivering, with the consequence that European nations had lost much of their political and economic influence on the international stage. The new power players were the United States and the Soviet Union. Against this backdrop, some Western European countries realised that in order to prosper, they had to cooperate. However, it was the efforts of the Commissioner-General of the French National Planning Commission Jean Monnet's and those of French Foreign Minister Robert Schuman that led to the establishment of the Coal and Steel Community (ECSC).

To form a closer relationship with Germany and avoid further strife between the nations, France pursued an innovative diplomatic solution masterminded by Jean Monnet. He envisaged that German heavy industry would be integrated within an international economic organisation governed by a supranational authority. Monnet believed that this would create genuine cooperation between the Western European countries and address the fears held by France and the Allies about German rearmament.[202] Germany's gain, from submitting itself to the control of an IGO (together with France) with a supranational authority would be the regaining of its territorial sovereignty, as this would lead to the Allies ending their control of Germany's industrial regions.[203] Hence German Chancellor Konrad Adenauer supported the Franco-German union.[204]

On 9 May 1950, the Schuman Declaration proposed the creation of a European Coal and Steel Community.[205] Four other countries—Belgium, Italy, Luxembourg and the Netherlands—after witnessing how the relations between France and Germany improved, joined them in the pursuit to establish the Coal and Steel Community. It took six more years of negotiations between the founding nations to create this multilateral network of preferential trade agreements.

Schuman insisted that the draft treaty, as it stood, had to include a supranational authority. This 'High Authority' was a conceptual control solution for the single genuinely independent supranational organisation.[206]

By creating a common market for coal—the primary source of energy—and steel—the most important raw material for industry (particularly the weapons industry)—and placing it under the control of an international organisation, Monnet ultimately sought to create genuine solidarity between the partners. He believed that

[202] On Franco-German problems, see CVCE (2019).

[203] The Ruhr Valley, Germany's industrial area, was occupied by the Allies and since 1949 had been under the International Authority for the Ruhr (IAR), the purpose of which was to regulate steel and coal production and trade practice. On the issue of the Ruhr, see CVCE (2019).

[204] On Franco-German problems, see CVCE (2019).

[205] EU (2019).

[206] It was financially independent and represented the whole community. See CVCE (2019).

'integrating key sectors of the economy' would eventually pave the way to a European free trade area and eventually to a federation.[207]

German cartels were partly blamed for Germany's military might, as their control over steel production in Germany had enhanced its weapons production.[208] Hence, to control cartels and monopolies, the Treaty of Paris introduced competition rules in Chapter VI—Agreements and rules on concentrations in Articles 65 and 66. The predecessor for state aid control was laid out in Chapter VII—Impairment of the conditions of competition (Article 67). It obliged the Member States to notify all their actions 'which might have noticeable repercussions on the conditions of competition in the coal and steel industries' to the High Authority of the Coal and Steel Community.[209] However, unlike in the succeeding treaty, The Treaty of Rome, the High Authority's role was restricted to recommending and consulting.[210] From this point, the first European Community began to take on an organisational structure, which would momentously alter the international order.

2.4.2 The Era of Integration: From the Treaty of Rome

Not long after the establishment of the ECSC, the fledgling European Community realised that it needed a better organisational shape and to cover more extensive areas of industry. Hence a similar, but more flexible, European treaty was introduced by the same founding states in the form of the 1957 Treaty of Rome. As explained by neo-functionalism, the European integration was to be achieved by Brussels-centred and steered polity, meant to spill over functionally and politically to the Member States. Yet not all policy areas were included by this treaty—for example, it did not include an IIA. Consequently, these two areas of international law, IIL and ECC law, functioned in parallel.

However, the authors of the Spaak Report visualised the common market as a highly integrated trade zone.[211] The rules governing this market would need effective competition policy, of which state aid was to be a part.[212] Specifically, the 1956 Spaak Report[213] foresaw the need to control the extent to which the individual

[207] The Jean Monnet Plan (CVCE 2019).

[208] On Franco-German problems, see CVCE (2019).

[209] The Treaty of Paris Chapter VII—Impairment of the conditions of competition (Article 67).

[210] Compare the Treaty of Paris Chapter VII—Impairment of the conditions of competition Article 67 to Articles 92–94 of the EEC.

[211] The Intergovernmental Committee on European Integration, *The Brussels Report on the General Common Market* (Spaak Report) was prepared by the Spaak Committee, which was commissioned at the Messina Conference in June 1955 (Spaak 1956). According to the Venice Conference of 29–30 May 1956, it was the main working document for the drafting of the EEC Treaty: see López (2015), p. 15.

[212] Verouden (2016), p. 129.

[213] Spaak (1956), Title II Ch. I section 2.

Member States of the future EEC would be able to provide financial assistance to their companies. Hence, the objective of European integration had state aid policy tied to it, which provided the impetus for the Member States to put restrictions on their sovereignty while assigning surveillance powers to the Commission. The state aid regime has a supranational character—which means that the rules on State aid apply within all Member States of the EU. Unlike GATT, which categorised subsidies as trade barriers, the European Economic Community integrated these 'aids granted by states' as part of rules of competition in Articles 92–94 of the EEC. Of these three provisions, which have been copied almost verbatim to the succeeding treaties, Article 92 of the EEC introduced the underpinning principle of state aid control: that state aid is 'incompatible' with the 'common market' and only acceptable under certain circumstances.[214] Since then, while the core provisions have remained basically the same, the EU's capacity and competence to steer and control state aid have evolved, adapted and expanded.

2.4.3 The Era of Coordinating External Actions: The Treaty of Maastricht

In 1993, the EU gained further powers to control and influence competition restrictions. For example, its control over subsidising practices was extended from internal actions to also cover external actions. To establish the EU's Common Foreign and Security Policy (CFSP) to help coordinate the union's external actions under Article J.1 of Title V, the Maastricht Treaty defined and implemented a common policy covering all security and foreign policy areas.[215] One policy area covered by the CFSP was trade and subsidies, effectively transferring the power to negotiate and enter these types of international agreements from the Member States.

2.4.4 The Era of Governance: From the Treaty of Amsterdam

As with each new ECC/EC/EU treaty, the Member States kept on conferring additional powers to the EU until some concerns about its decision-making process started to arise. The EU was perceived as undemocratic and lacking transparency. Hence, after the harmonisation of the internal market was achieved on several levels, the focus of policy objectives transformed into EU governance.[216] To calm concerns about the EU being able to wield its powers too intrusively, a fledgling approach by

[214] Merola (2016), p. 10.

[215] EUR-Lex glossary of summaries available at https://eurlex.europa.eu/summary/glossary/foreign_security_policy.html.

[216] Golberg (2018).

the EU to achieve 'better regulation', by setting out basic requirements for the preparation of 'good' EU legislation, was an annex to the Amsterdam Treaty of 1997.[217] This annex was a protocol on 'subsidiarity and proportionality'.[218] Simply put, all legislative initiatives had to respect the principles of subsidiarity and proportionality.[219] They also had to be prepared with a minimum of cost, and to be simple and subject to public consultation for transparency.[220]

Responding to changes in the Amsterdam Treaty, the state aid regime was also adapted. Through the introduction of secondary legislation in the form of Regulations[221] and soft law instruments,[222] state aid control—until then solely based upon negative integration—took steps towards including positive integration 'from above'.[223]

The era of governance was officially launched in 2001 by the White Paper on European Governance,[224] which witnessed developments in the EU's legislative process.[225] Improvements in consultation and impact assessment, in addition to new legislative methodology—for instance, self- and co-regulation[226]—simplification and improved application monitoring of law were implemented.

Naturally, state aid control kept on adjusting to the sweeping changes, and thus continued to develop its soft law approach,[227] which made it easier for the Member States to cope with the intrusive nature of state aid policy.[228] Four years after the

---

[217] Amsterdam Treaty amending the Treaty of the European Union, October 1997: see Golberg (2018), p. 19.

[218] *Subsidiarity* is the principle that the European Union should perform only those tasks that cannot be performed at national or local level. *Proportionality* is the principle that the European Union should act in a way that does not go beyond what is needed to meet the objectives of the measure under consideration.

[219] Golberg (2018), p. 19.

[220] Golberg (2018), p. 19.

[221] Such as Council Regulation No 659/1999 of 22 March 1999 laying down detailed rules for the application of Article 108 of the Treaty on the Functioning of the European Union, OJ L 83, 27.03.1999 and the first block exemption regulations.

[222] For example, the Commission notice on business taxation (EC 1998).

[223] Blauberger (2008). This was the period under Commissioners Van Miert and Monti.

[224] European Commission (2001); COM (2001), p. 428; EC (2001).

[225] As suggested by the Prodi Commission (2000–2005). For more information on this subject, see Mandelkern Report, 13 November 2001 at http://ec.europa.eu/smart-regulation/better_regulation/documents/mandelkern_report.pdf.

[226] The Inter-institutional Agreement on Better Law Making, 2003 C321/01 point 18 defines co-regulation and point 22 defines self-regulation. Co-regulation is the mechanism 'whereby a Community legislative act entrusts the attainment of the objectives defined by the legislative authority to parties which are recognized in the field'. Self-regulation allows some entities, such as economic operators, social partners and NGOs, to adopt guidelines that address themselves at a European level (EP, Council and EC 2003).

[227] The Commission has applied soft law instruments ever since the 1970s: see Biondi and Stefan (2018), p. 3.

[228] For more on European governance regarding state aid law, see Sects. 3.2.3 and 3.4 in Chap. 3.

introduction of the Governance White Paper, the Commission adopted the State Aid Action Plan (SAAP), which introduced a more economical approach.[229]

2.4.5 *The Era of Expansion of Competencies: From the Treaty of Lisbon*

The Lisbon Treaty, signed on 13 December 2007, entered into force on 1 December 2009. By means of this new treaty, all the EC's powers held under the previous EC Treaty were transferred to the EU.[230] Originally intended to be the Treaty establishing a Constitution for Europe (Constitutional Treaty) the nature of the Lisbon Treaty is constitutional. The removal of references to a constitution did not change its constitutional character.[231] Hence, the Lisbon Treaty provided the EU with a legal personality so that it could enter international treaties and join international organisations. It also clearly explains what the EU's powers are and honed the way it exercises these powers. Furthermore, it distinguishes the three different competencies that exist in the EU—exclusive (Article 3 TFEU), where only the EU can act and legislate; shared (Article 4 TFEU), where the Member States can act and legislate only if the EU has chosen not to; and supportive (Articles 5 and 6 TFEU).[232]

Following the signing of the Lisbon Treaty, the next substantial reform of the state aid regime was the State Aid Modernisation (SAM) of 2012. SAM revised and expanded the scope of secondary law and broadened the scope of the guidelines.[233] Recently, the EU has been assessing possibilities for directly tackling distortions that are caused by foreign subsidies granted to companies active in the EU market.[234] For this purpose, the Commission's White Paper on levelling the playing field as regards foreign subsidies (Vol. COM(2020) 253 final, pp. 49) (White Paper on Foreign Subsidies)[235] introduced a review of the EU's trade policy instruments and an

---

[229] For more on this, see Sect. 3.4.1 in Chap. 3.

[230] Craig and De Búrca (2011) p. 25.

[231] See the European Parliament website at http://www.europarl.europa.eu/factsheets/en/sheet/5/the-treaty-of-lisbon for the 2001 European Council declaration on the future of the European Union (the Laeken declaration).

[232] Article 6 TFEU stipulates that the EU can support certain actions by its Member States and Article 5 TFEU adds that the EU may provide arrangements for coordinated policy where the EU Member States must coordinate policy.

[233] For more on this see Sects. 3.2.3 and 3.4.1 in Chap. 3.

[234] Commissions media release, Commission adopts White Paper on foreign subsidies in the Single Market at https://ec.europa.eu/commission/presscorner/detail/en/ip_20_1070. For more on this see Sect. 3.5.5.

[235] European Commission (2020), p. 49. White Paper on levelling the playing field as regards foreign subsidies. The White Paper on Foreign Subsidies (EC 2020) discusses methods the EU could adopt to address such distortions.

initiative to further expand the state aid regime.[236] This would be achieved by adopting additional unilateral trade defence instruments targeting foreign subsidies that the Commission identifies as harmful to the EU's internal market.[237] According to the Commission, of particular concern are foreign subsidies that 'take the form of financial flows facilitating acquisitions of EU companies or where they directly support the operation of a company in the EU or facilitate bidding in a public procurement procedure'.[238]

However, the most substantial changes in the EU's competencies came in the area of foreign direct investment. In contrast to state aid law, investment law in the context of EU law is entirely new, as the EU did not have the competence to conclude investment agreements covering FDI before the entry into force of the Lisbon Treaty.[239] While intra-EU BITs, governed by two parallel legal frameworks, on one hand, by EU intra-BITs, and on the other hand, those under EU law and Member States domestic law had been deemed obsolete and incompatible with EU law by the Commission since 2006, these concerns did not extend to other BITs.[240] Before the Lisbon Treaty, investment provisions incorporated into the EU's international agreements merely had the purpose of encouraging investment flows between the EU and its trading partners without any specific procedural commitments.[241] Therefore, questions about the compatibility of ISA with EU law *vis-à-vis* external relations did not arise prior to the Lisbon Treaty.

This was to change after the Lisbon Treaty expanded the EU's Common Commercial Policy to cover FDI. Meunier describes this competence shift as finding its way into the text of the Lisbon Treaty 'by stealth', as the Member States did not embrace this change.[242] Soon after this transition of competence, the Member States realised that they had transferred more powers to the EU than they had wanted.[243] After the Commission enthusiastically started practising this new-found competence

---

[236] This was followed by the Commission's proposal for a Regulation on foreign subsidies distorting the internal market, Brussels 5 May 2021 COM(2021) 223 final (Draft Regulation on foreign subsidies EC 2021).

[237] The White Paper on Foreign Subsidies (EC 2020). For more on this, see Sect. 3.5.5.

[238] Commission's media release at https://ec.europa.eu/commission/presscorner/detail/en/ip_20_1070. For the outcome of the public consultations regarding this initiative, see https://ec.europa.eu/info/law/better-regulation/have-your-say/initiatives/12452-White-Paper-on-Foreign-Subsidies.

[239] TFEU, Art 207(1). Prior to the Lisbon Treaty, several agreements concluded by the EU contained investment-related provisions that were meant to complement Member State BITs. These agreements did not cover the treatment of investors/investments in the post-establishment phase or investor-state arbitration. The main exception is the Energy Charter Treaty: see Strik (2016), pp. 67–73, 90–100.

[240] See ECFIN (2006), p. 7. The Commission saw these BITs as discriminatory, causing legal uncertainty and in violation of the interpretive autonomy of the CJEU and the primacy of EU law. For more on issues regarding intra-EU BITs, see Chaps. 4 and 5.

[241] This matches the Commission's (unsuccessful) arguments about the lack of a disconnection clause in the ECT (see Sect. 5.7 in Chap. 5).

[242] Meunier (2017), p. 2.

[243] Lavranos (2013), pp. 1, 6.

by negotiating investment chapters into the EU's trade agreements, this activity also soon ran into 'teething troubles' due to the increased use of intra-EU litigation,[244] severe criticism from the civil society[245] and political and institutional differences[246] regarding the legal regime of ISDS.

Behind some of these 'teething troubles' was the Commission's approach to the application of investment protection standards. Before 2013, these standards negotiated by the Commission were traditional, covering ISDS and commonly used in IIAs.[247] Unfortunately, the recent period has seen IIAs, TIPs and IPAs involving the EU regarded as the repercussions of the Commission's action and non-action. Wielding its recently gained powers of exclusive competence in foreign direct investment, the Commission embarked on a grand pursuit to sign extensive trade agreements with nations such as the United States, Canada, Singapore, Japan and Mexico, which incorporated investment protection provisions within ISDS.[248] After the Commission's Public Consultations during 2014–2015 on ISDS under TTIP, the Commission made a significant effort to modernise international investment law and particularly ISDS to solve the issues related to for the EU's new investment provisions in trade agreements and IIAs.[249] Accordingly, the investment chapters in trade agreements concluded after these Commissions Public Consultations reformed ISDS to ICS.[250] Before negotiating these trade agreements, however, the Commission did not verify with the CJEU the combability of these provisions with EU law. Therefore, the extent of the Union's competence regarding ISDS clauses in IIAs remained unclear until *Opinion 2/15 of the Court* (2017) and *Opinion 1/17* (2019).

In *Opinion 2/15* the CJEU clarified that the EU investment treaties are mostly mixed agreements,[251] and as such, can be concluded only by the EU and its Member States acting together. ISDS particularly retains the shared competence of the EU

---

244 See EC (2016), Ch. 4.3, referring to UNCTAD database for data (UNCTAD, 2016a, b). See also EC (2015b), pp. 5, 6.

245 Byström (2016); EC (2015c); Ankersmit (2015, 2016a, b); Konttinen and Teivainen (2013); Fleming (2014); Schneiderman (2016); Van Harten (2015); Kleinheisterkamp (2015). See also (Albi et al. 2016). For pro ISDS, see Happ and Tietje (2013); Tietje et al. (2012); Ortolani (2015); Struckmann et al. (2016).

246 On TTIP, see Sims and Stone (2016); Gotev (2016). On CETA, Belgium requested CJEU's opinion on the compatibility of CETA's investment court with EU law ('*Opinion 1/17*', 2019). See also European Parliament think tanks workshop in April 2014 (EP 2014, p. 21; Bierbrauer 2014, Ch. 3.3; Cole 2014).

247 Gáspár-Szilágyi (2019). See also Matei (2015), p. 5; Lenk (2015); Gallo and Nicola (2015).

248 Gáspár-Szilágyi (2019), p. 3.

249 EC (2015a).

250 See *inter alia* CETA, JEEPA, EU–Korea. At the same time, the EU initiated discussion on reform of ISDS by the creation of a Multilateral Investment Court under UNCITRAL. See Negotiating Directives for a Convention Establishing a Multilateral Court for the Settlement of Investment Disputes, Introduction (Council 2018b).

251 Meaning that these agreements cover even areas outside the EU's exclusive competence. See opinion of AG Sharpston ('*Opinion 2/15*', 2016). See also *Opinion 1/17* (2019). For exclusive competence, see TFEU, Article 3, para. 1, p. 207.

and its Member States.[252] This means that the EU needs the Member States to ratify IIAs that include this type of provisions, which is why many trade agreements concluded after *Opinion 2/15 of the Court (Full Court)* (2017), such as the EUSFTA and the JEEPA, have been divided into a trade agreement and a separate Investment Protection Agreement (IPA).

However, further uncertainty on the fate of arbitrability in the EU's international agreements remained after the CJEU's ruling in *Achmea* and Belgium's referral to the CJEU for an opinion under Article 218(11) of the TFEU on the compatibility of the Investment Court System under CETA with EU law. This issue was partially resolved by the CJEU in *Opinion 1/17* (2019),[253] where the CJEU held that ICS in CETA could coexist with the EU judicial system under public international law.[254] After *Opinion 1/17* (2019), all international agreements with investment provisions that have been and are currently being negotiated by the EU[255] will use ICS. However, another consequence of *Opinion 1/17* (2019) is that the validity of IIAs negotiated by the EU in the past, which include ISDS instead of ICS, is highly doubtful. If these IIAs lack the mandatory guarantees for compatibility with EU law, these agreements (such as JEEEPA) are likely to conflict with EU law and therefore must be renegotiated.

2.5 Summary and Conclusions

The motivation for liberal trade policies is the notion that these boost economic development and wealth maximisation globally while avoiding protectionist measures that may lead to international conflicts (such as trade wars). Explicitly, elimination or reduction of different types of barriers to trade and FDI liberalisation are conceived to be crucial for a functional global free-market economy. The adoption of a rule-based world economic order with procedures for global trade and fiscal and monetary policies aims to achieve these goals. However, to implement such an order means that independent states must agree to restrict their capacity to make independent decisions within these policy areas.

A critical factor that revolves around the evolution of subsidies control and IIAs is the willingness to compromise on sovereignty. It took two World Wars before nations were willing to commit to international agreements where they transferred

[252] Paras 285–293 of *Opinion 2/15 of the Court (Full Court)* (2017).

[253] The Opinion of AG Bot on this matter came out at the end of January 2019: *Opinion Avis 1/17 (AG)* (2019).

[254] *Opinion 1/17* (2019) paras 106–61. These guarantees are procedural (say, guaranteeing the Tribunal's independence and impartiality) and normative (say, guaranteeing the effectiveness of EU competition law and particularly state aid law).

[255] Hence *Opinion 1/17* (2019) will also play a vital role in the Commission's plans to establish a Multilateral Investment Court, which potentially could develop into an international legal body responsible for resolving conflicts between investors and states.

some of their powers to international institutions. As a result, international rules governing trade and subsidies were successfully codified under a single institution, the GATT 1947, which later became the WTO (Sect. 2.3.1). In parallel, the EU's state aid regime developed into its own, unique system with a much broader scope (including investment incentives) than those of the GATT 1947 and WTO (Sect. 2.4).

Some separate incident markings distinguish this development. The first incident marker is the establishment of the IMF, the World Bank and the GATT, and it mutually applies to the EU and the global economic order. The second incident marking is the establishment of the European Coal and Steel Community by the Treaty of Paris. It created 'a fork in the road' by initiating the derivation of the EU's competition policy from the standing public international norms (Sect. 2.4.1). Since then, the Treaty of Rome (Sect. 2.4.2), The Treaty of Amsterdam (Sect. 2.4.3), the Treaty of Maastricht (Sect. 2.4.4) and the Treaty of Lisbon (Sect. 2.4.5) have markedly affected the development of the EU's Competition or FDI policy. IIAs, however, failed to achieve multilateralism due to their inability to satisfy the principles of sovereignty and nationality in a unified framework[256] and were instead implemented as a network of BITs (Sect. 2.3.2).

Indeed, (foreign) investment and competition policy are linked to trade and are supportive of each other by eliminating barriers to international trade and investment by restricting governments engaging in anti-competitive behaviour. These policies, however, have points of contradiction and divergence, despite their shared economic objective of wealth maximisation and close interrelationship. To reap the full benefits of foreign investment, government practises attracting it must be void of anticompetitive behaviour. Therefore, trade and investment policy must be aligned with efficient competition (and subsidies) policy. However, because of the fragmentation of international investment law in BITs combined with the States inability to agree on a comprehensive system to restrict investment incentives, which are anti-competitive subsidies aimed at attracting FDI, many nations engage in these types of measures. 'Subsidy' and 'incentive' are overlapping terms.

The Subsidies Agreement regulates some of these measures (explicitly good related); however, the EU's competition rules, covering all types of anti-competitive behaviour by private enterprises and states under the same law, catch most of these. Explicitly, these rules apply similarly to goods, services and capital, while other public international norms treat goods, services and capital movements differently. Consequently, many investment incentives offered by states to attract FDI run afoul of state aid rules but not the WTO rules.

Moreover, the regime of BITs aims to maintain regulatory stability for the benefit of foreign investors by attempting to uphold investment incentives while the EU state aid policy continues to adjust in line with the EU's other policies. The EU economy's increasing interlinkage with the international global economy is creating an increased need for tools that will protect the EU market from distortion via foreign

[256] Kirayoglu (2014), p. 9.

subsidies. Hence, the Draft Regulation on foreign subsidies represents a huge step towards bringing subsidies granted by third countries, which typically fall outside the scope of EU State aid regime, under EU's unilateral control. The EU is facing a situation where foreign subsidies facilitate the acquisition of EU companies and create a distortion of trade policies and investment decisions, including a negative effect on public procurement in the EU market. Thus, with the rules and regulations for trade defence not being sufficient to level the playing field for those operating in the EU market, there is a regulatory gap that needs to be filled (Sect. 2.4.5).

ISDS has increased. After the EU gained competence to conclude international investment agreements in 2009, the EU had exclusive competence of both FDI and state aid.[257] From this arose the need to slowly take over and adjust the IIA's previously negotiated arrangements with the Member States to match EU law correctly (Sect. 2.4). In particular, ISDS and subsidies in the form of investment incentives have proved to be a thorny issue, which even led to doubts about whether the EU's international investment agreements could be relied on. The solution has turned out to be the Commission's reform of ISDS to ICS, intended to guarantee that the EU's future international agreements will not collide with EU law and especially state aid law (Sect. 2.4.5).

Given that the EU's competition policy also has other objectives besides maintaining free markets, such as European integration and European governance that ISDS can undermine, this chapter has found that the crossfire of EU law and the BIT regime was bound to surface. In the EU's *sui generis* system, with its own political, structural and judicial norms and objectives, the inherent tensions behind the trade, competition and international investment norms become enhanced.

Cases

Advocate General's Opinion in Avis 1/17, ECLI:EU:C:2019:72 (Advocate General Bot, 2019)

Advocate General's Opinion in Opinion procedure 2/15, ECLI:EU:C:2016:992 (European Court of Justice, 2016)

Banco Nacional de Cuba v Sabbatino, 376 U.S. 398, 428 (Supreme Court of United States, 1964)

Criminal proceedings against Matteo Peralta, case C-379/92, ECLI:EU:C:1994:296 (European Court of Justice, 1994)

EDF (Services) Limited v Romania, Award, No. ICSID Case No. ARB/05/13 (ad hoc, 2009)

[257] Because the EU treaties did not include international investment agreements, these two areas of international law, IIL and EU law, functioned in parallel until the Treaty of Lisbon entered into force in 2009.

International Fruit Company NV and others v Produktschap voor Groenten en Fruit, joined cases 21 to 24-72, ECLI:EU:C:1972:115 (European Court of Justice, 1972)

Ioan Micula, Viorel Micula, S.C. European Food S.A, S.C. Starmill S.R.L. and S.C. Multipack S.R.L. v Romania, ICSID Award, Case No. ARB/05/20, Italaw (ICSID ad hoc, 2013)

Malicorp Limited v Arab Republic of Egypt (ICSID Case No. ARB/08/18) Award (ICSID ad hoc, 2011)

Metal-Tech Ltd v The Republic of Uzbekistan, ICSID Case No ARB/10/3 (ICSID ad hoc, 2013)

Opinion 1/17 of the Court (Full Court) ECLI:EU:C:2019:341 (European Court of Justice (Full Court), 2019)

Opinion 2/15 of the Court (Full Court), ECLI:EU:C:2017:376, Opinion 2/15 (European Court of Justice (Full Court), 2017)

The Queen, on the application of International Association of Independent Tanker Owners (Intertanko) and Others v Secretary of State for Transport, case-308/06, EU:C:2008:312 (European Court of Justice (Grand Chamber), 2008)

State aid SA.40348 (2015/NN)—Spain support for electricity generation from renewable energy sources, cogeneration and waste, C(2017) 7384 final (European Commission, 2017)

World Duty Free Company Ltd v The Republic of Kenya, Award, ICSID Case No. ARB/00/7 (ICSID ad hoc, 2006)

References

Abbott R, Erixon F, Ferracane MF (2014) Demystifying investor-state dispute settlement (ISDS). European Centre for International Political Economy, Brussels. https://ecipe.org/publications/isds

Ago R (1969) First report on state responsibility: Review of previous work on codification of the topic of the international responsibility of states. United Nations, Geneva

Albi A, Diamond A, Antoine B (2016) Legal statement on investment protection and investor-state dispute settlement mechanisms in TTIP and CETA. https://stop-ttip.org/wp-content/uploads/2016/10/28.10.16-Updated-Legal-Statement_EN.pdf

Ankersmit L (2015) Legality of investor-state dispute settlement (ISDS) under EU law. http://www.clientearth.org/health-environment/health-environment-publications/legality-of-investor-state-dispute-settlement-under-eu-law-3020

Ankersmit L (2016a) The compatibility of investment arbitration in trade agreements with the judicial system. J Eur Environ Plan Law 13(1):46–63

Ankersmit L (2016b) Is ISDS in EU trade agreements legal under EU law? Investment Treaty News, 29 February. https://www.iisd.org/itn/2016/02/29/is-isds-in-eu-trade-agreements-legal-under-eu-law-laurens-ankersmit

Bacon K (2017) European Union law of state aid, 3rd edn. Oxford University Press, Oxford

Bagwell K, Staiger RW (1999) Regionalism and multilateral tariff cooperation. In: Piggott J, Woodland A (eds) International trade policy and the Pacific Rim. St Martin's Press, New York

Bagwell K, Staiger RW (2006) Will international rules on subsidies disrupt the world trading system? Am Econ Rev 96(3):877–895

Bairoch P (1989) European trade policy. In: Mathias P, Pollard S (eds) The Cambridge economic history of Europe, vol 8. Cambridge University Press, Cambridge, pp 1815–1914

Baldwin R (1993) A domino theory of regionalism. In: Baldwin R, Haarapanta P, Kiander J (eds) Expanding Membership of the EU. Cambridge University Press, Cambridge

Baldwin R, Jaimovich D (2012) Are free trade agreements contagious? J Int Econ 88(1):1–16. S0022199612000591. https://doi.org/10.1016/j.jinteco.2012.03.009

Bergstrand JH (1990) The Heckscher-Ohlin-Samuelson model, the Linder hypothesis and the determinants of bilateral intra-industry trade. Econ J 100(403):1216–1229

Bermann GA (2012) Navigating EU law and the law of international arbitration. Arbitr Int 28(3): 397–446

Bierbrauer E (2014) Transatlantic Trade and Investment Partnership (TTIP) negotiations: State of play. http://www.europarl.europa.eu/RegData/etudes/BRIE/2014/536397/EXPO_BRI(2014)536397_EN.pdf

Biondi A, Stefan O (2018) The notice on the notion of state aid: Every light has its shadow. In: Nascimbene B, Di Pascale A (eds) The modernisation of state aid for economic and social development. Springer, Dordrecht

Blauberger M (2008) From negative to positive integration: European state aid control through soft and hard law. MPIfG Discussion Paper 08/4. https://ssrn.com/abstract=1660981 or https://doi.org/10.2139/ssrn.1660981.

Blauberger M, Krämer RU (2010) European competition vs global competitiveness: Transferring EU rules on state aid and public procurement beyond Europe. CCP Working Paper 10-10. https://www.uea.ac.uk/documents/107435/107587/1.168372!ccp10-10.pdf

Blomström M, Kokko A (2003) The economics of foreign direct investment incentives. NBER Working Paper 9489. https://econpapers.repec.org/paper/nbrnberwo/9489.htm

Boasson EL (2019) Constitutionalization and entrepreneurship: explaining increased EU steering of renewables support schemes. Polit Gov 7(1):70–80

Botta M, Schwellnus G (2015) Enforcing state aid rules in EU candidate countries: a qualitative comparative analysis of the direct and indirect effects of conditionality. J Eur Public Policy 22(3):335–352

Bourgeois J, Dawar K, Evenett, SJ (2007) A comparative analysis of selected provisions in free trade agreements. http://sro.sussex.ac.uk/id/eprint/59639

Brown AG (2009) Reluctant partners: a history of multilateral trade cooperation, 1850–2000. University of Michigan Press, Ann Arbor, MI

Brownlie I (1990) Principles of public international law. Oxford University Press, Oxford

Byström N (2016) TTIP vs Europeans: A wake-up call for the Commission. http://www.euractiv.com/section/trade-society/opinion/ttip-vs-europeans-a-wake-up-call-for-the-commission

Calvo C (1896) Le droit international: théorie et pratique précédé d'un historique des gens, vol 5. Rousseau, Paris

Clarke JL (2003) Competition policy and foreign direct investment. Paper presented at the fifth meeting of the European Trade Study Group, September

Cole T (2014) Legal instruments and practice of arbitration in the EU. European Parliament, Brussels. http://www.europarl.europa.eu/studies

Comín F, Hernández M, Agelán EL (2010) Historia económica mundial: siglos X-XX. Crítica, Barcelona

Commission of the European Communities (CEC) (1977) Sixth Report on Competition Policy 1976. http://ec.europa.eu/competition/publications/annual_report/ar_1976_en.pdf

Commission of the European Communities (CEC) (1998) Commission notice on the application of the state aid rules to measures relating to direct business taxation (98/C 384/03). Publications Office of the European Communities, Brussels

Craig P, De Búrca G (2011) EU law: text, cases, and materials, 5th edn. Oxford University Press, Oxford

Cremona M (2003) State aid control: Substance and procedure in the Europe agreements and the stabilisation and association agreements. Eur Law J 9:265

CVCE (2019) Historical events in the European integration process (1945–2014). https://www.cvce.eu/en

Damro C (2013) EU state aid policy and the politics of external trade relations. J Ind Compet Trade 13(1):159–157

Damro C, Guay T (2016) European competition policy and globalization. Springer, New York

Dixit A, Norman V (1986) Gains from trade without lump-sum compensation. J Int Econ 21(1–2): 111–122

DSU Appellate Body Report (n.d.) United States – Measures Affecting Trade in Large Civil Aircraft (Second Complaint) WT/DS353/AB/R12

Dugard JR (2000) First report on diplomatic protection by the Special Rapporteur, Mr. John R. Dugard. Retrieved from Geneva: http://legal.un.org/ilc/guide/9_8.shtml

Dür A (2010) Protection for exporters: Power and discrimination in transatlantic trade relations, 1930–2010. Cornell University Press, Ithaca

Duus P (1996) Imperialism without colonies: the vision of a greater east Asia co-prosperity sphere. Dipl Statecraft 7(1):54–72

ECFIN/CEFCPE (2006) REP/56882. Annual EFC Report to the Commission and the Council on the Movement of Capital and the Freedom of Payments

Eckes C (2016) International rulings and the EU legal order:Autonomy as legitimacy? CLEER Papers, 2016/2. http://www.asser.nl/media/3002/cleer16-2_complete_web.pdf

Egger P, Larch M (2008) Interdependent preferential trade agreement memberships: an empirical analysis. J Int Econ 76(2):384–399

Elkins Z, Guzman AT, Simmons BA (2006) Competing for capital: the diffusion of bilateral investment treaties, 1960–2000. Int Organ 60(4):811–846

European Commission (EC) (2001) White Paper of European Governance, COM(2001) 428. European Union, Brussels

European Commission (EC) (2015a) Investment in TTIP and beyond – the path for reform. European Union, Brussels. http://trade.ec.europa.eu/doclib/docs/2015/may/tradoc_153408.PDF

European Commission (EC) (2015b) Investor to State Dispute Settlement (ISDS) Some facts and figures Retrieved from Brussels: http://trade.ec.europa.eu/doclib/docs/2015/january/tradoc-153046.pdf

European Commission (EC) (2015c) Report on the online consultation on investment protection and investor-to-state dispute settlement in the Transatlantic Trade and Investment Partnership Agreement. Media release. http://europa.eu/rapid/press-release_MEMO-15-3202_en.htm

European Commission (EC) (2016) Commission staff working document on the movement of capital and the freedom of payments. DG FISMA, Brussels

European Commission (EC) (2018a) WTO – EU concept paper on WTO Reform, Brussels, 18 September. http://trade.ec.europa.eu/doclib/docs/2018/september/tradoc_157331.pdf

European Commission (EC) (2018b) Negotiating directives for a convention establishing a multilateral court for the settlement of investment disputes. European Union, Luxembourg

European Commission (EC) (2020) White paper on levelling the playing field as regards foreign subsidies. European Union, Brussels

European Commission (EC) (2021) Commission proposal for a Regulation on foreign subsidies distorting the internal market, Brussels 5 May 2021 COM(2021) 223 final

European Parliament (2003) Interinstitutional agreement between the European Parliament, the Council of the European Union and the European Commission on Better Law-Making. European Union, Brussels

European Parliament (2014) Investor-state dispute settlement (ISDS) provisions in the EU's international investment agreements. European Union, Brussels. http://www.europarl.europa.eu/thinktank/en/document.html?reference=EXPO_STU(2014)534979

European Union (2019). The Schuman Declaration. https://europa.eu/european-union/index_en

Farrell M (2005) EU external relations: exporting the EU model of governance? Eur Foreign Aff Rev 10(4):451–462

Fleming J (2014) ISDS clause: A gateway to future trade deals. http://www.euractiv.com/section/trade-society/news/isds-clause-a-gateway-to-future-trade-deals

Fornalczyk A (2004) State aid regulation in candidate countries: the case of Poland. In: Biondi A, Eeckhout P, Flynn J (eds) The law of state aid in the European Union. Oxford University Press, Oxford

Friedman M (1951) Capitalism and freedom. University of Chicago Press, Chicago

Friedman M (1956) Studies in the quantity theory of money. University of Chicago Press, Chicago

Gabisa H (2014) The fate of international human rights norms in the realm of bilateral investment treaties (BITs): has humanity become a collateral damage? Int Lawyer 48(2):153–167

Galindo BR (2015) State aid control in the context of globalisation. European Commission, Brussels

Gallo D, Nicola FG (2015) The external dimension of EU investment law: Jurisdictional clashes and transformative adjudication. Fordham Int Law J 39:1081

Gáspár-Szilágyi S (2019) The EU's cumbersome investment law and policy, and its effects on the protection of intellectual property rights. In: Geiger C (ed) Research handbook on intellectual property and investment law. Edward Elgar, Cheltenham

Gerber D (2000) Law and competition in twentieth century Europe: protecting Prometheus. Oxford University Press, Oxford

Ghouri A (2011) The evolution of bilateral investment treaties, investment treaty arbitration and international investment law. Int Arbitr Law Rev 14(6):189–204

Golberg E (2018) 'Better regulation': European Union style. Cambridge University Press, Cambridge

Gotev G (2016) Germany says TTIP dead in the water. http://www.euractiv.com/section/trade-society/news/germany-says-ttip-dead-in-the-water

Grin G (2003) The battle of the single European market: achievements and economic thought 1985–2000. Kegan Paul, London

Guzman AT (1997) Why LDCs sign treaties that hurt them: explaining the popularity of bilateral investment treaties. Va J Int Law 38:639

Haas EB (1961) International integration: the European and the universal process. Int Organ 15(3): 366–392

Haas EB (1975) The obsolescence of regional integration theory. Center for International Studies, Institute of International Studies, Berkeley

Haas EB, Dinan D (1958) The uniting of Europe: political, social, and economic forces, 1950–1957. Stanford University Press, Stanford

Hackworth GH (1940) Digest of international law. US Government Printing Office, Washington, DC

Happ R, Tietje C (2013) EU, investment treaties, and investment treaty arbitration: current developments and challenges. Transnatl Disp Manage 10(2) https://www.transnational-dispute-management.com/article.asp?key=1937

Haucap J, Schwalbe U (2011) Economic principles of state aid control. Düsseldorf Institute for Competition Economics (DICE), Düsseldorf

Heckscher E, Ohlin B (1991) Heckscher-Ohlin trade theory. MIT Press, Cambridge

Hoffmann S (1966) Obstinate or obsolete? The fate of the nation-state and the case of Western Europe. Daedelus 95(3):862–915

Hooghe L, Marks G, Marks GW (2001) Multi-level governance and European integration. Rowman & Littlefield, Lanham

International Code of Fair Treatment for Foreign Investment (1949). ICC, Quebec

International Trade Organization (ITO) (1948) Final Act of the United Nations Conference on Trade and Employment. Havana, Cuba

Irwin D (2016) Historical notes on subsidies and the trading system. In: Rubini L, Hawkins J (eds) What shapes law? European University Institute, Florence

Irwin DA, Mavroidis PC, Sykes AO (2008) The genesis of the GATT. Cambridge University Press, New York

Jackson MO, Nei S (2015) Networks of military alliances, wars, and international trade. Proc Natl Acad Sci 112(50):15277–15284
John TS (2018) The rise of investor-state arbitration: politics, law, and unintended consequences. Oxford University Press, Oxford
Johnson HG (1953) Optimum tariffs and retaliation. Rev Econ Stud 21(2):142–153
Kassim H, Lyons B (2013) The new political economy of EU state aid policy. J Ind Compet Trade 13(1):1–21
Kennedy KC (2000) Foreign direct investment and competition policy at the World Trade Organization. Geo Wash Int Law Rev 33:585
Keynes JM (1936) The general theory of employment, interest and money. Kessinger, Whitefish
Keynes JM (1978) The collected writings of John Maynard Keynes: Volume 25: Activities 1940–1944 – Shaping the Post-War World: the Clearing Union. Royal Economic Society, London
Kirayoglu S (2014) The bilateral investment treaty: its origins and effects. PhD dissertation, Florida State University, https://fsu.digital.flvc.org/islandora/object/fsu:254451/datastream/PDF/view
Kleinheisterkamp J (2012a) European policy space in international investment law. ICSID Rev Foreign Invest Law J 27(2):416–431
Kleinheisterkamp J (2012b) Investment protection and EU law: The intra- and extra-EU dimension of the Energy Charter Treaty. J Int Econ Law 15(1):85
Kleinheisterkamp J (2015) Investment treaty law and the fear for sovereignty: Transnational challenges and solutions. Mod Law Rev 78(5):793–825
Kleimann D (2013) EU preferential trade agreements: commerce, foreign policy, and development aspects. European University Institute, Florence
Kohler-Koch B (2003) The evolution and transformation of European governance. In: Jachtenfuchs M, Kohler-Kock B (eds) The transformation of governance in the European Union. Routledge, London
Kohler-Koch B, Eising R (2007) The transformation of governance in the European Union, 2nd edn. Routledge, London
Kohler-Koch B, Larat F (2009) European multi-level governance: contrasting images in national research. Edward Elgar, Cheltenham
Kohler-Koch B, Rittberger B (2006) The 'governance turn' in EU studies. JCMS J Common Mark Stud 44:27–49
Konttinen J, Teivainen A (2013) Professor: Finland's legislative power may be in jeopardy. Helsinki Times, 16 Dec. http://www.helsinkitimes.fi/finland/finland-news/domestic/8717-professor-finland-s-legislative-power-may-be-in-jeopardy.html
Krugman P (1979) Increasing returns, monopolistic competition, and international trade. J Int Econ 9(4):469–479
Krugman P (1991) Increasing returns and economic geography. J Polit Econ 99(3):483–499
Lavenex S, Schimmelfennig F (2009) EU rules beyond EU borders: theorizing external governance in European politics. J Eur Public Policy 16(6):791–812
Lavranos N (2013) In defence of Member States' BITs gold standard: the Regulation 1219/2012 establishing a transitional regime for existing extra-EU BITs-A Member State's perspective. Transnatl Disp Manage (TDM) 10(2) https://papers.ssrn.com/sol3/papers.cfm?abstract_id=2226979
League of Nations (1927) Report and Proceedings of the World Economic Conference held at Geneva, May 4th to 23rd, 1927. League of Nations, Geneva
League of Nations (1933) Monetary and Economic Conference: Reports Approved by the Conference on the 27th July 1933. League of Nations, London
Lenin V (2016) Second All-Russia Congress of Soviets – 04. https://www.marxists.org/archive/lenin/works/1917/oct/25-26/26d.htm
Lenk H (2015) Challenging the notion of coherence in EU foreign investment policy. Eur J Legal Stud 2:6–20
Lindblom C (1977) Politics and markets. Basic Books, New York

López JJP (2015) The concept of state aid under EU law: From internal market to competition and beyond. Oxford University Press, Oxford

Lowenfeld AF (2009) The ICSID convention: Origins and transformation. Ga J Int Comput Law 38:47–61

Maduro M (2007) Interpreting European law: Judicial adjudication in a context of constitutional pluralism. Eur J Legal Stud 1:137

Matei E (2015) The chamber of secrets: The repudiation of the ISDS. RRDE 83. https://heinonline.org/HOL/LandingPage?handle=hein.journals/rianrwioe13&div=46&id=&page=

Mattli W (1999) The logic of regional integration: Europe and beyond. Cambridge University Press, Cambridge

Meade JE (1951) The balance of payments: trade and welfare, vol 1–2. Oxford University Press, Oxford

Meade JE (2013) The economic basis of a durable peace. Routledge, London

Merola M (2016) The forces shaping state aid control in the EU. In: Rubini L, Hawkins J (eds) What shapes the law? Reflections on the history, law, politics and economics of international and European subsidy disciplines. European University Institute, Florence

Meunier S (2017) Integration by stealth: how the European Union gained competence over foreign direct investment. J Common Mark Stud 55(3):593–610

Meunier S, Nicolaïdis K (2006) The European Union as a conflicted trade power. J Eur Public Policy 13(6):906–925

Milward A (2000) The European rescue of the nation state, 2nd edn. Routledge, London

Miroudot S, Bartók C (2008) The interaction amongst trade, investment and competition policies. OECD, Paris

Moravcsik A (1993) Preferences and power in the European Community: a liberal intergovernmentalist approach. J Common Mark Stud 31(4):473–524

Moravcsik A (1998) The choice for Europe: social purpose and state power from Messina to Maastricht. Cornell University Press, New York

Moravcsik A, Nicolaidis K (1999) Explaining the treaty of Amsterdam: interests influence institutions. JCMS: J Common Mark Stud 37(1):59–85. https://doi.org/10.1111/1468-5965.00150

Newcombe AP, Paradell L (2009) Law and practice of investment treaties: standards of treatment. Kluwer Law International, The Hague

Nichols JP (1951) Roosevelt's monetary diplomacy in 1933. Am Hist Rev 56(2):295–317

Niemelä PJ (2017) The relationship of EU Law and bilateral investment treaties of EU Member States: treaty conflict, harmonious coexistence and the critique of investment arbitration. University of Helsinki. http://urn.fi/URN:ISBN:978-951-51-3730-2

OECD (1976) Declaration on international investment and multinational enterprises. OECD, Paris

OECD (1995) OECD begins negotiations on a multilateral agreement on investment. Media release. http://www.oecd.org/daf/inv/internationalinvestmentagreements/43389907.pdf

OECD (2017) Investment, conference on investment treaties: policy goals and public support. OECD, Paris

OECD (2019) Decision of the council on international investment incentives and disincentives. OECD, Paris

Olsson S-O (2006) Nordic trade policy in the 1930s. Paper presented at the Papers of the XVI International Economic History Congress, Helsinki, 21–25 August

Ortolani P (2015) Intra-EU Arbitral Awards vis-à-vis Article 107 TFEU: State aid law as a limit to compliance. J Int Disp Settlement 6(1):118–135

Papadopoulos AS (2010) The international dimension of EU competition law and policy. Cambridge University Press

Paulsson J (1987) Third world participation in international investment arbitration. ICSID Rev 2(1): 19–65

Ricardo D (1891) Principles of political economy and taxation. George Bell, London

Richard, Baldwin Dany, Jaimovich (2012) Are Free Trade Agreements contagious?. Journal of International Economics 88(1) 1-16 S0022199612000591 10.1016/j.jinteco.2012.03.009

Rosen DH, Hanemann T (2009) China's changing outbound foreign direct investment profile: Drivers and policy implications. https://econpapers.repec.org/paper/iiepbrief/pb09-14.htm
Rubini L (2004) The international context of EC state aid law and policy: the regulation of subsidies in the WTO. The Law of State Aid in the European Union. Oxford University Press, New York
Rubini L (2010) The definition of subsidy and state aid: WTO and EC law in comparative perspective. Oxford University Press, New York
Salacuse JW (2015) The law of investment treaties, 2nd edn. Oxford University Press, Oxford
Salacuse JW, Sullivan NP (2005) Do BITs really work? An evaluation of bilateral investment treaties and their grand bargain. Harv Int Law J 46(1):67–130
Samuelson PA, Stigler GJ (1963) A dialogue on the proper economic role of the state. University of Chicago School of Business, Chicago
Sandholtz W, Sweet AS (1997) European integration and supranational governance. Oxford University Press, Oxford
Sauter W (1997) Competition law and industrial policy in the EU. Oxford University Press, Oxford
Schneiderman D (2016) On suffering and societal constitutionalism: at the border of international investment arbitration and human rights. In: Kahana T, Scolnicov A (eds) Boundaries of state, boundaries of rights: human rights, private actors, and positive obligations. Cambridge University Press, Cambridge
Schreuer C (2001) The ICSID convention: a commentary. Cambridge University Press, Cambridge
Shafaeddin M (1998) How did developed countries industrialize? The history of trade and industrial policy: the cases of Great Britain and the USA. Paper presented at the United Nations Conference on Trade and Development, Geneva. http://unctad.org/en/Docs/dp_139.en.pdf
Shalakany AA (2000) Arbitration and the third world: a plea for reassessing bias under the specter of neoliberalism. Harv Int Law J 41:419
Simmons BA (2014) Bargaining over BITs, arbitrating awards: the regime for protection and promotion of international investment. World Polit 66(1):12–46
Sims A, Stone J (2016) TTIP has officially failed – but no one is admitting it, says German Vice-Chancellor Sigmar Gabriel. News, Europe, 28 Aug. http://www.independent.co.uk/news/world/europe/ttip-trade-deal-agreement-failed-brexit-latest-news-eu-us-germany-vice-chancellor-a7213876.html
Smith A (1776) An inquiry into the nature and causes of the wealth of nations. W Strahan and T Cadell, London
Smith MP (1998) Autonomy by the rules: the European commission and the development of state aid policy. J Common Mark Stud 36(1):55–78
Snyder F (1994) Soft law and institutional practice in the European Community. In: Martin S (ed) The construction of Europe: Essays in Honour of Emile Noël. Springer, Dordrecht
Spaak C (1956). The Brussels report on the General Common Market. http://aei.pitt.edu.ludwig.lub.lu.se/995/1/Spaak_report.pdf
Stigler GJ (1971) The theory of economic regulation. Bell J Econ Manage Sci 2(1):3–21
Stiglitz JE (2005) Is central bank independence all it's cracked up to be? Project Syndicate, 4 November. https://www.project-syndicate.org/commentary/is-central-bank-independence-all-it-s-cracked-up-to-be?barrier=accesspaylog
Strik P (2016) Shaping the single European market in the field of foreign direct investment. Hart, London
Struckmann K, Forwood G, Kadri A (2016) Investor-state arbitrations and EU state aid rules: Conflict or co-existence. Eur St Aid LQ 15(2):258–269
Svechkar I, Glushchenko S (2018) State aid 2018 – Ukraine. https://www.asterslaw.com/press_center/publications/getting_the_deal_through_state_aid_2018_ukraine
Sykes AO (2010) The questionable case for subsidies regulation: a comparative perspective. J Leg Anal 2(2):473–523
Tavares-Lehmann AT, Toledano P, Johnson L, Sachs L (2016) Rethinking investment incentives: trends and policy options. Columbia University Press, New York

Thielemann ER (1999) Institutional limits of a Europe with the regions: EC state-aid control meets German federalism. J Eur Public Policy 6(3):399–418
Thomas KP (2007) Investment incentives: Growing use, uncertain benefits, uneven controls. International Institute for Sustainable Development, Geneva
Thomas KP (2016) Regulation of investment incentives: national and subnational efforts to regulate competition for investment through use of incentives. In: Tavares-Lehmann AT, Toledano P, Johnson L, Sachs L (eds) Rethinking investment incentives. Columbia University Press, New York
Tietje C, Sipiorski E, Töpfer G (2012) Responsibility in investor-state-arbitration in the EU: Managing financial responsibility linked to investor-state dispute settlement tribunals established by EU's International Investment Agreements. European Union, Brussels
UNCTAD (1994) World investment report 1994 Transnational corporations, employment and the workplace. United Nations, Geneva. http://unctad.org/en/pages/PublicationArchive.aspx?publicationid=642
UNCTAD (1996) Incentives and foreign direct investment. UNCTAD. (1996b). World investment report 1996: Overview – investment, trade and international policy arrangements. United Nations, Geneva. https://unctad.org/topic/investment/world-investment-report
UNCTAD (1997) World investment report 1997: Transnational corporations, market structure and competition policy. United Nations, Geneva. http://unctad.org/en/pages/PublicationArchive.aspx?publicationid=648
UNCTAD (1999) World investment report 1999: Foreign Direct Investment and the Challenge of Development. United Nations, Geneva. http://unctad.org/en/pages/PublicationArchive.aspx?publicationid=652
UNCTAD (2004) Incentives. United Nations, Geneva. https://unctad.org/en/Docs/iteiit20035_en.pdf
UNCTAD (2014) The impact of international investment agreements on foreign direct investment: an overview of empirical studies 1998–2014. In: World investment report 2014. United Nations, Geneva
UNCTAD (2015) World investment report 2015: Reforming international investment governance. United Nations, Geneva. http://unctad.org/en/pages/PublicationWebflyer.aspx?publicationid=1245
UNCTAD (2016a) International investment agreements navigator. http://investmentpolicyhub.unctad.org/IIA
UNCTAD (2016b) Investor-state dispute settlement: Review of developments in 2015. United Nations, Geneva. http://unctad.org/en/PublicationsLibrary/webdiaepcb2016d4_en.pdf
UNCTAD (2017a) Special update on investor-state dispute settlement: Facts and figures. United Nations, Geneva. http://unctad.org/en/PublicationsLibrary/diaepcb2017d7_en.pdf
UNCTAD (2017b) World investment report 2017: Overview. United Nations, Geneva. http://unctad.org/en/Pages/DIAE/World%20Investment%20Report/World_Investment_Report.aspx?Re=1,30
UNGA (1962a) UNGA Res. 1803 (XVII) of December 14. United Nations, New York
UNGA (1962b) Permanent sovereignty over natural resources (Vol. RES/1803 (XVII)). United Nations, New York
UNGA (1974) Charter of Economic Rights and Duties of States (Vol. RES/3281 (XXIX)). United Nations, Geneva
UNICTRAL (2018a) Possible reform of investor-state dispute settlement (ISDS). https://uncitral.un.org/en/working_groups/3/investor-state
UNICTRAL (2018b) Status – Convention on the Recognition and Enforcement of Foreign Arbitral Awards (New York, 1958). http://www.uncitral.org/uncitral/en/uncitral_texts/arbitration/NYConvention_status.html
UNICTRAL (2019) Report of Working Group III (Investor-State Dispute Settlement Reform) on the work of its thirty-seventh session (New York, 1–5 April 2019). https://uncitral.un.org/en/working_groups/3/investor-state

United Nations (1946) Preparatory Committee of the International Conference on Trade and Employment. United Nations, Geneva
United Nations (1976) United Nations Commission on International Trade Law. In UNCITRAL Rules (Vol. General Assembly of the United Nations by resolution No. 31/98). United Nations, Geneva
United Nations (2017) The World Economic and Social Survey 2017 Reflecting on seventy years of development policy analysis. United Nations, Geneva. https://www.un.org/development/desa/dpad/wp-content/uploads/sites/45/publication/WESS_2017-FullReport.pdf
US Department of State (2001) The Bretton Woods Conference, 1944. https://2001-2009.state.gov/r/pa/ho/time/wwii/98681.htm
Van de Casteele K (2006) The international dimension of state aid. In: Rydelski MS (ed) The EC state aid regime: distortive effects of state aid on competition and trade. Cameron May, London
Van de Casteele K (2016) Changes and what drives them: evolution of state aid control. In: Rubini L, Hawkins J (eds) What shapes the law? Reflections on the history, law, politics and economics of international and European subsidy disciplines. European University Institute, Florence
Van Harten G (2015) A parade of reforms: The European Commission's latest proposal for ISDS. Osgoode Legal Studies Research Paper No. 21/2015
Vandevelde KJ (2005) A brief history of international investment agreements. UC Davis J Int Law Policy 12(1):157–194
Venables AJ (1987) Trade and trade policy with differentiated products: a Chamberlinian-Ricardian model. Econ J 97(387):700–717
Verouden V (2016) EU state aid control: the quest for effectiveness. In: Rubini L, Hawkins J (eds) What shapes law? European University Institute, Florence
von Mises L (1949) Human action, 3rd edn. Mises Institute, New York
Working Group on the Relationship between Trade and Investment (1998) The relationship between foreign investment and competition policy, communication from the European Community and its Member States. WTO, Geneva. https://docs.wto.org/dol2fe/Pages/FE_Search/FE_S_S005.aspx
World Trade Organization (1996) Trade and foreign direct investment. Media release. https://www.wto.org/english/news_e/pres96_e/pr057_e.htm
World Trade Organization (1998a) Foreign direct investment and economic development. WTO, Geneva
World Trade Organization (1998b) Synthesis paper on the relationship of trade and competition policy to development and economic growth. WTO, Geneva
World Trade Organization (2020) WTO homepage. http://www.wto.org/index.htm
World Trade Organization (WTO) World Trade Report (2011) The WTO and preferential trade agreements: from co-existence to coherence. WTO, Geneva

Chapter 3
The EU State Aid Regime

3.1 Introduction

This chapter explains the core legal framework and the reasons behind the gradual emergence of a vast amount of complex rules governing different aspects of the EU's unique state aid law and policy.[1] It's state aid law and policy aims to remove frictions within the EU's legal order, and beyond, as caused by subsidies-based competition, and to promote fair competition within the internal market.[2] State aid control prevents the Member States from favouring some firms above others to protect the internal market, effectively prohibiting discrimination between firms that are comparable.[3]

As stressed by De Cecco, Maduro and Sauter,[4] state control is one of the cornerstones of EU law and a crucial component of the European economic constitution. Within the EU system, state aid control is part of the competition rules that, as defined by Article 3 of the TFEU, fall under the exclusive competence of the EU.[5] Thus, the Member States have transferred their rights to regulate or decide on matters regarding state aid control for internal and external actions to the EU.[6] Not only has state aid control been a tool for the economic integration of the EU internal market

[1] State aid law is part of the EU's public policy.

[2] Thus preventing discrimination against undertakings that are in a comparable factual and legal situation: see *C-20/15 P – Commission v World Duty Free Group* (2016).

[3] In a similar situation in law or in fact.

[4] Maduro (1998); De Cecco (2012) and Sauter (1997).

[5] See Article 3.1 stating that 'The Union shall have exclusive competence in the following areas'. Para 3.1(b) of the TFEU declares competition rules to be one of these: 'the establishing of the competition rules necessary for the functioning of the internal market'. Title VII, Chapter 1 'Rules on Competition' can be found both rules applicable to undertakings (Section 1) and 'Aids granted by States' (Section 2).

[6] Article 207 of TFEU.

P. Finckenberg-Broman, *Weaponizing EU State Aid Law to Impact the Future of EU Investment Policy in the Global Context*, Studies in European Economic Law and Regulation 23, https://doi.org/10.1007/978-3-031-10108-3_3

but it has also developed to cover broader policy objectives.[7] EU's state aid rules have a robust policy dimension as they are more likely to have an effect on national sovereignty and interest issues than other competition provisions,[8] as the state aid rules govern Member States' budgetary policies.[9]

Yet, extraterritoriality of state aid policy has remained surprisingly neglected by legal academia until recently.[10] Therefore, this chapter contributes to the legal discipline by discussing the external dimension of State aid broadly. It has six parts (with subchapters). It begins by providing an overview of the contents and literature used for the chapter, then explains the legal framework. The chapter then examines the notion of state aid/subsidies control before exploring the development of state aid law and policy. The state aid procedures and consequences of a breach of them are then elaborated before the final part of the chapter summarises the content and reaches some conclusions.

3.2 The Legal Framework

The treaty provisions for state aid law are Articles 107–109 TFEU. The scheme is composed of the TFEU provisions, binding secondary law, non-binding instruments such as Commission guidelines and communications, and CJEU judgments and Commission decisions.

3.2.1 EU State Aid Legislation

Under the central provision of EU state aid law, Article 107 of the TFEU, state aid is prohibited unless reasons of general economic development can justify it. It is the first part of Article 107(1) TFEU that sets out the general prohibition on all

[7] Blauberger (2008); Koenig (2014); López (2015); Van de Casteele (2016). See also Biondi and Righini (2014); Chari and Cavatorta (2002); Griswold and Marine (1996); Paemen (2016).

[8] Bacon (2017), p. 3.

[9] Blauberger (2008); Ehlermann (1994); Smith (1998).

[10] For more on these authors, see Sect. 3.4.2 in this chapter. Some of these authors, like Blauberger (2008) and Lavenex and Schimmelfennig (2009) have addressed the different ways and conditions under which regulatory export of state aid control has been successful. Most legal literature on this area, such as Hoekman and Holmes (1999), Rubini (2010) and Goyette (2006), discuss the similarities of the definitions of subsidy and state aid in the WTO and EU law from a comparative perspective. Others analyse the influence the EU (and American) policies have had on the WTO (Damro and Guay 2016; Hoekman and Holmes 1999). Some legal practitioners, like Papadopoulos (2010), provide a global overview from an EU standpoint, which covers the whole competition policy, including state aid control by particularly discussing multilateral, plurilateral and bilateral agreements that contain competition policy provisions.

Article 107

(ex Article 87 TEC)

1. Save as otherwise provided in the Treaties, any aid granted by a Member State or through State resources in any form whatsoever which distorts or threatens to distort competition by favouring certain undertakings or the production of certain goods shall, in so far as it affects trade between Member States, be incompatible with the internal market.

2. The following shall be compatible with the internal market:

(a) aid having a social character, granted to individual consumers, provided that such aid is granted without discrimination related to the origin of the products concerned;

(b) aid to make good the damage caused by natural disasters or exceptional occurrences;

(c) aid granted to the economy of certain areas of the Federal Republic of Germany affected by the division of Germany, in so far as such aid is required in order to compensate for the economic disadvantages caused by that division. Five years after the entry into force of the Treaty of Lisbon, the Council, acting on a proposal from the Commission, may adopt a decision repealing this point.

3. The following may be considered to be compatible with the internal market:

(a) aid to promote the economic development of areas where the standard of living is abnormally low or where there is serious underemployment, and of the regions referred to in Article 349, in view of their structural, economic and social situation;

(b) aid to promote the execution of an important project of common European interest or to remedy a serious disturbance in the economy of a Member State;

(c) aid to facilitate the development of certain economic activities or of certain economic areas, where such aid does not adversely affect trading conditions to an extent contrary to the common interest;

(d) aid to promote culture and heritage conservation where such aid does not affect trading conditions and competition in the Union to an extent that is contrary to the common interest;

(e) such other categories of aid as may be specified by decision of the Council on a proposal from the Commission.

Fig. 3.1 Article 107 TFEU

intervening public measures favouring certain enterprises, which distort or threaten to distort competition.

This strict prohibition is eased by a narrow category of exemptions, defined in Article 107(2) and (3), where the aid is compatible with the internal market. If one of the 107(2) TFEU criteria is in place, the aid is EU compatible *per se*, whereas in the context of Article 107(3) TFEU (Fig. 3.1), where the exemptions are more generally applicable, state aid must fulfil specific requirements to be internal market compatible.[11] Essentially, aid allowed covers measures for the common interest.[12] Enforcement procedures for state aid law are established by Article 108 TFEU. It is for the Commission and the CJEU to apply these, with the possibility of intervention by the Council when acting unanimously. Article 108(2) TFEU establishes the exclusive

[11]Subject to notification obligation and a balancing test. A balancing test weights the negative effects v the positive effects of the intervention. On one side is the possible damage it can cause to the internal market trade and competition, and on the other side are the positive effects of common interest (Coppi 2011).

[12]Commission Regulation No. 651/2014 (EC 2014a) Ch. 1 p. (5).

power of the Commission to assess, approve or disapprove all state aid measures, as well as financial compensation measures adopted by the Member State.[13]

Nevertheless, the Commission decisions can be appealed to the General Court, which is the ultimate decision-maker.[14] Article 108(2) also links to the notification obligation in the standstill clause in Article 108(3). Accordingly, 'any plans to grant or alter' state aid must be notified to the Commission before they are implemented or altered by a Member State.

The Commission's ability to adopt block exemptions is set by Article 109 TFEU. Further, there is a fair amount of secondary legislation on state aid[15] *vis-à-vis* both procedural and substantial matters. With the purpose to define and clarify the meaning of Article 107(2) and (3) TFEU exemptions for improved legal certainty, the Commission also publishes Guidelines and Communications. These documents ease the identification process of applicable exemptions designed to maintain the balance of free competition and common interest for the Member States.

3.2.2 The Four Cumulative Criteria

EU state aid control balances free competition and common interest to enable aid beneficiary for the common interest. The key for state aid to be compatible with the state aid rules is for it to be appropriate, necessary and proportionate. According to the CJEU case law, for state aid to be present in a measure, four cumulative criteria must be in place.[16] These criteria, drawn from Article 107(1) TFEU, are that the aid must: (1) be an intervention by the state or be derived from state resources; (2) confer a selective advantage to the recipient; (3) distort or potentially distort competition; and (4) be likely to affect intra-community trade.[17]

Article 107(1) TFEU, however, lacks details on what this notion entails, and therefore the Commission's decisions and the CJEU's judgments have been crucial for interpreting this.[18] Therefore the CJEU has discussed each criterion on several occasions in a significant body of case law and the Commission has published

[13] See Article 108 TFEU 1st section. See also *C-78/76 - Steinike & Weinlig* (1977) para 9, confirming the Commission's powers. See also *C-119/05 – Lucchini* (2007) for a decision made by national court being *res judicata* within the context of recovery of state aid granted.

[14] Article 108 TFEU 2nd section.

[15] Especially block exemptions.

[16] As can be seen in *C-280/00 – Altmark* (2003) para. 75. In this case, the CJEU analysis of the concept of the aid conferring an advantage on the recipient undertaking. *C-280/00 – Altmark* (2003) concerned compensation for public service in Germany. The CJEU analysed whether licences and public subsidies received by a private transport company—Altmark Trans GmbH—to enable the operation of scheduled transport services for public interest were state aid.

[17] For an example of how state aid cases repeat this requirement, see *C-20/15 P – Commission v World Duty Free Group* (2016), para 53 and *C-280/00 – Altmark* (2003), paras 74 and 75.

[18] Biondi (2013); Blauberger (2008); López (2015). The notion of aid is still developing.

several policy documents to ease the task of national courts and public authorities in assessing whether a planned measure falls within the ambit of article 107 TFEU and subsequently under the notification and standstill obligations under Article 108(3) TFEU.[19]

Criterion 1: 'Derived from State Resources'

The concept of 'state resources' is broad, and covers resources from the Member States at all levels, both central and local governments,[20] together with public/private bodies controlled by the state, which use state resources.[21] This ensures that state aid law is not circumvented through the creation of autonomous enterprises charged with allocating aid.[22] Both positive transfers, such as grants and capital participation, or foregone revenues, such as the sale of assets below market price, loans with interest below market rates or tax waivers or deferrals, are included. Additionally, the intervention must be imputable to a Member State.[23] Explicitly, for a measure to be deemed state aid, the state must have granted the revenue independently. Primarily, the action and the decision behind the benefit should be made by the Member State, not be a consequence of complying with an obligation as mere compensation for damage caused by the state[24] or implementation of community provisions.[25]

[19] For details on the notification and standstill obligations, see Sect. 3.5.1. The Commission Notice on the Notion of State Aid as Referred to in Article 107(1) of the Treaty on the Functioning of the European Union (2016/C 262/01) OJ C 262/1, 19 July 2016 (Notice on the Notion of State Aid) (EC 2016), provides an extensive clarification 'of the Commission's understanding of Article 107(1) of the Treaty.

[20] See *C-78/76 – Steinike & Weinlig* (1977). Paragraph 21 on fiscal advantages found that a crucial element for this concept was that the aid was the consequence of action taken by public authority: *C-345/02 – Pearle and Others* (2004) para 34 referring to *C-379/98 – PreussenElektra* (2001) para 58.

[21] *C-482/99 – France v Commission (Stardust Marine)* (2002) paras 32–43; *Joined Cases 67, 68 and 70/85 – Van der Kooy and others v Commission* (1988) and *C-150/16 – Fondul Proprietatea* (2017) paras 19–20.

[22] *C-482/99 – France v Commission(Stardust Marine)* (2002) para. 23.

[23] *T-351/02 – Deutsche Bahn v Commission* (2006) para 101 and *C-413/15 Farrel* (2017) for a private body as an emanation of the state. For further details on imputability, see Clayton and Segura Catalan (2015).

[24] *C-61/79 – Denkavit* (1980), paras 29, 31 and 32; *Joined Cases 97 and 193/86 – Asteris* (1988) paras 23–24 and *T-62/08 – ThyssenKrupp Acciai Speciali Terni v Commission* (2010) regarding compensation for expropriation. See also Ortolani (2015), pp. 123–24 and Tietje and Wackernagel (2014), Ch. I.

[25] *T-351/02 – Deutsche Bahn v Commission* (2006) para 102; see also Tietje and Wackernagel (2014), p. 6.

Criterion 2: 'Selective Advantage'

Selective advantage criteria include three sub-parts. First, for the state aid rules to apply, the recipient of the measure must be an undertaking. Therefore, before the evaluation of a selective advantage,[26] it must be assessed whether the recipient of a measure qualifies as an 'undertaking' according to the rules. An undertaking is an entity that engages in economic activity in competition with other operators.[27] Their legal form and how they are financed are irrelevant to this assessment.[28]

Second, to establish whether a recipient undertaking will derive an 'advantage', an evaluation of whether the undertaking has gained an economic advantage which it could not have obtained without state intervention is necessary. For this evaluation, the Commission applies a Market Economy Investor Principle test.[29] Notably, the only relevancy is the effect of the measure on the undertaking, without consideration of the reason behind the state intervention.[30]

Finally, the measure must favour certain undertakings, regions and economic activities over other undertakings in a similar legal and factual situation to be considered selective.[31]

Criterion 3: 'Potential to Distort Competition'

The third aspect of these four cumulative criteria is whether the selective advantage received by the firm has the potential to distort competition within the internal market. This means that criteria 3 and 4 (see below) are interwoven.[32] Because these criteria aim to hinder distortion of competition from occurring, there is no requirement for an actual distortion to be proved. As a general rule, as can be seen

---

[26] *C-280/00 – Altmark* (2003). These two are criteria are inextricably linked: see *T-298/97 – Alzetta and Others v Commission* (2000) and Biondi (2013), p. 1720.

[27] *Klaus Höfner and Fritz Elser v Macrotron GmbH, case C-41/90* (1991) (GmbH, 1991).

[28] Notice on the Notion of State Aid (EC 2016) p. 3 referring to *Joined Cases C-180/98 to C-184/98 – Pavlov and Others* (2000), para 74 and *C-222/04 – Cassa di Risparmio di Firenze and Others* (2006), para 107.

[29] *C-124/10 P – Commission v EDF* (2012), para 78; *C-300/16 P – Commission v Frucona Košice* (2017), paras 21 and 22 and *C-579/16 P – Commission v FIH Holding and FIH Erhversbank* (2018), para 45. See also Anestis and Mavroghenis (2006); Kavanagh et al. (2011); Nicolaides (2017), Ch 4.

[30] EC (2016), p. 5 referring to *C-173/73 – Italy v Commission* (1974), para 13.

[31] *C-399/08 P – Commission v Deutsche Post* (2010) para 40 and *C-74/16 – Congregación de Escuelas Pías Provincia Betania* (2017), para 65. The concept of selectivity was stretched substantially in *C-20/15 P – Commission v World Duty Free Group* (2016), which was about amortisation of financial goodwill resulting from acquisitions by Spanish firms of shareholdings in foreign firms for tax purposes. According to the CJEU, all types of derogations that result in firms being treated differently are selective. It makes no difference that the derogation is not available to all undertakings.

[32] *T-298/97 – Alzetta and Others v Commission* (2000), para. 81.

from the CJEU's case law and the Commission's Notice on the Notion of State Aid, this part of the test is easy to satisfy.[33] Often the selective advantage will be found to have the potential to distort competition in the internal market.[34] Moreover, the wording of Article 107 TFEU does not require the beneficiary of state aid to be internal market-based. It is enough that the effect is potentially distortive to the internal market.

Criterion 4: Affecting Intra-Community Trade

According to CJEU case, law distortion of competition may *per se* happen in the presence of any intra-EU cross border activity.[35] How ever, even local activities may be caught as the wide way of interpreting 'effect on intra Community trade' occurs after the *de minimis* roof is surpassed.[36] By its Notice on the Notion of State Aid,[37] the Commission has attempted to change its strict approach to determining whether state aid affects trade between the Member States.[38] The adoption of a more lenient approach to the notion of affecting intra-Community trade lends support to the notion that the nature of state aid control is mainly for controlling macro-economic competition between Member States. The policy documents published by the Commission also allow the Commission to influence Member States' choices about how these allocate and design their public measures.

3.2.3 *State Aid Law: Complex and Immense*

Indeed, state aid policy has led to an increasing amount of complex and elaborate rules to cover specific state aid objectives to align national budgetary policies concerning the objectives defined by the EU.[39] Modern state aid regulation in the

---

[33] See the CJEU case *(T-298/97 – Alzetta and Others v Commission* (2000), para. 80: 'A measure granted by the State is considered to distort or threaten to distort competition when it is liable to improve the competitive position of the recipient compared to other undertakings with which it competes.'

[34] *T-298/97 – Alzetta and Others v Commission* (2000), paras 141–147. See also *C-280/00 – Altmark* (2003).

[35] According to *C-197/11 – Libert and Others* (2013) and *T-50/06 RENV II – Ireland v Commission* (2016), there is no threshold below which trade between Member States can be said not to be affected.

[36] *C-142/87 – Tubemeuse* (1990) and *C-280/00 – Altmark* (2003). See also the (*de minimis*) regulation (EU) no 1407/2013 (EC 2013a).

[37] Notice on the Notion of State Aid (EC 2016).

[38] However, the Notice does not bind the EU courts, nor can the Commission deviate from the case law of the EU courts (EC 2016), Ch 1.3.

[39] Blauberger (2008).

EU has evolved from a purely hard law instrument to a hybrid framework employing both 'binding and non-binding legal instruments… in order to achieve a scaling down and a better rationalization of subsidies throughout the EU.'[40] Different EU institutions have published an increasing number of (in order of precedence) regulations, case law, communications and guidelines. Primarily, the Commission has published a wide range of policy documents on government intervention, based on a strong urge to protect competition from such intervention.

To achieve this, the Commission has applied both soft and hard law instruments to tempt, convince and coerce the Member States to fall in line with state aid rules. As an outcome, it is a legal framework that aims to minimise subsidies and rationalise the subsidy schemes being implemented by the Member States within the EU. The soft law instruments draw from the primary law and the CJEU's case law. Though not legally binding on the Member States, these provide preemptive, by explanation, legal certainty on current law and what the Commission's views are on the law.[41] They are published by the Commission and thus also bind the Commission,[42] and the Commission will not raise state aid infringement procedures against a Member State that has followed them. Therefore, it is both practical and tempting for the Member States to design their subsidy schemes in compliance with the whole general state aid framework.[43] This linkage of governance and enforcement is of such an extent that some authors hold that in the EU, state aid is regulated by information.[44]

Extensively, the main instrument for state aid regulation has applied a soft law approach,[45] subsequently 'formalised by the adoption of Commission (hard law) decisions in individual cases based on the various soft law instruments'[46] or by the CJEU's endorsement.[47] This has led to the EU's state aid policy, from its humble origins as a few articles in the Treaties, to develop into an elaborate system of governance, with rules incorporating a wide range of policy sectors and forms of government measures.[48] Modern state aid regulation is horizontally focused on supporting objectives that are in the EU's interest,[49] such as research, renewable energy and employment. For example, since 2014 the CJEU and the Commission

[40] Biondi and Stefan (2018), p. 3.

[41] Biondi and Stefan (2018), p. 4.

[42] *C-189/02 P – Dansk Rørindustri and Others v Commission* (2005), para. 211; *C-526/14 – Kotnik and Others* (Case C-526/14), para 40; *C-431/14 P – Greece v Commission* (2016), paras 69 and 70.

[43] Szyszczak (2011), p. 38. A great example of this is the energy policy. After the Commission published soft law instruments regarding 'softer approach' on subsidies for green energy, several Member States—for instance, Denmark, Italy, Spain and the Czech Republic—implemented subsidy schemes that supported renewable energy.

[44] Snyder (1994), pp. 199–201; Hofmann (2006), pp. 169–70; Benz (2000), p. 33.

[45] Biondi and Stefan (2018), p. 3.

[46] Cini (2001), pp. 192, 200.

[47] Snyder (1994).

[48] Bacon (2017); Blauberger (2008); Nyberg (2017).

[49] Biondi and Stefan (2018), p. 4.

have successfully orchestrated an exceptional expansion of the adoption of renewable energy within the EU by the support of relevant subsidy schemes.[50] Supported by the CJEU's case law, the Commission took action *vis-à-vis* the national schemes for renewable energy by introducing new guidelines on state aid designed for environmental protection and energy.[51]

New administrative procedures have been introduced to the Member States, with a whole range of different government activities put into place to keep the Member States from providing state aid. An exchange system for information and best practices utilising national competitions agencies has been structured in a European Competition Network.[52]

3.3 The Notion of State Aid

Fundamentally, state aid control confronts Member States' measures, projected to achieve redistributive justice or allocative efficiency, with the Lisbon Treaty's market economy presumptions.[53] State aid and subsidies are at odds with the idea that free competition leads to economic efficiency. Granting state aid is considered a wasteful use of public funds.[54] Government interventions tamper with market signals, generating allocative inefficiencies and ultimately leading to market distortions.[55] State aid control, being tied to public procurement, even hinders corruption and insider deals.[56]

In a sense, the EU has a negative investment policy.[57] It restricts the incentives (including investment incentives, which are designer subsidies) that the Member States can offer to national or foreign enterprises for establishing economic activities within their borders.[58] The Member States' interventions to provide goods and

[50] Eurostat, Renewable energy statistics: see https://ec.europa.eu/eurostat/statistics-explained/index.php/Renewable_energy_statistics#Renewable_energy_produced_in_the_EU_increased_by_two_thirds_in_2007-2017.

[51] Community Guidelines on State Aid for Environmental Protection and Energy 2014–20 (EC 2014b); European Commission Impact Assessment on State aid for Environmental Protection and Energy for 2014–20 (EC 2014c). Boasson (2019, p. 70) notes that these guidelines requesting the Member States to implement subsidys schemes favouring investments in renewables was uncommon in the EU at that time. She argues (p. 76) that the Member States were not likely to 'have endorsed this shift in the strength and direction of EU steering if it had been up for decision in an ordinary legislative procedure'.

[52] Bacon (2017); Blauberger (2008); López (2015); Nyberg (2017).

[53] Friederiszick et al. (2006), p. 1.

[54] OECD (2011), Ch 2.

[55] OECD (2011), Ch 2.

[56] See *C-280/00 – Altmark* (2003). See also Blauberger and Krämer (2010).

[57] Rosenthal and Nicolaides (1997), p. 362.

[58] Rosenthal and Nicolaides (1997), p. 362.

services on preferential terms for specific companies are also constrained and controlled. However harmful, protectionist and distortive state aid is identified to be, and how much it is prohibited, good state aid that is used to promote imperative social and economic policies is accepted. As noted by Blauberger, EU state aid control is a compromise that aims for undistorted competition while recognising the potentially positive effects of state aid.[59]

The challenge to distinguish the 'good' subsidies from 'bad' subsidies is not restricted to the EU's internal market. It is a global phenomenon, and as such has established the case for a need to control state aid/subsidies and their responses in international trade agreements, through clearly defined obligations for the participating governments.[60] Therefore, subsidies control for global trade usually is (explicitly in the absence of specific trade agreements) governed by the WTO.[61] The EU is a WTO member as it represents all its Member States as a single voice.[62] Together with the United States, it was one of the driving forces behind the introduction of the Subsidies Agreement in 1995[63] and continues to promote the development of effective subsidies control within the WTO system.

Damro and Guay note that state aid/subsidies policy affects the global political economy via a two-level game.[64] According to their two-level game theory, when subsidising public and private actors of the EU to protect the interest of these enterprises (level one), the EU also creates barriers to market access, which may infringe on WTO rules. Consequently (level two), other nations can insist on dispute-settlement mechanisms taking place and retaliate by raising countervailing measures. The political decision-making relating to subsidies/state aid policy in trade is a Prisoner's Dilemma with the potential to launch tit-for-tat strategies from other countries.[65]

Consequently, non-tariff measures such as subsidies[66] are the most significant remaining challenge for free trade in the current global environment, where direct barriers—namely customs—are controlled by trade agreements.[67] In fact, due to the

---

[59] Blauberger (2008).

[60] According to Rubini (2010), p. 5, 'State aid [systems] used in the WTO and EU are the most developed systems of control of this type of policy instrument in the world.'

[61] For more on the history of the WTO and the development of international subsidisation and efforts to establish a mechanism to control governments to implement subsidies see Chap. 2.

[62] After the establishment of the EU's Common Foreign and Security Policy (CFSP).

[63] Paemen (2016), p. 52.

[64] Damro and Guay (2016).

[65] Damro and Guay's (2016) two-level game theory on the state aid/subsidies policy effects on the global political economy, although created for multilateral trade, is also applicable on a bilateral level.

[66] The main complaint about policies that support domestic prices, or subsidise production in some other way, is that they encourage over-production. This squeezes out imports or leads to export subsidies and low-priced dumping on world markets: see WTO (2015), p. 28.

[67] Multilaterally, the WTO, by plurilateral regional agreements (such as the EU Treaties) and bilateral trade agreements between nations.

growing interdependence between states with the distortive effect of subsidies on the EU internal market spilling over into external competition and vice versa, the WTO's subsidies rules constitute a substantial part of the extraterritorial dimension of the EU's state aid policy.[68] EU state aid law and the WTO's subsidies rules, therefore, complement each other and interact continuously.

3.3.1 *State Aid or Subsidies: Non-Identical Twins*

As established in Chap. 2, state aid interacts with the WTO Subsidies Agreement and GATT.[69] Hence it is logical that a high level of heterogeneity exists among systems for control of state aid and subsidies at both the supranational and national levels.[70] In general, if there is no specific trade agreement in place between the EU and a third country, the EU's and its Member States' trade relations with third countries are governed by the WTO.[71] This means that if a Member State of the EU, such as France, decides to subsidise French-produced aeroplane parts meant to be exported to the United States, the United States can register a complaint against the EU at the WTO.[72]

Because this book examines the effect of state aid policy on investment, it is of interest to carefully examine the extent to which the notion of subsidy, as governed by the WTO rules, overlaps with the notion of state aid. In this way, it is possible to pinpoint which government measures are caught by the WTO's subsidies rules, as a part of the extraterritorial dimension of the EU's state aid policy. The WTO provisions on subsidies, notably the Subsidies Agreement, bear a close resemblance to

---

[68] To protect state aid policy in the internal market from erosion of external distortions and actors, the export of state aid has taken place in diverse forms. In addition to being one of the driving forces behind the introduction of the Subsidies Agreement in 1995, the EU has negotiated state aid provisions into its international agreements, such as the EU's Accession, Associate, and Free Trade agreements.

[69] In the same way as other regional and national subsidy regulation does. For example, many states that lack domestic rules on subsidies have rules that provide competition neutrality, which aims to maintain a level playing field between public and private business. Competitive neutrality aims to maintain a level playing field between public and private business (OECD 2012). Some of the countries with which the EU has Association Agreements (AA), as well as other regional trade blocs such as the West African Economic and Monetary Union (WAEMU, also called UEMOA), have also implemented state aid rules as part of their competition policies: see OECD (2011), p. 10; UNCTAD (2007), p. 11.

[70] OECD (2011), p. 9.

[71] See Sect. 2.4.1 in Chap. 2.

[72] The EU does not have a trade agreement with the United States. Therefore, the trade relations between the United States and the EU fall under the WTO rules. See WTO case on subsidies for large aircraft (WTOAP 2018).

EU's state aid rules due to mutual influence on each other's trade systems.[73] However, the scope of WTO subsidies provisions was never extended beyond those related to goods, while the EU state aid rules have no such limitations, covering almost all measures where a firm benefits from government action.[74] Another substantial difference between these two legal frameworks is that, unlike the WTO Treaty and the agreements under it, the EU's law is to a much greater extent hard law.

Hence, contrary to the WTO's rules—which do not provide legal remedies for individual rights—EU law provides rights and obligations to the Member States, the EU institutions and private parties, and these are legally binding. An EU Member State is obliged to either implement EU law in its domestic law or apply EU law directly (depending on the type of rule that is applicable). Further, because the EU has executive power over the state aid regime, the EU enforcement state aid rules that are breached is far more aggressive[75] than the enforcement of the Subsidies Agreement by the legal framework of the WTO.[76] Instead, the effect of WTO rules on a country's domestic law is contingent on the general effect of international law on the legal system of that country. Even though the WTO dispute-settlement system may sanctify WTO members' action to impose countervailing duties against imports from WTO members who grant harmful subsidies,[77] the WTO lacks executive power.

Nevertheless, on a surface level, the WTO's Subsidies Agreement provisions have similar patterns to those of Articles 107–109 TFEU.[78] As discussed previously, the Subsidies Agreement covers three of the four cumulative criteria of Article 107(1) TFEU that identifies a measure constituting a subsidy: (1) it involves a

[73] GATT Article XIV contains rules for export subsidies by providing countervailing measures. The Subsidies Agreement is an evolution of GATT Article XIV.

[74] For exemptions, see Sect. 3.2 above. Therefore, the WTO rules catch only a narrow category of investment incentives. For example, see United States and EUs disputes on measures affecting trade in large civil aircraft (WTOAP 2018; WTO Panel 2011). In 1996, in the *Certain Pasta from Italy* US countervailing duty case, the United States held that several Italian pasta-makers had been subsidised by Italy and the EU (USDoC 2017). Many of these subsidies were investment aids (Thomas 2007), p. 43.

[75] Sykes (2010), pp. 14–15. While repayment of illegal aid is a typical remedy in the EU, this is not the case in the WTO. According to Thomas (2007), a repayment of prohibited subsidies has occurred only once in the WTO, when the United States raised a complaint against Australia: see *Australia – Automotive Leather-Recourse to Article 21.5 of the DSU* (2000); *Australia – Automotive Leather I* (1998); *Australia – Automotive Leather II* (1999). For repayment *(Australia – Automotive Leather – Recourse to Article 21.5 of the DSU*, 2000), the panel held that Article 4.7 of the Subsidies Agreement covered repayments under certain circumstances. This ruling has been strongly criticized.

[76] Also, as noted in Sect. 2.4.1, unlike in the EU, where the Commission can take the initiative, the WTO cannot act unless a WTO member state raises a complaint against another nation's subsidising practices.

[77] Annex 2 of the Subsidies Agreement.

[78] Schön (2004), p. 284.

financial contribution derived from the state; (2) it confers a benefit upon its recipients; and (3) it is specific to a company, an industry or a group of industries. However, state aid law definitions differ from those of the Subsidies Agreement regarding the types of measures considered to constitute aid.

WTO law interprets 'state resources' more broadly than EU law, by covering horizontal transfers between private companies initiated by government instruction, even where the financial contribution has not depleted government resources. 'Selectivity', in contrast, is interpreted quite narrowly. The CJEU has denied the direct effect of the GATT, and WTO law cannot be invoked to challenge a measure adopted by the EU.[79] However, while state aid law exercises ex-ante control, the WTO Subsidies Agreement applies ex post facto assessment.[80]

Under WTO law, there are two categories of subsidies: actionable and non-actionable. Actionable subsidies are based on a two-track system. The first is 'Track I actionable subsidies', which are subsidies where one signatory state impositions countervailing duties on imports from another signatory state, hurting the duty-imposing state's domestic industry. The second is 'Track II', which consists of the prohibited subsidies. These consist of export subsidies and 'import substitution'.[81] They allow for a signatory state to challenge the subsidy of another signatory state before the WTO dispute-settlement body.[82] Here the assessment of a type of 'subsidy' is not acceptable differs from the EU's assessment of justifiable State aid. Under the WTO system, every measure that fulfils the essential criteria of a subsidy breaches the Subsidies Agreement.[83] State aid law, however, has codified justifications in Article 107 (2–3) TFEU for granting subsidies, which makes the application of state aid rules dynamic and enables it to be shaped by the EU's policies, the Commission's decisions and the CJEU's rulings.

3.4 Development of State Aid Law and Policy

Since the establishment of the European Coal and Steel Community (ECSC) in 1956, the main rationale behind state aid control has been the integration of the internal market.[84] It is why state aid control was introduced to the core legislation

[79] *C-27/76 – United Brands v Commission*' (1978); *C-377/02 – Van Parys* (2005); *C-120/06 P – FIAMM and Others v Council and Commission* (2008).

[80] Goyette (2006), p. 717.

[81] Article 3.1(a) and (b) of the Subsidies Agreement.

[82] OECD (2011), p. 21. With the consequence of that dispute outcomes are more unpredictable than the EU's.

[83] Rubini shows how, (very) frequently, the legal definition of aid or subsidy is combined with the justifications given for granting them in both the EU and the WTO (Rubini 2010).

[84] 'Competition policy is one of the fundamental means for preserving the unity of the market.' Commission of the EC, Sixth Report on Competition Policy, 1976 (EC 1977) p. 9. See also Grin (2003), p. 7 and Sauter (1997) p. 118.

from the very beginning in the forerunner of the EU. Further, to ensure that state aid control would be effective, it was made to cover all trading and have far-reaching enforcement powers.[85] Certainly, the EU has the strictest state aid/subsidies control in the world, initially revealed by the *prima facie* prohibition in Article 107 TFEU of all state aid, unless there are specific reasons why state aid is seen as necessary, non-discriminatory and fair.

Nevertheless, although state aid provisions remain relatively unchanged from the Treaty of Rome,[86] state aid control has evolved into an immense and complex legal framework and a potent policy tool for the EU to harmonise and influence the policies of Member States. By correlating state aid policy-making and regulation policies with changes in the EU's political and economic circumstances, the EU has been able to 'steer' Member States' economic choices. Hence scholars such as Lopez,[87] Blauberger[88] and Biondi[89] have found the evolution of the state aid policy to be dynamic. It is shaped by adopted policies and decisions made by the Commission and judgments by the CJEU; the key institutions withhold power over state aid decisions and enforcement.

This process has not always been painless. A nation typically attempts to respond to political and economic changes through adjustment of its budget by the allocation of resources to economic activities it considers to be in the general interest of the country. Because state aid rules restrict the ability of Member States to do so unless proper justification exists, the Member States have at times resisted these rules.[90] Hence, there has been a need to overcome this resistance while maintaining the effectiveness and enforcement of state aid rules, which has strongly influenced the development of state aid policy.[91] This type of process is displayed in, *inter alia*, the *Micula* proceedings and their aftermath.[92] Conceivably, this is the reason for the Treaties equipping the Commission with wide-ranging powers, from normative, procedural and executive to judicial, in the area of state aid policy.[93]

On the other hand, the Commission addresses concerns expressed by the Member States. A typical example of this is the Commission's White Paper on Foreign Subsidies,[94] which introduces measures to protect the Member States and their

---

[85] Bacon (2017), p. 3; Rubini (2010).

[86] Biondi and Righini (2014), p. 1.

[87] López (2015), pp. 3, 7.

[88] Blauberger (2008).

[89] López (2015), pp. 3, 7; Biondi and Rubini (2005); Biondi (2013). See also Chari and Cavatorta (2002).

[90] Paemen (2016), p. 49.

[91] López (2015), p. 3. This type of reasoning was partially indicated by Biondi (2006), p. 1428 et seq. See also Hölscher et al. (2017).

[92] For details, see Chap. 4.

[93] The EU implements separation of powers in accordance to teachings of De Montesquieu (1989).

[94] European Commission (2020b).

firms from unfair foreign competition which is empowered by foreign subsidies.[95] The White Paper aims to unilaterally regulate a wide range of 'distortive subsidies' originating from non-EU countries that are beyond the scope of Article 107 TFEU, the GATT and the Subsidies Agreement.[96]

Another notable driver behind the evolution of state aid control is the case law of the CJEU. Being the only court that provides the binding interpretations of the treaties[97] and how these are to be applied in effect causes European integration by 'judicial activism'.[98] Consequently, the Member States have, through different periods of the integration process, adapted their policies to fit the specific state aid regime of the time, causing the national subsidy schemes to partly echo the European model.[99]

In a similar vein, the exportation[100] of state aid control has also taken place on a global scale through the EU's dynamic promotion of this policy, and participation in activities related to competition policy and enforcement.[101] Certainly, the EU has demanded its accession and neighbouring countries to adopt strict state aid-related obligations directly derived from EU law in exchange for enhanced cooperation and trade.[102] After all, the exportation of state aid rules is an essential method of ensuring that the competition within the internal market is not threatened by external actors. As Neelie Kroes asserted in a speech for the Informal Competitiveness Council early in 2007, the reason for the Commission being active both externally and internally is that an active trade policy abroad and the EU internal discipline on state aid are two sides of the same coin.[103]

Being aware that a comprehensive competition policy calls for state aid rules to be recognised and respected also in the international field the EU actively promotes

---

[95] See Commissions website Commission adopts white paper on foreign subsidies in the single market at https://ec.europa.eu/commission/presscorner/detail/en/ip_20_1070. On 5 May 2021 the Commission released the Commission's proposal a Regulation on foreign subsidies distorting the internal market, Brussels 5 May 2021 COM(2021) 223 final (Draft Regulation on foreign subsidies EC 2021); European Commission (EC) (2020a).

[96] For more information, see Sects. 3.4 and 3.5.5 below.

[97] Due to the primacy and direct effect of EU law, established by the CJEU in the early 1960s in *Case 26-62 – van Gend & Loos* (1963) and *Case 6-64 – Costa v ENEL* (1964).

[98] Stone Sweet (2010) p. 7. This influence of the CJEU on the EU's policy-makers has, in turn, also widely affected all EU policy.

[99] Smith (1998), p. 57; Szyszczak (2011), p. 38; López (2015), p. 3. The Member States are obliged to follow the CJEU rulings.

[100] This book adopts a broad concept of Europeanisation (Featherstone and Radaelli 2003), where the term implies situations when a national political system is somewhat affected by the European system (Vink 2003).

[101] European Commission (2017b); European Commission (2017a), p. 5. The Commission identified improvement of subsidies control as part of important objectives on the multilateral and plurilateral agenda for 2017.

[102] See EEA agreement and association agreements with Turkey and Albania and bilateral agreements with Switzerland and Israel (EC 2015b). See also Cremona (2003); Rydelski (2004).

[103] Kroes (2007), p. 4.

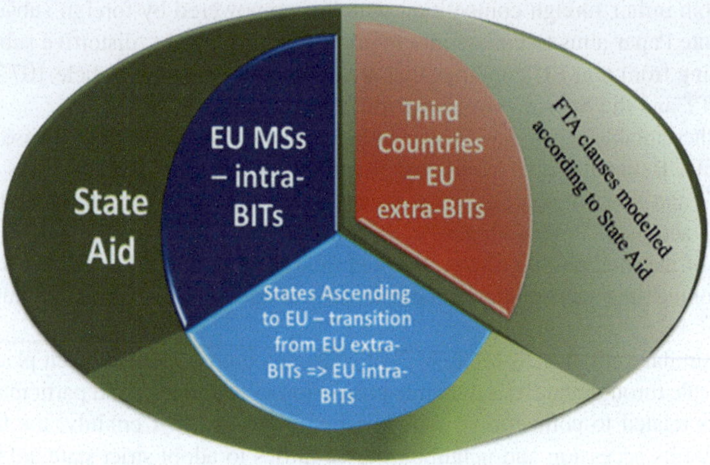

Fig. 3.2 EU state aid global influence

multilateral subsidies control in line with its Common Commercial Policy (CCP) Articles 206 and 207 TFEU.[104] See Fig. 3.2 for the EU's state aid global influence.

Besides the general notion that State aid control is fundamental to a global competition strategy,[105] Lavenex and Schimmelfennig explain that the driving force behind the regulatory export of the EU's internal policies to third countries is the EU's *acquis communautaire*.[106] In their opinion, this exportation contains much more than a formal membership of an international trade or cooperation agreement. The notion of the EU's 'external governance' is meant to capture this process.[107] According to Lavenex and Schimmelfennig, the regulatory transfer takes place through the CCP and a wide array of external relations developed by the EU.[108]

Article 21(1) TEU, read together with Article 207 TFEU, drives the EU to emphasise and apply globally the core values and internal policies of the EU, particularly the policy areas covered by the EU's CCP. The Commission is also compelled by Article 17(1) TEU to promote and act according to the general interest of the EU and to ensure the application of the EU Treaties, including measures

[104] EU (2008). Accordingly, the EU shall contribute towards harmonisation of global trade, especially in removing trade barriers on, *inter alia*, foreign direct investment (Article 206) and protection of distortion of trade by dumping or subsidies. See also Rubini (2004), p. 1.

[105] See Sect. 3.2 above.

[106] Lavenex and Schimmelfennig (2009); Lavenex and Uçarer (2004).

[107] Lavenex and Uçarer (2004).

[108] Lavenex and Schimmelfennig (2009).

adopted by EU's institutions pursuant to the same.[109] The development of an external dimension of state aid rules and policies to third countries and international organisations is an expected consequence of this. Indeed, this evolution of state aid law from a simple prohibition offers a great example of a legal tool capable of remarkable adaptation with the potential to tackle an enormous variety of issues.[110] As we will see in the following chapters, legal research and literature analysing CJEU case law and actions taken by the Commission observe and demonstrate this development.

3.4.1 Internal Dimension

Until the twenty-first century, legal research and literature on state aid law within the internal market concentrated on this concept as a prohibition. Contributions focused on discussing and analysing the criteria included in this concept, reacting to judgments of the CJEU[111] and deliberating on one or more of the cumulative criteria[112]—state resources, selective advantage, distortion of competition and the effect on trade.[113] Incidentally, the broad meaning that the CJEU applies to the notion of state aid, covering most forms of state intervention, is stressed by authors who tend to emphasise the tensions caused by the breadth of this notion and how the CJEU fine-tunes it by excluding some measures from its scope.[114] The same literature has also analysed the notion of state aid concerning specific forms of state intervention in the economy.

Of these, two have been studied substantially: the application of aid for social measures[115] and fiscal state aid (which is often the form investment incentives take),[116] especially at times when the Commission has escalated its combat against

[109] Otherwise, the Commission risks facing possible action from the European Parliament (Article 234 TFEU) or becoming a subject for complaint to the CJEU by an EU citizen, legal or natural alike, under Article 265 TFEU.

[110] Chari and Cavatorta (2002); Griswold and Marine (1996), p. 361; Koenig (2014), p. 611.

[111] Bartosch (2010, 2011); Biondi (2006, 2013); Clayton and Segura Catalan (2015); Nicolaides (2015).

[112] See Sect. 3.2.2 above for the four cumulative criteria.

[113] Bartosch (2010, 2011); Biondi (2006, 2013); Clayton and Segura Catalan (2015); Slotboom (1995).

[114] For example, Biondi (2013), which considers critically how the definition of state aid has developed through the jurisprudence of the CJEU. See also Biondi and Righini (2014); Chari and Cavatorta (2002); Griswold and Marine (1996); López (2015); Paemen (2016).

[115] Biondi and Rubini (2005); Davies (1995).

[116] Bobby (2017); Brokelind (2014); Englisch (2013); Luja (2006, 2016, 2017); Nicolaides (2001, 2004); Quigley (2004); Schön (2004).

harmful tax practices[117] caused by Member State resistance to these rules. A significant body of literature has also analysed the relationship between the notion of state aid and State participation in the economy,[118] and between this notion and the financing of public services.[119]

Two policy initiatives that combine soft and hard law instruments—the SAAP[120] launched by the Commission in 2005 and the latest reform, SAM,[121] implemented in 2012—introduced a more economical approach to state aid control.[122] As well as introducing new secondary legislation and guidelines, the development by these two policy initiatives inspired many authors to engage in economic narratives covering the economic rationale behind the granting and control of subsidies.[123]

In the SAAP, the Commission affirmed the role of EU state aid control for addressing the EU's fundamental purpose of providing undertakings in the Union with a level playing field, and as a response to market mechanism interruptions caused by state aid.[124] In conjunction with SAAP, literature has engaged in a discussion on the objectives and the nature of the state aid rules, and on the interpretation of the notion of aid that would best suit those objectives and the nature of the rules.[125] Since the Commission issued the SAAP, the handling of individual cases has, in practice, revolved around the 'balancing test'.[126]

SAM broadened the scope of the guidelines by creating new ones to the extent of covering nearly all areas of state aid control, including horizontal and sector-specific rules. SAM further refined an economic approach, both in the design of the rules and

---

[117]In the late 1990s, by publication of the Code of Conduct 1998 (European Council 1998) and European Commission notice on business taxation (European Commission 1998). Another major push took place in 2013, when the Commission initiated in-depth probes into the tax ruling practices of Member States. This led to several rulings on the breach of state aid rules, by schemes allowing for tax avoidance by multinational corporations—for example, *SA.38373 $ Apple* (2016); *SA.38374 Starbucks* (2015).

[118]Kavanagh et al. (2011); Nicolaides (2017), Ch 4; Anestis and Mavroghenis (2006).

[119]Biondi (2004); Biondi and Rubini (2005); Hettne (2011); Szyszczak and van de Gronden (2014).

[120]State aid action plan (EC 2005).

[121]Communication on EU State Aid Modernization (SAM) (EC 2012).

[122]Biondi and Stefan (2018), p. 3.

[123]Biondi (2013); De Vries (2011); Fidrmuc and Tunali (2015); Nitsche and Heidhues (2006).

[124]State aid action plan (EC 2005), paras 6–7.

[125]Two main groups stand out in this debate. Those in the first group, including authors such as Buendia-Sierra (2006), argue that state aid provisions are more closely related to those of the internal market (e.g. free movement of capital and establishment) than to other competition law. As a result, similarly to the internal market field, economics has a limited role in the field of state aid. Group two includes scholars such as Friederiszick et al. (2006). These authors promote the adoption of a more effects-based approach to the EU's competition law (including state aid rules) by increasing the role of economics when analyzing the potential distortion on competition of state aid measures.

[126]This means that 'the compatibility of state aid is fundamentally about balancing the negative effects of aid on competition with its positive effects in terms of common interest'. State aid action plan (EC 2005), para 11.

in the assessment of individual cases. This led to a thorough analysis of the current legal and economic principles of EU state aid by literature.[127] In 2015, López analysed the notion of aid in the wider context of the role and purpose of the state aid regime within the economic constitution of the EU.[128]

The Commission's White Paper on Foreign Subsidies, published in June 2020, proposed the adoption of unilateral legal instruments to protect the EU's internal market and companies from unfair competition by foreign companies subsidised by third countries. Around a year later, on 5 May 2021, the Commission published the Draft Regulation on foreign subsidies.[129] This marks a strong new development in the area of state aid law.[130] However, the regulatory instruments proposed by the Commission would substantially enhance the EU's capacity to offer a level playing field to all firms within the internal market, and therefore comprehensive literal works that elaborate on this subject are bound to emerge.[131]

Many contributions have also covered the relationship between state aid law and intra-EU BITs, particularly on the problems relating to investor-state agreements (ISAs)[132] and the substantial and procedural matters and issues arising therefrom. Disputes caused by the opposite views of the principle of legitimate expectations in state aid law and FET provisions of investment protection and the enforcement of Awards that constituted state aid have inspired several articles on the subject.[133]

In contrast to the ample literature on the concept of state aid and the development of the application of state aid law within the internal market, the development of extraterritorial state aid policy remains a relatively under-studied area, as shown by the scarcity of academic contributions.[134]

3.4.2 *Extraterritorial Dimension*

Extraterritoriality and regulatory export of competition policy for state aid have taken place slowly but steadily, so they have not gained as much attention as other

[127] Especially after several controversial rulings from the CJEU, such as *T-210/02 – RENV I* (2012), *C-487/06 P – British Aggregates v Commission* (2008) and *C-487/06 P – British Aggregates v Commission* (2008). See also Biondi (2013); Mause and Gröteke (2017); Werner and Verouden (2016).

[128] López (2015).

[129] EC (2021).

[130] See, for example, Cunha Rodrigues (2021); Nicolaides (2020).

[131] For more on this subject, see Sect. 3.5.5.

[132] See Andersen and Hindelang (2016); Dimopoulos (2011); Hindelang (2012a, b); Kende (2015); Gubrynowicz and Wierzbowski (2009); Gallo and Nicola (2015); Ortolani (2015); Happ and Tietje (2013); Tietje (2013); Tietje et al. (2012); Tietje and Wackernagel (2014, 2015); Matei (2015, 2016); Matei and Ciurtin (2016); Saavedra Pinto (2016).

[133] Saavedra Pinto (2016); Tietje and Wackernagel (2015); Matei (2016).

[134] Blauberger and Krämer (2010); Van de Casteele (2006).

areas of the EU's competition policy.[135] One reason could be that state aid rules are understood by many legal scholars more as part of the internal market rules—like the four freedoms—than as competition law.[136] Differing from antitrust law, state aid/subsidies control is also not part of competition networks like the ICN.[137] State aid has been and still is, a useful tool to expand the scope of Europeanisation beyond the EU.[138] This is the external dimension of state aid, explicitly linked to the EU's external trade policy, and it has developed in step with increases in the EU's global trade.[139]

Authors writing about the external dimension of state aid can be divided into two categories: the political scientist and practitioners of legal academia, especially persons with connections to the Commission or the Parliament.[140] Political scientists, like Lavenex, Schimmelfennig and Blauberger, are seemingly focused on the EU's goals and the 'mechanisms' of the regulatory transfer by the use of state aid policy,[141] while the emphasis of the written contributions by legal academia has been on analysing different type of trade instruments, especially those of the WTO. Issues and disputes relating to a specific aspect of trade instruments, as well as comparative studies, have also inspired authors.

Prior to 2006, the Commission's state aid policy was focused mainly on the development of the internal market.[142] Despite several FTAs concluded between the EU and third countries often including state aid provisions, these were vaguely formulated and hardly enforceable.[143] Only a few papers, such as those of Szepesis[144] and Geradins,[145] review state aid provisions in EU bilateral FTAs. Fornalczyks'[146] analysis of regulation of state aid in non-EU countries, published

---

[135] Van de Casteele (2006).

[136] State aid and obstacles to trade are discussed in Biondi et al. (2004), p. 103; Biondi (2006); Kassim and Lyons (2013), p. 2.

[137] Some competition practitioners in the United States (A.B. Association 2010) have expressed the appeal and usefulness of expanding ICNs to cover subsidies control.

[138] Lavenex and Schimmelfennig (2009). Usually legal authors study the Europeanisation of the EU's Member States (Eliantonio 2013; Jans et al. 2007) and countries in the accession process, as well as countries that are possible future accession countries. Some authors, such as Featherstone and Radaelli (2003) have shown that the scope of Europeanisation can go beyond Europe. See also Schimmelfennig (2012a, b); Radaelli (1997); Grabbe (2003).

[139] Damro (2013); Damro and Guay (2016) p. 72.

[140] Papadopoulos (2010); Van de Casteele (2006, 2016); Laprévote et al. (2015); Jarosz-Friis et al. (2010); Galindo (2015); Bourgeois et al. (2007).

[141] Blauberger (2008) discusses the adoption of these policies through 'negative integration'—that is, the abolition of national barriers—and 'positive integration'—that is, the formal harmonisation of national rules.

[142] Even though the notion of global governance was introduced in 2001 by the Commissions White Paper (EC 2004), p. 5.

[143] Jarosz-Friis et al. (2010), p. 78; Szepesi (2004).

[144] Szepesi (2004).

[145] Geradin (2004).

[146] Fornalczyk (2004).

in this era, reveals that state aid was considered to have only a minor role in bilateral trade agreements.

Exceptions to these FTAs are the plurilateral regional agreements of EEA and EFTA[147] and the obligation to establish internal state aid control for EU candidate and accession countries.[148] Although the enforcement of state aid rules in EEA countries, due to the establishment of the EFTA surveillance authority was highly successful, the situation differed vastly in the acceding Central and Eastern European countries. National authorities lacking proper authority experienced severe issues when it came to enforcing the state aid rules pre-accession.[149] Yet there are fewer written contributions about state aid control in EEA and EFTA than in the candidate and accession countries. The effect of an obligation to establish an operationally independent state aid control for the Western Balkans, which are considered potential accession countries by the EU, through Stabilisation and Association Agreements (SAAs), have also been scrutinised by Cremona, and by Popović and Caka.[150]

For association countries in the EU's geographical vicinity—the likes of Ukraine, Moldova and Georgia—the post SAAP literature has documented a trend to include substantial national state aid regulation.[151] Markedly, the national laws of the Eastern neighbourhood are those of state aid, not subsidies control.

On global multilateral trade instrument rules and their correlation with state aid, Hoekman and Holmes,[152] Rubini[153] and Goyette,[154] in their contributions on the interplay of EU state aid law and the Subsidies Agreement, have adopted a global multilateral approach on trade remedies.[155] Accordingly, the development of the WTO and state aid rules have affected each other.[156] Although the EU's campaign to evolve WTO rules towards state aid has had limited success, mainly due to resistance from the United States,[157] the Subsidies Agreement is a notable result of the EU's

[147] Bourgeois et al. (2007); Rosenthal and Nicolaides (1997); Rydelski (2004).

[148] Atanasiu (2001); Schutterle (2002); Cremona (2003). For more recent literature on the subject, see Birnstiel and Heinrich (2011); Blauberger (2008); Botta and Schwellnus (2015); Hölscher et al. (2017).

[149] Hölscher et al. (2017) p. 782; Hargita and Filep (2004), p. 585. This problem is also displayed by *Micula*.

[150] Popović and Caka (2017).

[151] Dimitrova and Dragneva (2013).

[152] Hoekman and Holmes (1999).

[153] Rubini (2004).

[154] Goyette (2006).

[155] A similar approach has been adopted by more recent literature (Damro and Guay 2016; Rubini 2010).

[156] Damro (2013); Blauberger and Krämer (2010).

[157] Blauberger and Krämer (2010), p. 19; de Madrid (2007), p. 87. The United States has not adopted subsidies disciplines. The Shearman Antitrust Act (1890) Sec. 1. was worded ambiguously enough to potentially cover subsidies prohibition. The Congress, empowered by Article I of the US Constitution, and the High Court can regulate subsidies, but have mostly chosen not to use it: see Sykes (2010).

efforts to align the two regimes with one another.[158] Since the implementation of SAAP, after the Commission received criticism about its inward-looking perspective and its lack of global considerations,[159] the Commission has stepped up its efforts to promote state aid globally.[160] The literature presented in this chapter shows this process, although on the state aid regime in a megaregional context. This is perhaps due to the relevant case law from the CJEU, on the specific subject, being mainly approached from a WTO angle[161] and mostly concentrated to a specific country.[162] In 2007 and 2008, the Commission commissioned reports on state aid provisions in FTAs, which included some agreements with regional trading blocs.[163]

The need for enforceability of subsidies control in multiregional FTAs became relevant during the EU–Korea FTA negotiations.[164] Inclusion of provisions with clear referral to the right to regulate,[165] and with binding arbitration provisions for disputed state aid, made this FTA the first of the EU's new generation of FTAs. Many of the new-generation FTAs signed since then by the EU with countries like Singapore, Japan, Mexico, and regional trade blocs like Central America and the Andean countries, include rules on subsidies. Some of these agreements expand the scope of subsidies to cover services.[166] Post-*Micula*, a new trend has been to include provisions in TIPs investment Chapters, or IIAs, guaranteeing that measures related to state aid are expressively outside the scope of expropriation (see Appendix 1).

In the wake of SAM, more literature has surfaced on the state aid regulation in specific non-EU countries. State aid in Switzerland became a relevant subject after the Commission accused Switzerland of its cantonal tax regime constituting state aid under the rules of the EU–Switzerland FTA, thus being incompatible with the FTA.[167] Brexit brought up questions about the status of state aid control in the United Kingdom after it has departed from the EU.[168] How state aid law will look

---

[158] Blauberger and Krämer (2010), p. 19.

[159] For results of the Consultation on the State Aid Action Plan, see EC (2006), p. 8; EU Consultation-Liason Association (2005), p. 2; MEDEF (2004), pp. 2–3.

[160] Galindo (2015); Jarosz-Friis et al. (2010).

[161] The EU is the party in disputes even though the infringing measure would be an act of a Member State. See WTO, *EC sugar case* (WTOAB 2005). However, on competition law in an extra-EU BIT, see *C-126/97 – Eco Swiss* (1999).

[162] For Switzerland, see Hoffet (2016).

[163] Bourgeois et al. (2007); see also European Commission (2008).

[164] Jarosz-Friis et al. (2010).

[165] EU–South Korea FTA, Art. 7.1(4); see also the preamble and Articles 13.3, 13.4.3, 13.5.2 and 13.7.

[166] See, for example, JEEPA, EU–Singapore FTA and EU–Mexico FTA.

[167] Obrist (2013); Hoffet (2016).

[168] Peretz and Bacon (2016); Peretz (2016); Peretz et al. (2017); Schonberg (2017), p. 51. See also Lyons et al. (2017), discussing the United Kingdom's new trade arrangements, setting limits on future state aid policy.

after Brexit has inspired several articles and a substantial study from the British House of Lords.[169]

Overall, scrutiny of the subsidies management of the EU's trading partners reveals that most are subject to some type of control on subsidies. From the literature reviewed for this chapter, it becomes clear that the compatibility with the internal market state aid regime for these countries varies from a general similarity to vague compatibility, based on their geographical closeness to the EU.

3.5 State Aid Procedures in the EU: The Commission as the King of the Hill

Whereas the EU's external state aid control for its trading partners takes place nationally, the same control within the internal market is extremely centralised at the EU level.[170] Within the internal market, the Commission is an EU institution responsible for enforcing the EU state aid rules. The CJEU 'controls the legality of Commission decisions, in particular on the notion of aid' through the appeal process, but does not have the authority to decide on compatibility of a state aid measure with the internal market.[171] The CJEU can naturally also make preliminary rulings on questions regarding state aid upon request from national courts. Most state aid cases, however, do not proceed to the CJEU.[172]

Hence, the Commission's clever use of the CJEU's rulings has increased its power and autonomy over the area of state aid.[173] National courts have a role in determining the existence of aid and whether the required notification obligation has been fulfilled.[174] However, the Commission's competence regarding the assessment and decision of the compatibility of the state aid is exclusive according to Article 108(2) TFEU. It is therefore left to the Commission only to decide, after examining measures subject to Article 107(2) and (3) TFEU, whether to accept or decline a Member State's interventions, depending on their compatibility with the internal market. For Article 107(3) exemptions, which are complex to assess, the Commission wields a margin of discretion to announce whether aid falls under the provision. The Commission, with a mandate from the Council, can even adopt block exemptions in line with Article 109 TFEU procedure, which pre-approves certain state aid

---

[169] House of Lords (2018); Davis, May and Union (2017). See introduction by the Secretary of State for Exiting the EU in the fourth paragraph, ensuring that laws and regulations deemed 'practical and sensible' will apply post Brexit. See also Letter by MP Andrew Griffits to Lord Witty, Chair, EU Internal Market Sub-Committee House of Lords on 28 March 2018 (Griffits 2018).

[170] Hettne (2011) p. 6.

[171] Buendia Sierra (2016), p. 124.

[172] Buendia Sierra (2016), p. 124.

[173] Blauberger (2009).

[174] *T-542/11 RENV – Alouminion tis Ellados v Commission* (2018) paras 51–54.

as internal market compatible.[175] For other than block exemptions, the Commission's decisions can be positive, conditional[176] or negative.[177] Should the Commission decide not to raise objections after a preliminary examination of the measure, the notified measure would be deemed compatible with the internal market and implementable by the Member State.[178]

3.5.1 Thou Shall Not Proceed Un-Notified

The block exemptions are an exception to the mandatory pre-notification. All measures that do not qualify as existing aid or that fall under block exceptions or other relevant provisions thereof[179] are subject to an *ex-ante* notification obligation under Article 108(3) TFEU. A simple notification, post-implementation of the measure, is adequate to satisfy the 'standstill clause' in Article 108(3) TFEU and Article 2.1 of the 'Council Regulation (EU) 2015/1589 of 13 July 2015 laying down detailed rules for the application of Article 108 of the Treaty on the Functioning of the European Union' (Council of the European Union 2015). Otherwise, due to the standstill obligation in Article 108(3) TFEU and clarified by Article 2.1 of the Procedural Regulation, the Member States are prohibited from implementing any state aid measures without ex-ante notification to and approval by the Commission.

The notion of existing aid covers aid that the Member State already had in place before joining the EU[180] or schemes that have been in place for more than 10 years (even if of illegal origin, as ten years is the time for the measure to be statute-barred).[181] Naturally, aid that has been implemented according to state aid rules also qualifies as existing aid.[182] Article 108(3) TFEU also includes a standstill clause; hence, it is prohibited to implement measures classified as notifiable aid before the

[175] *T-542/11 RENV – Alouminion tis Ellados v Commission* (2018) paras 51–54 referring to *C-78/76 – Steinike & Weinlig* (1977) and *C 120/73 – Lorenz v Germany* (1973) para 8.

[176] Meaning, as stated in Article 7 of the Procedural Regulation, that the Commission will open an in-depth investigation. The implementation of the measure will be frozen until the Commission has completed its investigation. The measure may become acceptable after certain amendments in line with Article 9.3 of the Procedural Regulation. For example, see *2005/346/EC – MobilCom* (2004).

[177] EC (2013b), p. 1.

[178] Article 4 of the Procedural Regulation.

[179] Like measures deemed too small to distort the competition within the internal market covered by the *de minimis* (EC 2013a) or block exemption (giving automatic approval for a range of aid measures defined by the Commission), the GBER.

[180] The Procedural Regulation Article 1(b)(i). The Procedural Regulation replaced the former Regulation (EC) No. 659/1999 laying down detailed rules for the application of Article 93 of the EC Treaty Text with EEA relevance (European Council 1999).

[181] The Procedural Regulation Articles 1(b)(iv) and 17, unless interrupted by an action by the Commission or the Member State. See also *C-276/03 – P Scott v Commission* (2005), para 26.

[182] The Procedural Regulation Article 1(b)(ii), (iii) and (v).

Commission has issued or is deemed to have issued its approval.[183] If a measure has been adopted contrary to the notification obligation procedure, it becomes unlawful.[184]

3.5.2 *Unlawful or Incompatible Aid*

When a Member State has implemented a state aid measure without prior Commission authorisation, it is considered unlawful state aid.[185] This does not necessarily mean that the aid is incompatible with the internal market, as the sole reason for its unlawfulness is the failure to notify ex-ante implementation. Because the unlawfulness of the measure is caused only by the supranational character of the conditional prohibition in Article 107 TFEU,[186] the measure would otherwise be lawful. Therefore, it is the Commission's internal market compatibility assessment that delivers the final verdict on the fate of a Member State's state aid measure, unlawful or not. A Member State discovered to have granted illegal state aid faces immediate scrutiny by the Commission. Unlawful state aid may also be subject to suspension of payments of the aid or a provisional clawback mechanism[187] until the Commission has finished internal market compatibility assessment.

3.5.3 *Clawback Procedure*

If unlawful and internal market-incompatible state aid has been paid, the Commission issues a decision directed to the Member State concerned on the discontinuation of the measure and recovery of the allocated aid from its beneficiaries. The standard procedure of retroactive recovery used is aimed at re-establishing the previously existing situation, returning the benefit to the Member State granting it. The Member State must use all necessary measures available in the domestic legal system to

---

[183] The Procedural Regulation Articles 2.1, 4.3 and 4.6.

[184] The Procedural Regulation Article 1(f) defines new aid put into effect in breach of Article 108(3) 3 TFEU as illegal. New aid is defined as either non-existing aid or altered existing aid.

[185] See Article 108(3) TFEU and the Procedural Regulation; Articles 1(f) and (c).

[186] See Matei and Curtin (2016) p. 54, referring to the judgment in *C-74/76 – Ianelli v Meroni* (1977) paras 14–17. According to Matei and Curtin, the examination of the compatibility under Article 108(2) TFEU takes into consideration compliance with other supranational norms, especially the respect due to economic freedoms within the EU.

[187] The Procedural Regulation Articles 10(2), 11(2) and 16. See also *C-278/92 – Spain v Commission (Hytasa)* (1994), para 75; *Micula II (EU)* (2014), paras 103 and 154 et seq; *C-301/87 – France v Commission (Boussac)* (1990), paras 9–24; *C 120/73 – Lorenz v Germany* (1973) para 8 for direct effect of Article 108(3) and *Micula I (EU)* (2014), paras 6, 22 and 74 for suspension injunction.

recover the aid plus interest from the beneficiary.[188] The Commission will seek recovery, including a commercial rate of interest,[189] from all undertakings under control of the same individuals to which the recipient's assets have been transferred.[190]

Unless the Commission's right of recovery has expired due to surpassing the 10-year time limit[191] or it cannot be enforced being contrary to the General Principles of EU Law, the Member State avoids the obligation for retroactive recovery of the aid only if it is impossible.[192] Despite that, the notification must be done by the Member State, not the beneficiary of the aid, as it is the recipient who pays the price of the illegal aid. It is crucial to understand that the recipient of this type of aid is not protected by the principle of legitimate expectations. By settled EU state aid practice, a beneficiary's unawareness of the unlawful status of the state aid does not make it legal. This means that recipients of unlawful state aid, including recipients of investment incentives, lack the legal rights to claim the restitution of illegal payments or to reclaim retroactively recovered state aid except under exceptional circumstances.[193] The obligation goes as far as negating a national *res judicata*.[194] Furthermore, a third-party firm that has suffered damage caused by the measure may seek damages from the Member State that granted the aid, following the *Francovich* doctrine.[195]

The Member State that has awarded the aid cannot avoid the recovery without being guilty of failing to fulfil its obligations under the Treaties.[196] Ultimately, a Member State that does not comply with EU law may face Article 258 TFEU infringement proceedings launched by the Commission.[197] If the CJEU, as established by 260 TFEU, decides that a Member State has failed to fulfil an obligation under the Treaties, the Member State is obliged to comply with the

---

[188] Article 14(3) of the Procedural Regulation; see also *C-142/87 – Tubemeuse* (1990), para 66.

[189] The Procedural Regulation, Article 14(2).

[190] The 24th Report on Competition Policy 1999 (EC 2001), point 314.

[191] The Procedural Regulation, Article 15.

[192] See, for example, *C-404/97 – Commission v Portugal* (2000).

[193] See *C-24/95 – Alcan Deutschland* (1997) para 25; *C-5/89 BUG – Alutechnik* (1990), para 16.

[194] See, for example, *C-119/05 – Lucchini* (2007) and *C-505/14 – Klausner Holz Niedersachsen* (2015).

[195] See *C-173/03 – Traghetti del Mediterraneo* (2006) paras 41 and 45 (referring to *C-224/01 – Köbler* (2003) para 51; *Francovich Joined Cases C-6 & 9/90* (1991) para 40; *Joined cases C-46/93 and C-48/93 Brasserie du Pêcheur* (1996) para 51. Case *C-173/03 – Traghetti del Mediterraneo* concerned state liability in situations where illegal state aid granted by Italy had caused damage to individuals. According to the CJEU, there is a 'right to obtain redress ... where it has been established that the rule of law infringed is intended to confer rights on individuals and there is a direct causal link between the breach of the obligation incumbent on the State and the loss or damage sustained by the injured parties.'

[196] See Sects. 3.4.1 and 3.4.2 in Chap. 3.

[197] For example, see the infringement proceedings against five Member States (McKenzie 2015) and European Commission (2015a).

CJEU's judgment. If this does not occur, the Member State may face severe consequences.[198] In general, Member States stop granting incompatible state Aid at the latest after the CJEU has decided on its incompatibility with EU law.

3.5.4 Member States Under a Magnifying Glass

As established in the previous chapters, the clawback mechanism is intended to re-establish the balance of the internal market.[199] However, before initiating the recovery of state aid that has already been paid out, the Commission opens a formal investigation as stated by Article 108(2) TFEU. This investigation is initiated where the Commission is unsure about the measure's compatibility with EU state aid provisions, or where the acquisition of necessary information faces procedural difficulties.[200]

The risk of a breach of EU law by a Member State is what makes it a target for action by the Commission under the Procedural Regulation.[201] Internal market-incompatible measures must be discontinued and state aid that has already been paid out must be recovered—that is, clawed back. The Member State is informed by a Commission decision if there is a formal investigation being initiated against them. This decision provides the Member State with a summary of the factual and legal basis for the investigation, including the Commission's preliminary assessment. It outlines the issues and concerns around the measure's compatibility with EU state aid rules. The published decision, which appears in the EU's official journal, provides one month for the submission of comments by the Member State and interested third parties.[202] Observations published by interested third parties can be commented on by the Member State concerned. However, even though the EU can stop a Member State from selectively financing a third-country firm[203] the principle of international comity hinders the EU from applying EU state aid rules on third countries that subsidise firms doing business within the EU internal market.

---

[198] Article 14 of the Procedural Regulation. See also *C-142/87 – Tubemeuse* (1990) para 66; *C-37/14 – Commission v France* (2015); *Case C-204/21 R Commission v Poland*. Further disciplinary methods are laid down by the Article 7 TEU procedures enabling the EU cutting off EU funding or suspending specific rights from to the rebellious Member State. See *C-157/21 - Poland v Parliament and Council; C-156/21 Hungary v European Parliament and Council* on breaching the rule of law.

[199] See *C-120/73 – Lorenz v Germany* (1973) para 8 for direct effect of Article 108(3). See also the Procedural Regulation, Articles 10(2), 11(2) and *C-301/87 – France v Commission (Boussac)* (1990), paras 9–24.

[200] European Commission (2013b), p. 2.

[201] European Commission (2013b), p. 2.

[202] European Commission (2013b) p. 2.

[203] See tax rulings—for example, *SA.38373 $ Apple* (2016); *SA.38375 Fiat* (2015) and *SA.38374 Starbucks* (2015).

3.5.5 State Aid Control and Enforcement: Third Countries

As a result of strict EU state aid rules, European enterprises may have disadvantages in global competition compared with third-country firms, which may benefit from state aid. Therefore, from time to time the Commission has come under pressure to be more lenient about the state aid rules.[204] However, this might jeopardise maintaining fair competition in the EU's internal market. For the protection of 'fairness' in competition, particularly for EU enterprises within the internal market and globally, the EU has turned its trade policy 'into an external competitiveness tool', the purpose of which is 'to deal with unfair foreign subsidies'.[205] By promoting norms on state aid control past EU borders through bilateral or plurilateral agreements, the EU attempts to fight unfair foreign subsidies where multilateral subsidies control[206] and trade defence instruments[207] have failed.

An active trade policy abroad and the EU internal discipline on state aid are two sides of the same coin.[208] This kind of reasoning is supported by the wording of Article 107 TFEU, which does not require the receiver of the subsidy to be based in the internal market, only that the effect be potentially distortive to the internal market. For reasons of international comity, even though the EU can stop a Member State from selectively financing a third-country undertaking,[209] it cannot use state aid law to stop the third country from subsidising companies that compete with other

[204] See, for example, Valejo (2019). See also Commission consultations in the wake of implementing SAAP (MEDEF 2004) and reflected in the speech of former Competition Commissioner Kroes (2007), p. 2.

[205] For example, see the latest modernisation of trade defences at the Commission's web page at http://ec.europa.eu/trade/policy/accessing-markets/trade-defence. See also Commission's 'Europe's trade defence instruments now stronger and more effective' trade instrument fact sheet (EC 2018). In April 2016, Trade Commissioner Malmstrom's speech, 'Way ahead for the global steel industry', identified subsidies as one of the issues behind the Chinese steel dumping (Malmström 2016).

[206] These WTO-based rules are implemented into EU law by Regulation (EU) 2016/1037 of the European Parliament and of the Council of 8 June 2016 on protection against subsidised imports from countries not members of the European Union, OJ L 176, 30.6.2016, p. 55–91 (European Parliament & Council 2016).

[207] These WTO-based rules are implemented into EU law by Regulation (EU) 2015/476 of the European Parliament and of the Council of 11 March 2015 on the measures that the Union may take following a report adopted by the WTO Dispute Settlement Body concerning anti-dumping and anti-subsidy matters OJ L 83, 27.3.2015, p. 6–10 (Parliament & Council 2015). See also Regulation (EU) 2015/476 of the European Parliament and of the Council of 11 March 2015 on the measures that the Union may take following a report adopted by the WTO Dispute Settlement Body concerning anti-dumping and anti-subsidy matters OJ L 83, 27.3.2015, pp. 6–10 (Parliament & Council 2015).

[208] Kroes (2007) p. 4.

[209] See *SA.38373 $ Apple* (2016); *SA.38375 Fiat* (2015); *SA.38374 Starbucks* (2015).

firms within the internal market.[210] Hence, the state aid criteria of state resources do not cover third-country resources apart from the EEA countries.[211]

However, while the EU still has no legal tools to directly control subsidisation of third countries, this situation is subject to change soon. Responding to the Member States' concerns about 'unfair foreign competition' and calls to relax the state aid rules, the Commission's White Paper on Foreign Subsidies proposed a plan on how to bring companies benefiting from foreign subsidizing in line with the EU firms.[212] The White Paper, followed by the Draft Regulation on foreign subsidies,[213] visualises new unilateral legal instruments that tackle unfair competition by foreign companies subsidised by third countries from distorting the EU's internal market.

The rules introduced by the Draft Regulation on foreign subsidies are structured as three 'tools', each with a specific function. The Commission would be in charge to see to the enforcement of these rules.[214] The modules constitute one general investigation tool and two notification based tools:

- Tool 1 contains a general instrument empowering the Commission to initiate investigations or request ad-hoc notifications to conduct a balancing test to deem if the specific foreign subsidies distort competition in the internal market.[215] If the Commission finds that distortion occurs redressive measures may be imposed, or it may accept enterprise offered commitments.
- Tool 2 found in Chapter 3 is designed to manage or stop acquisitions and mergers of EU companies enabled by 'distortive subsidies' provided by a third country government. As a prerequisite; the turnover inside EU must be equal to or higher than €500 million for the acquired company, or at a minimum of one of the parties to a merger, with the foreign financial contribution having been at least €50 million in the last three years. Besides providing the Commission authority ex-ante control over acquisitions enabled by foreign subsidies before these occur by introducing a compulsory notification requirement.
- Tool 3 found in Chapter 4 aims to stop unfair bidding from occurring in public procurement. A notification requirement for firms participating in tender procedures would cover subsidies received from a third country government when an estimated procurement value equals or exceeds €250 million. Recipients of these, if found to have gained an unfair advantage in comparison to other firms, would not be granted the contract.

---

[210] For example, the United States from subsidising American companies that export to the EU, thus competing within the internal market with the European undertakings.

[211] Articles 109 and 110 of the EEA Agreement authorise the Commission to apply EEA competition rules within the EEA territory.

[212] See the Commission's website: 'Commission adopts white paper on foreign subsidies in the single market | Internal Market, Industry, Entrepreneurship and SMEs' (europa.eu).

[213] EC (2021).

[214] See Chapter 1 Articles 3-6 Draft Regulation on foreign subsidies.

[215] Draft Regulation on foreign subsidies Chapters 2-4.

Notably, the planned rules target all types of subsidies, hence mimicking the scope of Article 107 TFEU. This way the proposed rules would catch foreign measures that escape the prohibitions by GATT and the Subsidies Agreement such as subsidies for services or in form of foreign investment. Fundamentally, the effect of inbound subsidies (such as inbound capital flows) would be substantially diminished and would calm the Member States' concerns. According to the public consultations, the Member States and other EU stakeholders mostly supported this initiative. Not surprisingly, though, participating third countries objected to any addition to the existing rules.[216]

Until the abovementioned plan is realised, the control must take place indirectly by national laws influenced by EU state aid laws[217] based on an international agreement, such as multilateral trade rules (WTO[218] and UNICTRAL rules on competition) or relevant plurilateral[219] or bilateral agreements.[220]

When countries agree to abide by common norms through trade agreements, it is for the reason of diffusing adverse cross-border effects.[221] Sometimes, as a spillover effect or as required by the agreement, internal measures are adopted to maintain those norms. In this way, state aid and subsidies control may indirectly find their way to domestic courts and national law. Further, unilateral political pressure, the modern gunship diplomacy, can be proven to cause a change in national laws[222] even when outside of the scope of a free or preferential trade agreement.[223] The EU is also highly active at the multilateral level. The future will show whether the EU's Investment Court System, which has been endorsed by the CJEU in *Opinion 1/17* (2019) is successful; the same applies to the attempt at establishing a multilateral investment court, MIC.

---

[216]The Summary of the responses to the public consultation on the White Paper on levelling the playing field as regards foreign subsidies is available at https://ec.europa.eu/info/law/better-regulation/have-your-say/initiatives/12452-White-Paper-on-Foreign-Subsidies/public-consultation.

[217]See Ch 6 of this thesis for the Switzerland cantonal banking case (Obrist 2013) and Ukraine's Antimonopoly Committee's (UMC) state aid decisions.

[218]For example, mini trade wars EU-USA (Schön 2004), p. 293 and (Breuss 2004), p. 373 et seq. As an example, see WTOAP (2018).

[219]For example, EFTA, Cariforum.

[220]For example, EU–Ukraine FTA.

[221]In the EU's geographic nearness, there are specific theories explaining this process, such as the domino theory of regionalism, which was provided by Baldwin (1993) and further discussed by Baldwin and Jaimovich (2012), Dür (2010) and Mattli (1999).

[222]For more on this topic see Chap. 6 for. See also Obrist (2013).

[223]Some literature addresses 'the EU as a conflicted power' (Meunier and Nicolaïdis 2006), which by use of its market power (e.g. by offering access to the EU's internal market or customs union) pressures weaker powers, such as other trading blocs or countries, into accepting trade arrangements that are aligned with EU law (Farrell 2005; Grabbe 2003; Lavenex and Schimmelfennig 2009) such as the EEA Agreement.

Apart from WTO Trade remedies,[224] restoring the balance of the internal market is not without difficulties. Where the EU has applied state aid rules extraterritorially, by the initiation of clawback measures targeting third-country companies operating in the EU[225] that have received illegal/incompatible state aid, countries like the United States may protest.[226] These nations complain that the EU's clawback of unlawfully obtained state aid from companies that are national enterprises of these states impairs their vital national interests. Therefore, to ensure that competition works on an equal basis in the global markets, the EU must work together with its trading partners to keep government subsidies under control. Positively, restricting international anti-competitive action with global effects not only affects the EU's internal market but those of other nations as well.

3.6 Summary and Conclusions

This chapter has found that the dimensions of law, policy and institutions of state aid are as follows. Regarding the dimensions of law, the primary legal source for the state aid regime is set out in Articles 107–109 TFEU. These provisions address states instead of private actors and are under the exclusive competence of the EU. State aid law prohibits unjustified spending of a Member State's revenue for the benefit of certain firms in a way that might disturb the competition on the internal market. In principle, the nationality of the beneficiary of the aid is irrelevant.

Regarding the dimension of state aid policy, state aid control is part of EU Competition rules and policy, which is one of the fundamental cornerstones of EU law. As crucial components of the European economic constitution, state aid law and policy function both as a shield, by defending the EU's internal market from harmful subsidy wars, and a sword, by acting as a tool for further integration. Certainly, since the Treaty of Rome, the state aid regime has served a wide range of policy purposes, preventing crowding out of existing investment, fostering competition, contributing to market liberalisation and ensuring a level playing field for all operators in a competitive EU market.

Above all, the state aid policy has served as an essential tool for the constitutionalisation of European values and the deepening integration of the internal market. In addition, the rationale for state aid control rests on the theory of a market economy presuming free competition leading to economic efficiency, yet state aid policy also aims to achieve redistributive justice. Globally, the implementation of

[224] The EU's trade defence mechanism is based on WTO rules, but the EU 'applies a number of extra conditions to the WTO rules to make sure their use is measured'. European Commission home page at http://ec.europa.eu/trade/policy/accessing-markets/trade-defence.

[225] Which are, according to the Commission, established in a Member State only as letterbox companies. See *SA.38373 $ Apple* (2016).

[226] See US Treasury White Paper (Treasury, 2016) and US Senate finance committee press release including letter.

free-market theories has led to subsidies control codified by the WTO framework into the multilateral GATT and the Subsidies Agreement. Contrary to the state aid regime, these international agreements are limited only to measures related to goods.

As shown by Lopez, Biondi and Rubini, the evolution of state aid policy is dynamic,[227] as it has adapted to the decisions made by two institutions: The Commission's application of state aid provisions and the judgments by the CJEU. While the Commission is empowered by the treaties to fine-tune state aid policy and secondary legislation to correlate with existing political and economic needs based on the ongoing development of the EU, it is the CJEU that decides the scope of the state aid criteria.

This development initially happened only internally, but later spilt over into external relations, to protect the EU internal market from subsidising practices by third nations. Further, the exportation of key EU rules, including state aid control, is being driven by the EU's *acquis communautaire*. For internal market protection and successful exportation of state aid control policies, the EU uses trade instruments and collaborates with its trading partners. The EU is also planning to utilise unilateral trade defence tools to curb the negative effect of inbound subsidies (such as inbound capital flows).

Further, state aid control within the internal market is extremely centralised at the EU level. Within the procedural sphere, the Commission reigns supreme. The mandatory ex-ante notification duty under Article 108(3) TFEU ensures that subsidies measures implemented by the Member States are internal market compatible. A failure by the Member State to notify an implemented measure renders it illegal and subject to clawback procedures, leading to suspension or discontinuation of the measure and potential recovery of the allocated aid from its beneficiary.

This chapter has also confirmed the finding of Chap. 2 that deep in this process lies the potential trigger for the collision of the state aid regime and the international investment regime. If a Member State is also a signatory to an international investment agreement, the Member State may find itself to be in breach of that agreement. Hence, the trigger launching the collision of the state aid regime and international investment regime lies within the scope of the clawback procedures.

Cases

Aid to Apple SA.38373 $, IP/16/2923 (Alouminion tis Ellados VEAE, formerly Alouminion AE v European Commission case T-542/11 RENV (General Court, 2018)

[227] The argument about state aid being dynamic is proposed by, for example, López (2015), pp. 3, 7. On the evolution of state aid, see and Biondi (2013); Biondi and Rubini (2005).

Alzetta Mauro and others v Commission of the European Communities, joined cases T-298/97, T-312/97, T-313/97, T-315/97, T-600/97 to 607/97, T-1/98, T-3/98 to T-6/98 and T-23/98, ECLI:EU:T:2000:151 (European Court of Justice, 2000)

Amministrazione delle finanze dello Stato v Denkavit italiana Srl, case 61/79, ECLI: EU:C:1980:100 (European Court of Justice, 1980).

Asteris AE and others and Hellenic Republic v Commission of the European Communities, joined cases 97, 193, 99 and 215/86, ECLI:EU:C:1988:199 (European Court of Justice, 1988)

Australia-Automotive leather I (1998)

Australia-Automotive Leather – Recourse to Article 21.5 of the DSU (Panel Report 2000)

Brasserie du Pêcheur SA v Bundesrepublik Deutschland and The Queen v Secretary of State for Transport, ex parte: Factortame Ltd and others, joined cases C-46/93 and C-48/93, ECLI:EU:C:1996:79 (European Court of Justice, 1996)

British Aggregates Association v Commission of the European Communities and United Kingdom, case C-487/06 P, ECLI:EU:C:2008:757 (European Court of Justice, 2008)

British Aggregates Association v European Commission, case T-210/02 RENV, ECLI:EU:T:2012:110 (Court of Justice of the European Union (GC), 2012)

Commission Decision of 14 July 2004 on the state aid implemented by Germany for MobilCom AG 2005/346/EC (European Commission, 2004)

Commission of the European Communities v Federal Republic of Germany, case C-5/89, ECLI:EU:C:1990:320 (European Court of Justice, 1990)

Commission of the European Communities v Portuguese Republic, case C-404/97, ECLI:EU:C:2000:345 (European Court of Justice, 2000)

Congregación de Escuelas Pías Provincia Betania, case C-74/16, ECLI:EU:C:2017:496 (European Court of Justice (Grand Chamber), 2017)

Dansk Rørindustri A/S (C-189/02 P), Isoplus Fernwärmetechnik Vertriebsgesellschaft mbH and Others (C-202/02 P), KE KELIT Kunststoffwerk GmbH (C-205/02 P), LR af 1998 A/S (C-206/02 P), Brugg Rohrsysteme GmbH (C-207/02 P), LR af 1998 (Deutschland) GmbH (C-208/02 P) and ABB Asea Brown Boveri Ltd (C-213/02 P) v Commission of the European Communities, joined Cases C-189, 202, 205, 208 & 213/02 Dansk Rørindustri and others v Commission, No. ECLI:EU:C:2005:408 (European Court of Justice (Grand Chamber) 2005)

Deutsche Bahn AG v Commission of the European Communities, T-351/02, ECLI: EU:T:2006:104 (Court of Justice of the European Union (GC), 2006)

Eco Swiss China Time Ltd v Benetton International NV, case C-126/97, ECLI:EU: C:1999:269 (European Court of Justice, 1999)

Eric Libert and Others v Gouvernement flamand (C-197/11) and All Projects & Developments NV and Others v Vlaamse Regering (C-203/11), joined Cases C-197/11 and C-203/11, ECLI:EU:C:2013:288 (European Court of Justice, 2013)

European Commission v Deutsche Post AG, case C-399/08 P, EU:C:2010:481 (European Court of Justice, 2010)
European Communities – Export Subsidies on Sugar (2005) WT/DS265/AB/R
European Commission v Électricité de France (EDF), case C-124/10 P, EU:C:2012:318 (European Court of Justice (Grand Chamber), 2012)
European Commission v Banco Santander and Santusa, joined Cases C 20/15 P and C 21/15 P, ECLI:EU:C:2016:981 (European Court of Justice (Grand Chamber), 2016)
European Commission v FIH Holding A/S and FIH Erhvervsbank A/S, case C-579/16 P, ECLI:EU:C:2018:159 (European Court of Justice (Grand Chamber), 2018)
European Commission v French Republic case C-37/14, ECLI:EU:C:2015:90 (European Court of Justice, 2015)
European Commission v Frucona Košice a.s., case C-300/16 P, EU:C:2017:706 (European Court of Justice, 2017)
European Commission v Republic of Poland, case C-204/21 R, ECLI:EU:C:2021:878 (Court of Justice of the European Union, 2021)
Fabbrica italiana accumulatori motocarri Montecchio SpA (FIAMM) and Fabbrica italiana accumulatori motocarri Montecchio Technologies LLC (C-120/06 P), Giorgio Fedon & Figli SpA and Fedon America, Inc. (C-121/06 P) v Council of the European Union and Commission of the European Communities, ECLI:EU:C:2008:476 (European Court of Justice, 2008)
Farrell and others (Grand Chamber), case C-413/15, ECLI:EU:C:2017:745 (European Court of Justice 2017)
Flaminio Costa v E.N.E.L, case 6-64, No. 61964J0006, ECLI:EU:C:1964:66, Eurlex (European Court of Justice (ECJ), 1964)
Fondul Proprietatea SA v Complexul Energetic Oltenia SA, case C-150/16, ECLI:EU:C:2017:388 (European Court of Justice, 2017)
Francovich Joined Cases C-6 & 9/90, ECLI:EU:C:1991:428, [1991] ECR I-5357 (European Court of Justice, 1991)
French Republic v Commission of the European Communities, case C-301/87, ECLI:EU:C:1990:67 (European Court of Justice 1990)
French Republic v Commission of the European Communities, case C-482/99, ECLI:EU:C:2002:294 (European Court of Justice, 2002)
Gebrüder Lorenz GmbH v Federal Republic of Germany and Land Rheinland-Pfalz, case 120-73, ECLI:EU:C:1973:152 (European Court of Justice, 1973)
Gerhard Köbler v Republik Österreich, case C-224/01, ECLI:EU:C:2003:513 (European Court of Justice, 2003)
Hellenic Republic v European Commission, case C-431/14 P, ECLI:EU:C:2016:145 (European Court of Justice (Grand Chamber), 2016)
Hungary v European Parliament and Council of the European Union, case C-156/21, not yet published (European Court of Justice (Grand Chamber), 2022)
Iannelli & Volpi SpA v Ditta Paolo Meroni, case 74/76, ECLI:EU:C:1977:51 (European Court of Justice, 1977)

Ireland and Aughinish Alumina Ltd v European Commission, joined cases T-50/06 RENV II and T-69/06 RENV II, ECLI:EU:T:2016:227 (European Court of Justice, 2016)
Italian Republic v Commission, of European Communities, case 173/73, ECLI:EU: C:1974:71 (European Court of Justice, 1974)
Kingdom of Belgium v Commission of the European Communities (Tubemeuse) C-142/87, ECLI:EU:C:1990:125, 1990 I-00959 (European Court of Justice, 1990)
Kingdom of Spain v Commission of the European Communities, joined cases C-278/92, C-279/92 and C-280/92, ECLI:EU:C:1994:325 (European Court of Justice, 1994)
Klaus Höfner and Fritz Elser v Macrotron GmbH, case C-41/90, ECLI:EU:C:1991: 161 (European Court of Justice (Sixth Chamber), 1991)
Klausner Holz Niedersachsen GmbH v Land Nordrhein-Westfalen, case C-505/ 14, ECLI:EU:C:2015:742 (European Court of Justice, 2015)
Kwekerij Gebroeders van der Kooy BV and others v Commission of the European Communities., joined cases 67, 68 and 70/85, ECLI:EU:C:1988:38 (European Court of Justice, 1988)
Land Rheinland-Pfalz *v* Alcan Deutschland GmbH, case C-24/95, ECLI:EU: C:1997:163 (European Court of Justice, 1997)
Léon Van Parys NV v Belgisch Interventie- en Restitutiebureau (BIRB), case C-377/ 02, ECLI:EU:C:2005:121 (European Court of Justice, 2005)
Ministero dell'Economia e delle Finanze v Cassa di Risparmio di Firenze SpA, Fondazione Cassa di Risparmio di San Miniato and Cassa di Risparmio di San Miniato SpA, case C-222/04, ECLI:EU: C:2006:8 (European Court of Justice, 2006)
Ministero dell'Industria, del Commercio e dellArtigianato v. Lucchini SpA, case 119/05, ECLI:EU:C:2007:434 (European Court of Justice (Grand Chamber), 2007)
NV Algemene Transport- en Expeditie Onderneming van Gend & Loos v Netherlands Inland Revenue, case 26-62, ECLI:EU:C:1963:1, Eur-Lex (European Court of Justice, 1963)
Pavel Pavlov and Others v Stichting Pensioenfonds Medische Specialisten, joined cases C-180/98 to C-184/98, ECLI:EU:C:2000:428 (European Court of Justice, 2000)
Pearle BV, Hans Prijs Optiek Franchise BV and Rinck Opticiëns BV v Hoofdbedrijfschap Ambachten, Case C-345/02, ECLI:EU:C:2004:448 (European Court of Justice, 2004)
PreussenElektra AG v Schhleswag AG, in the presence of Windpark Reußenköge III GmbH and Land Schleswig-Holstein, case C-379/98, ECLI:EU:C:2001:160 (European Court of Justice, 2001)
Regierungspräsidium Magdeburg v Nahverkehrsgesellschaft Altmark GmbH C-280/00, ECLI:EU:C:2003:415, 2003 I-07747 (European Court of Justice, 2003)

Republic of Poland v European Parliament and Council of the European Union, Case C-157/21, not
yet published, (European Court of Justice (Grand Chamber), 2022)

SA Intermills v Commission of the European Communities, case 323/82, ECLI:EU:C:1984:345 (European Court of Justice, 1984)

SA.38374 State aid implemented by the Netherlands to Starbucks, 2014/C (European Commission, 2015)

SA.38375 State aid which Luxembourg granted to Fiat, 2014/C (European Commission, 2015)

SA.38517 Micula v Romania, 2014/NN (Commission DG Comp, 2014)

Scott SA v Commission of the European Communities, case C-276/03 P, ECLI:EU:C:2005:590 (European Court of Justice, 2005)

State Aid SA.38517(2014/C) Romania Implementation of Arbitral award Micula v Romania of 11 December 2013, No. (ex 2014/NN), C(2014) 6848 final, Italaw (European Commission, 2014)

Steinike & Weinlig v Federal Republic of Germany case 78-76, ECLI:EU:C:1977:52 (European Court of Justice, 1977)

Tadej Kotnik and Others v Državni zbor Republike Slovenije, case C-526/14, ECLI:EU:C:2016:570 (European Court of Justice (Grand Chamber), 2016)

ThyssenKrupp Acciai Speciali Terni SpA v European Commission, case T-62/08, ECLI:EU:T:2010:268 (Court of Justice of the European Union (GC), 2010)

Traghetti del Mediterraneo SpA v Repubblica italiana, case C-173/03, ECLI:EU:C:2006:391 (European Court of Justice (Grand Chamber), 2006)

United Brands Company and United Brands Continentaal BV v Commission of the European Communities, case 27/76, ECLI:EU:C:1978:22 (European Court of Justice, 1978)

References

American Bar Association (ABA) (2010) Competition as public policy. ABA Book Publishing, Chicago

Andersen TT, Hindelang S (2016) The day after: alternatives to intra-EU BITs. J World Invest Trade 17(6):984–1014

Anestis P, Mavroghenis S (2006) The market investor test. In: Rydelski MS (ed) The EC state aid regime: distortive effects of state aid on competition and trade. Cameron May, London

Atanasiu I (2001) State aid in Central and Eastern Europe. World Compet 24:257

Bacon K (2017) European Union law of state aid, 3rd edn. Oxford University Press, Oxford

Baldwin R (1993) A domino theory of regionalism. In: Baldwin R, Haarapanta P, Kiander J (eds) Expanding membership of the EU. Cambridge University Press, Cambridge

Baldwin R, Jaimovich D (2012) Are free trade agreements contagious? J Int Econ 88(1):1–16

Bartosch A (2010) Is there a need for a rule of reason in European state aid law – or how to arrive at a coherent concept of material selectivity. Common Mark Law Rev 47:17

Bartosch A (2011) The concept of selectivity. In: Szyszczak E (ed) Research handbook on European state aid law. Edward Elgar, Cheltenham

Benz A (2000) Two types of multi-level governance: Intergovernmental relations in German and EU regional policy. Reg Federal Stud 10(3):21–44

Biondi A (2004) Justifying state aid: the financing of service of general economic interests. In: Tridimas T (ed) European Union law for the 21st century. Hart, Oxford

Biondi A (2006) Some reflections on the notion of state resources in European Community state aid law. Fordham Int Law J 30:1426

Biondi A (2013) State aid is falling down, falling down: an analysis of the case law on the notion of aid. Common Mark Law Rev 50(6):1719–1743

Biondi A, Righini E (2014) An evolutionary theory of EU state aid control. In: Arnull A, Chalmers D (eds) The Oxford handbook of European law. Oxford University Press, Oxford

Biondi A, Rubini L (2005) Aims, effects and justifications: EC state aid law and its impact on national social policies. In: Dougan M, Spaventa E (eds) Social welfare and EU law. Hart, Oxford

Biondi A, Stefan O (2018) The notice on the notion of state aid: every light has its shadow. In: Nascimbene B, Di Pascale A (eds) The modernisation of state aid for economic and social development. Springer, Dordrecht

Biondi A, Eeckhout P, Flynn J (2004) The law of state aid in the European Union. Oxford University Press, Oxford

Birnstiel A, Heinrich H (2011) State aid in the accession states. In: Szyszczak E (ed) Research handbook on European state aid law. Edward Elgar, Cheltenham

Blauberger M (2008) From negative to positive integration: European state aid control through soft and hard law. MPIfG Discussion Paper 08/4. https://ssrn.com/abstract=1660981 or https://doi.org/10.2139/ssrn.1660981

Blauberger M (2009) Of 'good'and 'bad'subsidies: European state aid control through soft and hard law. West Eur Polit 32(4):719–737

Blauberger M, Krämer RU (2010) European competition vs global competitiveness: transferring EU rules on state aid and public procurement beyond Europe. CCP Working Paper 10-10. https://www.uea.ac.uk/documents/107435/107587/1.168372!ccp10-10.pdf

Boasson EL (2019) Constitutionalization and entrepreneurship: explaining increased EU steering of renewables support schemes. Polit Gov 7(1):70–80

Bobby C (2017) A method inside the madness: understanding the European Union state aid and taxation rulings. Chicago J Int Law 18:186

Botta M, Schwellnus G (2015) Enforcing state aid rules in EU candidate countries: a qualitative comparative analysis of the direct and indirect effects of conditionality. J Eur Public Policy 22(3):335–352

Bourgeois J, Dawar K, Evenett, SJ (2007) A comparative analysis of selected provisions in free trade agreements. http://sro.sussex.ac.uk/id/eprint/59639

Breuss F (2004) WTO dispute settlement: four EU–US mini trade wars – a rejoinder. J Ind Compet Trade 4:373–378

Brokelind C (2014) International tax law and new challenges by constitutional and legal pluralism: competing constitutional concepts relevant for international taxation: prohibition of tax subsidies. Paper presented at the the 9th GREIT conference, Munich

Buendia Sierra J (2016) EU state aid control: competition between undertakings or between Member States. In: Rubini L, Hawkins J (eds) What shapes law? European University Institute, Florence

Buendia-Sierra JL (2006) Not like this: some skeptical remarks on the "refined economic approach" to state aid. In: Proceedings of the 4th Experts' Forum on New Developments in European State Aid Law. Lexxion, Berlin

Chari RS, Cavatorta F (2002) Economic actors' political activity in 'overlap issues': privatisation and EU state aid control. West Eur Polit 25(4):119–142

Cini M (2001) The soft law approach: commission rule-making in the EU's state aid regime. J Eur Public Policy 8(2):192–207

Clayton M, Segura Catalan M (2015) The notion of state resources: so near and yet so far. Eur State Aid Q 14(2):260–270
Commission of the European Communities (1977) Sixth Report on Competition Policy: 1976. http://ec.europa.eu/competition/publications/annual_report/ar_1976_en.pdf
Commission of the European Communities (1998) Commission Notice on the application of the State aid rules to measures relating to direct business taxation. European Communities, Brussels
Commission of the European Communities (2005) State aid action plan: less and better targeted state aid: a roadmap for state aid reform 2005–2009. European Communities, Brussels
Coppi L (2011) The role of economics in state aid analysis and the balancing test. In: Szyszczak E (ed) Research handbook on European state aid law. Edward Elgar, Cheltenham
Council of the European Union (1998) Council Conclusions 9 March 1998, concerning the establishment of the Code of Conduct Group (business taxation). Official Journal of the European Communities C 099, 01/04/1998: 0001–0002
Council of the European Union (1999) Council Regulation (EC) No 659/1999 laying down detailed rules for the application of Article 93 of the EC Treaty Text with EEA relevance. European Union, Luxembourg
Council of the European Union (2015). Council Regulation (EU) 2015/1589 of 13 July 2015 laying down detailed rules for the application of Article 108 of the Treaty on the Functioning of the European Union (Text with EEA relevance). Official Journal of the European Union OJ. doi:32015R1589
Cremona M (2003) State aid control: Substance and procedure in the Europe agreements and the stabilisation and association agreements. Eur Law J 9:265
Cunha Rodrigues N (2021) Filling the regulatory gap to address foreign subsidies: the EC's search for a level playing field within the internal market. In extraterritoriality of EU economic law. Springer, Cham, pp 197–227
Damro C (2013) EU State aid policy and the politics of external trade relations. J Ind Compet Trade 13(1):159–170
Damro C, Guay T (2016) European competition policy and globalization. Springer
Davies P (1995) Market integration and social policy in the Court of Justice. Ind Law J 24:49
Davis D, May T (2017) Legislating for the United Kingdom's withdrawal from the European Union. Goverment of United Kingdom, London
De Cecco F (2012) State aid and the European economic constitution. Bloomsbury, London
de Madrid GE (2007) Regulation of subsidies and state aids in WTO and EC law: conflicts in international trade law. Kluwer, Amsterdam
De Montesquieu C (1989) Montesquieu: the spirit of the laws. Cambridge University Press, Cambridge
De Vries SA (2011) Services of general economic interest in the interplay between public and private in Europa after Lisbon: the search for more coherence. Europarättslig Tidskrift 3:462–482
Dimitrova A, Dragneva R (2013) Shaping convergence with the EU in foreign policy and state aid in post-orange Ukraine: weak external incentives, powerful veto players. Europe-Asia Stud 65(4):658–681
Dimopoulos A (2011) The validity and applicability of international investment agreements between EU Member States under EU and international law. Common Mark Law Rev 48(1): 63–93
Dür A (2010) Protection for exporters: power and discrimination in transatlantic trade relations, 1930–2010. Cornell University Press, Ithaca
Ehlermann C-D (1994) State aid control in the European Union: sucess or failure? Fordham Int Law J 18(4):1212
Eliantonio M (2013) Europeanization of legal principles? The influence of the CJEU's case law on the principle of legitimate expectations in the Netherlands and the United Kingdom. Eur Public Law 19(4):715–738
Englisch J (2013) EU state aid rules applied to indirect tax measures. EC Tax Rev 22(1):9–18

EU Consultation-Liason Association (2005) Comments on the European Commission consultation document on the state aid action plan: A road map for reform 2005–2009. European Union, Birmingham

European Commission (EC) (2001) XXIXth Report on competition policy 1999. https://publications.europa.eu/en/publication-detail/-/publication/106c34b6-7227-4ecd-beb3-43bad2093cca

European Commission (EC) (2004) Commission white paper on services of general economic interest. European Communities, Brussels

European Commission (EC) (2006) Results of the Consultation on the State Aid Action Plan (SAAP) – detailed summary. http://ec.europa.eu/competition/state_aid/reform/comments_saap/index.html

European Commission (EC) (2008) Provisions on international relations in EU competition policy: Situation as of 1 January 2008. https://publications.europa.eu/en/publication-detail/-/publication/50fd3279-5b8b-4f81-b534-b00fbedbff85/language-en

European Commission (EC) (2012) EU state aid modernization. European Union, Brussels

European Commission (EC) (2013a) Commission Regulation (EU) No 1407/2013 of 18 December 2013 on the application of Articles 107 and 108 of the Treaty on the Functioning of the European Union to de minimis aid. Official J Eur Union 50(352):8

European Commission (EC) (2013b) Competition: State aid procedures. European Union, Luxembourg

European Commission (EC) (2014a) Commission Regulation (EU) No 651/2014 of 17 June 2014 declaring certain categories of aid compatible with the internal market in application of Articles 107 and 108 of the Treaty. European Union, Brussels

European Commission (EC) (2014b) Guidelines on state aid for environmental protection and energy 2014–2020. European Union, Brussels

European Commission (EC) (2014c) Impact assessment. Accompanying the document Communication from the Commission guidelines on state aid for environmental protection and energy for 2014–2020. European Union, Brussels

European Commission (EC) (2015a) Commission asks Member States to terminate their intra-EU bilateral investment treaties. Media release. http://europa.eu/rapid/press-release_IP-15-5198_en.htm

European Commission (EC) (2015b) Provisions on international relations in EU competition policy. http://ec.europa.eu/competition/international/legislation/legislation.html

European Commission (EC) (2016) Commission notice on the notion of state aid as referred to in Article 107(1) of the Treaty on the Functioning of the European Union. European Union, Brussels

European Commission (EC) (2017a) Management Plan 2017. https://ec.europa.eu/info/publications/management-plan-2017-trade_en

European Commission (EC) (2017b) State aid: Commission and China start dialogue on state aid control. Media release. http://europa.eu/rapid/press-release_IP-17-1520_en.htm

European Commission (EC) (2018) Europe's trade defence instruments now stronger and more effective. http://trade.ec.europa.eu/doclib/docs/2018/june/tradoc_156921.pdf

European Commission (EC) (2020a) Commission adopts white paper on foreign subsidies in the single market. Media release. https://ec.europa.eu/commission/presscorner/detail/en/ip_20_1070

European Commission (EC) (2020b) White paper on levelling the playing field as regards foreign subsidies. European Union, Brussels

European Commission (EC) (2021) Commission's proposal for a Regulation on foreign subsidies distorting the internal market, 5 May 2021 COM(2021) 223 final. European Union, Brussels

European Parliament and European Council (2015) Regulation (EU) 2015/476 of the European Parliament and of the Council of 11 March 2015 on the measures that the Union may take following a report adopted by the WTO Dispute Settlement Body concerning anti-dumping and anti-subsidy matters. European Union, Brussels

European Parliament and European Council (2016) Regulation (EU) 2016/1037 of the European Parliament and of the Council of 8 June 2016 on protection against subsidised imports from countries not members of the European Union. In Official Journal of the European Union. European Union, Brussels

Farrell M (2005) EU external relations: exporting the EU model of governance? Eur Foreign Aff Rev 10(4):451–462

Featherstone K, Radaelli CM (eds) (2003) The politics of Europeanization. OUP Oxford

Fidrmuc J, Tunali C (2015) State aid policy in the European Union. J Common Mark Stud 53(5). https://doi.org/10.1111/jcms.12247

Fornalczyk A (2004) State aid regulation in candidate countries: the case of Poland. In: Biondi A, Eeckhout P, Flynn J (eds) The law of state aid in the European Union. Oxford University Press, Oxford

Friederiszick HW, Röller L-H, Verouden V (2006) European state aid control: an economic framework. In: Buccirossi P (ed) Handbook of antitrust economics. MIT Press, Cambridge

Galindo BR (2015) State aid control in the context of globalisation. European Commission, Brussels

Gallo D, Nicola FG (2015) The external dimension of EU investment law: Jurisdictional clashes and transformative adjudication. Fordham Int Law J 39:1081

Geradin D (2004) Competition law and regional economic integration: an analysis of the southern Mediterranean countries. World Bank, Washington, DC

Goyette C-D (2006) The interface between EU state aid control and the WTO disciplines on subsidies. Eur State Aid Law Q 4:695–718

Grabbe H (2003) Europeanization goes east: power and uncertainty in the EU accession process. In: Featherstone K, Radaelli CM (eds) The politics of Europeanization. Oxford University Press, Oxford

Griffits A (2018) Letter by MP Andrew Griffits to the Lord Witty, Chair, EU Internal Market Sub-Committee House of Lords

Grin G (2003) The battle of the single European market: Achievements and economic thought 1985–2000. Kegan Paul, London

Griswold CP, Marine GM (1996) Political influences on state policy: higher-tuition, higher-aid, and the real world. Rev High Edu 19(4):361

Gubrynowicz A, Wierzbowski M (2009) Conflict of norms stemming from intra-EU BITs and EU legal obligations: some remarks on possible solutions. Oxford University Press, Oxford

Happ R, Tietje C (2013) EU, investment treaties, and investment treaty arbitration: current developments and challenges. Transnatl Disp Manage 10(2) https://www.transnational-dispute-management.com/article.asp?key=1937

Hargita E, Filep ZR (2004) State aid control in Hungary. Eur State Aid Law Q 3(4). https://doi.org/10.21552/estal/2004/4/49

Hettne J (2011) Public services and state aid: Is a decentralisation of state aid policy necessary? European Policy Analysis. https://www.sieps.se/en/publications/2011/public-services-and-state-aid%2D%2Dis-a-decentralisation-of-state-aid-policy-necessary%2D%2D201114epa

Hindelang S (2012a) Circumventing primacy of EU law and the CJEU's judicial monopoly by resorting to dispute resolution mechanisms provided for in inter-se treaties: the xase of intra-EU investment arbitration. Leg Iss Econ Integr 39:179

Hindelang S (2012b) Member State BITs: there's still (some) life in the old dog yet: Incompatibility of eexisting Member State BITs with EU law and possible remedies. In: Coleman J, Sachs L, Johnson L (eds) Yearbook on international investment law & policy. Oxford University Press, Oxford

Hoekman B, Holmes P (1999) Competition policy, developing countries and the WTO. World Econ 22(6):875–893

Hoffet F (2016) State aid 2016: Switzerland. https://globalcompetitionreview.com/insight/know-how/state-aid/report/switzerland

Hofmann HC (2006) Negotiated and non-negotiated administrative rule-making: the example of EC competition policy. Common Mark Law Rev 43(1):153–178
Hölscher J, Nulsch N, Stephan J (2017) State aid in the new EU Member states. J Common Mark Stud 55(4):779–797
House of Lords (2018) Brexit: competition and state aid. Authority of the House of Lords, London. https://publications.parliament.uk/pa/ld201719/ldselect/ldeucom/67/6702.htm
Jans JH, de Lange R, Prechal A, Widdershoven RJ (2007) Europeanisation of public law. Europa Law, Groningen
Jarosz-Friis A, Pesaresi N, Kerle C (2010) EU–Korea FTA: a stepping stone towards better subsidies control at the international level. Competition Policy Newsletter 1. http://ec.europa.eu/competition/publications/cpn/2010_1_19.pdf
Kassim H, Lyons B (2013) The new political economy of EU state aid policy. J Ind Compet Trade 13(1):1–21
Kavanagh J, Niels G, Pilsbury S (2011) The market economy investor: an economic role model for assessing state aid. In: Szyszczak E (ed) Research handbook on European state aid law. Edward Elgar, Cheltenham
Kende T (2015) Arbitral awards classified as state aid under European Union law. ELTE LJ 37
Koenig C (2014) Where is state aid law heading to? Heinemann, New York
Kroes N (2007) State aid and globalization – the competition perspective. European Commission, Würzburg
Laprévote F-C, Frisch S, Can B (2015) Competition policy within the context of free trade agreements. The E15 Initiative, September. http://e15initiative.org/publications/competition-policy-within-the-context-of-free-trade-agreements
Lavenex S, Schimmelfennig F (2009) EU rules beyond EU borders: theorizing external governance in European politics. J Eur Public Policy 16(6):791–812
Lavenex S, Uçarer EM (2004) The external dimension of Europeanization: the case of immigration policies. Cooperat Confl 39(4):417–443
López JJP (2015) The concept of state aid under EU law: from internal market to competition and beyond. Oxford University Press, Oxford
Luja R (2006) Investment funds, tax planning and state aid. Eur Tax 46(12):565–569
Luja R (2016) Do state aid rules still allow European Union Member States to claim fiscal sovereignty? EC Tax Rev 25(5/6):312
Luja R (2017) State aid recovery & investor protection for non-EU taxpayers. https://cris.maastrichtuniversity.nl/en/publications/state-aid-recovery-amp-investor-protection-for-non-eu-taxpayers-h
Lyons B, Reader D, Stephan A (2017) UK competition policy post-Brexit: taking back control while resisting siren calls. J Antitrust Enforce 5(3):347–374
Maduro M (1998) We the court: the European Court of Justice and the European economic constitution. Bloomsbury, London
Malmström C (2016) Way ahead for the global steel industry. In: Trade OECD High-Level Symposium on Steel. European Union, Brussels
Matei E (2015) The chamber of secrets: the repudiation of the ISDS. RRDE 83
Matei E (2016) SA.38517 – Commission Decision of 30 March 2015 on state aid granted by Romania to Micula. Eur State Aid Law Q 15(1):134
Matei E, Ciurtin H (2016) Turning enemies into adversaries: TTIP negotiations and the quest for a new Westphalia momentum. Turkish Commer Law Rev 2(1):27
Mattli W (1999) The logic of regional integration: Europe and beyond. Cambridge University Press, Cambridge
Mause K, Gröteke F (2017) The economic approach to European state aid control: a politico-economic analysis. J Ind Compet Trade 17(2):185–201
McKenzie B (2015) Commission targets five EU Member States over Intra-EU BITs. Global Arbitration News. http://globalarbitrationnews.com/european-commission-targets-five-eu-member-states-intra-eu-bits

MEDEF (2004) Position adopted by MEDEF concerning the European Commission's State AID Action State Aid Action Plan. European Union, Brussels
Meunier S, Nicolaïdis K (2006) The European Union as a conflicted trade power. J Eur Public Policy 13(6):906–925
Nicolaides P (2001) Fiscal aid in the EC: a critical review of current practice. World Compet 24(3): 319
Nicolaides P (2004) Fiscal state aid in the EU: the limits of tax autonomy. World Compet 27:365
Nicolaides P (2015) New limits to the concept of selectivity: the birth of a 'general exception' to the prohibition of state aid in EU competition law. J Eur Compet Law Pract 6(5):315–323
Nicolaides P (2017) State aid uncovered: critical analysis of developments in state aid 2016. Lexxion Verlagsgesellschaft mbH, Berlin
Nicolaides P (2020) The Commission's white paper on foreign subsidies: a real problem that needs sharper tools. https://www.lexxion.eu/en/stateaidpost/the-commissions-white-paper-on-foreign-subsidies-a-real-problem-that-needs-sharper-tools
Nitsche R, Heidhues P (2006) Study on methods to analyse the impact of state aid on competition. Directorate General Economic and Financial Affairs (DG ECFIN), European Commission, Brussels
Nyberg L (2017) Neoliberalism, competition, and EU state aid policy. PhD dissertation, Lund University. http://portal.research.lu.se/portal/files/23600808/Avhandling_till_tryck_Nyberg_vers_2.pdf
Obrist T (2013) The end of Switzerland's cantonal tax regimes is near: what's next? Tax Notes Int 71(7):647
OECD (2011) Roundtable on Competition, State Aids and Subsisdies. OECD, Paris. http://www.oecd.org/competition/sectors/48070736.pdf
OECD (2012) Competitive neutrality: maintaining a level playing field between public and private business. OECD, Paris
Ortolani P (2015) Intra-EU arbitral awards vis-à-vis Article 107 TFEU: State aid law as a limit to compliance. J Int Disp Settlement 6(1):118–135
Paemen H (2016) Forces that (may) have shaped subsidy regulation. In: Rubini L, Hawkins J (eds) What shapes the law? Reflections on the history, law, politics and economics of international and European subsidy disciplines. European University Institute, Florence
Papadopoulos AS (2010) The international dimension of EU competition law and Policy. Cambridge University Press, Cambridge
Peretz G (2016) A star is torn: Brexit and state aid. Eur State Aid Law Q 15(3):334–337
Peretz G, Bacon K (2016). Post-Brexit options for state aid. http://uksala.org/paper-on-post-brexit-options-for-state-aid
Peretz G, Bacon K, Taylor I (2017) Bringing state aid home: Could an effective domestic state aid regime be devised for the UK? http://uksala.org/bringing-state-aid-home-could-an-effective-domestic-state-aid-regime-be-devised-for-the-uk/#_ftn1
Popović DV, Caka F (2017) State aid control in south-east Europe: waiting for a wake-up call. Eur Bus Organ Law Rev 18(2):333–349
Quigley C (2004) General taxation and state aid. In: Biondi A, Eeckhout P, Flynn J (eds) The law of state aid in the European Union. Oxford University Press, Oxford
Radaelli CM (1997) How does Europeanization produce domestic policy change? Corporate tax policy in Italy and the United Kingdom. Comp Polit Stud 30(5):553–575
Rosenthal DE, Nicolaides P (1997) Harmonizing antitrust: the less effective way to promote international competition. In: Richardson JD, Graham EM (eds) Global Competition Policy. Peterson Institute for International Economics, Washington, DC
Rubini L (2004) The international context of EC state aid law and policy: the regulation of subsidies in the WTO. The law of State Aid in the European Union. Oxford University Press, New York
Rubini L (2010) The definition of subsidy and state aid: WTO and EC law in comparative perspective. Oxford University Press, New York

Rydelski MS (2004) The EEA state aid regime. In: Biondi A, Eeckhout P, Flynn J (eds) The law of state aid in the European Union. Oxford University Press, Oxford
Saavedra Pinto C (2016) The 'narrow' meaning of the legitimate expectations principle in state aid law versus the foreign investor's legitimate expectations. Eur State Aid Law Q 15(2):270–285
Sauter W (1997) Competition law and industrial policy in the EU. Oxford University Press, Oxford
Schimmelfennig F (2012a) EU external governance and Europeanization beyond the EU. In: Levi-Faur D (ed) The Oxford handbook of governance. Oxford University Press, Oxford
Schimmelfennig F (2012b) Europeanization beyond Europe. Living Reviews in European Governance 7. https://doi.org/10.12942/lreg-2012-1
Schön W (2004) World Trade Organization law and tax law. International Bureau of Fiscal Documentation, Washington, DC
Schonberg M (2017) Continuity or change? State aid control in a post-Brexit United Kingdom. Compet Law J 1:47–57
Schutterle P (2002) Implementing of the EC state aid control: an accession criterion. Eur St Aid LQ 1(1):79–86
Slotboom M (1995) State aid in community law: a broad or narrow definition? Eur Law Rev 20:289
Smith MP (1998) Autonomy by the rules: the European commission and the development of state aid policy. J Common Mark Stud 36(1):55–78
Snyder F (1994) Soft law and institutional practice in the European community. In: Martin S (ed.), The construction of Europe:essays in honour of Emile Noël. Springer, Dordrecht
Stone Sweet A (2010) The European Court of Justice and the judicialization of EU governance. Living Reviews in EU Governance. https://papers.ssrn.com/sol3/papers.cfm?abstract_id=1583345
Sykes AO (2010) The questionable case for subsidies regulation: a comparative perspective. J Legal Anal 2(2):473–523
Szepesi S (2004) Comparing EU free trade agreements competition policy state aid. ECDPM, Maastricht
Szyszczak E (2011) Research handbook on European state aid law. Edward Elgar, Cheltenham
Szyszczak E, van de Gronden JW (2014) Financing services of general economic interest: reform and modernization. Springer, Dordrecht
Thomas KP (2007) Investment incentives: growing use, uncertain benefits, uneven controls. International Institute for Sustainable Development, Geneva
Tietje C (2013) Bilateral investment treaties between EU Member States (intra-EU-BITs): challenges in the multilevel system of law. Transnatl Disp Manage (TDM) 10(2) https://www.transnational-dispute-management.com/article.asp?key=1945
Tietje C, Wackernagel C (2014) Outlawing compliance? The enforcement of intra-EU investment awards and EU state aid law. Transnational Dispute Management (TDM) 3. https://www.transnational-dispute-management.com/article.asp?key=2116
Tietje C, Wackernagel C (2015) Enforcement of Intra-EU ICSID awards. J World Invest Trade 16(2):205–247
Tietje C, Sipiorski E, Töpfer G (2012) Responsibility in investor-state-arbitration in the EU: managing financial responsibility linked to investor-state dispute settlement tribunals established by EU's International Investment Agreements. European Union, Brussels
UNCTAD (2007) Voluntary peer review of competition policy: West African Economic and Monetary Union, Benin and Senegal – Overview. https://unctad.org/en/Docs/ditcclp20071overview_en.pdf
US Treasury (2016). The European Commission's recent state aid investigations of transfer pricing rulings. http://www.treasury.gov/resource-center/tax-policy/treaties/Documents/White-Paper-State-Aid.pdf
Valejo J (2019) Commission to strengthen anti-subsidies measures by end of year, Euractiv 14 March. https://www.euractiv.com/section/economy-jobs/news/commission-to-strengthen-anti-subsidies-measures-by-end-of-year

Van de Casteele K (2006) The international dimension of state aid. In: Rydelski MS (ed) The EC state aid regime: distortive effects of state aid on competition and trade. Cameron May, London

Van de Casteele K (2016) Changes and what drives them: Evolution of state aid control. In: Rubini L, Hawkins J (eds) What shapes the law? Reflections on the history, law, politics and economics of international and European subsidy disciplines. European University Institute, Florence

Vink M (2003) What is Europeanisation? And other questions on a new research agenda. Eur Polit Sci 3(1):63–74

Werner P, Verouden V (2016) EU state aid control: Law and economics. Kluwer, Geneva

WTO (2015) Understanding the WTO. https://www.wto.org/english/thewto_e/whatis_e/tif_e/understanding_e.pdf

WTO Panel (2011) United States: measures affecting trade in large civil aircraft (Second Complaint) – Second Complaint DS353. WTO, Geneva

WTOAP (2018) European communities: measures affecting trade in large civil aircraft. WTO, Geneva

Chapter 4
The Breaking Point: The *Micula Award*

4.1 Introduction

The *Micula* case is the most (in)famous case regarding intra-EU investment arbitration stemming from collisions between EU state aid law and intra-EU BITs.[1] This case is complicated to follow, as it has gone through several stages (see Appendix 3 of this book), which can roughly be divided into four phases.

- *Phase 1:* Initially the *Micula* case was a dispute settled under the rules of the ICSID Convention about a breach of the Sweden–Romania BIT FET provisions. The claimants were the *Micula* brothers and their three corporates, S.C. Starmill SRL, SC Multipack and SC European Food SA. The respondent was Romania. The ICSID Tribunal deemed Romania, by discontinuing incentives that had been scheduled to last for 10 years, to be in breach of the FET standard under the Sweden–Romania BIT and ordered Romania to pay €178 million to the claimants.
- *Phase 2:* The next phase of the *Micula* case was about a breach of EU law, as the Commission held that Romania's payments of the Award to the Miculas constituted illegal state aid. Therefore, Romania remained the respondent, but the claimant was now the Commission. The Commission ordered Romania to stop payments towards the *Micula Award*. Further, the Commission ordered Romania to claw back sums that it had already paid towards fulfilling the Award.
- *Phase 3:* The claimants, the Miculas, shopped for the enforcement of the Award in multiple jurisdictions against the respondent, Romania. Romania's plea was that it did not have the competence to go against the Commission's decision unless the CJEU annulled it. The Commission became part of this process as *amicus curie.*

[1] As can be read from Chaps. 1, 2 and 4.

P. Finckenberg-Broman, *Weaponizing EU State Aid Law to Impact the Future of EU Investment Policy in the Global Context*, Studies in European Economic Law and Regulation 23, https://doi.org/10.1007/978-3-031-10108-3_4

- *Phase 4:* The Miculas, again the claimants, appealed the decision of the Commission (the defendant) to the General Court.[2] The GC did not dispute that an ICSID Award could constitute illegal state aid.
- *Phase 5:* The Commission appealed this GC judgement to the ECJ. The ECJ set aside the General Court's decision regarding the applicability of EU law on Romania's pre-accession actions.[3]

However, this case is not the only collision between EU state aid law and intra-EU BITs. Investors have initiated intra-EU ISDS with increasing frequency since 2006.[4] In 2014, 16 per cent of all investment arbitrations brought globally was intra-EU in nature.[5] By 2016, intra-EU investment arbitration accounted for about a quarter of all investment disputes.[6] This is because:

- the Western European Members States mostly ignored the Commission's pressure and pleas from the Central and Eastern European Members States to phase out their intra-EU BITs.[7]
- the international investment tribunals systematically rejected these arguments, despite the Commission's protests that these proceedings and intra-EU BITs were incompatible with EU law and hence, wanted to phase them out. The intra-EU BITs obliged the Member States to honour the BIT provisions even when in direct violation of the EU treaties and threatened the autonomy of EU law.[8] However, investors preferred to rely on investment protection by intra-EU BITs

[2]The General Court annulled the Commission's decision in June 2019 because it held that state aid rules were not in conflict with intra-EU BITs and Awards stemming from these BITs where the measures related to the Tribunal's ordered compensation predated the EU law's entry into force. This took place on 1 January 2007 when Romania acceded to the EU: see *Micula V (EU)* (2019) paras 67 and 109. Therefore, the Commission lacked the competence to review Romania's pre-accession actions pursuant to Article 108 TFEU: see *Micula V (EU)* (2019) paras 74 and 77. See, to that effect, judgment of 20 March 2013, *Rousse Industry v Commission, T-489/11*, not published, EU:T:2013:144. The effect of this judgment was that two courts where the enforcement of the *Micula Award* had been stayed allowed for the enforcement of this Award. These two were the US District Court for the District of Columbia in *Ioan Micula et al. v. Goverment of Romania, Case No. 17-cv-02332 (APM)* 11 September 2019 (*Micula VI (USA)* and the UK Supreme Court in *Micula and others v Romania* [2020] UKSC 5, 19 February 2020 (*Micula UK3*).

[3]See the appeal brought on 27 August 2019 by the European Commission against the judgment of the General Court (Second Chamber, Extended Composition) delivered on 18 June 2019 in *Case T-624/15: European Food e.a. v Commission, Case C-638/19 P*.

[4]See European Commission (2016), Ch. 4.3, referring to UNCTAD database for data (UNCTAD 2016a, b). See also Commission (EC) (2015), pp. 5 and 6. By now there have been over 100 intra EU ISDS cases.

[5]UNCTAD IIA Issues Note 2015: UNCTAD (2015).

[6]UNCTAD IIA Issues Note 2017: UNCTAD (2017).

[7]See, for example, AFFGN (2016).

[8]For more on this, see Sects. 4.3 and 4.4. See also Chap. 5, elaborating on the issues that created conflict between intra-EU BITs and EU law that were the reasons the Commission wanted to phase these out. Chapter 5 also elaborates on why investors prefer to use intra-EU BITs rather than EU law.

as this system awards larger amounts of compensation and pays less heed to state interests.

Therefore, countries acceding to the EU found themselves targeted by claims arising from mandatory pre-accession streamlining of domestic legislation (particularly by removing incompatibilities with the EU *acquis*) with that of EU law in accordance with Article 4 TEU and Article 351 TFEU. Some of these awards have encompassed, at their core, the termination of an agreement due to its clash with EU state aid rules.

For example, in *AES v Hungary (III) Award* (2010), *Electrabel* (2012) and *EDF v Hungary* (2014) investor-state arbitration against Hungary was brought up by several investors under the Energy Charter Treaty's FET standard regarding Power Purchase Agreement termination claims. Dunamenti (the formerly publicly owned operator of Hungary's main power plant) and MVM (Hungary's only wholesale electricity buyer) had established this Power Purchase Agreement and, since 1995, foreign private investors had invested in it. In June 2008, the Power Purchase Agreement was found by the Commission to be illegal state aid.[9] The related annulment proceedings by the CJEU upheld the Commission's decision.[10] During the same time period, investor-state arbitration—for instance, *US Steel v Slovakia* (2013), based on the Netherlands-Slovak Republic BIT owing to Slovakia terminating the provision for exemptions to payment of electricity consumption charges and the *Micula* proceedings which led to the *Micula Award*, 2013—was also ongoing under intra-EU BITs. Behind both disputes were claims arising from the discontinuation of unlawful state aid.[11]

The Commission's role is to guard the EU Treaties,[12] so it can hardly ignore these continuous collisions of EU law with international investment law. By 2013, the Commission was losing its patience with the escalating number of intra-EU ISDS[13] and proclaimed that intra-EU BITs were not compatible with EU law.[14] Nonetheless,

[9] Commission's Decision 2009/609/EC (EC 2008) on State Aid C 41/2005. Hungary acceded to the EU in 2004.

[10] For example, see *Case T-179/09 Dunamenti Erőmű Zrt v Commission* (2014); *Joined cases T-80/06 and T-182/09 Budapesti Erőmű Zrt v Commission* (2012); *C-357/14 P – Electrabel and Dunamenti Erőmű v Commission* (2015).

[11] *Commission Amicus Curiae Brief in US Steel Global Holdings v The Slovak Republic* (2014) and Commission decision *C (2014) 1676 final US Steel* (2014). See also Sect. 4.3.3 below.

[12] The Commission being the executive organ of the EU.

[13] This is visible in the Commission's decision C (2014) 1676 final US Steel, para 5 which states that 'US Steel is not entitled to continue to receive what appears to be State aid ... nor is it entitled to receive compensation for the elimination by the Slovak Republic of that aid measure.'

[14] Paras 7 and 8 of this decision clarified that intra-EU BITs 'can only continue to be applied to the extent that they are compatible with the Member States' obligations under Union law' and that the Commission held 'that bilateral investment treaties between Member States may be contrary to Union law'.

the *Micula Award*,[15] which surfaced after the Lisbon Treaty added FDI to the EU's exclusive competence, was about ISDS proceeding *vis-à-vis* the collision of state aid law and a BIT.[16] After these proceedings resulted in an Award in direct violation of state aid law, the Romanian court chose to follow international investment law over EU law.[17] Effectively, this disregard of EU law brought the clash between state aid rules and intra-EU BITs to a point where the Commission felt compelled to act.

4.2 Overview

This chapter builds on the know-how provided in the previous chapters of state aid law and the international investment regime. The purpose of the chapter is to determine the issues arising from situations when a Member State's investment policy is not in line with EU state aid law, and there exists an international investment treaty entered into between EU Member States that challenges the EU judicial system. This chapter particularly asks what problems follow where the international investment regime, as applied and interpreted by international investment tribunals, necessitate that Member States act against the EU state aid law.

Fundamentally, what are the Member States to do when, to fulfil their obligations stemming from an international investment treaty, they (1) are to act in direct violations of the EU treaties, (2) effectively reclaim the power to mandate state aid measures from the EU, and (3) disobey decisions made by the Commission and the CJEU. This chapter examines the consequences of the Member States' actions, depending on the choices made.[18]

The previous chapter explained and outlined the reasons why economic benefits given by the Member States to firms are governed by state aid law and how this is regulated and enforced within the EU. Fundamentally, the Member States have given the EU exclusive power on matters regarding state aid control. This means that it is the EU and its institutions, not the Member States, that are the source of power on state aid law. Article 107(1) TFEU is the legal basis that prohibits all intervening public measures favouring certain undertakings, which distort or threatens to distort competition between the Member States, omitting their purpose unless justified as being in the common interest.

As explained in Sects. 3.5.1 to 3.5.3 in Chap. 3, a measure that has been implemented by the Member State and provided to a firm in a breach of Article 107(1) TFEU, State aid law requires that it must be suspended or discontinued by the

[15] *Micula Award* (2013). See also *Micula I (USA)* (2015a); *Micula III (USA)* (2016); *Micula I (USA)* (2015b); *Micula IV (USA)* (2017); *Micula II (USA)* (2015); *Micula V (USA)* (2017).

[16] The *Micula Award* (2013) is likely the first ISDS proceeding *vis-à-vis* the collision of state aid law and a BIT with which the Commission had to deal directly after the Lisbon Treaty.

[17] The Award was not set aside by the Romanian national court.

[18] Namely, to obey international investment law as governed by BITs or EU law.

Member State. It is the Commission that initiates this clawback procedure (see Sect. 3.5.3). The Commission may order the Member State, which has granted unlawful state aid to firms, to recover it. When there are no other international legal obligations involved, this is a relatively straightforward system; however, in an opposite situation, it becomes much more complicated. The clawback procedure is identified as the likely cause of the collision between the state aid regime and the international investment regime.

This chapter confirms that these treaty conflicts are often initiated by the clawback procedures,[19] which in turn lead to a breach of the principle of legitimate expectations (by IIL but not by state aid law) due to the completely opposite ways in which the international investment tribunals and the sphere of state aid law interpret and apply this principle.[20] Further, the broader implications of court shopping are considered, particularly where investors seek indirect ways to force Member States to breach EU law in favour of the international investment regime by bringing their enforcement claims for Awards to courts of third countries. If the outcome of such a process would lead to a decision in favour of the investor, this decision would effectively rebuff the EU's mandate within the core of its powers and transfer this power to the international investment regime.

Moreover, because state aid control prevents the Member States favouring some firms over others where it potentially harms the internal market, it effectively prohibits discrimination against undertakings in a comparable situation. Therefore, this chapter also implicitly discusses the second argument of this book: that intra-EU BITs are inherently discriminatory. Indeed, this chapter shows that intra-EU BITs have empowered foreign investors to receive and keep unlawful state aid received by way of investment incentives, such as tax breaks designed to attract FDI or individual long-term contracts with fixed tariffs, where other investors cannot. This is demonstrated through the judgements of international investment tribunals, which have perceived these state aid measures as protected under fair and equal treatment, umbrella or expropriation clauses in BITs,[21] as demonstrated by the *Micula case*.[22]

Using a case study of the *Micula Award*,[23] and the substantial and procedural legal complications that followed,[24] as an example of how this situation can play out in practice, this chapter reveals how confusing and onerous legal debates between the international bodies may be to states and individuals alike. In addition to causing substantial legal uncertainty to all parties, a sovereign Member State faces two

---

[19] Because state aid granted contrary to Articles 107 and 108 TFEU launches enforcement procedures as codified by the Procedural Regulation.

[20] See Sect. 3.5.3 in Chap. 3 for more details on this subject.

[21] Hindelang (2012b), p. 223.

[22] *Micula Award* (2013).

[23] *Micula Award* (2013). See also Commission's decisions: *Micula I (EU)* (2014); *Micula II (EU)* (2014); *Micula III (EU)* (2016); and for CJEU proceedings, *Micula V (EU)* (2019) and *Micula VI (EU)* (2022). See also *Micula I (USA)* (2015a); *Micula I (USA)* (2015b); *Micula III (USA)* (2016).

[24] See Appendix 3 of this thesis for a detailed timeline regarding the *Micula* proceedings.

conflicting obligations: one to follow the terms of the BIT and the other to abide by EU state aid law. Subsequently, a Member State acting in compliance with one legal framework leads to its non-compliance with the other legal framework, resulting in possible sanctions.[25]

Furthermore, although the *Micula* case study is of an intra-EU nature, it is applicable to a broader setting when examined by analogy in situations where the same core issues are replicated unless IIAs of which the EU is a part sufficiently guarantee that these do not breach state aid law. Therefore, this chapter supports the theoretical basis for the hypotheses of this book. In effect, it provides an essential building block that connects the other chapters of this monograph by visualising the continuous power struggle of international bodies—in this case, the EU and international investment regime—over state policy and law as it applies to and affects the actions of sovereign states.

This chapter is divided into three sub-chapters, reflecting the different stages of the legal process that *Micula* has gone through, as well as the spillover effects this case has had on the EU, its Member States, third states and the international trade and investment regime in general.

The first sub-chapter focuses on the *Micula* proceedings and consists of four parts, which address the breach of EU state aid measures on several stages in different processes for the *Micula* case, deliberate on the disputes of the compliance by the Member State (here Romania) with the Award, elaborate the conflict between compliance, and which legal order gets to decide over the matter, and address the legal actions the state aid beneficiary may take to claim this benefit despite it being in breach of EU law by using the international investment regime.

The second sub-chapter discusses the legal dilemma at hand. It begins by discussing the treaty conflict and its effect on the Member States before discussing the trigger that initiates this conflict then elaborating the struggle faced by public international law when dealing with distinct legal regimes like that of the EU.[26]

The third sub-chapter provides analyses of the issues discussed and concludes that where an IIA is covering the international relations of an EU Member State or perhaps even the EU itself with a third country, there is an unresolved conflict between state aid law and the implementation of these laws by the Member States.

---

[25] For breaching an international investment agreement, the sanctions are Awards. For breaching EU law, the sanctions are EU infringement procedures, which may lead to fines, penalty payments and liability for damages. For more on this, see Sect. 3.4.4 in Chap. 3.

[26] *Saluka* was followed by, *inter alia*, *Eastern Sugar – Final Award* (2007); *Eastern Sugar – Partial Award*, (2007); *Binder v Czech Republic Award* (2007); *Achmea v Slovak Republic* (2008); *AES v Hungary (III) Award* (2010); Eureko (2010); *Oostergetel v Slovak Republic* (2010); *Achmea BV Final Award* (2012); *Electrabel Decision on Jurisdiction* (2012); *US Steel v Slovakia* (2013); *EDF v Hungary* (2014); *Electrabel Award* (2015); *Charanne Final Award* (2016); *RREEF Infrastructure* (2016); *Isolux Award* (2016); *WNC Award* (2017); *Anglia Auto Accessories Final Award* (2017); *Eiser Award* (2017); *Novoenergia Award* (2018). For more on this subject, see Chap. 5.

4.3 The Bad Beginnings

The *Micula*[27] case was very likely the first state aid case the Commission had to deal with directly after the Lisbon Treaty conferred on the EU exclusive competence in FDI. It is rooted to a Romanian (pre-accession to EU) fiscal aid scheme including exemptions from profit tax, customs duties and granting of privileged subsidies[28] by Emergency Government Ordinance ('EGO 24') for disfavoured regions.[29] EGO 24, intended to exist for 10 years only, and launched in April 1999, clashed initially with EU state aid rules, implemented into the Romanian legal framework by Statutory Act No. 143/1999.[30] Romania, however, had already committed to harmonising its domestic legislation with that of the EU's *acquis communautaire* by entering an Association Agreement (European Agreement) with the EU in 1993, which entered into force in 1995.[31] European Agreement Article 64.1(iii) notably prohibits state aid.[32] Therefore, EGO 24 was incompatible with the EU's internal market rules from the day Romania implemented it.

4.3.1 *The Incompatibility Issues*

Already incompatible with the EU's internal market rules, according to the ex-ante evaluation by the Romanian Council of Competition,[33] this scheme laid the seed for future conflict, as the Romanian Government chose to disregard the decision of its

---

[27] The *Micula Award* (2013) started a lengthy procedure of appeals and cases. See *Micula I (EU)* (2014); *Micula II (EU)* (2014); *Micula III (EU)* (2016). The first *Micula* appeal to the CJEU was withdrawn by the appellant for amendment as of 29 February 2016. The second appeal, *Micula V (EU)* (2019) was decided in favour of the claimants by the CJEU (General Court). The General Court held that state aid rules were not in conflict with intra-EU BITs and Awards stemming from these BITs, provided the measures related to the Tribunal's ordered compensation predated the EU law's entry into force. In *Micula VI (EU)* (2022) the CJEU's Grand Chamber found in favor of the Commission, i.e., that the General Court erred in law in its assessment that EU law did not apply to the arbitral award. For more on this, see Sect. 4.3.3 below. See also *Micula I (USA)* (2015a); *Micula I (USA)* (2015b); *Micula III (USA)* (2016).

[28] *Micula Award* (2013).

[29] Article 107(3)(a) and (c). TFUE covers disfavoured regions for regional aid. Disfavoured regions are socio-economically disadvantaged by, *inter alia*, high unemployment or economic development. The EU publishes a map, drawn by the Member States, which identifies the regions qualifying as disfavoured, which may be considered for internal market-compatible state aid. See European Commission Regional policy Maps at http://ec.europa.eu/regional_policy/en/information/maps.

[30] For the full timeline, see Appendix 3.

[31] By Articles 69 and 71 of the European Agreement.

[32] On State aid, see SA.38517 (2014/C) (ex 2014/NN) implemented by Romania) para 12.

[33] Romanian Competition Council (2000); *Micula Award* (2013) para 205. See also *Micula II (EU)* (2014) para 16. the Romanian Council of Competition was and still is the national administrative body in charge of upholding competition laws.

own competition authority.[34] Effectively, the EGO 24 scheme, selective due to its regional character and sponsored by the Romanian state, provided advantages to the undertakings receiving aid. The incentives—some of which distorted competition—should have been terminated in 2000 when the Romanian Council of Competition declared them state aid for operating purposes and subject to removal. However, the amending Act, Emergency Government Ordinance 75/2000 ('EGO 75'),[35] failed to implement the amendments that the Competition Council stated were necessary. The incompatibility with EU state aid of EGO 24 and EGO 75 was even pointed out by the Commission in the context of the Romanian accession to the EU negotiations.[36]

A year after ratification of the Romania–Sweden BIT in 2003,[37] Romania repealed all economic incentives in force due to amending its legislation in accordance with EU state aid rules. However, this revocation was four years ahead of the original schedule.[38] Revocation, which took effect on February 2005, was followed by initiation of *Micula v Romania* infringement proceedings based on the Romania–Sweden BIT four months later.[39] In 2013, an ICSID ad hoc tribunal awarded the Miculas some €85 million plus interest as damages due to a disregard of the principle of legitimate expectations.[40] By not maintaining the incentives for the scheduled 10-year period as the investor had expected, Romania was in breach of the fair and equitable standard under the BIT. However, the execution of the *Micula Award* proved to be a lengthy process.

4.3.2 Execution Proceedings in Romania

Because Romania discontinued incentives that had been scheduled to last for 10 years, an ICSID tribunal decided it was in breach of the fair and equitable standard under the Sweden–Romania BIT. However, the execution of the *Micula Award* proved to be a complicated process. In early 2014, to execute the *Micula Award,* Romania proceeded to pay the Award to the claimants[41] but failed to notify

---

[34] *Micula Award* (2013), para 207.

[35] *Micula II EU Final* (2015), para 16.

[36] See *Micula II EU Final* (2015) para 19 and *Micula III (USA)* (2016), p. 14 n. 11 referring to the Conference on Accession to the European Union – Romania, European Union Common Position of 21 November 2001 on Chap. 6 – Competition Policy, CONF-RO 43/01 (Dkt. 43, Ex. 5).

[37] For the Sweden–Romania BIT, see https://investmentpolicy.unctad.org.

[38] See European Commission final Decision ('*Micula II EU final,*' 2015) para 18.

[39] See https://investmentpolicyhub.unctad.org/ISDS/Details/180. The Micula claimants are Romanian brothers who gained Swedish citizenship—Ioan in 1992 and Viorel in 1995 (Knahr 2010).

[40] *Micula Award* (2013).

[41] See EC (2014) para 3 and *Micula II EU Final* (2015) para 3. According to the Commission (*Micula II EU Final*, 2015, para 11), these payments were made voluntarily by the Romanian Ministry of Finance.

these payments *ex-ante* to the Commission in line with the notification obligation outlined in Article 108(3) TFEU.[42]

A month later, four[43] of the five claimants also succeeded in their application for execution of the Award based on Article 54 of the ICSID Convention to a Bucharest Court of the first instance.[44] The execution of the *Micula Award* was interrupted by the Bucharest Tribunal,[45] due to a Commission injunction order, addressed to Romania, on May 2014 because the execution of the remaining part of the *Micula Award* would constitute unlawful state aid, and was thus invalid.[46]

Four months later, the Bucharest Tribunal lifted the suspension after an ICSID ad hoc committee, in September 2014, ruled the enforcement of the *Micula Award* to take place regardless of ongoing ICSID annulment proceedings. This decision was due to Romania's refusal to pay the full award unconditionally in case the appeal failed.[47] The Bucharest Tribunal also ignored the Commission's request to refer the matter to the CJEU for a preliminary ruling based on Article 267 TFEU.[48] As a result, the claimants received approximately €10 million more in direct violation of two separate Commission decisions regarding state aid.[49] On 24 February 2015, the Bucharest Court of Appeal intervened and stayed the required ICSID enforcement proceedings of the Award. Since then, Romania has passed a law suspending all these enforcement actions and has sealed the remaining amount from access by the *Micula* claimants unless the Commission releases the payments by approval of the aid as internal market compatible.[50]

4.3.3 *Micula Award* Was Unlawful State Aid

Further payments of the *Micula Award* being conditional on the Commission's approval of the aid as internal market compatible caused Romania to put these on hold.[51] Because the Commission held that the payments (by Romania) to

[42] See EC (2014), paras 2 and 3. For the 108(3) TFEU notification obligation, see Sect. 3.5.1 in Chap. 3.

[43] These were Ion Micula and the four corporate claimants (*Micula II EU Final*, 2015) para 31.

[44] See EC (2014), para 21; *Micula II EU Final* (2015) para 32. See also *Micula Anullment Proceedings* (2016), para 70.

[45] *Micula II EU Final* (2015) para 33.

[46] Suspension injunction proceedings are regulated by Article 11 of Regulation (EC) No 659/1999. (Council 1999). This Regulation is replaced as of 14.10.2015 with Council Regulation (EU) 2015/1589 (Council 2015).

[47] *Micula II EU Final*, 2015) paras 28, 29 and 34.

[48] *Micula II EU Final* (2015) paras 28, 29, 33 and 34.

[49] For the Commission decisions of 26 May 2014 and 1 October 2014, see *Micula II EU Final* (2015) paras 11, 35, 37.

[50] *Micula II EU Final* (2015), paras 11, 35, 37.

[51] *Micula II EU Final* (2015), paras 11, 35, 37.

compensate the *Micula Award* constituted internal market-incompatible state aid within the meaning of Article 107(1) TFEU, the release of these payments did not take place before 18 June 2018 on order of the CJEU's General Court.[52] The GC implied that a post-accession ICSID Award could constitute illegal state aid.[53] Unfortunately, the GC chose not to analyse such a situation in more detail. However, further clarity on the subject will be forthcoming because the Commission's successful appeal against the GC's decision, case *C-638/19 P - Commission v European Food and Others (Micula VI (EU))* to the European Court of Justice. The ECJ (Grand Chamber) held that EU law was applicable, *ratione temporis*, to the arbitral award because it was adopted post-accession and therefore the Commission had the competence to decide on state aid under Article 108 TFEU. I.e., the GC has now to analyse if the Commission's findings were accurate and the *Micula Award* constituted illegal state aid.

The Commission had held that the payments by Romania against the Award constituted new aid,[54] as Romania granted these after its accession to the EU, and as a definite advantage for the claimants only arising from the ICSID Convention.[55] The sum of the Award equalled advantages predicted under the obliterated EGO 24 scheme, from the date it was repealed until its expected expiry *plus* predicted profits lost.[56] In effect, it restored incompatible state aid subject to recovery (as the basis for the *Micula Award*, the EGO 24 never fulfilled the criteria for existing aid as featured in the Act of Accession of Romania, Annex V, Chapter 2, n. 1).[57] Further, the failure of Romania to notify the Award *ex-ante* in line with Article 108(3) TFEU renders the Award unlawful state aid.[58] Illegal state aid is subject to an immediate

[52] The General Court annulled the Commission state aid decision SA.38517(2014/C because it held that state aid rules were not in conflict with intra-EU BITs and Awards stemming from these BITs provided the measures related to the Tribunal's ordered compensation predated the EU law's entry into force: *Micula II EU Final* (2015), paras 11, 35, 37. According to the General Court it made no difference that the *Micula Award* was rendered after Romania's accession to the EU because the Award referred mostly to measures had been implemented before pre-accession: *Micula V (EU)* (2019), paras 71–93. Further, the General Court explained that the Commission could not retroactively apply its executive powers under Article 108 TFEU and Procedural Regulation 1999 to a time when EU law was not yet in force in Romania: *Micula V (EU)* (2019), para 92.

[53] Because the CJEU's decisions to annul the Commission's decision was based on the fact that the Commission had not clarified the distinction between the pre- and post-accession periods in its decision: *Micula II EU Final* (2015). Otherwise, the CJEU's decision might have had a different outcome.

[54] The Award did not qualify as existing aid or fit into the block exemptions. See Sect. 3.5.2 in Chap. 3 for incompatible or illegal state aid.

[55] *Micula II EU Final* (2015), paras 134 and 137.

[56] *Micula II EU Final* (2015), para 135.

[57] *Micula II EU Final* (2015), para 136. The CJEU in *C-357/14 P – Electrabel and Dunamenti Erőmű v Commission* (2015), paras 59–62 confirms this type of reasoning.

[58] Procedural Regulation Article 1(f) defines new aid put into effect in breach of Art 108(3)3 TFEU as illegal. New aid is defined as either non-existing aid or altered existing aid. See also Council (2015) Art 1(c).

suspension of payments, and a clawback including a commercial rate of interest counted from the date which the beneficiary had access to the sum of the aid granted so far.[59]

On these bases, in March 2015 the Commission, after finding the new state aid incompatible with the internal market, ordered Romania to initiate clawback procedures to recover payments it had carried out to compensate the Award winners.[60] Since then, the claimants—the Micula brothers and the three companies—have tried to access the money from the Award via other jurisdictions.

4.3.4 Going on a Forum Shopping Spree

Since the Commission's decision in March 2015[61] and Romania's failed appeal to an ICSID tribunal,[62] the *Micula Award* winners have applied for enforcement in many different countries,[63] displaying a vibrant example of court shopping. In Europe, these award winners appealed to the CJEU.[64] Further, they have raised enforcement proceedings on a national level in several EU countries without much success. The five claimants have sought recognition of the Award in Belgium, France, Luxembourg, Romania and the United Kingdom.[65] However, only in Belgium and Romania have enforcement proceedings been commenced, with a Belgian court refusing enforcement in deference to the final decision.[66] In the United Kingdom, the High Court of Justice of England and Wales (Commercial Court) stayed the enforcement in January 2017 until a decision from the CJEU and another decision from the same High Court rejected the applicants' requests for a Security Order on 15 June 2017.[67]

[59] *C-120/73 – Lorenz v Germany* (1973) para 8 for the direct effect of Article 108(3). See also 'the Procedural Regulation' Articles 10(2), 11(2); *C-301/87 – France v Commission (Boussac)* (1990), paras 9–24 and *Micula II (EU)* (2014). For more details on the clawback procedure, see Chap. 3.

[60] European Commission Decision (*Micula II (EU)*' 2014). It was incompatible as the scheme filled the cumulative criteria of Art 107.1 TFEU and was not exempted individually or by a block exemption. For state aid legislation, see Chap. 1. Because Romania had not fully recovered these payments, which totalled €92 million, by the Commission's deadline (31 July 2015), the Commission decided in December 2018 to refer Romania to the ECJ for violation of EU state aid rules regarding failure to abide by the Commission's decision (*Micula II (EU)*, 2014; Commission, 7 December 2019).

[61] European Commission Decision (*Micula II (EU)* (2014).

[62] See *Micula Anulment Proceedings* (2016).

[63] *Micula I (UK)* (2017); *Micula UK2* (2017).

[64] *Micula V (EU)* (2019).

[65] See Commissions *Amicus Curia* for the US Court of Appeals brief p. 16: *Micula III (USA)* (2016).

[66] See European Commission, *Amicus Curiae* Brief: *Micula III (USA)* (2016).

[67] *Micula I (UK)* (2017) and *Micula UK2* (2017), which recognised that essentially any substantive finding of EU law would give rise to a significant risk of conflict with ongoing proceedings in the CJEU to annul the final decision (Struckmann et al. 2017).

The *Micula Award* winners also took the dispute outside the EU, to a Washington and New York district court, for enforcement.[68] While the Washington court deemed that the Foreign Sovereign Immunities Act of 1976, 28 USC §1650a[69] did not permit *ex parte* recognition of ICSID Awards, the New York court ruled in favour of the appellants.[70] Romania, backed by the Commission, successfully appealed this decision to the Court of Appeals of the Second Circuit of the USA.[71] The Court of Appeals for the Second Circuit rejected *ex parte* enforcement of ICSID Awards against foreign states in July 2017, in line with an earlier decision on Exxon Mobil subsidiaries against Venezuela *(Mobil II).*[72] Because the conduct behind the claim lacked any connection to New York, the District Court of New York lacked subject matter and personal jurisdiction over Romania.[73]

4.4 The Thorny Dilemma

The *Micula* case resulted out of two conflicting obligations of a sovereign state, one to follow the terms of the BIT and the other to abide by EU state aid law. Consequently, for a Member State, the application of one legal framework would

---

[68] *Micula Annulment Proceedings* (2016); *Micula I (USA)* (2015); *Micula II (USA)* (2015). The same New York court also ruled to enforce the *Eiser Award (USA I)* (2017) in June 2017.

[69] *Arbitration Awards Under the Convention* (2011).

[70] See note 71 below for the Southern District of New York's reasoning for its decision.

[71] *Micula III (USA)* (2016); *Micula IV USA* (2017). This decision also enabled Spain to vacate the New York Court enforcement decision in November 2017 in *Eiser Award (USA I)* (2017).

[72] *Mobil II* (2017). According to the Court of Appeals, the Southern District of New York had erred in rejecting the Foreign Sovereign Immunities Act as the governing rule over the enforcement of ICSID awards against foreign sovereigns. 28 USC § 1608 (Foreign Sovereign Immunities Act of 1976, 1976). The US Court of Appeals held that the Foreign Sovereign Immunities Act was the sole basis for jurisdiction over foreign sovereigns and its procedures and therefore venue requirements must be met before enforcement of the Award may take place: *Mobil II* (2017); *Micula IV USA* (2017), pp. 5–6. It further held that as the conduct behind the claim lacked any connection to New York, the District Court of New York lacked subject matter and personal jurisdiction over Romania. By its decision that baulked at the use of streamlined procedures based on the Foreign Sovereign Immunities Act against sovereign defendants, it is quite clear that the US Court of Appeals applied the principles of comity and negative comity. These principles are international and apply to all nations; hence it follows that national courts lacking a direct connection to the dispute are reluctant to take a stance against foreign sovereign states regarding conflicting treaty obligations.

[73] *Micula IV USA* (2017), p. 6. The principle of negative comity should also be applicable here. According to the OECD (2015), p. 1, negative comity 'involves a country's consideration of how to prevent its laws and law enforcement actions from harming another country's important interests'. Essentially, negative comity is conflict avoidance, yet several more intra-EU arbitration cases under the Energy Charter Treaty were brought to the US District Court for Columbia in 2018 for enforcement—three cases in June (*Novenergia II (USA)*, pending; *Antin (USA)*, pending; *Eiser Award (USA III)*, pending) and one in September by Masdar Solar & Wind Cooperatief UA, a United Arab Emirates-owned and Dutch-incorporated company: *Masdar v Spain (USA)* (pending).

constitute a breach of the other, resulting in possible sanctions.[74] The Member States, like Romania in *Micula*, may be torn between which set of rules to follow. As demonstrated, there may be an internal conflict between public organs within the Member State on the application of EU state aid law. Also, due to the sky-high costs of arbitration,[75] the Member State authorities could be hesitant to enforce EU state aid law when facing the threat of arbitration.

4.4.1 The Treaty Conflicts

The authorities of Member States, as happened in Romania in *Micula*, may be uncertain about which set of rules to follow.[76] Also, by following one legal framework, the Member State may be in breach of another legal framework, resulting in possible sanctions that may even go beyond economic compensation. According to the *Micula Award* Tribunal, restitution in the form of the reinstitution of the terminated legal framework was theoretically possible under the ICSID Convention, as the treaty does not articulate exclusion of this remedy.[77] In other words, investors may attempt to intimidate Member States to revive schemes that contradict state aid law in direct violation of EU primary law. This is an impossible requirement, as a Member State cannot act and legislate contrary to state aid law, as it is exclusively the competence of the EU.

Indeed, the position rejecting any de jure conflicts 'between intra-EU BITs and state aid law' that has been adopted by several scholars and arbitrators[78] is incorrect. An international treaty does not annul state aid law, and an external tribunal cannot make decisions on EU law that bind the EU institutions—for example, so that they cannot regulate.[79] The same circumstances should be valid for extra-EU BITs as

---

[74] Kokott and Sobotta (2016), pp. 11–12.

[75] See UNICTRAL (2018), paras 14–16; Sands (2016), p. 893; Kokott and Sobotta (2016), pp. 11–12; Van Harten and Malysheuski (2016), p. 9; European Commission (2016). See also Gaukrodger and Gordon (2013), p. 19; Friedland (2015), p. 2.

[76] The legal practice of tribunals, even now: Roberts (2013), p. 95; Koutrakos (2016), p. 880. See also Koskenniemi and Leino (2002), p. 558.

[77] *Micula Award* (2013), paras 1309–1312. However, due to procedural grounds and based on merits, the claimants' request for definitive injunctive relief was dismissed by the tribunal: *Micula Award* (2013), paras 1315–1319.

[78] Ortolani (2015), p. 121 et seq; Tietje and Wackernagel (2014), p. 3 et seq, referring to *T-384/08 – Elliniki* (2011); *T-62/08 – ThyssenKrupp Acciai Speciali Terni v Commission* (2010); *Joined Cases C-448/10 P to C-450/10 P – ThyssenKrupp Acciai Speciali Terni and Others v Commission* (2011) para 101 and *C-61/79 – Denkavit* (1980), para 31. See also Struckmann et al. (2016) and Lavranos (2015). For counter-arguments, see Hindelang (2012a); Kende (2015), pp. 41–43 referring to *T-384/08 – Elliniki* (2011); Lamadrid de Pablo (2015); Rovetta and Gambardella (2015).

[79] See *Achmea C-284/16* (2018) and *Micula II EU Final* (2015). In *Micula II EU Final* (2015), the GCEU held that acts occurring post-EU law coming into force and being applied could cause situations of incompatibility between observance of rendered arbitral awards and state aid: *Micula V*

well, unless these include disconnection clauses that safeguard the primacy of EU law. A treaty conflict leading to liability for Member States to compensate investors for implementing 'non-expected' EU measures or repealing illegal state aid to restore the competitive neutrality between the investors is harmful from an EU perspective. Behind this conflict is the radical difference in how state aid law and investment treaty law interpret and apply the concept of legitimate expectations.

4.4.2 *Legitimate Expectations Challenging the Validity of EU Law*

The opposite approach to the principle of legitimate expectations is the issue that triggers the treaty conflict between EU state aid law and the international investment regime.[80] In the sphere of state aid, the acceptance of an undertaking's legitimate expectations is extraordinarily narrow, while the same notion is overly broad and ambiguously formulated under FET clauses in investment treaty law.[81] *Micula* underlined the immense difference between the principle of legitimate expectations under fair and equal treatment (FET), the most successfully invoked BIT clause for challenging regulatory measures of host countries,[82] and legitimate expectations under EU state aid law.

Protection of legitimate expectations has emerged as a distinct category within the extensive scope of the FET standard.[83] FET clauses are usually vaguely worded, leaving much to interpretation but without sufficient guidance to aid the

(EU)' (2019) para. 91 'as regards the amounts granted as compensation for the period subsequent to Romania's accession to the European Union, namely, the period from 1 January 2007 to 1 April 2009, even assuming that the payment of compensation relating to that period could be classified as incompatible aid, given that the Commission did not draw a distinction between the periods of compensation for the damage suffered by the applicants before or after accession, the Commission has, in any event, exceeded its powers in the area of State aid review'.

[80] Saavedra Pinto (2016), p. 285.

[81] Saavedra Pinto (2016), p. 285.

[82] *Micula Award* (2013), para 667. See also Johnson and Volkov (2014), p. 3; Matei and Ciurtin (2016), p. 33; Gaukrodger (2017), p. 5. FET clauses are also incorporated in FTAs that include investment chapters. Se, for example, EU–Singapore Free Trade Agreement (EUSFTA) (EU and Singapore 2017), Article 9.4; and CETA (EU and Canada 2016), Article 8.10.

[83] Rösch (2017), p. 44; Hindelang (2012a), p. 232; Saavedra Pinto (2016), p. 277; Matei (2015). This fact was confirmed by the *Micula* Tribunal. The Tribunal also noted that the claims on legitimate expectations were most successful: *Micula Award* (2013), para 677.

interpreter.[84] Also, neither the variable context of FET clauses[85] nor the narrowing of the definition by some international investment tribunals practice has been reflected in the application of legitimate expectations by other international investment tribunals.[86] Instead, this concept has expanded.[87]

In EU law, there is no single provision for FET; instead, there are different legal principles that combine to protect the individual. Since the EU focuses on the rule of law, the scope of interpretation for legitimate expectations varies.[88] FET standards of BITs are deeply incompatible with EU competition law, where a beneficiary of state aid cannot enjoy the protection derived from the principle of legitimate expectations before a measure has been notified and approved by the Commission,[89] as stipulated by the provisions of Article 108(3) TFEU. Before Romania's accession, the Romanian Competition Council retained this authority. It exercised its authority by endorsing the removal of internal market-incompatible elements in EGO 24, in May 2000, two years ahead of signing the Sweden–Romania BIT. Subsequently,

---

[84] Saavedra Pinto (2016), p. 267; Gélinas and Jadeau (2016), p. 2 referring to a doctoral thesis written in French; Raux (2010), p. 179; Gaukrodger (2017), p. 5; Vandevelde (2010), p. 46. See also *EDF (Services) Limited v Romania, Award* (2009) para 215. Relevant cases for attempts of establishing a definition for legitimate expectations are ICSID Case No. ARB(AF)/00/2 (*Tecmed*) (2003) para 154; *Saluka* (2006), paras 305–306 and *LG&E* (2006). *Tecmed* set the standard of protection as extremely broad for investors, while the host states needed to uphold a regulatory limbo: *LG&E* (2006). The scope was narrowed later by *Saluka* and *LG&E*, which recognised the nation's right to regulate and the necessity of separating normal business risk from legitimate expectations.

[85] Vandevelde (2010), p. 47; Gaukrodger (2017), p. 5.

[86] Saavedra Pinto (2016), p. 277; Gaukrodger (2017), p. 5.

[87] Van Harten (2013), pp. 101–103; Saavedra Pinto (2016), p. 277; Johnson and Volkov (2014), p. 3.

[88] Kleinheisterkamp (2012), p. 418. Legal certainty and legitimate expectations are general principles of EU law. However, economic operators are expected to do proper due diligence and 'reckon with regulatory change as business risk'; see Saavedra Pinto (2016), p. 270 and Sharpston (1990). The EU investors also enjoy the protection of NT by the prohibition of discrimination on grounds of nationality in Article 18 TEU. Also, Article 26 TFEU highlights that the internal market rules embrace the principle of non-discrimination. Free movement of establishment, Article 54(1) TFEU, and free movement of capital, Articles 63 and 64 TFEU, ensure that investors can establish a business in any EU country and move their capital. Further, Articles 56, 62, 52 TFEU enable EU companies (including investors) to provide their services in all the Member States. Foreign investors are also protected by the Charter Articles 6, 15, 17, 41 and 47 which establish fundamental rights such as the right to property, fair compensation, good administration and access to effective justice. EU law also covers state liability where the Member States of the EU institutions have caused damages to individuals by violating their freedoms and rights in line with the Francovich doctrine. For more on the Francovich doctrine see Sect. 3.5.3 of Chap. 3, fn. 194.

[89] This has been confirmed repeatedly by the CJEU case law, which has held that beneficiaries of aid have a duty to check the lawfulness of the aid: Jestaedt et al. (2006). See also generally Hindelang (2012a), p. 232; Saavedra Pinto (2016); Tietje and Wackernagel (2014); Matei and Ciurtin (2016).

the investors relying on fiscal incentives from the EGO24 scheme were never entitled to be protected by legitimate expectations due to the unlawful origins.[90]

Despite the underlying legitimacy issues[91] and the fact that the Tribunal recognised that Romania had acted reasonably and non-discriminatorily,[92] the decision was in favour of the claimants. In contrast to *Eastern Sugar*[93] and *EES v Hungary*,[94] the status of Romania as an accession state was not given any weight. Nor did the Tribunal apply an objectivity test.[95]

The Tribunal in *Micula* chose to not consider the impact of EU law on the dispute or the arguments on the enforceability of the Award due to technicalities, even though the Tribunal acknowledged that EU law might be relevant to the case.[96] By solely concentrating on practice by prior investment arbitration award Tribunals, CJEU case law essential to the *Micula Award*, legitimate expectations under state aid law were ignored.

4.4.3 In a Void, There Can Be a Conflict

Micula[97] demonstrates a clash of these supranational parallel international legal frameworks, each with its legal systems, procedures, rules and agendas. Where there is a dilemma about the relationship between investment treaty laws, the

[90] Tietje and Wackernagel (2014), p. 3, Matei and Ciurtin (2016) and Ortolani (2015) agree that reinstating illegal state aid by means of an Award does not 'whitewash' the economic benefit.

[91] Stanivukovixc informs us that the Micula brothers were familiar with the Romanian market, had full access to domestic justice and ought to have been aware of the uncertain future of the EGO 24 scheme. The disputed initial investment was made before the launch of the EGO 24 scheme, with additional investment made in the following years despite the legitimacy of scheme being contested by the Commission and the Romanian Competition Council. In fact, The Miculas' efforts to claim tax exemptions were coupled with tax evasion: *Micula Anulment Proceedings* (2016) para 133 and the brothers ignored advice from their accountants on the risk of legislative change: *Micula Award* (2013) para 641. See also Stanivukovixc (2017).

[92] *Micula Award* (2013), paras 813–827.

[93] *Eastern Sugar* (2007).

[94] *AES v Hungary (III) Award* (2010).

[95] As was done in *Electrabel Decision on Jurisdiction* (2012) para 177, by taking into account insights offered by a World Bank document of 1999 that new owners were prepared for changes caused by Hungary's EU accession in their mid-term and longer term marketing strategies and plans.

[96] *Micula Award* (2013) paras 329, 341. The Tribunal deemed only the Europe Agreement from 1 April 2005 and the BIT from 1 April 2003 applicable (para 319). Since neither the BIT nor the Accession Treaty mentions the other, the Tribunal elaborated that the countries never intended to deny or modify their obligations under either of the Treaties applicable (paras 321–329).

[97] *Micula Award* (2013). See also *Micula I (USA)* (2015a); *Micula I (USA)* (2015b); *Micula III (USA)* (2016).

VCLT[98] is supposed to solve the issue. On the flip-side, where a dispute is subject to inter-state court or tribunal jurisdiction, a universal agreement on which interpretive approach to adopt is missing.[99] Innately, this void incorporates elements of disputes, unless the transnational judicial bodies involved are deferential.

Another void in the VCLT is that it is tailored to recognise only sovereign states as its subjects, hence identify only national law and part of international law.[100] It does not deal with the relations of IGOs or a state with an IGO.[101] An EU legal order is *sui generis* of a semi-constitutional character and hence does not fit well within the scope of the VCLT.[102] Where an EU legal order clashes with another supranational order, due to its *sui generis* character, a tribunal may assess EU law as either international law or national law under the VCLT.[103] Thus application of VCLT rules of conflict in disputes involving the EU varies according to the perspective the arbitrating judicial body adopts on the nature of EU law. In the same vein, rulings on intra-EU awards (this should apply for extra-EU Awards as well) in conflict with EU state aid rules before an independent arbitration tribunal are contingent upon the depth to which they examine the implications of EU law on the matter.[104] However, for matters concerning EU law, the national courts of the Member States and the CJEU must follow the EU law, which gives superiority of EU primary law over other international treaties and agreements.[105] *Vis-à-vis* intra-EU BITs, this was made

[98] Vienna Convention on the Law of Treaties United Nations, Treaty Series, vol. 1155 CRF (1969).

[99] Roberts (2013) Ch 2. 'Inter-state' dispute resolution takes place between two or more states and 'transnational' dispute resolution involves disputes between non-state actors and state (Keohane et al. 2000).

[100] For more details on the subject, see Sect. 5.4.1 in Chap. 5.

[101] The Vienna Convention on the Law of Treaties Between States and International Organizations or Between International Organizations (VCLTIO), Vienna, 21 March 1986 is supposed to do this but it has not entered into force.

[102] See *Case 6-64 – Costa v ENEL* (1964); *Case 26-62 – van Gend & Loos* (1963). See also Barents (2004); Weiler and Haltern (1996) and Tietje and Wackernagel (2015), p. 215.

[103] Tietje and Wackernagel (2015), pp. 215–217. For the EU's *sui generis* nature, see Sect. 5.3 in Chap. 5.

[104] For conflicting ITA rulings, see, *inter alia*, *AES v Hungary (III) Award* (2010; *Eastern Sugar – Partial Award* (2007); *Electrabel Decision on Jurisdiction* (2012); *Micula Award* (2013). For EU Commission decisions, see *Micula I (EU)* (2014); *Micula II (EU)* (2014). For CJEU rulings see *Micula VI (EU)* (2022).

See also; *Achmea C-284/16* (2018) for the incompatibility of intra-EU ISDS with EU. See also *C-205/06 – Commission v Austria* (2009), C-249/06 – *Commission v Sweden* (2009) and *C-118/07 – Commission v Finland* (2009) on the obligation for acceding Member States to align their extra EU-BITs in accordance with Article 351 TFEU and Article 4(3) TEU with EU law.

[105] *Case 6/64 – Costa v ENEL*' (1964); *C-308/06 – Intertanko and Others* (2008) paras 42, 53. For primacy over agreements concluded between Member States ex ante an EEC Treaty entered into force, see *Case 10/61 – Commission v Italy* (1962) and *Case 235/87 – Matteucci* (1988), para 22. For primacy of EU law in agreements concluded by EC Member States, see *C-469/00 – Ravil* (2003), para 37. See also rejection of EU accession of the ECtHR: *Opinion 2/13 of the Court (Full Court)* (2014), paras 150, 170 and 201. Further, see the decision by the German Federal Court of Justice (*Bundesgerichtshof beschluss I ZB 2/15 – (Achmea)* (2018), which decided to set aside the

quintessentially clear by the Declaration of the Member States on the legal consequences of *Achmea*,[106] which proclaimed the Member States' commitment to mutually terminate these intra-EU BITs at the latest by 6 December 2019. This commitment was confirmed by signing and implementing the Intra-EU BIT Termination Agreement.

The *Micula* case also draws attention to some of the particular legal challenges related to ICSID Awards stemming from intra-EU BITs in comparison to Awards under other international investment arbitration systems.[107] Unlike the *Electrabel Award* (2015),[108] settled under the New York convention,[109] which recognised the *sui generis* nature and primacy of EU law over ECT due to obligations of an EU Member State under international law,[110] the *Micula Award* (2013) ICSID tribunal dismissed EU law as irrelevant.[111] The reason behind ICSID decisions being particularly intrusive to the EU legal order is that unlike other enforcement treaties, such as the New York Convention and the UNCITRAL Model Law on International Commercial Arbitration,[112] the ICSID Convention does not include public policy exceptions. Hence, unless these are included in a BIT (and intra-EU BITs notoriously lack provisions on public policy) investors have a wide margin to raise litigations against Member Sates implementing EU law as required by the EU Treaties.[113] This way the combined BIT/ICSID regime, by being fixed on bilateral

Achmea BV Final Award (2012) decision in response to the CJEU (*Achmea C-284/16*, 2018) and the Swedish Svea court of appeals (*Novenergia II v Spain Award*' 2018) staying the enforcement in *T 4658-18 Spanien v Novenergia II* –suspension of enforcement (2018). See also Sect. 5.3 in Chap. 5.

[106] FISMA (2019a, b, c).

[107] International Centre for Settlement of Investment Dispute (UNICTRAL), Stockholm Chamber of Commerce, and International Chamber of Commerce. For more on ICSID related issues regarding EU law see Sect. 5.5.1 below.

[108] In contrast to the *Micula* claimants, the *Electrabel* claimants did not go on a forum shopping spree.

[109] 'The New York Convention on the Recognition and Enforcement of Foreign Arbitral Awards' (1958) (UNCITRAL 1958).

[110] For the *sui generis* nature, see *Electrabel Decision on Jurisdiction* (2012) paras 4.119–4.124; for primacy due to EU Treaties (*lex posterior* status due to the former EC Treaties), see para 4.178. The *Electrabel Award* (2015) Tribunal also took notice that Electrabel, together with Dunamenti, had appealed to the CJEU (*C-357/14 P – Electrabel and Dunamenti Erőmű v Commission*, 2015) on the Commission's final decision on state aid (2009/609/EC of 4 June 2008 on the state aid C 41/05 (EC), 2008a) awarded by Hungary. The CJEU dismissed the claimants' appeal: *Electrabel Award* (2015), para 115.

[111] The Tribunal held that it was 'inappropriate for the Tribunal to base its decisions in this case on matters of EU law that may come to apply after the Award has been rendered'. Therefore, the tribunal found it to be sufficient to rely only on Articles 53 and 54 ICSID Convention for its assessment: *Micula Award* (2013), paras 340 and 341.

[112] See the Convention on the Recognition and Enforcement of Foreign Arbitral Awards (New York Convention) (UN 1958), Article V.2(b) and UNCITRAL Model Law on International Commercial Arbitration (1985), with amendments as adopted in 2006 (UN 2006), Article 34b(ii).

[113] Jennings (2016), p. 133.

contractual obligations, may overlook factual concerns of legitimacy and even the purpose behind BITs.[114]

Indeed, in the *Micula Award* proceedings, a Member State was obliged to award damages based on the abolition of an illegal advantage, which should not have been granted in the first place. The ICSID Tribunal in *Micula* twice overrode the Commission's verdict on illegal state aid in the same case[115]—first by awarding the investor damages that accounted for unlawful state aid then, after the Commission's clawback procedure, awarding the investor damages as compensation for the reclaimed subsidies.[116]

4.5 The Shock and the Reverberations: Analysis and Conclusions

In effect, the Micula brothers' business empire receiving tax breaks and subsidies from the Romanian government that other firms did not receive gave them a competitive edge over other investors. Hindering this kind of preferential treatment of the few privileged firms at the cost of taxpayers is the reason for the existence of state aid law, whether it takes place directly or indirectly—for example, as an Award. As established in Chaps. 1, 2 and 3, state aid law is the primary law of the EU and an essential part of the EU legal order.[117] Still, after being subject to clawback procedures, investors may raise—and have raised—claims against Member States based on breach of the principle of legitimate expectations under a BIT.

Consequently, legal practice based on international investment agreements that leads to circumventing and negating state aid law also undermines the autonomy of the EU legal order, carrying the risk of weakening the legitimacy of the EU and the authority of its bodies.[118] Therefore, Member States being trapped between choosing EU law or international investment law, with no sanctuary from facing sanctions from one or the other or even both sides generates conflict within the EU's legal order (see Sects. 4.3 and 4.4). It also manifests as disruptions to the ongoing internal

[114] The primary reasoning behind BITs was to protect foreign investments against expropriation by the host states, which were lacking well-developed property rights—thereby making redress through action in domestic courts uncertain and at times impossible: Abbott et al. (2014), p. 5; Salacuse (2015), p. 657.

[115] The *Micula Award* (2013) started a lengthy procedure of appeals and cases. See *Micula I (EU)* (2014); *Micula II (EU)* (2014); *Micula III (EU)* (2016). The first *Micula* appeal to the CJEU was withdrawn for amendment by the appellant as of 29 February 2016. See also *Micula I (USA)* (2015a); *Micula I (USA)* (2015b); *Micula III (USA)* (2016).

[116] See *Micula Anulment Proceedings* (2016).

[117] Kleinheisterkamp (2012).

[118] *Van Gend en Loos* (1963). *Case 6-64 – Costa v ENEL* (1964) established the EU as a new legal order—that is, a legal entity that was autonomous and supreme. See also Eckes (2016), pp. 3, 10. For more on this subject see Chap. 5.

market integration and the Commission's capacity to correct competition distortions. Nonetheless, as will be demonstrated in Chap. 5, the regime of intra-EU BITS rejects the interpretive autonomy of the CJEU. As a rule, international investment arbitrators adopt a perspective that gives priority to IIL over EU law,[119] in contrast to the courts of the EU, which must upkeep the legal autonomy of the EU and the primacy of EU law.[120]

In effect, by their legal practice, tribunals claim the right, independently of the EU, to set the borders and occasionally the status of EU law regarding investment protection. However, if external international legal obligations can trump EU law, to the extent of potentially legitimising illegalities,[121] the prohibition of state aid would be easily evaded. EU state aid law aims for a neutral playing field for all undertakings, including investors in the internal market. A comprehensive application of the principle of legitimate expectations under FET standards in BITS, establishing a bilateral MFN status, stands in stark contrast to with the purpose of state aid law. The Commission's uses of state aid law in the *Micula* case are based on real and relevant legal concerns (see Sects. 4.3 and 4.4).

Hence this chapter concludes that where an IIA is covering the international relations of an EU Member State, or perhaps even the EU itself, with a third country, there is an unresolved conflict between state aid law and the implementation by Member States of these laws. Indeed, since 2006 there have been several cases where collisions between EU state aid law and intra-EU BITs have led to intra-EU ISDS. These have stemmed from investors initiating claims against countries acceding to the EU streamlining their domestic legislation with that of EU law.[122] The *Micula Award*,[123] however, emerged as a final award in favour of the investor after the Lisbon Treaty. The substantial court shopping relating to the *Micula Award* and proceedings that lasted for almost a decade attracted worldwide attention. For this reason, the *Micula Award* has had substantial spillover effects, which are identifiable by observing the reactions and activities adopted by the different actors, namely the EU, its Member States, investors and groups representing them and arbitration circles, all with stakes in this conflict between different legal frameworks.

[119] See all ISDS cases discussed in this chapter, except *Electrabel* (2012).

[120] *Case 6-64 – Costa v ENEL* (1964).

[121] Namely by applying their own system in such a manner that it legitimises measures that are illegal by the other legal order. This can be seen in *C-346/03 – Atzeni and Others* (2006).

[122] See European Commission (2016), Ch 4.3, referring to UNCTAD database for data (UNCTAD 2016a, b). See also European Commission (EC) (2015a), pp. 5 and 6. By now there have been over 100 intra EU ISDS cases.

[123] *Micula Award* (2013). See also *Micula I (USA) (2015a)*; *Micula I (USA)* (2015b); *Micula III (USA)* (2016).

Besides aggravating the Commission,[124] ISDS has come under significant criticism from several sources,[125] including a rejection by the European Parliament.[126] As noted previously, since the end of 2017, the Commission has removed traditional investment treaty arbitration from new EU bilateral agreements and added state aid provisions in investment protection chapters.[127] To prevent harmful effects to the EU legal order, the CJEU rejected intra-EU arbitration in *Achmea C-284/16* (2018), which led to the majority of the Member States mutually terminating their intra-EU BITs, contrary to EU law, on 5 May 2020.[128] Some Member States have even started renegotiating their extra-EU BITs to include state aid provisions.[129] Clearly the Member States, obliged to act (and acting) upon the consequences of the *Achmea C-284/16* (2018) judgment, demonstrate that ultimately it is the actions of the sovereign states that either strengthen or weaken the international body.[130]

The intervention of state aid law in international investment protection system has also caused anger, opposition[131] and careful planning for how to avoid enforcement issues within the EU.[132] Indeed, as seen in Sect. 4.4, to circumvent EU law, several petitions to enforce intra-EU BIT Awards were brought to the US Washington DC District Court in 2018.[133]

---

[124] See the Commission's infringement procedures against five Member States of the EU with active intra-EU BITs, European Commission Press release (EC 2015b). See also Chap. 1 of this book.

[125] For the opinion of NGOs, see for example Client Earth (Ankersmit 2015) and Transnational Institute (Olivet 2013; Cecilia Olivet 2016; Olivet and Eberhardt 2012). See also Politico (2015); Euractiv (2016). Even academia, which is of the opinion that BITs and state aid are not generally a problem, is highly critical of the *Micula Award*, to the extent of questioning the legitimacy of ISDS relating to intra-EU BITs: Tietje and Wackernagel (2015), p. 246.

[126] European Parliament (2014) think-tank workshop in April 2014, p. 21. See Matei (2015), pp. 5–6; Griller et al. (2017), p. 89.

[127] See Chap. 6 below.

[128] Accordingly, termination of these BITs does not awake either sunset or grandfathering provisions because: 'An arbitral tribunal established on the basis of investor-state arbitration clauses lacks jurisdiction, due to a lack of a valid offer to arbitrate by the Member State party to the underlying bilateral investment Treaty.' See the Agreement for the Termination of Bilateral Investment Treaties between the Member States of the European Union, SN/4656/2019/INIT, OJ L 169, 29.5.2020, pp. 1–41 (FISMA 2020), Articles 2 and 3. See also the Declaration of the Member States on the legal consequences of Achmea DG (FISMA) (2019a, b, c), p. 1.

[129] The model BIT was published on 16 May 2018. See the Netherlands government website at https://www.internetconsultatie.nl/investeringsakkoorden.

[130] See Chap. 5.

[131] For example, from business lobby groups such as B. Businesseurope (2016), arbitration lawyers such as Lavranos (2015) and Fietta (2015).

[132] For example, Lavranos (2015), Fietta (2015) and Wehland (2016). Kende (2015) brings up how to counter avoidance of state aid-related enforcement when taken to third countries for litigation.

[133] Despite these disputes having no connection to the United States, *Micula IV USA* (2017) rejected enforcement of the arbitration Award against foreign sovereign states where such a link did not exist.

As illustrated, the EU's new generation trade agreements[134] protect competition policy and state aid law from external measures and tribunal practice, and state aid provisions limit the scope of investment protection.[135] Indeed, the EU has established itself as an external as well as internal force in its pursuit of a modernised ISDS.[136] As future challenges to the EU, this book identifies the following:

1. reducing/negating the current and forthcoming legal disputes on IIAs v State aid law eroding the EU's public policy of governance[137]
2. preplanning by the EU and the Member states to negate future treaty collisions of investment protection and State aid law,[138]
3. ensuring that investors in the EU receive fair and equal treatment in every Member State[139]
4. hindering the multinational corporations and arbitration industry from continuing practices in breach of EU law by proceedings and enforcement of Awards taking place in courts outside the EU.[140]

This chapter has reflected on actions taken by the different actors involved and found support for the argument put forward by this monograph—explicitly that EU state aid law is affecting the future of EU investment policy in a global context.

Cases

Achmea B.V. (formerly known as Eureko B.V.) v Slovak Republic Final Award, PCA Case No 2008-13) (UNCITRAL, 2012)

AES Summit Generation Limited and AES-Tisza Erömü Kft v The Republic of Hungary, ICSID Award, ICSID No. ARB/07/22, Italaw (International Centre for Settlement of Investment Disputes, 2010)

Amministrazione delle finanze dello Stato v Denkavit italiana Srl, case 61/79, ECLI: EU:C:1980:100 (European Court of Justice, 1980)

---

134 Such as the EU's FTAs with Vietnam, Singapore, Canada and Mexico. For the EU's basis for the EU–Australia FTA negotiations, see European Commission (EC 2017). Subsidies and their enforcement are particularly mentioned, as well as the right to regulate and public policy objectives exemption under the Investment chapter.

135 See Chap. 6 for empirical observations on this.

136 This happens by, for example, rejecting ISDS and promoting a new type of ISDS that, among other things, includes public policy limitations to investment protection claims and enhanced transparency.

137 Analogically, DG (FISMA 2019b), p. 3, paras 1–4.

138 Analogically, DG (FISMA 2019b), p. 3, paras 1 and 2.

139 Analogically, DG (FISMA 2019b), p. 4, para 6.

140 Analogically, DG (FISMA 2019b), p. 3, para 2.

Annunziata Matteucci v Communauté française of Belgium and Commissariat général aux relations internationales of the Communauté française of Belgium, case 235/87, ECLI:EU:C:1988:460 (European Court of Justice, 1988)
Appeal brought on 27 August 2019 by European Commission against the judgment of the General Court (Second Chamber, Extended Composition) delivered on 18 June 2019 in Case T-624/15: European Food e.a. v Commission, case C-638/19 P (European Court of Justice, pending)
Budapesti Erőmű Zrt v European Commission, joined cases T-80/06 and T-182/09, ECLI:EU:T:2012:65 (Court of Justice of the European Union (GC), 2012)
Bundesgerichtshof Beschluss des I. Zivilsenats vom 31.10.2018–I ZB 2/15 (Bundesgerichtshof, 2018)
Commission decision (EU) 2015/1470 on state aid SA.38517 (2014/C) (ex 2014/NN) implemented by Romania – Arbitral award Micula v Romania of 11 December 2013 (European Commission, EC 2015)
Commission of the European Economic Community v Italian Republic, case 10/61, ECLI:EU:C:1962:2 (European Court of Justice, 1962)
Dunamenti Erőmű Zrt v European Commission, case T-179/09, ECLI:EU:T:2014:236 (Court of Justice of European Union (GC), 2014)
Eastern Sugar B.V. (Netherlands) v. The Czech Republic, Partial Award SCC case no. 088/2004- Partial award, Italaw (Stockholm Chamber of Commerce (SCC), 2007)
EDF (Services) Limited v. Romania, Award, No. ICSID case no. ARB/05/13 (ad hoc, 2009)
Eiser Infrastructure Limited and Energía Solar Luxembourg S.à r.l. v Kingdom of Spain, ICSID case no. ARB/13/36 – Order Granting Ex Parte Recognition of the Award, No. Case 1:18-cv-01686 (US Court for the Southern District of New York, 2017)
Eiser Infrastructure Limited and Energia Solar Luxembourg S.A.R.L. v Kingdom of Spain – Petition to Enforce Arbitral Award No. Case 1:18-cv-01686 (United States District Court for Columbia, pending)
Electrabel S.A. v Hungary Award, ICSID case no. ARB/07/19 (International Centre for Settlement of Investment Disputes, 2015)
Electrabel S.A. v The Republic of Hungary Decision on Jurisdiction, Applicable Law and Liability, ICSID case no. ARB/07/19 Italaw (ICSID, 2012)
Electrabel SA and Dunamenti Erőmű Zrt v European Commission, C-357/14 P, ECLI:EU:C:2015:642 (European Court of Justice, 2015)
Elliniki Nafpigokataskevastiki AE Chartofylakeiou, Howaldtswerke-Deutsche Werft GmbH and ThyssenKrupp Marine Systems AG v European Commission, T-384/08, ECLI:EU:T:2011:650 (Court of Justice of the European Union (GC), 2011)
European Commission Amicus Curiae Brief in PCA case No.2013-6 U.S. Steel Global Holdings I B.V. v The Slovak Republic (2014)
European Food e.a. v Commission, Case C-638/19 P, Infocuria. http://curia.europa.eu/juris/document/document.jsf?text=&docid=219134&pageIndex=0&doclang=EN&mode=lst&dir=&occ=first&part=1&cid=2253128

Flaminio Costa v E.N.E.L, case 6-64 No. 61964J0006, ECLI:EU:C:1964:66, Eurlex (European Court of Justice (ECJ), 1964)
French Republic v Commission of the European Communities, case C-301/87, ECLI:EU:C:1990:67, Case C-301/87 (European Court of Justice, 1990)
Gebrüder Lorenz GmbH v Federal Republic of Germany and Land Rheinland-Pfalz, ECLI:EU:C:1973:152, Case 120-73 (European Court of Justice, 1973)
Giuseppe Atzeni and Others (C-346/03), Marco Scalas and Renato Lilliu (C-529/03) v Regione autonoma della Sardegna, joined cases C-346/03 and C-529/03, ECLI:EU:C:2006:130 (European Court of Justice, 2006)
Guernsey Limited v Republik Usbekistan, No. 5A_942/2017 (Bundesgericht Tribunal Fédéral, 2018)
Infrastructure Services Luxembourg S.A.R.L. (formerly Antin Energia Termosolar B.V.) v Kingdom of Spain – Petition to Enforce Arbitral Award, Case 1:18-cv-01753 (pending)
Ioan Micula et al. v Goverment of Romania, case no. 17-cv-02332 (APM) (United States District Court for the District of Columbia, 2019)
Ioan Micula, Viorel Micula, S.C. European Food S.A, S.C. Starmill S.R.L. and S.C. Multipack S.R.L. v Romania, No. WL 4643180, at *1 No. 15 MISC. 107, 2015 (Southern District of New York, 2015)
Ioan Micula, Viorel Micula, S.C. European Food S.A, S.C. Starmill S.R.L. and S.C. Multipack S.R.L. v Romania, No. No. 1:14-cv-00600 (APM) (U.S. Dist. LEXIS 64461 (DC), 2015)
Ioan Micula, Viorel Micula, S.C. European Food S.A, S.C. Starmill S.R.L. and S.C. Multipack S.R.L. v Romania, ICSID Award, case no. ARB/05/20, Italaw (ICSID ad hoc, 2013)
Ioan Micula, Viorel Micula, S.C. European Food S.A, S.C. Starmill S.R.L. and S.C. Multipack S.R.L. v Romania, Brief for Amicus Curiae the Commission of the European Union in Support of Defendant-Appellant before the US Court of Appeals, No. 15-3109-cv (United States Court of Appeals Second Circuit, 2016)
loan Micula, Viorel Micula and others v. Romania ICSID case no. ARB/05/20 annulment proceedings (ICSID ad hoc Committee, 2016)
Konungariket Spanien v Novenergia II – Energy & Enviroment (SCA), SICAR, B 124550, inhibition Mål nr T 4658-18 (Svea hovrätt, 2018)
LG&E Energy Corp., LG&E Capital Corp., and LG&E International, Inc. v Argentine Republic, Decision on Liability, ICSID case no. ARB/02/1 (ad hoc, 2006)
Masdar Solar & Wind Cooperatief U.A. v. Kingdom of Spain – Petition to Enforce Arbitral Award, No. Case 1:18-cv-02254 Masdar Solar & Wind Cooperatief U.A. v Kingdom of Spain (United States District Court for Columbia, pending)
Micula and Others v Commission, case T-646/14, ECLI:EU:T:2016:135, OJ C 136 removal from the register (Court of Justice of the European Union (GC), 2016)
Micula and Others v Commission, joined cases T-624/15, T-694/15 and T-704/15, ECLI:EU:T:2019:423, Curia (Court of Justice of the European Union (GC), 2019)
Micula and others v Romania UKSC 5 (UK Supreme Court, 2020)

Micula and others v Romania [2017] EWHC 1430 (Comm), [2017] BUS LR 1147 (England and Wales High Court (Commercial Court), 2017)
Micula et al. v Romania [2017] EWHC 31 (Comm) No. CL-2014-000251 (High Court of Justice, UK, 2017)
Micula v Gov't of Romania, 15-3109-cv (2d Cir. 2017) summary order, 15-3109-cv (Court of Appeals for the Second Circuit, 2017)
Novenergia II – Energy & Environment (SCA), Société d'Investissement à Capital Risque v The Kingdom of Spain – petition to confirm foreign arbital Award, Case 1:18-cv-01148 (United States District Court for Columbia, pending)
Novenergia II – Energy & Environment (SCA)SICAR v Spain, Award, SCC case no. 063/2015 (SCC (Stockholm Chamber of Commerce), 2018)
NV Algemene Transport- en Expeditie Onderneming van Gend & Loos v. Netherlands Inland Revenue Administration. English special edition 1963 00001, case 26-62 (European Court of Justice (ECJ), 1963)
NV Algemene Transport – en Expeditie Onderneming van Gend & Loos v Netherlands Inland Revenue, case 26-62, ECLI:EU:C:1963:1, Eur-Lex (European Court of Justice, 1963)
Mobil Cerro Negro Ltd v Bolivarian Republic of Venezuela (2017). http://law.justia.com/cases/federal/appellate-courts/ca2/15-707/15-707-2017-07-11.html
Opinion 2/13 of the Court (Full Court), ECLI:EU:C:2014:2454, Opinion 2/13 (European Court of Justice (Full Court), 2014)
The Queen, on the application of International Association of Independent Tanker Owners (Intertanko) and Others v Secretary of State for Transport, case-308/06, EU:C:2008:312 (European Court of Justice (Grand Chamber), 2008)
Ravil SARL v Bellon import SARL and Biraghi SpA, case C-469/00, ECLI:EU:C:2003:295 (European Court of Justice, 2003)
SA.38517 Micula v Romania, 2014/NN (Commission DG Comp, 2014)
Saluka Investments B.V v The Czech Republic partial Award (Permanent Court of Arbitration (PCA), 2006)
Slowakische Republik (Slovak Republic) v Achmea BV Case C-284/16, ECLI:EU:C:2018:158 (European Court of Justice (Grand Chamber), 2018)
State aid SA.38517(2014/C), Romania Implementation of Arbitral Award Micula v Romania of 11 December 2013 (ex 2014/NN), C(2014) 6848 final, Italaw (European Commission, 2014)
Técnicas Medioambientales Tecmed, S.A. v The United Mexican States Award, ICSID Case No. ARB(AF)/00/2 (ad hoc, 2003)
ThyssenKrupp Acciai Speciali Terni SpA (C-448/10 P), Cementir Italia Srl (C-449/10 P) and Nuova Terni Industrie Chimiche SpA (C-450/10 P) v European Commission, ECLI:EU:C:2011:642, Joined cases C-448/10 P to C-450/10 P (European Court of Justice, 2011)
ThyssenKrupp Acciai Speciali Terni SpA v European Commission, case T-62/08, ECLI:EU:T:2010:268 (Court of Justice of the European Union (GC), 2010)
Viorel Micula v Goverment of Romania Memorandum opinion (2015)
Viorel Micula, Ioan Micula, S.C. Starmill S.R.L, S.C. Multipack and S.C. European Food S.A v Romania and Europe Petition to confirm ICSID arbitration and enter

judgement Civil Action No. 17-CV-2332 (The District of Columbia courts in Washington, DC, 2017)

References

Abbott R, Erixon F, Ferracane MF (2014) Demystifying investor-state dispute settlement (ISDS). European Centre for International Political Economy, Brussels. https://ecipe.org/publications/isds

AFFGN (2016) Intra-EU Investment treaties – non-paper Austria, Finland, France, Germany and the Netherlands. http://www.s2bnetwork.org/wp-content/uploads/2016/05/Intra-EU-Bits2-18-05.pdf

Ankersmit L (2015). Legality of investor-state dispute settlement (ISDS) under EU law. http://www.clientearth.org/health-environment/health-environment-publications/legality-of-investor-state-dispute-settlement-under-eu-law-3020

Barents R (2004) The autonomy of community law, vol 45. Kluwer, Amsterdam

Businesseurope (2016) A strong investment protection mechanism should be created before intra-EU BITs are terminated. 15 April. https://www.businesseurope.eu/publications/businesseurope-headlines-no-2016-13

Cecilia Olivet PV (2016) Proposal to expand investors' rights for all intra-EU investment will be the next nail in the coffin of European integration. https://www.tni.org/en/publication/proposal-to-expand-investors-rights-for-all-intra-eu-investment-will-be-the-next-nail-in

Council of the European Union (1999) Council Regulation (EC) No 659/1999 laying down detailed rules for the application of Article 93 of the EC Treaty Text with EEA relevance. European Union, Luxembourg

Council of the European Union (2015) Council Regulation (EU) 2015/1589 of 13 July 2015 laying down detailed rules for the application of Article 108 of the Treaty on the Functioning of the European Union (Text with EEA relevance). European Union, Luxembourg

Eckes C (2016) International rulings and the EU legal order: autonomy as legitimacy? CLEER Papers, 2016/2. http://www.asser.nl/media/3002/cleer16-2_complete_web.pdf

Euractiv (2016) Is ISDS dead? No, multi-million lawsuits still on the horizon. http://www.euractiv.com/section/trade-society/opinion/is-isds-dead-no-multi-million-lawsuits-still-on-the-horizon

European Commission (EC) (2008) Commission decision of 4 June 2008 on the state aid C 41/05 awarded by Hungary through power purchase agreements. European Commission, Brussels

European Commission (EC) (2014) European Commission's letter to Romania on state aid SA.38517(2014/C) (ex 2014/NN) – Romania implementation of arbitral award Micula v Romania of 11 December 2013. European Commission, Brussels

European Commission (EC) (2015a) Investor to state dispute settlement (ISDS): some facts and figures. http://trade.ec.europa.eu/doclib/docs/2015/january/tradoc-153046.pdf

European Commission (EC) (2015b) Commission asks Member States to terminate their intra-EU bilateral investment treaties. Media release. http://europa.eu/rapid/press-release_IP-15-5198_en.htm

European Commission (EC) (2016) Commission staff working document on the movement of Capital and the freedom of payments. European Commission, Brussels

European Commission (EC) (2017) Recommendation for a Council Decision authorising the opening of negotiations for a Free Trade Agreement with Australia (Vol. COM/2017/0472 final). Publications Office of the European Union, Brussels

European Parliament (2014) Investor-state dispute settlement (ISDS) provisions in the EU's International Investment Agreements. European Commission, Brussels. http://www.europarl.europa.eu/thinktank/en/document.html?reference=EXPO_STU(2014)534979

European Union and Canada (2016) EU–Canada Comprehensive Economic and Trade Agreement. European Union. European Commission, Brussels

European Union and Singapore (2017) The EU–Singapore Free Trade Agreement. European Commission, Brussels

Fietta V (2015) Further attempts by the European Commission to eradicate intra-EU BITs. http://www.volterrafietta.com/further-attempts-by-the-european-commission-to-eradicate-intra-eu-bits

FISMA (2019a) Declaration of the representative of the Goverment of Hungary of 16 January 2019 on the legal consequences of the judgment of the Court of Justice in Achmea and on investment protection in the European Union. European Union, Brussels

FISMA (2019b) Declaration of the eepresentative of the foverments of the Member States of 15 January 2019 on the legal consequences of the judgment of the Court of Justice in Achmea and on investment protection in the European Union. European Union, Brussels

FISMA (2019c) Declaration of the representative of the goverments of the Member States of 16 January 2019 on the legal consequences of the judgment of the Court of Justice in Achmea and on investment protection in the European Union: The representatives of Goverments of Finland, Luxembourgh, Malta, Slovenia and Sweden. European Union, Brussels

FISMA (2020) Agreement for the termination of bilateral investment treaties between the Member States of the European Union. European Union, Brussels

Friedland P (2015) 2015 International Arbitration Survey: Improvements and Innovations in International Arbitration. https://www.whitecase.com/publications/insight/2015-international-arbitration-survey-improvements-and-innovations

Gaukrodger D (2017) Addressing the balance of interests in investment treaties: the limitation of Fair and equitable treatmenr provisions to the minimum standard of treatment under customary international law. https://doi.org/10.1787/0a62034b-en

Gaukrodger D, Gordon K (2013) Investor-state dispute settlement: a scoping paper for the investment policy community. https://www.oecd-ilibrary.org/finance-and-investment/investor-state-dispute-settlement_5k46b1r85j6f-en

Gélinas F, Jadeau F (2016) CETA's definition of the fair and equitable treatment standard: toward a guided and constrained interpretation. Transnatl Dispute Manag 13(1). https://www.transnational-dispute-management.com/article.asp?key=2319

Griller S, Obwexer W, Vranes E (2017) Mega-regional trade agreements – CETA, TTIP, and TiSA: new orientations for EU external economic relations. Oxford University Press, Oxford

Hindelang S (2012a) Circumventing primacy of EU law and the CJEU's judicial monopoly by resorting to dispute resolution mechanisms provided for in inter-se treaties: the case of intra-EU investment arbitration. Leg Issues Econ Integr 39:179

Hindelang S (2012b) Member State BITs: there's still (some) life in the old dog yet: incompatibility of eexisting Member State BITs with EU law and possible remedies. In: Coleman J, Sachs L, Johnson L (eds) Yearbook on international investment law & policy. Oxford University Press, Oxford

Jennings MB (2016) The international investment regime and investor-state dispute settlement: states bear the primary responsibility for legitimacy. Bus Law Int 17(2):25

Jestaedt T, Derenne J, Ottervanger T (2006) Study on the enforcement of state aid law at national level. http://ec.europa.eu/competition/state_aid/studies_reports/study_part_1.pdf

Johnson L, Volkov O (2014) Investor-state contracts, host-state 'commitments' and the myth of stability in international law. Am Rev Int Arbitr 24(3):361–415

Kende T (2015) Arbitral awards classified as state aid under European Union law. ELTE LJ 37. https://eltelawjournal.hu/arbitral-awards-classified-state-aid-european-union-law

Keohane RO, Moravcsik A, Slaughter A-M (2000) Legalized dispute resolution: interstate and transnational. Int Organ 54(3):457–488

Kleinheisterkamp J (2012) European policy space in international investment law. ICSID Rev – Foreign Invest Law J 27(2):416–431

Knahr C (2010) Ioan Micula, Viorel Micula, S.C. European Food S.A., S.C. Starmill S.R.L., & S.C. Multipack S.R.L. v. Romania. ICSID Case No. ARB/05/20, Decision on Jurisdiction and Admissibility. 48 ILM 51 (2009). Arbitral Tribunal, September 24, 2008. Am J Int Law 104(1): 81–86

Kokott J, Sobotta C (2016) Investment arbitration and EU law. In: Armstrong K (ed) Cambridge yearbook of European legal studies. Cambridge University Press, Cambridge

Koskenniemi M, Leino P (2002) Fragmentation of international law? Postmodern anxieties. Leiden J Int Law 15(3):553–579

Koutrakos P (2016) The relevance of EU law for arbitral tribunals: (Not) managing the lingering tension. J World Invest Trade 17(6):873–894

Lamadrid de Pablo A (2015) State aid and investment arbitration: an improbable (and fascinating) conflict. https://chillingcompetition.com/2015/02/05/state-aid-and-investment-arbitration-an-improbable-and-fascinating-conflict

Lavranos N (2015). Micula vs. (Brussels) Dracula. http://www.globalinvestmentprotection.com/index.php/micula-vs-brussels-dracula

Matei E (2015) The chamber of secrets: the repudiation of the ISDS. RRDE 83. https://heinonline.org/HOL/LandingPage?handle=hein.journals/rianrwioe13&div=46&id=&page=

Matei E, Ciurtin H (2016) Turning enemies into adversaries: TTIP negotiations and the quest for a new Westphalia momentum. Turk Commer Law Rev 2(1):27

OECD (2015) Provisions of negative comity in OECD competition co-operation and enforcement - inventory of co-operation agreements. OECD, Paris

Olivet C (2013) A test for European solidarity: the case of intra-EU bilateral investment treaties. https://www.tni.org/files/download/briefing_on_intra-eu_bits_0.pdf

Olivet C, Eberhardt P (2012) Profiting from injustice: how law firms, arbitrators and financiers are fuelling an investment arbitration boom. http://corporateeurope.org/sites/default/files/publications/profiting-from-injustice.pdf

Ortolani P (2015) Intra-EU Arbitral Awards vis-à-vis Article 107 TFEU: state aid law as a limit to compliance. J Int Dispute Settlement 6(1):118–135

Politico (2015) ISDS: the most toxic acronym in Europe. http://www.politico.eu/article/isds-the-most-toxic-acronym-in-europe

Raux M (2010) La responsabilité de l'etat sur le fondement des traités de promotion et de protection des investissements: Etude du fait internationalement illicite dansle cadre du contentieux investisseur-etat. PhD thesis, Panthéon-Assas University, Paris

Roberts A (2013) Subsequent agreements and practice: the battle over interpretive power. In: Nolte G (ed) Treaties and subsequent practice. Oxford University Press, Oxford

Romanian Competition Council (2000) Fiscal aid scheme EGO 24. Romanian Government, Bucharest

Rösch KÖ (2017) May the European Court of Justice tame intra-EU investment tribunals? Lund Student EU Law Rev 1(1):25. http://www.law.lu.se/WEBUK.nsf/(MenuItemByDocId)/ID588ED585F0F7F68DC125815B0025794E/$FILE/LSEUR_2017_1.pdf

Rovetta AD, Gambardella AM (2015) Intra-EU BITs and EU law: what to learn from the Micula battle. Global Trade Customs J 10(6):194–197

Saavedra Pinto C (2016) The 'narrow' meaning of the legitimate expectations principle in state aid law versus the foreign investor's legitimate expectations. Eur State Aid Law Q 15(2):270–285

Salacuse JW (2015) The law of investment treaties, 2nd edn. OUP Oxford, New York

Sands P (2016) Reflections on international judicialization. Eur J Int Law 27(4):885–900

Sharpston E (1990) European Community Law and the doctrine of legitimate expectations: how legitimate, and for whom. Northwest J Int Law Bus 11(1):87

Stanivukovixc M (2017) Legitimate expectations: a commentary of Micula v. Romania. YB Int Arb 5:165

Struckmann K, Forwood G, Kadri A (2016) Investor-state arbitrations and EU state aid rules: conflict or co-existence. Eur St Aid LQ 15(2):258–269

Struckmann K, Forwood G, Kadri A, Wallin A (2017) Micula and Others v Romania [2017] EWHC 31 (Comm) Annotation by Kai Struckmann, Genevra Forwood, Aqeel Kadri and Adam Wallin. Eur State Aid Law Q 16(2). https://doi.org/10.21552/estal/2017/2/19
Tietje C, Wackernagel C (2014) Outlawing compliance? The rnforcement of intra-EU investment awards and EU state aid law. Transnatl Dispute Manag 3. https://www.transnational-dispute-management.com/article.asp?key=2116
Tietje C, Wackernagel C (2015) Enforcement of Intra-EU ICSID Awards. J World Invest Trade 16(2):205–247
UNCITRAL (1958) New York Convention on the Recognition and Enforcement of Foreign Arbitral Awards. https://www.uncitral.org/pdf/english/texts/arbitration/NY-conv/New-York-Convention-E.pdf
UNCTAD (2015) Recent trends in IIAS and ISDS. UNCTAD, Geneva
UNCTAD (2016a) International Investment Agreements Navigator. http://investmentpolicyhub.unctad.org/IIA
UNCTAD (2016b) Investor-state dispute settlement: review of developments in 2015. UNCTAD, Geneva. http://unctad.org/en/PublicationsLibrary/webdiaepcb2016d4_en.pdf
UNCTAD (2017) Investor-state dispute settlement: review of developments in 2016. https://investmentpolicyhub.unctad.org/Upload/Documents/diaepcb2017d1_en.pdf
UNICTRAL (2018) Possible reform of investor-state dispute settlement (ISDS). https://uncitral.un.org/en/working_groups/3/investor-state
United Nations (1958) Convention on the Recognition and Enforcement of Foreign Arbitral Awards. United Nations, New York
United Nations (2006) UNCITRAL Model Law on International Commercial Arbitration (1985), with amendments as adopted in 2006. United Nations, New York
Van Harten G (2013) Sovereign choices and sovereign constraints: judicial restraint in investment treaty arbitration. Oxford University Press, Oxford
Van Harten G, Malysheuski P (2016) Who has benefited financially from investment treaty arbitration? An evaluation of the size and wealth of claimants. https://doi.org/10.2139/ssrn.2713876
Vandevelde KJ (2010) A unified theory of fair and equitable treatment. N Y Univ J Int Law Pol 43: 43–106
Wehland H (2016) The enforcement of intra-EU BIT awards: Micula v Romania and beyond. J World Invest Trade 17(6):942–963
Weiler JH, Haltern UR (1996) The autonomy of the community legal order-through the looking glass. Harv Int Law J 37(2):411

Chapter 5
New Centre of Gravity

5.1 Introduction

An appeal by the claimants to allow the enforcement of the *Micula Award* to the CJEU took six years, and therefore the focus in scholarly publications on the subject of intra-EU BITs, extra-EU BITs and the EU's IIAs shifted. Much happened during this period. For example, a surge of intra-EU ISDS under the ECT[1] relating to state measures was initiated by investors both inside and outside of the EU, and the first preliminary ruling on the status of intra-EU BITs (*Achmea C-284/16*, 2018) from the CJEU was concluded in 2018. Further clarity on the EU's investment policy—namely whether the ICS in CETA is compatible with the autonomy of the EU's legal order regarding its external dimension—was provided by the CJEU on 30 April in *Opinion 1/17* (2019).[2] Therefore, the focus of discussions on ISDS involving the EU or its Member States (both state aid-related and other) has gravitated from *Micula* to the CJEU's *Achmea C-284/16* (2018) decision and *Opinion 1/17* (2019).

The origin of the *Achmea C-284/16* ruling is a claim raised by Achmea (formerly Eureko), a Dutch multinational financial corporation, to the Permanent Court of Arbitration based on the Netherlands–Slovak Republic BIT in 2008.[3] Accordingly, the new law introduced by the Slovak Republic, which limited corporations operating within the healthcare sector from freely distributing their profits, breached this

[1] See Sect. 5.6.2.

[2] This Opinion was initiated by Belgium asking for a referral from the CJEU under Article 218(11) TFEU on the compatibility of the Investment Court System under CETA with EU law. See Sect. 2.5.5 in Chap. 2.

[3] Agreement on encouragement and reciprocal protection of investments between the Kingdom of the Netherlands and the Czech and Slovak Federative Republic was concluded in 1991. International Investment Agreements Navigator, UNCTAD database at http://investmentpolicyhub.unctad.org/IIA/treaty/2650.

P. Finckenberg-Broman, *Weaponizing EU State Aid Law to Impact the Future of EU Investment Policy in the Global Context*, Studies in European Economic Law and Regulation 23, https://doi.org/10.1007/978-3-031-10108-3_5

BIT.[4] For the investor, it was clearly a tactical choice to bring this case to an international investment tribunal. The Achmea corporation had already won court proceedings on the same claims at the Slovakian constitutional court, which abolished this new law as unconstitutional.[5] Furthermore, the Commission had held this law to be incompatible with EU law (free movement of capital) and hence initiated infringement proceedings against Slovakia.[6] However, instead of raising claims for damages at the national court based on infringement of EU law,[7] the Achmea corporation turned to the ISDS system under the Netherlands–Slovak Republic BIT, as this system awards larger amounts of compensation and pays less heed to state interests.[8]

Indeed, the investment tribunal awarded Achmea corporation damages of €22.1 million for breaching this BIT. However, Slovakia was not ready to accept this and therefore fought this Award in the German courts. Slovakia's challenge, claiming that the investment tribunal lacked jurisdiction under an intra-EU BIT, escalated to the German Supreme Court, which referred the matter to the European Court of Justice. The outcome of the preliminary ruling was that the arbitration clause in the Netherlands–Slovak Republic BIT violated EU law. However, while the *Achmea v Slovak Republic* (2008) BV case shook the landscape of the EU's investment policy and raised doubts about whether the EU's international agreements remained arbitrable at all, the CJEU calmed these fears to some extent with its *Opinion 1/17* (2019) on the compatibility of the Investment Court System under CETA with EU law.

5.2 Overview

Chapter 2 examined the similarities, differences and tensions between state aid control and the international investment regime of FDI governed by BITs and how these arrived at a crossroad in the recent decade, while Chap. 3 explained state aid law and policy. Jointly, these two chapters identified and explained how, at the core of the tensions between international investment regime for foreign direct investments are the different rules governing state aid and investment incentives. Chapter 4 then went on to demonstrate how these conflicts and tensions work out in practice. Building upon discussion and analysis of these chapters, this chapter adds another dimension: the procedural issues relating to the EU legal order and the ISDS.

---

[4] *Achmea v Slovak Republic* (2008), BV, para 54.

[5] Niemelä (2017).

[6] *Achmea v Slovak Republic* (2008) BV para 55. These proceedings were discontinued after the Slovak laws had been annulled by the Slovakian constitutional court.

[7] It is possible to claim damages based on non-contractual liability for infringing EU law.

[8] Niemelä (2017).

It explains the unique status of sui generis in the EU's legal system and how this status translates to the legal aspects behind investment protection and state aid.[9] It further examines how a critical common denominator, behind the current treaty collision, is that both regimes have gradually expanded their scope through their jurisprudence until the overlap has the potential to lead to a crossfire. These collisions are both legal procedural (investor-state arbitration process with the European Court of Justice and State aid procedures that are administered by the European Commission) and substantial, which stems from their procedural (principle of legitimate expectations) nature. Possible consequences range from the risk of eroding the autonomy of the EU legal order and its capacity to regulate public policy objectives. This situation can also arise in any setting that involves the EU or one or more of its Member States, including relations with non-EU countries, as the web of IIAs operates in different forms on an international scale. This chapter mainly aims to cover all these scenarios.

While this chapter identifies and discusses the manifest critical differences—structural, procedural, substantial and in priority of values—between the regimes of international investment law and EU law through a state aid lens, the main concern addressed by this chapter is the challenges created by the international BIT regimes for the EU's legal order and the autonomy of EU law. It does so by answering the question:

> How and why do the EU's procedural rules collide with ISDS?

Further, to explain how the notion of the EU's external autonomy differs from the notion of internal autonomy, this chapter uses the sub-question:

> Why and how is ISC in the EU's international agreements compatible with the autonomy of EU law?

A logical starting point for this chapter is therefore to discuss the principle of autonomy of EU law which is the reason behind the CJEU's rejection of ISDS in *Achmea C-284/16* (2018). Next, the CJEU's unexpected move to redeem investor-state arbitration for the EU's IIAs in *Opinion 1/17* (2019) will be examined. From there, the debate will move on to cover dilemmas mainly related to state aid law and ISDS, focusing particularly on how ISDS, as practised by international investment tribunals in their interpretation of FET provisions in intra-EU BITs, has disregarded the procedural requirement for legitimacy in EU state aid law.

The discussion and analysis in this chapter build on the EU's primary and secondary law, case law from the CJEU and Commissions decisions and documented legal interpretations on bilateral international investment agreements by international investment tribunals, particularly on intra-EU BITs. Scholarly works regarding the autonomy of the EU's legal order, the protection of the EU's judicial system and the collision of state aid with ISDS are profoundly drawn upon. Observations of recent policy changes on the subject, as reflected in the

[9] See *C-6/64 Costa v ENEL* (1964), summary para 3.

Commission's policy documents,[10] the EU's international agreements and declarations by the Member States are also relied upon.

While the CJEU ruling rejecting ISDS in *Achmea C-284/16* (2018) generated angry protests from the arbitration circles, these welcomed the CJEU's *Opinion 1/17* (2019).[11] Nevertheless, the CJEU's case law on the principle of autonomy of EU law is not new, nor is it the first time this particular case law has been subject to a heated debate by authors.[12] Opinions expressed in scholarly works on the principle of autonomy of EU law, as it has been developed through CJEU case law[13] to protect its judicial monopoly as the final interpreter of EU law, are diverse. As this case law is still under development, this subject will remain topical. Scholarly works on this subject can be divided roughly into those who approve and those who disapprove of this development. Many of these choose to discuss a specific case related to this subject,[14] while others elaborate upon the concept of the autonomy as it has developed through time,[15] focusing on specific treaty articles upon which the CJEU has based this doctrine.[16]

The principle of autonomy of EU law as developed by the CJEU is a logical consequence of EU constitutionalism, and it adds to legal certainty and a more comprehensive legal system, and contributes to a stronger and more integrated EU.[17] Some even note that this case law upholds important values and therefore affects the rest of the international legal system positively.[18] Critics, however, argue, *inter alia*, that the EU is not following its international legal obligations, that due to its *sui generis* nature the EU is no longer international law, that the EU and the CJEU are 'power-grabbing'[19] and that this erodes the 'rule of law within the EU'.[20]

---

[10] Particularly the European Commission communication on protection of intra-EU investment (EC 2018b).

[11] For example, see blogs by Croisant (2019) and Lavranos.

[12] Eckes (2018), Hindelang (2019), Kochenov (2015), Schilling (1996) and Weiler and Haltern (1996).

[13] For example, see *Opinion 1/91* (1991), EEA Agreement of 14 December 1991, paras 40 and 70; *Opinion 1/00* (2002) on the establishment of a European Common Aviation Area of 18 April 2002; *Opinion 1/09* (2011), Agreement creating a unified patent litigation system of 8 March 2011, paras 74 and 76; and *Opinion 2/13 of the Court (Full Court)* (2014) paras 182 and 183 on the accession to the ECHR of 18 December 2014. See also *Achmea C-284/16* (2018) and *Opinion 1/17* (2019).

[14] Hindelang (2019) and Niemelä (2017).

[15] Cremona and Thies (2014) and Koutrakos (2016).

[16] De Búrca (2010) and Kokott and Sobotta (2012).

[17] Fouchard and Krestin (2018).

[18] In the aftermath of *Joined Cases c-402/05 p and c-415/05 p Kadi* (2008), the United Nations created the Office of the Ombudsperson (UN 2015).

[19] On this particular point, expression varies from the CJEU's position that 'Investment arbitration poses a threat to the autonomy of EU law is somewhat inflated'(Niemelä 2017) to outright calls for the national courts to rebel against this judgement as it allegedly violates the principle of proportionality in Article 5 of the TEU (Gaffney 2018).

[20] Lavranos (2018a, b).

Achmea however, was particularly about ISDS and how it fits with the principle of autonomy of EU law, more specifically about intra-EU dispute resolution vis-à-vis intra-EU BITs as practised by international arbitration tribunals under the UNICTRAL rules. After the initial reactions to this case, ranging from welcome[21] to uproar,[22] different stakeholders in this matter have realised they faced a new reality depending on the scope of *Achmea*'s applicability.[23] The profound legal uncertainty resulting from the *Achmea* case has led to an accumulation of judicial processes and debates. The Commission seized this situation as an opportunity to expand the applicability of *Achmea* on the ECT.[24] In doubt of the legality of intra-EU ISDS, the national courts of the EU have set aside[25] or stayed enforcement of intra-EU investment Awards[26] with the consequence that the investors have turned to the US courts to appeal for enforcement of awards already secured.[27]

Furthermore, the international investment tribunals have resisted adapting to this decision by the CJEU.[28] For these tribunals, *Achmea* is an unpopular decision as it severely diminishes their influence in an intra-EU arbitration and cuts deeply into their revenue.[29] However, in *Opinion 1/17* (2019),[30] the CJEU did not wholly obliterate all types of ISDS in EU trade deals. Instead, the CJEU drew a line that investment protection provisions and international investment tribunals cannot cross, forcing an alignment with the general requirement of compatibility with the EU constitutional framework. The aftermath of the *Achmea* judgment and *Opinion 1/17* appears to be multidimensional.[31] Some authors note that the first area of EU

[21] Bizikova (2018) and Nikitin (2018).

[22] Gaffney (2018) and Lavranos (2018a, b).

[23] See, for example, Dimopoulos (2018), Eckes (2018), Hess (2018), Hindelang (2018, 2019) and Szilágyi (2018).

[24] In its decision in the Spanish renewable energy schemes, which prohibited Spain from proceeding with paying the Awards stemming from the new and un-notified state aid, the Commission cast doubt on the legality of intra-EU ISDS for the ECT: *State aid SA.40348 (2015/NN)* (2017), paras 161–163. In its policy document, 'Protection of Intra-EU investment', the Commission set that it holds *Achmea C-284/16* (2018) applicable to all intra-EU ISDS proceedings, including those under the ECT (EC 2018a). See also Cross and Kube (2018), p. 5 and *Blusun v Italy* (2016), para 288.

[25] The German Supreme Court set aside the *Achmea Award (Bundesgerichtshof beschluss – I ZB 2/15 (Achmea)*, 2018).

[26] The Swedish Svea Court of Appeals stayed the enforcement of an Award to Novoenergia that was based on the ECT (*T 4658-18 – Spanien v Novenergia II*, 2018; *T 4658-18 Spanien v Novenergia II – Suspension of Enforcement,* 2018), while the UK courts have declined to enforce the *Micula Award* until the CJEU has decided this pending case: *Micula UK2* (2017); *Micula I (UK)* (2017).

[27] *Micula III (USA)* (2016); *Micula I (USA)* (2015b); *Micula IV USA* (2017); see also *Eiser Award (USA III)* (pending); *Masdar v Spain (USA)* (pending; *Novenergia II (USA)* (pending).

[28] *Vattenfall II (Decision on the Achmea Issue)* (2018).

[29] According to UNCTAD, in 2016 about 25 per cent of all investor-state arbitration cases originated from intra-EU ISDS. See UNCTAD IIA Issues Note 2017 issue 1 (UNCTAD 2017). In 2017 the number of these disputes was about 20 per cent of the global total (UNCTAD 2017).

[30] The Opinion of AG Bot on this matter came out in January 2019: *Opinion Avis 1/17 (AG)* (2019).

[31] Hindelang (2019).

law impacted will be state aid law,[32] as these cases have been prominent in an intra-EU ISDS context. Nevertheless, while overall academics,[33] judges and institutions[34] debating this issue have focused mostly on the procedural aspects as applied by the courts,[35] only a few have considered the role of state aid procedures administered by the Commission in this dilemma.[36] Even less attention has been paid to substantive problems.[37]

This chapter finds that the ISDS indeed imposes a risk of eroding the autonomy of EU law. Due its *sui generis* character, the legitimacy of EU law—including state aid measures—can only be interpreted and decided by the EU law itself. International investment tribunals' rejection of the CJEU's exclusivity as the final interpreter of EU law and their disregard of state aid procedures that are a requirement for legitimacy put these two in the situation where they cannot peacefully coexist.

This chapter begins with an overview of the procedural issues relating to the EU legal order and the ISDS, providing an insight into how the principle of autonomy of EU law has emerged and developed through the CJEU's case law. It then explains how the scope of the principle of autonomy of EU law has, over the years, expanded from an internal relations focus to cover the external dimension. The chapter then elaborates how the principle of autonomy of EU law also applies to ISDS. With the EU, via the Commission and the CJEU, establishing itself as an independent entity with absolute jurisdiction inside the internal market, there is a challenge issued to external, specialised and ad hoc courts operating and acting outside of EU's legal system but within the internal market.

The chapter goes on to provide an in-depth explanation of, and to compare, the different court and award systems affecting state aid and investment protection. Part V investigates how the different systems have gone from occasional minor clashes to increasingly serious controversies. It shows how Awards can be considered as state aid in the internal market. By looking at the purpose behind the procedural structures, this chapter maps changes that have affected the path of international investment protection and how that inevitably has led to a conflict with the new and very different approach taken by the EU in this area. As such, this chapter delves into both the similarities between these legal regimes policies implemented and the different stands taken by different parties on the issue of international investment protection. It reaches the conclusion that, between FDI and competition law, the expansion of investment protection scope, through practice by the tribunals, and the CJEU's

[32] Righini (2018).

[33] Bermann (2012), Ortolani (2015), Tietje (2013), Tietje and Baetens (2014) and Tietje and Wackernagel (2014).

[34] European Parliament (2014) think-tank workshop, April 2014; see also Matei (2015a), pp. 5–6; Griller et al. (2017), p. 89.

[35] Happ and Tietje (2013), Kleinheisterkamp (2012a, b, 2015), Tietje (2008), Tietje et al. (2012) and Tietje and Wackernagel (2015).

[36] Gallo and Nicola (2015), Lamadrid de Pablo (2015) and Lavranos (2015).

[37] Lamadrid de Pablo (2015), Matei (2016) and Saavedra Pinto (2016).

extension in the case law of its public policy scope have caused a head-on collision of the two regimes.

5.3 The EU's Legal Order and the Autonomy of EU Law

A key area in terms of understanding this book is the EU's protection of its own autonomous status within both the European and the international legal order. It has an immense impact on how the EU perceives its international obligations and therefore affects both the EU's internal and external policies. However, the principle of autonomy of EU law cannot be found in the Treaties; instead, it has emerged and developed over the years from the CJEU's case law.[38] The EU legal order has some unique features,[39] as its original focus was internal. The intention was to bolster the emerging legal order's normative features from the beginning, especially in the context of supremacy, to enable its capacity to stand up to challenges from national law.[40]

The European Community (EC) was replaced as a legal entity by the EU when the Lisbon Treaty, signed on 13 December 2007, entered into force on 1 December 2009.[41] With the new treaty, named the Treaty on the Functioning of the European Union, the EU took over all the ECs powers held under the previous EC Treaty.[42]

In the 1960s, the European Court of Justice (ECJ) made a critical judgment that set a precedent for how EU law was positioned internally: *C-6/64 Costa v ENEL.*[43] In this case, the ECJ firmly established the supremacy of EU law. With reference to Article 189 EEC (Article 288 TFEU), the court firmly established EU legislation as *lex superior* internally, with confirmation of its binding nature and direct applicability in all Member States and to all their nationals. The motive for this reasoning was that without this, EU legislation would be meaningless since it would create the possibility for national legislative measures to unilaterally nullify it.[44]

With regard to the EU's commitment to respect public international law, the decision of the ECJ in *Joined Cases C-402/05 P and C-415/05 Kadi* has been heavily criticised.[45] In this case, the CJEU made it clear that the then EC, now the EU, when exercising its powers to adopt measures based on international law, must respect these measures as interpreted and limited in scope by the relevant parts of

[38] Koutrakos (2016).

[39] These unique features make it a *sui generis* legal order IGO. The UN is a *sui generis* international organisation.

[40] Koutrakos (2016).

[41] Art 47 TEU.

[42] Craig and De Búrca (2011), p. 25.

[43] *Case 6-64 – Costa v ENEL* (1964).

[44] *Case 6-64 – Costa v ENEL* (1964), p. 594.

[45] Kokott and Sobotta (2012), Abstract.

international law.[46] However, in his Opinion on the case, the EU's Advocate General Maduro emphasised the lack of institutional safeguards in the UN system at the time. He highlighted the constitutional principles behind the EU's legal order that provided rules for its interaction with international law by finding that 'international law can permeate that legal order only under the conditions set by the constitutional principles of the Community'.[47]

In this case, the ECJ agreed with the AG's Opinion, establishing the primacy of the EU Treaties over international law, though at the time of the decision it only applied to EU primary legislation.[48] The ECJ clarified that this does not imply that there is an automatic immunity from judicial review of a Community measure, with its basis in EU primary law, based on the primacy of obligations under international law.[49] The ECJ also clarified that under Article 307 EC (Article 351 TFEU), there could be no challenge to the principles at the foundation of the EU's legal order, in this specific case the Fundamental Human Rights under the Charter.[50]

For the purpose of this book, a relevant example of the constitutional approach the EU has taken to establish its autonomous role within the sphere of international law is the ECJ's *Opinion 2/94* from 1996. This Opinion, on the EU's accession to the European Convention of Human Rights (ECHR), clarified that the EU lacked any conferred powers under the Treaties to 'enact any rules on human rights or conclude international conventions in this field',[51] and that no such power was implied.

Therefore, the then EC, now the EU, would have to amend the Treaty to be able to accede to the European Convention of Human Rights.[52] The new Lisbon Treaty maintained a requirement under Article 2018(6) TFEU that any crucial international agreement needed 'consent' from the directly elected European Parliament. In this way, the European Parliament restricted the EU Commission's power of attorney in this matter.

In *Opinion 2/13*, on the latest draft of the ECHR accession treaty, the ECJ ruled it out due to it conflicting with EU law.[53] The ECJ, in paragraph 178(a), raised the issue of the 'specific characteristics and the autonomy of EU law'.[54] It continues in paragraphs 179–186 to define its stance, relying on previous rulings, on international agreements. In particular, para 813 of the Opinion clarifies the showstopper in that 'there is no adverse effect on the autonomy of the EU legal order'.[55]

[46] *Joined cases c-402/05 p and c-415/05 p Kadi* (2008), para 291.

[47] *Joined cases c-402/05 p and c-415/05 p Kadi* (2008) and AG Opinion *Joined cases c-402/05 p and c-415/05 p Kadi* (2008), para 24.

[48] *Joined cases c-402/05 p and c-415/05 p Kadi* (2008), paras 306–307.

[49] *Joined cases c-402/05 p and c-415/05 p Kadi* (2008), para 327.

[50] *Joined cases c-402/05 p and c-415/05 p Kadi* (2008), paras 299–300, 304–305.

[51] *Opinion 2/94* (1996) on Accession of the EC to the ECHR, para 27.

[52] *Opinion 2/94* (1996) on Accession of the EC to the ECHR, paras 35–36.

[53] *Opinion 2/13 of the Court (Full Court)*, 2014) on Accession by the Community to the ECHR.

[54] *Opinion 2/13 of the Court (Full Court)*, 2014), para 178(a).

[55] *Opinion 2/13 of the Court (Full Court)*, 2014), para 183.

The ECJ stopped the EU accession to the European Convention of Human Rights, saying it was incompatible with EU law. In particular, the court referred to Article 6(2) TEU itself and Protocol (No 8), which is related to Article 6(2) TEU on the EU's accession to the European Convention of Human Rights. The court found the blocking of the accession by the argument that it would place the EU and the ECJ under the jurisdiction of the European Convention of Human Rights court in Strasbourg outside its jurisdiction. This was what the Council of Europe,[56] which is not an EU entity but an international organisation, was looking to achieve: 'the EU will be bound to respect the ECHR and will be placed under the external control of the European Court of Human Rights'.[57] The ECJ noted that EU legislation does not allow the Union or its Member States to be bound by external interpretations of EU law.[58]

This particular concern for the autonomy of EU law was further addressed on 6 March 2018, when the ECJ ruled against ISDS clauses relating to intra-EU BIT disputes in *Achmea C-284/16* (2018). The ECJ's conclusion in the ruling was that common arbitration clauses in intra-EU BITs violate EU law, specifically Articles 267 TFEU, 344 TFEU and A19.1(2) TEU, since rulings made by investment tribunals cannot be reviewed by domestic courts for conformity with EU law. As these tribunals are exceptions to the legal system of the EU, they cannot make reference to the ECJ for a preliminary ruling according to Article 267 TFEU. Therefore, according to the ECJ in *Achmea*, tribunals potentially threaten the autonomy of the EU legal order and compromise its specific characteristics.[59] The ECJ determined that the meaning of Articles 267 and 344 TFEU read together is that intra-EU ISDS provisions in international agreements entered among the Member States, 'such as art.8 of the [NCS BIT]',[60] are not compatible with EU law.

In its controversial *Opinion 1/17*, the CJEU refined the scope of its *Achmea C-284/16* (2018) decision concerning the EU's external autonomy.[61] *Opinion 1/17* focused on this aspect by discussing the constitutional principles and the legal framework that apply to the EU's international agreements. For this purpose, the

---

[56] The Council of Europe is the European organization monitoring Human Right's issue under the ECHR, authors own description—see also Council website at http://www.coe.int/en/web/about-us/who-we-are.

[57] The Council of Europe website at https://www.coe.int/en/web/human-rights-intergovernmental-cooperation/accession-of-the-european-union-to-the-european-convention-on-human-rights.

[58] *Opinion 2/13 of the Court (Full Court)*, 2014), para 184.

[59] *Achmea C-284/16* (2018) paras 31–37. For primacy, see *Case 6-64 – Costa v ENEL* (1964); for direct effect, see *Case 26-62 – van Gend & Loos* (1963); for mutual trust, see Article 2 TEU; and for sincere cooperation, see Article 4(3)1 TEU. See also *Achmea C-284/16* (2018), para 58 and *Opinion 2/13 of the Court (Full Court)* (2014), para 176.

[60] *Achmea C-284/16* (2018).

[61] For reactions to the Opinion, see blogs such as those of Duarte (2019), Holterhus, Krajewski (2019), Bungenberg and Titi (2019), and Peers. The comments and analysis on this specific Opinion have ranged from Peer's 'an unusually strong acceptance by the Court of the EU legal system's co-existence with international law' to Duarte's 'the incoherent move'.

ECJ held that the EU's external autonomy permits international courts that arbitrate international agreements to which the EU is a party under certain conditions[62]—namely, if

- these tribunals are authorised only to interpret and apply the provisions of that distinct international agreement according to international law[63]
- these tribunals are not able to issue awards that affect the EU institutions from operating consistent with the EU constitutional framework.[64]

After examining and analysing the CETA provisions, the ECJ found that ICS in CETA was confined to these conditions. Explicitly, CETA had no direct effect,[65] and the CETA tribunals could only apply EU law 'as a matter of fact'.[66]

Moreover, because ICS in CETA provides enough guarantees that EU law will not be breached, the ECJ held that the EU judicial system could coexist with ICS in CETA under public international law.[67] These guarantees are procedural (say, guaranteeing the Tribunal's independence and impartiality)[68] and normative (say, guaranteeing the effectiveness of EU law by introducing police power exceptions under the concept of indirect expropriation). As a result, a CETA tribunal cannot order the EU to be liable for damages.[69] The ECJ distinguished ICS for CETA from the *Achmea* case by emphasising that the principle of mutual trust applies only for relations between Member States. That is, different principles—such as the necessity of reciprocity and the necessity to protect EU investors when investing abroad—apply to the relations between the EU and third countries. Further, unlike the international arbitration tribunal in *Achmea*, a CETA tribunal has no jurisdiction to decide on the legality of domestic or EU law.

As has been shown above, through the EU's *sui generis* nature and with the support of these cases, the CJEU has established the EU's autonomous position within the international legal order. The EU has therefore established its position: external courts and rulings that are not compliant with primary legislation cannot and should not have legal force within the EU.

[62] The ECJ confirmed that the CETA tribunals were not 'part of the judicial system of either of the Parties' (*Opinion 1/17,* 2019), para 114.

[63] See *Opinion 1/17* (2019), para 118: 'Since those Tribunals stand outside the EU judicial system, they cannot have the power to interpret or apply provisions of EU law other than those of the CETA or to make awards that might have the effect of preventing the EU institutions from operating in accordance with the EU constitutional framework.'

[64] *Opinion 1/17* (2019), paras 106–161.

[65] *Opinion 1/17* (2019), para 131.

[66] *Opinion 1/17* (2019), paras 122, 130, 131 referring to CETA Article 8.21.

[67] *Opinion 1/17* (2019), paras 106–161.

[68] Instead of the traditional system of ad hoc tribunals, the ICS also establishes a permanent court with two instances: a tribunal (CETA Article 8.27) and an appellate body (CETA Article 8.28).

[69] *Opinion 1/17* (2019), para 153.

5.4 ISDS Is Not Compatible with EU Law

Despite the regimes of state aid control and rules governing international investment—namely investment protection—both being built on economic policy, these two regimes have often become contradictory in the EU over the last few years.[70] The EU and the IIAs, however, do have something in common. Explicitly, as was made clear in Chaps. 3 and 4, these cover natural and legal persons alike.[71] Unlike conventional trade agreements, where rights and obligations are applied and enforced vertically, these two cover horizontal relations and provide for monetary remedies for firms in case of a trade law violation.[72] Due to their European origin, BITs have become especially prevalent in the EU.[73] Therefore, despite the investment tribunals generally having avoided direct confrontation with the EU,[74] the paths of these two were bound to cross eventually.

Yet, until 2006, the law of international arbitration and EU competition law largely occupied separate worlds.[75] These intersections have mostly been intra-EU[76] after the 2004 enlargement, when 10 European Sates acceded to the EU. Several of these BITs, agreed upon in the 1990s, were concluded as extra EU-BITs between the Member States and other countries looking to accede to the EU during a series of enlargements in 2004, 2007 and 2013.[77] Explicitly, the intra-EU BITs—the product of accession of new Member States to the EU—started their life cycle as extra-EU BITs.

Since the EU enlargements, and the conversion of extra-EU BITs to intra EU-BITs, investment protection within the EU has been driven under two parallel legal frameworks: on the one hand, those driven by international investment law, governed primarily by EU intra-BITs;[78] and on the other, those under EU law and

---

[70] See Chap. 2.

[71] For investors under IIAs, see OECD (2005) and for investors that are natural and legal persons under EU law, see for free movement of establishment, Article 54(1) TFEU and for free movement of capital, Articles 63 and 64 TFEU and the Council Directive of 24 June 1988 for the implementation of Article 67 of the Treaty (88/361/EEC) (Directive 88/361 (EC 1988) Article 1.

[72] Alan O Sykes (2005) informs us that parties under NAFTA and the WTO disputes may agree to a settlement that includes monetary damages in cases of a trade violation. This occurs rarely.

[73] Anderer (2010), p. 853.

[74] Tribunals have tended to side-step EU law by either denying any existing conflict while applying Articles 59 and 30 VTCL as expressions of *lex posterior*. See Chap. 4.

[75] Shelkoplyas (2003) and (Basener 2017) part I. See also ECOFIN (2006), p. 7 and *Eastern Sugar – Partial Award* (2007) para 119, for DG FISMA letter to Czech Republic, and para 126 for the informal note from the DG FISMA on strong opposition against intra-EU BITs.

[76] *AES v Hungary (III) Award* (2010); *Eastern Sugar-Final Award* (2007); *Eureko* (2010); *Saluka* (2006); *Vattenfall 1* (2011).

[77] EC (2015b).

[78] Including the Energy Charter Treaty (ECT) (signed 17 December 1994, entered into force 16 April 1998), to which the EU is a signatory, as a relevant instrument in that context. See Andersen and Hindelang (2016); Hindelang (2012a), pp. 2 179, 191 et seq.

Member States' domestic law.[79] This parallelism entered a global aspect post the Lisbon Treaty, as the Member States extended the existing framework for the EU's Common Commercial Policy and conferred on the EU the exclusive power to negotiate FDI under Article 207 TFEU.[80] As FDI became an EU exclusive competence, the Member States lost the mandate to conclude new BITs without receiving an individual mandate from the EU. Since 2009, the EU has been able to choose to conduct the IIA itself[81] or permit an individual Member State to do so. This led to Member State BITs becoming challengeable under EU law.

Since then, the EU's investment regime has faced turbulent times. Especially the intra-EU BITs have been laden with procedural and substantial controversies.[82] The Commission persisted in making the intra-EU BITs obsolete, and Tribunals are insisting on the opposite. This situation came about mainly due to the lack of explicit expression in the relevant Treaties (the Europe Agreements,[83] the Accession Treaties[84] and the Treaty of Lisbon)[85] on the matter,[86] and the failure of coherent measures by different actors within the EU.[87] The Declaration of the Member States

---

[79]For the most part, the EU's freedoms of establishment and capital ensure an unlimited investments regime in the EU. These rules are at the core of the mechanisms of European company law, which serves to protect intra-EU investments as argued by Papadopoulos (2019). Further, freedom of establishment enables investors from one Member State to establish easily in another Member State. Hence, similarly to tax planning (or avoidance), a company may seek additional advantages by establishing letterbox companies in another Member States to obtain the status of 'foreign' investor to raise claims under an intra-EU BIT. Hereof, national treatment may be present as the foreign investor may lack any real subject due to a national investor being the actual owner, as suggested by van Os and Knottnerus (2011) and Lenk et al. (2016).

[80]See European Commission (2017c) and Basener (2017).

[81]To mention a few, TTIP information is available at Commission (2017d); EU–Canada Comprehensive Economic and Trade Agreement (CETA) text is available at EU and Canada (2016) and EU–Singapore Free Trade Agreement (EUSFTA) text is available at EU and Singapore (2017). For a list of all EU existing trade agreements and those under negotiation, see https://ec.europa.eu/trade/policy/countries-and-regions/negotiations-and-agreements. For the opposition of ISDS, see Sects. 1.1 and 1.2 in Chap. 1. See also Parliament (2015) paras (xiv)–(xv) and Euronews (2015).

[82]Despite CJEU case law (*Case 10/61 – Commission v Italy*, 1962, para 10) holding that relations between Member States, before their accession, have been automatically taken over by their obligations under the Treaties.

[83]See EC (2016) for information on the Europe agreements. Full texts available from the Commissions database at http://ec.europa.eu/world/agreements/default.home.do.

[84]For the Accession Treaties, see the EUR-Lex at http://eur-lex.europa.eu/collection/eu-law/treaties/treaties-accession.html.

[85]Treaty of Lisbon amending the Treaty on European Union and the Treaty establishing the European Community (EU 2007).

[86]The Treaty of Lisbon, the Europe Agreement and the Accession Treaties not expressly providing that their terms superseded the BITs: see, for example, *Eastern Sugar – Partial Award* (2007), pp. 32–33 Arts 143–149. The consequence is that some arbitral Tribunals have concluded that Article 351 TFEU is more lenient with regard to intra-EU BITs (Matei 2015d).

[87]The EU and many academics recognise this. To mention a few: the publication by some EU organs, such as the European Parliament (Cole et al. 2014), p. 15; publications by Commission Directorate-General for Financial Stability, financial services and capital markets union

on the legal consequences of *Achmea* finally made it clear that they held intra-EU ISDS (some reserved this to intra-EU BITs only while others held this applicable for all intra-EU ISDS) incompatible with EU law. As a consequence, ISDS provisions in those BITs became obsolete from the moment these were signed.[88]

The intersection of the international investment regime with EU law has displayed the manifest critical differences (structural, procedural, formal and in priority of values) between these two different legal orders. For example, in contrast to the EU legal order, which has a solid core provided by the EU Treaties that strongly influences and interacts with the law of its Member States and their judiciary system,[89] investment rules are completely decentralised. BITs and TIPs exist as a web of bilateral and regional treaties.[90]

5.4.1 *A Bit About BITs and TIPs*

The intersecting of the international investment regime with EU law has displayed the manifest critical differences (structural, procedural, formal) between these two different legal orders. For example, compared with the EU legal order, which has a solid core provided by the EU Treaties that strongly influences and interacts with the law of its Member States and their judiciary system, investment rules are utterly decentralised. BITs and TIPs therefore exist as a web of bilateral and regional treaties.

As explained in Sect. 2.4.2 in Chap. 2, the IIAs cover horizontal relations, where rights and obligations are applied and enforced horizontally. Namely, IIAs usually come with investment protection provisions, which include ISDS, which enables investors to sue states on the grounds of breach of investment protection obligations. Unlike in the EU (the CJEU), for ISDS procedures there is no single central court of appeal. Within this system, investors can bypass national courts by bringing a case

(DG FISMA); Commission Staff working documents (Commission 2012), pp. 4 and 13; Commission (2017b), p. 27. See also Directorate General for Competition (DG COMP) decision *Micula II (EU)* (2014). On scholarly literature on the subject, see also Reinisch (2013), pp. 111–157; Hindelang (2012b); Kleinheisterkamp (2011); Tietje and Wackernagel (2014); Wehland (2016).

[88] According to the Member States, these provisions 'do not produce effects including as regards provisions that provide for extended protection of investments made prior to termination for a further period of time (so-called sunset or grandfathering clauses)'. The Declaration of the Member States on the legal consequences of *Achmea*, p. 1. See also the Intra-EU BIT Termination Agreement Articles 2 and 3, SN/4656/2019/INIT, OJ L 169, 29.5.2020, p. 1–41.

[89] The EU's internal market has established a general adoption of the MFN principle instead of a web of BITs. If selective MFN treatment between selected Member States is allowed, it may cause fragmentation of European unity. (The WTO provides a prime example by losing a lot of its influence due to several bilateral agreements bypassing WTO rules.)

[90] Simmons (2014), p. 14. According to Juillard, BITs were never meant to 'be a charter of the economic rights and duties of either the MNEs or the sovereign States'. However, this does not mean MNEs have no duties and sovereign states have no rights: see Juillard (2001), p. 6.

directly before an international tribunal.[91] This setup provides a basis for these tribunals to interpret and apply EU law.[92]

While the primary purpose of ISDS is to encourage international investment by protecting the property rights of investors in foreign jurisdictions, IIAs are also supposed to boost investor confidence by ensuring a steadier regulatory framework in the host state.[93] However, the approach adopted towards regulatory stability clearly depends on the views of the individual arbitral tribunals.[94] Due to the diversity of the investment arbitration community, some tribunals hold that a regulatory status quo should be upheld, while other tribunals adopt a wider contextual approach regarding broader regulatory governance matters.[95]

The goal of 'promotion and protection of investments' is often the investment tribunal's focus when assessing the BITs envisioned content of standards for investors' protection. Given that the purpose and goals of the agreement are usually spelt out in the treaty introduction, this approach emphasises the role of the preamble. A more integrated approach is taken by the Vienna Convention on the Law of Treaties (VCLT), Article 31. It requires that text, context and purpose be considered equally in an integrated approach to the interpretation of the agreement. An illustration of the departure from the VCTL's requirements for interpretation is the very close

---

[91] The UNICTRAL Working Group III report pinpointed this being a serious issue and agreed that as part of the ISDS reform it should be seriously considered that investors would be required to exhaust local remedies before bringing their claims to investment arbitration: UNICTRAL (2019), para 30.

[92] *Achmea C-284/16* (2018), para 42.

[93] Niemelä (2017). For arguments that ISA is a 'neutral' and 'depoliticised' venue, and for arguments about investment tribunals developing human rights jurisprudence, see Brower (2014). See also Schreuer and Kriebaum (2011), p. 1088, arguing more cautiously that 'investment law has certain similarities with human rights law in that it protects an individual or corporate investor against infringements' by the host state.

[94] Notably, in *Genin v Estonia* (2001), para. 370, the tribunal took into account the context of post-communist economic transition.

[95] For example, see *Electrabel* compared with *Micula*. The international investment tribunals practice has given rise to concerns about the risk of regulatory chill: see Tienhaara (2010), Hazzaa and Kumpf (2015) and Brown (2013). The report of UNICTRAL's ongoing project on the reform of ISDS (April 2019) notes that some members of the working group held that: 'ISDS or the mere threat of using ISDS had resulted in regulatory chill and discouraged States from undertaking measures aimed to regulate economic activities and to protect economic, social and environmental rights'. See also report of Working Group III (Investor-State Dispute Settlement Reform) (UNICTRAL 2018, 2019). Then again, Tietje and Baetens (2014), pp. 39–48 argue that, due to multiple variables in play behind political decisions, it is hard to identify ISDS as the cause of chilling effects. Jennings (2016), pp. 132–133 points out that it is a correct analysis that multiple variables are in play behind political decisions; however, that does not necessarily close out ISDS being one of them. Schill (2007) concludes that investment treaties do not lead to a regulatory chill; however, his paper counts police power exception provisions to restrict the use of indirect expropriation. These are not present in many BITs—for example, intra-EU BITs. Niemelä (2017), p. 207; Brower and Schill (2008), p. 477 argue that it is misplaced to criticise investment treaties and arbitration as undermining the right to regulate as the states consented to this when ratifying investment treaties.

connection between the pro-investor outcome of many investment cases and the stated teleological interpretation of the 'promotion and protection of investments' goal.[96]

Within this context, as Srilal M. Perera explains, a 'prolific phenomenon in the past decade'[97] is the increased usage of Customary International Law (CIL) as part of investment arbitration, through notions of fairness and equity filtered through the FET standard.[98] Besides, the legal practice of narrowing the legitimate expectations under FET[99] has not been systematically reflected in the investment tribunal's application of the same.[100] Rather, some tribunals have expanded the concept.[101] Indeed, Tienhaara notes that, 'While originally devised to deal with issues such as government seizure of property in the context of the postcolonial period, ISDS cases now frequently revolve around the impacts of public policies on Investments.'[102]

FET clauses are often vaguely worded and of variable context,[103] leaving much to interpretation but without sufficient help to aid the interpreter.[104] Perera shows that the reason for generally inconsistent Awards is that there were no established criteria and no line of precedent through which to interpret equity-based decisions more objectively.[105] This evolution of CIL interpretation, to assess the FET standard, has a major issue due to the subjectivity of judgments based on the arbitrators' discretion of interpretation. This subsequently creates a situation where the imposed degree of liability varies due to a lack of criteria for a standard of damages.[106]

---

[96] Djajić (2017), p. 27.

[97] Perera (2012), p. 210.

[98] Perera (2012), pp. 210, 212. See also Rösch (2017), p. 44; Hindelang (2012b), p. 232; Saavedra Pinto (2016), p. 267; Gallo and Nicola (2015).

[99] Relevant cases for attempts at establishing a definition for legitimate expectations are ICSID Case No. ARB(AF)/00/2 (*Tecmed*, 2003) para 154; *Saluka* (2006), paras 305–306; and *LG&E* (2006). *Tecmed* set the standard of protection as extremely broad for investors, while the host states needed to uphold a regulatory limbo: *LG&E* (2006). The scope was narrowed later by *Saluka* and *LG&E*, which recognised a nation's right to regulate and the necessity of separating normal business risk from legitimate expectations. Tietje and Baetens (2014) argue (by referring to *Saluka)* that investment tribunals have in practice interpreted FET narrowly by applying proportionality principles: Tietje and Baetens (2014), p. 57. However, this has not been consistent practice, especially for intra-EU BITs, as shown in this dissertation.

[100] Saavedra Pinto (2016), p. 277; Gaukrodger (2017), p. 5.

[101] Van Harten (2013), pp. 101–103; Saavedra Pinto (2016), p. 277; Johnson and Volkov (2014), p. 3.

[102] Tienhaara and Downie (2018), p. 452.

[103] Vandevelde (2010), p. 47; Kleinheisterkamp (2015), p. 802; Gaukrodger (2017), p. 5; OECD (2005), p. 74.

[104] Saavedra Pinto (2016), p. 267; Perera (2012), pp. 210, 212; Gaukrodger (2017), p. 5; Vandevelde (2010), p. 46. See also *EDF (Services) Limited v Romania, Award* (2009), para 215.

[105] Perera (2012), p. 213.

[106] Perera (2012), p. 215.

ISDS and especially investment state arbitration is currently facing a legitimacy crisis.[107] Sands mentions that the sky-high legal fees for even small, rather insignificant, cases and the practice of double hatting[108] leading to lack of transparency and conflict of interests concerns,.[109] As the main concern, Sands pinpoints the ethics of the appointments. To most reasonable observers, the material and political interests of the international lawyers seem to trump independence and impartiality.[110] Available evidence also suggests that ISDS is not limited to being only an insurance policy by some international investors, but is regarded as an added profit-source.[111]

In combination with the increasing use of ISDS, these actions and concerns have led to a growing number of collisions where the BIT regime and the EU exercise international rules of conflict of laws regarding party autonomy. This is particularly because the EU 'is a polity based on the rule of law'[112] and, like any such entity, does assert its right to ascribe fundamental importance to some of its own norms—thus warranting protection from the exercise of party autonomy and the operation of ordinary conflict of law rules.[113]

5.4.2 *The EU Is Not Like Other IGOs*

Further, for the EU this right for self-assertion has evolved to take on more of a constitutional nature. Besides being an entity based on the rule of law, the EU holds an international legal personality,[114] which utilises CIL in its external relationships. This practice applies to both relationships with other intergovernmental

---

[107] Sands (2015). See also Giorgetti (2013), Olivet and Eberhardt (2012) and Puig (2016). Especially on indirect expropriation, see Dani and Akhtar-Khavari (2016).

[108] Langford et al. (2017), pp. 3–4. In an empirical study Langford, Behn, and Hilleren Lie found that in 47 per cent of cases (509 of 1077 in total) at least one arbitrator double hats. Moreover, 'in a fifth of cases both the bench and bar are playing the opposite role somewhere else'. The term 'double hatting' refers to the practice of simultaneously combining the roles of arbitrator and counsel in different cases.

[109] Sands (2015). Philippe Sands is a senior figure in international law and international arbitration. Similar concerns and warnings have also been raised before from other senior figures. See Mackenzie and Sands (2003), Sands (2011) and Buergenthal (2006). For example, several attempts to disqualify arbitrator Gary Born on the grounds of partiality have been unsuccessful. This is likely because the arbitrators in the ICSID system judge their colleagues. For example, one of the judges deciding on the challenge against Mr Born in *Kruck and others v. Spain, Decision on the Proposal to Disqualify Mr. Gary B. Born* (2018) was facing similar charges himself on alleged prejudgment in another case: Peterson (2018b).

[110] Langford et al. (2017), p. 2.

[111] Tienhaara and Downie (2018), p. 458.

[112] Bermann (2012), p. 410.

[113] Bermann (2012), pp. 410–411.

[114] Article 47 TEU. Hence the EU has a power to conclude treaties in line with Articles 216(1) TFEU and 37 TEU.

organisations and third countries, and the relationships between its Member States and third countries. The EU is, however, a very different legal entity from standard intergovernmental organisations and constitutional polities, with its structure falling in between the two. It is an intergovernmental organisation, created and based on treaties, and therefore a creature of public international law.[115]

The EU has put itself in a special position *vis-à-vis* the application and implementation of public international law. As Ziegler notes, the EU combines the features of an intergovernmental organisation and a state.[116] The CJEU, the supreme court of the EU, declared the *sui generis* nature of EU law in two landmark cases, *C-26/62 van Gend & Loos* (1963) and *C-6/64 Costa v. E.N.E.L* (1964), and thereby it positioned EU law and the European Union, *a fortiori*, within public international law.[117]

Certainly, the development of the EU legal order shows that an intergovernmental entity can evolve to contain a legal regime that has specific and even unique features compared with other entities of public international law.[118] EU law has made a unique version of public international law. While a contracting state makes public international law applicable by virtue of an act of the state, EU law is incorporated and applied within the Member State's national legal order due to its supranational source.[119] That makes EU law part and in force of the national law of the Member State by virtue of an international agreement concluded by the state.[120]

As a result, while EU law has primacy over national law, with provisions having a direct effect for EU citizens and Member States, it also has an autonomous position in relation to both national and international law.[121] Not only is EU law superior to the law of its Member States, but the same principle applies to international law and

---

[115] Finckenberg-Broman (2019) referring to De Búrca (2010). See Amerasinghe (2005) for the criteria for an intergovernmental organisation. The CJEU in *Achmea C-284/16* (2018) para 33 underlines the constitutional structure of the EU.

[116] Ziegler (2013). This makes EU law a *sui generis* legal order.

[117] Interdependent treaties are recognised by the 1969 Vienna Convention on the Law of Treaties regarding the modification, suspension and termination of treaties (Articles 41, 58 and 60) with implications for the relevant rights and duties of state parties to treaties. Thus, 'under "normal" international law sovereign states can, within the limits of peremptory norms, establish an international organisation, with as extensive powers as they agree upon whether it affects their national legislation or not' (Hartley 2004).

[118] Weiler and Haltern (1996), p. 419; Tietje and Wackernagel (2015), p. 215. Supranational organisations, despite being *lex specialis*, remain entities of public international law: Hartley (2004), pp. 1–2.

[119] Tietje and Wackernagel (2015), p. 215.

[120] *Achmea C-284/16* (2018), para 33 referring to *Opinion 2/13 of the Court (Full Court)* (2014), paras 165–167.

[121] These principles were developed by early case law of the CJEU. Direct effect means that under certain conditions individuals can assert European provisions in a national or European court: *Case 26-62 van Gend & Loos* (1963). The primacy of EU law means that, in case of conflict of laws, EU law prevails: *Case 6-64 – Costa v ENEL* (1964). The principle of primacy applies even on national norms of constitutional status in conflict situations: *Case 106/77 – Simmenthal* (1978).

the agreements of its Member States within the scope of EU law.[122] Notably, EU law is hard law, meaning that besides being binding, it also contains legal obligations to individuals as well as providing legal remedies for individual rights.

The Lisbon Treaty, like its predecessors, is an integral part of the legal system of the Member States and must be applied by their courts.[123] As stressed by AG Maduro,[124] the source of the validity of EU law, being integrated and applied within the national legal orders of its Member States because of its supranational source, is not merely dependent on a wilful act of its Member States. This differs from international law, where the application of international law depends on the intent of the state.[125] Hence the EU law is not subject to a change of a specific state's will, nor can a Member State act contrary to the EU Treaties.[126] Explicitly, a Member State cannot change these laws by unilateral action.[127] Yet in the wake of the ongoing internal market integration, the Member States' relative capacity to influence their economies, and to reach their own policy goals has eroded.[128]

As stated earlier, the EU's autonomy serves as the base for its legitimacy.[129] Within the EU, the notion of EU public policy encompasses and the specific characteristics of the EU.[130] As the EU imbues its legal norms with a public policy dimension expansively, as part of EU's most fundamental objectives, it does not fit well with the regime of international investment arbitration, which has a substantially different point of view of procedural autonomy and public policy.[131]

---

[122]For intra-EU BITs, see *Case 10/61 – Commission v Italy* (1962) ECLI:EU:C:1962:2; *Case 235/87 – Matteucci* (1988) ECLI:EU:C:1988:460 para 22; *C-3/91 – Exportur v LOR and Confiserie du Tech* (1992); *Achmea C-284/16* (2018). For agreements concluded by EC Member States, see *C-478/07 Budějovický Budvar* (2009) ECLI:EU:C:2009:521 and *C-469/00– Ravil* (2003) para 37; *C-377/98 – Netherlands v Parliament and Council* (2001), para 52, where the CJEU clarified that 'the lawfulness of a Community instrument does not depend on its conformity with an international agreement to which the Community is not a party'. The primacy of the EU's primary law applies over international agreements. In *C-308/06 – Intertanko and Others* (2008), paras 42 and 53, the CJEU confirmed that International Agreements of which the EU is part have primacy over secondary legislation but not primary legislation. See also the rejection of EU accession of the ECtHR: *Opinion 2/13 of the Court (Full Court)* (2014), paras 150, 170 and 201.

[123]Latif (2017).

[124]Maduro (2007), p. 4 et seq.

[125]Tietje and Wackernagel (2015), pp. 215–216.

[126]See the initial version of Article 9 of the Treaty Establishing the European Coal and Steel Community, opened for signature 18 April 1951 (entered into force 23 July 1952).

[127]Tietje and Wackernagel (2015). The procedure of changing of Treaties is laid down in Article 48 TEU.

[128]Finckenberg-Broman (2019).

[129]See Sect. 1.2 in Chap. 1, referring to *Achmea C-284/16* (2018) paras 33 and 34. See also Bermann (2012), p. 431; Eckes (2016), pp. 10 and 31; Gallo and Nicola (2015).

[130]Bermann (2012), p. 410.

[131]See Sect. 1.2 in Chap. 1.

5.4.3 The Procedural Paradox

Consequently, when assessing disputes stemming from breaches of IIAs, as Tietje and Wackernagel put it, there are more than the 'internal' or 'international' legal and political conditions under the law for an area and people to consider; they need to think about the EU.[132] Nevertheless, Tribunals have failed to recognise this several times, as demonstrated by numerous ISDS cases.[133] According to *Electrabel Decision on Jurisdiction* (2012), this is the outcome of the arbitrators deciding these cases not being equally competent in EU law and international investment law.[134] Due to this *sui generis* character of EU law, the legitimacy of state aid measures can only be decided by the EU law itself.

However, its relationship with other international law is generally being determined by international rules of conflict laid down in the VCLT.[135] The VTCL is neutral on the interpretive approach to be adopted by the disputing parties.[136] Occasionally, this type of neutrality courts conflict. Explicitly, conflict arises over disputes between non-state actors where transnational courts and tribunals have jurisdiction. As Roberts puts it, transnational judicial bodies tasked with interpreting and applying treaties that create rights or benefits for non-state actors are likely to view themselves, at least partially, as trustees tasked with protecting the interests of the treaty's beneficiaries.[137] Therefore, these judicial bodies are less likely to be deferential to subsequent interpretations adopted by the treaty parties.[138] Inherently, this type of self-perception incorporates conflicts of interest between transnational courts and tribunals. From the perspective of investment tribunals when applying the VCTL, the EU legal order comes across as a new species.[139]

[132]Tietje and Wackernagel (2015), p. 215.

[133]Sometimes the investment tribunals deem EU law to be international law; at other times it is viewed as domestic law: see *Eastern Sugar-Final Award* (2007); *Eastern Sugar – Partial award* (2007); *AES v Hungary (III) Award* (2010); *Electrabel Decision on Jurisdiction* (2012); *Electrabel Award* (2015); *EDF v Hungary* (2014); *Binder v Czech Republic Award* (2007); *Oostergetel v Slovak Republic* (2010); *Achmea BV Final Award* (2012); *Achmea v Slovak Republic* (2008); *Charanne Final Award* (2016); *RREEF Infrastructure* (2016); *Isolux Award* (2016); *WNC Award* (2017); *Anglia Auto Accessories Final Award* (2017); *Eiser Award* (2017). In *Electrabel Decision on Jurisdiction* (2012), paras 4.117 et seq. *(Electrabel Award*, 2015), which considered that EU law as a *sui generis* legal order, the investment tribunal decided to treat thus EU law as international law. The tribunals in *Achmea BV Final Award* (2012) and *Euram v the Slovak Republic* (2012) reached similar conclusions.

[134]*Electrabel Award* (2015).

[135]Burgstaller et al. (2013).

[136]Roberts (2013), Ch 2(b). 'Inter-state' dispute resolution is where the dispute resolution takes place between two or more states and 'transnational' dispute resolution involves disputes between non-state actors and states: see Keohane et al. (2000).

[137]Roberts (2013), Ch 2(b); Alter (2008), pp. 33, 38–39.

[138]Roberts (2010), pp. 180, 182–185.

[139]The VCLT recognises only states as its subjects, and thus covers only domestic and international law. This complicated situation exhibits itself, for example, in the intra-EU–ECT practice under

While the investment tribunals have mostly avoided direct confrontation with the EU by denying any existing conflict while applying VTCL,[140] they do not feel bound to respect EU law when deciding on subject matter covered and regulated by EU *acquis*.[141] As a further aggravation for the EU, the regime of international investment law has been rejecting the interpretive autonomy of the CJEU.[142] Indeed as Hindelang notes, 'This principle of self-assertion became centre stage when answering the question of whether ISDS in an intra-EU context was compatible with EU law.'[143]

Another issue is that rulings made by investment tribunals cannot be reviewed by domestic courts for conformity with EU law. Because these tribunals are exceptions to the legal system of the EU, they cannot make a reference to the CJEU for a preliminary ruling according to Article 267 TFEU. Therefore, according to the CJEU in *Achmea*, tribunals potentially threaten the autonomy of the EU legal order and compromise its specific characteristics.[144] The CJEU, as the ultimate guardian of the

---

which the tribunals have perceived EU law as being: (1) national law in *Achmea BV Final Award* (2012) and *Achmea v Slovak Republic* (2008); (2) international law in *Electrabel Award* (2015); and (3) a matter of fact in *AES v Hungary (III) Award* (2010).

[140] Articles 59 and 30 VTCL as expressions of *lex posterior*. This type of denial has been consistent even post *Achmea C-284/16* (2018) and seems to have escalated in *Vattenfall II (Decision on the Achmea issue)* (2018), which took place on 31 August 2018. Not only did the *Vattenfall II* tribunal reject all arguments on EU law being relevant but, according to the *Vattenfall II* Tribunal, 'Article 16 ECT prevents the EU Treaties from being construed so as to derogate from more favourable rights of the Investor in Parts III and V ECT, including the right to dispute resolution' (para 221).

[141] Cole et al. (2014), p. 15. This is also presented in *Micula* as well as *Achmea C-284/16* (2018), previously *Eureko* (2010). Other cases, such as *AES v Hungary (III) Award* (2010) were settled by the parties *AES v Hungary (Anulment)* (2012). The *EDF v Hungary* (2014) Award was set aside by the Swiss Federal Supreme Court (*EDF International SA v Republic of Hungary, Swiss*, 2015) and *US Steel v Slovakia* (2013) was withdrawn by the claimant-stipulated termination order (*Stipulated Termination Order US Steel*, 2014). See also *Saluka* (2006). In *Achmea C-284/16* (2018), the ECJ underlines the importance of respecting EU law at para 34.

[142] See *Eastern Sugar – Final Award* (2007); *Eastern Sugar – Partial Award* (2007); *AES v Hungary (III) Award* (2010); *EDF v Hungary* (2014); *Electrabel Decision on Jurisdiction* (2012); *Electrabel Award* (2015); *Binder v Czech Republic Award* (2007); *Oostergetel v Slovak Republic* (2010); *Achmea BV Final Award* (2012); *Achmea v Slovak Republic* (2008); *Charanne Final Award* (2016); *RREEF Infrastructure* (2016); *Isolux Award* (2016); *WNC Award* (2017); *Anglia Auto Accessories Final Award* (2017), *Eiser Award* (2017); *Masdar v Spain Award* (2018); *Antin Infrastructure and Others v Spain Award* (2018); *Vattenfall II (Decision on the Achmea Issue)* (2018).

[143] Hindelang (2019), p. 3.

[144] *Achmea C-284/16* (2018), paras 31–37. For primacy, see *Case 6-64 – Costa v ENEL* (1964); for direct effect, see Van Gend en Loos (1963); for mutual trust, see Article 2 TEU and sincere cooperation Article 4(3)1 TEU (*Achmea*, para 58). See also *Opinion 2/13 of the Court (Full Court)* (2014) para 176. Before *Achmea*, several authors recognised these complications connected to investor-state arbitrations, including Kleinheisterkamp (2012b, 2015); Konttinen and Teivainen (2013); Fleming (2014); Schneiderman (2016); Van Harten (2015); Matei (2015a, b); Happ and Tietje (2013); Tietje (2008); Tietje et al. (2012); Tietje and Wackernagel (2015); Ortolani (2015); Struckmann et al. (2016); Gallo and Nicola (2015); Bermann (2012).

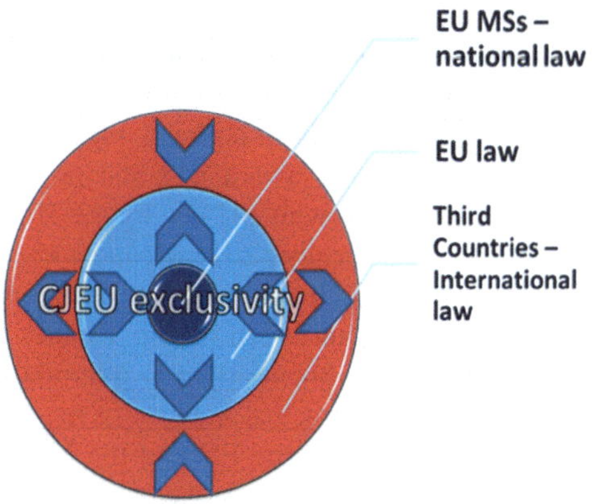

Fig. 5.1 The CJEU's exclusivity as the final interpreter of EU law

EU Treaties, protects the autonomy of the EU's legal order as well as its judicial system against any external intrusions and influences that breach it. The CJEU also aims at durable protection against the same illegal external influences for the parts of the European judicial system that are technically under Member State jurisdiction—the national courts.[145] For the CJEU's exclusivity as the final interpreter of EU law, see Fig. 5.1.

In effect, by their legal practice, Tribunals have been setting the borders and occasionally the status of EU law regarding investment protection. From the EU's viewpoint, this authority belongs to the CJEU. Sworn to upkeep the legal autonomy of the EU and the specific characteristics of EU law for matters concerning EU law, the courts of the Member States and the CJEU must follow EU law.

To preserve the autonomy of EU law, the CJEU has consistently rejected the ability of international courts to interpret the provisions of an international agreement that are binding on EU institutions if this adversely affects the autonomy of the EU legal order.[146] In principle, a judge of an EU Member State, when faced with the dilemma of having to choose between respecting their country's obligations under international law[147] or preserving the integrity of the legal order of the EU Treaties, is obliged to privilege the latter.[148] This situation manifested recently via the German Federal Supreme Courts (Bundesgerichtshof) final decision on *Achmea* (*Joined*

---

[145] Hindelang (2019), p. 2.

[146] *Opinion 1/91* (1991); EEA Agreement of 14 December 1991, paras 40 and 70; *Opinion 1/09* (2011); Agreement Creating a Unified Patent Litigation System of 8 March 2011, paras 74 and 76; *Opinion 2/13 of the Court (Full Court)* (2014), paras 182 and 183. See also *Achmea C-284/16* (2018). For an international court to not threaten the autonomy of EU law, the CJEU created a test in *Opinion 1/17* (2019). See Sect. 5.3 above.

[147] *AES v Hungary (III) Award* (2010) para 7.6.9. For arguments that EU law is not international law for the purposes of Article 26(6) of the ECT and thus not applicable law, see Roe (2016), pp. 95–97. However, the CJEU in *Achmea C-284/16* (2018) para 41 firmly sets EU law as international law.

[148] Kleinheisterkamp (2012b), p. 93. See also *Opinion 1/91* (1991), paras 35, 71; *C-459/03- Mox Plant* (2006) para 123; *Joined cases c-402/05 p and c-415/05 p Kadi* (2008), paras 282, 286. The

Cases c-402/05 p and c-415/05 p Kadi, 2008) in October 2018.[149] It was the Bundesgerichtshof that sent the request for a referral (*Bundesgerichtshof beschluss – I ZB 2/15 – (Achmea)*, 2018) on the compatibility of intra-EU BITs with EU law. After the CJEU's *Achmea* decision, rejecting intra-EU BITs, the Bundesgerichtshof set aside the arbitral award that had previously been in favour of *Achmea* and deemed compatible with EU law by the Higher Regional Court of Frankfurt in its decision of 18 December 2014 (*Achmea C-284/16*, 2018).

For international market disputes within the ambit of EU law, the CJEU claims exclusive jurisdiction based on the Treaties and case law. This exclusivity covers topics such as an ultimate right to interpret EU law within the EU legal order,[150] rulings on non-contractual liability of the EU[151] and decisions on the division of competences between the EU and the Member States.[152] Further, the CJEU also claims the right to decide whether a given Member State's administrative or judicial system meets the adequacy standard set by EU case law.[153]

By applying a wide range of interpretative methods in its case law,[154] the CJEU has also challenged a central premise of international arbitration law, by advancing a far-reaching and advanced notion of EU public policy.[155] For investment tribunals, public policy is subject to a narrow interpretation when invoked as a ground for annulling arbitral awards or denying them recognition or enforcement,[156] due to the

---

role of national courts since *Van Gend en Loos* (1963) has been to ensure full effectiveness of EU law by applying the principles of direct effect and supremacy when EU law is relevant.

[149] *Bundesgerichtshof beschluss – I ZB 2/15 – (Achmea)* (2018) beschluss I ZB 2/15 vom 31; *Achmea C-284/16* (2018).

[150] Thus, rejecting any external judicial or quasi-judicial body that attempts to interpret or apply EU law. See *Opinion 2/13 of the Court (Full Court)* (2014) para 183; *Opinion 1/09* (2011), para 76.

[151] Articles 340 TFEU and 19 TEU. See *C-377/09 – Hanssens-Ensch* (2010), para 16; *C-275/00 – European Community v First NV and Franex NV* (2002) para 43; *C-282/90 – Vreugdenhil v Commission* (1992), para 14; *Case 281/84 – Zuckerfabrik Bedburg v Council and Commission* (1987), para 12. Dimopoulos (2014) argues that this does not hinder the EU from concluding an international agreement containing investment protection and ISDS provisions. However, these fall within the field of mixed competence, so all the Member States must also be signatories of IIAs with these type of provisions: *Opinion 2/15 of the Court (Full Court* (2017).

[152] *Opinion 2/13 of the Court (Full Court)* (2014) para 234; and *Opinion 2/15 of the Court (Full Court)* (2017).

[153] Ankersmit (2016); Bermann (2012), p. 410. See also *Case 14/83 von Colson* (1984).

[154] In addition to literal interpretation used in public international law, other interpretation methods used frequently by the CJEU, *inter alia* contextual interpretation and teleological interpretation. See VCTL, Articles 31–33 and Maduro (2007), p. 4. Unlike many other courts from a different jurisdiction, the CJEU does not refer to any literature other than the opinion of the Advocate General in its judgments. The EU also merges civil law and common law elements. Generally, for mixed legal systems, see Picker (2008) and Tetley (1999).

[155] *C-126/97 – Eco Swiss* (1999) para 39 established EU competition policy as EU public policy in an arbitration setting.

[156] Saavedra Pinto (2016) and Bermann (2012).

tribunal's inherent function of overriding party autonomy or circumventing/overriding the enforcement of an applicable judgment or even law.[157]

It is a conflict arising out of a Member State's national court duty to deny effect to an otherwise valid award, on the grounds of it offending EU public policy norms.[158] Thus a Member State might undertake dubious actions under international investment law, enforced by tribunals, when under pressure from EU law. It leads to both the tribunals and the Member State courts facing competing legal claims.[159]

Neither side of the conflict, the investment tribunals and the EU, has been willing to yield jurisdictive authority. Eventually, the tribunals' expansion of the scope of investment protection through their practice, colliding with the CJEU's case law equally extending its public policy scope, arrived at the rejection of ISDS by the EU in *Achmea*.[160] Clearly, the CJEU's main concern was the protection of the autonomy and the *sui generis* character of the EU, as well as the principles of effectiveness and mutual trust. The fundamental importance of these principles cannot and should not be overcome by shared economic interests, such as the global race for capital and investment.

5.5 State Aid Regime vs ISDS (The Requirement for Legitimacy)

General economic policies over the last six decades have been promoting the positive effects of foreign direct investment. It is therefore not surprising that countries, in their attempt to attract FDI, try to outbid each other by offering elaborate incentive schemes (see Sect. 2.4.3 in Chap. 2). While this type of action is common, it does not necessarily make these incentives legal by all international norms. According to the UNCTAD report in 1998, these benefits tend to mostly end up in the pockets of MNEs instead of consumers and local businesses,[161] distorting competition in favour of these MNEs. This type of market distortion is what competition laws governing private and public entities are particularly meant to hinder from taking place. For example, behind some WTO cases based on the Subsidies Agreement[162] lurk fiscal incentive schemes. However, the WTO only

---

[157] Bermann (2012), p. 419.

[158] Bermann (2012).

[159] Bermann (2012). As was shown to have occurred in the *Micula* case (see Chap. 4).

[160] Accordingly, critics of investment treaties and ISA have welcomed the judgment, whereas the proponents of investment treaties have held it to be bad law, leading to weaker 'rule of law within the EU' (Niemelä 2017).

[161] Tavares-Lehmann et al. (2016), p. 2. Accordingly, 80 per cent of all cross-border flows are internal transactions of multinational firms or through supply chains supervised by them.

[162] See, *inter alia*, European Communities and Certain Member States – Measures Affecting Trade in Large Civil Aircraft, WT/D316/R (*EC – Aircraft (Panel)*, 2010; *EC - Aircraft AB-2010-1*, 2011)

catches incentive schemes that are related to goods, where EU state aid law covers all these schemes. Furthermore, in the EU, the economic nature of the Treaties has been softened by the systematic embedment of the fundamental principles of EU law[163] through the case law of the CJEU and by the adoption of the Charter.

Moreover, BIT regimes diverge from state aid policy in the *de facto* application and implementation of rules, and the target group at which the ultimate benefit is aimed. Unlike IIAs, which solely cover foreign investors, EU competition law strives for a fair competition of all undertakings. Likewise, state aid control limits preferential treatment to a selected group unless it contributes to the common interest (see Chap. 3). Competition policy provides for the ability of governments to uphold sound competition domestically by preventing the market from being distorted by unfair competition or monopolisation;[164] otherwise, it cannot be ensured that consumers will benefit and the competitive process of a national economy, irrespective of the origin of a producer or service provider, will be upheld.

Unless competition laws are neutral in their application, anticompetitive practices, regardless of whether domestic or foreign companies undertake them, cannot be dealt with.[165] Nevertheless, the global granting of FDI incentives stand in contradiction to this awareness, 'in the sense that they target or give preferential treatment to foreign investors, are by nature discriminatory'.[166]

Explicitly, FDI incentives consist of *capital import subsidies*,[167] which means that in effect subsidy wars are very real regarding capital flows. Therefore, appropriate and effective competition laws are essential to control this kind of harmful behaviour. In the EU, these are already in place in the form of state aid control. EU competition law and policy, one of the cornerstones of EU law,[168] is there to defend fair competition for all enterprises with operations in the EU and to prohibit anti-

---

and 'US –Measures Affecting Trade in Large Aircraft DS353 (second complaint)', WTOAB (2012).

[163] Such as human rights, public health, labour rights, consumer protection and environmental protection.

[164] The Relationship Between Foreign Investment and Competition Policy, Communication from the European Community and its Member States Retrieved from Geneva (Working Group on the Relationship Between Trade and Investment 1998; Clarke 2003).

[165] WTO (Working Group on the Relationship Between Trade and Investment 1998), p. 14.

[166] OECD Report 2003 (The Organisation for Economic Co-operation and Development (OECD) 2003), p. 11; see also Coyne and Moberg (2015).

[167] Not to be confused with import substitution subsidies (WTO), which are contingent upon the use of domestic over-imported goods, or the OECD's definition of import subsidies, which is otherwise the same as that of the WTO but with a broader scope encompassing both goods and services (OECD glossary of statistical terms, Import Subsidies, at https://stats.oecd.org/glossary/detail.asp?ID=1298). The concept of capital import subsidies is *e contrario* to import substitution subsidy as it is contingent upon the use of imported capital and has been created by the author of this dissertation to explain the connection of FDI and state aid policy.

[168] State aid policy is part of EU competition policy. The *Eco Swiss case* paragraph 39 established EU competition policy as EU public policy in an arbitration setting. Later cases, such as *C-295/04-Manfredi* (2006) para 31 and *T-Mobile Netherlands BV v Raad van beestuur van de Nederlandse*

competitive practices for skewing the level playing field within the EU and across the world.[169] Many Member State government actions result in a benefit to an enterprise, thus national initiatives to attract FDI may easily classify as a state aid measure.[170]

In this situation, it is the investment incentives that constitute the elephant in the room. If Member States do not abide by the Article 108(3) TFEU standstill clause before implementing investment incentives,[171] these will constitute unlawful state aid.

5.5.1 *Investment Incitements Can Be Unlawful State Aid*

Therefore, initiatives offered to attract foreign direct investment must follow EU state aid law to be legal and/or internal market compatible, or an underlying possibility of conflict between state aid law and investment protection is ever-present. Ironically, the EU state aid policy constitutes almost an antithesis of FDI incentives, as it prohibits preferential treatment of a select group. As this preferential treatment also provides an advantage to the enterprises receiving the incentives from a Member State, which potentially affects the competition on the internal market, the elements for state aid are in place.

Whether these incitements constitute state aid depends on the character of the incentives that have been offered by the Member State to the enterprise to obtain the foreign direct investment. Hence, to ensure compatibility with state aid law, all incentives offered by Member States to investors that contain the 107 TFEU criteria must be approved (or pre-approved) by the Commission.[172] Nevertheless, the revocation of a Member State's measures, implemented without the Commission's consent, to attract FDIs has not prevented investors from invoking the BITs investment protection provisions—that is, FET—in order to launch claims against them.

Mededingingsautoriteit (2009) para 49, affirmed this. Competition law is one of the cornerstones of EU law: De Cecco (2012); Maduro (2007); Sauter (2013).

[169] A global application of state aid rules is actively lobbied for by EU companies (Businesseurope 2015) and trade ministers of many of the Member States and the Commission.

[170] American Bar Association (2010), Ch 6.

[171] Secondary law, namely the procedural regulation, explains how these procedures, as administered by the Commission, are implemented and applied.

[172] As explained in Sect. 3.5 in Chap. 3.

5.5.2 *Legitimate Expectations: State Aid vs FET*

In EU law, there is no single provision for FET. Instead, there are different legal principles that combine to protect the individual. Because the EU focuses on the rule of law, as Kleinheisterkamp informs us, the scope of interpretation for legitimate expectations varies.[173] Due to the strict case law from the CJEU on the subject, the lack of legitimate expectations does not protect an investor under EU state aid law,[174] except under exceptional circumstances.[175]

Misguided assumptions that the principle of legitimate expectations covers similar requirements in both fields, in EU state aid law and FET under investment treaty law, have further enhanced the apparent dissimilarities. In fact, these two fields of law interpret and apply these in completely diverse ways. See Fig. 5.2 to visualise the situation where FDI incentives that constitute illegal state aid are perceived by international investment tribunals compared with the EU courts and the Commission The scope of acceptance of the expectations of undertakings regarding state aid law is extremely narrow, while in investment treaty laws FET clauses the acceptance is overly broad.[176]

Several authors emphasise that the incompatibility of the FET standard of BITs is enhanced in EU competition law, where a beneficiary of state aid cannot enjoy the protection derived from the principle of legitimate expectations before a measure has been notified and approved by the Commission, as stipulated by the provisions of Article 108(3) TFEU.[177] Hence arguments on legitimate expectations from an intra-

---

[173] Kleinheisterkamp (2012a), p. 418.

[174] *C-24/95 – Alcan 2* (1997), paras 25, 49. *C-24/95 – Alcan 2* (1997) was a request for a preliminary ruling by the German Federal Administrative Court regarding unlawful state aid received by Alcan Deutschland GmbH from the German territory of Land RheinlandPfalz. The economic benefit received by Alcan had been prescribed according to national law, so was protected by the general principle of legitimate expectations. However, according to the CJEU (para 49 referring to para 25), an 'undertakings receiving aid cannot have a legitimate expectation as to the lawfulness of the aid unless it has been granted in compliance with the procedure laid down in Article 93 of the Treaty'. Indeed, 'A diligent businessman should normally be able to determine whether that procedure has been followed' (para 25 referring to *Case C-5/89 – Commission v Germany* (1990), paras 13 and 14 and *C-169/95 – Spain v Commission* (1997), para 51.

[175] If there is a violation of the general principles of European Union law (Article 16(1) of the Procedural Regulation). The CJEU has applied this exemption restrictively, accepting the invocation of legitimate expectations only if, and to the extent that, the Member State or undertaking concerned was given consistent, unconditional, and precise assurances that the EU would act in a specific way: *C-630/11 P – HGA and Others v Commission* (2013) para 132. See also *T-328/09 - Producteurs de légumes de France v Commission* (2009); *T-177/10 Alcoa v Commission* (2014)) and *joined cases T-427/04 and T-17/05 France and France Télécom v Commission* (2009). It is possible that an investor might rely on legitimate expectations under FET provisions for 'extra-EU situation' under the ECT (*State aid SA.40348 (2015/NN)* (2017), para 164.

[176] Saavedra Pinto (2016), p. 285.

[177] This has been confirmed repeatedly by the CJEU case law, which has held that beneficiaries of aid have a duty to check the lawfulness of the aid: Jestaedt et al. (2006); see also Hindelang (2012b),

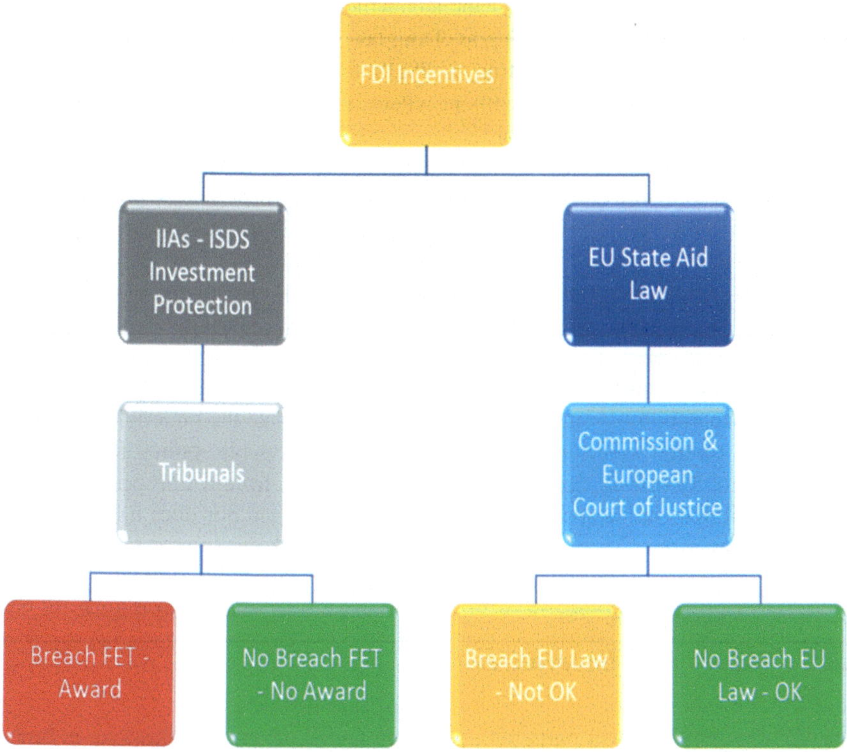

Fig. 5.2 How ISDS Awards become state aid

EU BIT angle have not solved any conflicts between state aid law and FET, leading to a competition of authority between the EU and the international investment law.

5.6 From Casual Collisions to Recurrent Clashes

In the aftermath of these claims, a competition of authority between the EU and the international investment law, as applied by arbitration tribunals, has occurred.[178] Neither any argument on origins of illegality nor autonomy from the EU has

p. 232; Reinisch (2013), pp. 111–157; Saavedra Pinto (2016); Tietje and Wackernagel (2014); Matei and Ciurtin (2016).

[178] In contrast to the idealistic position adopted by many judges of the International Court of Justice (ICJ) in 2003, the fragmentation of the international law has led to contradictory jurisprudence: Simma (2009); Guillaume (2000). Koskenniemi did, however, warn of managerial anti-formalism (Broude 2013)—in particular, the investment protection regime and ISDS (Konttinen and Teivainen

prevailed in front of the investment tribunals, which have insisted upon their right to determine these claims—although, as Douglas shows, depending on the rules governing the investor-state arbitration, ISDS may have the legal infrastructure necessary to regulate foreign investment where issues are raised about the legality of the acquisition of the investment.[179]

Consequently, in an investment agreement, where the measure acquiring the foreign investment has taken place in violation of the host state's laws in some ISDS system (such as the UNICTRAL rules), the tribunal lacks jurisdiction to determine the claim.[180] However, when illegality stems from the conduct of an entity of a state in connection with the acquisition of the investment, the arbitrators have been unwilling to impeach their right to arbitrate.[181] By choosing to enforce this type of agreement, the courts have effectively upheld an agreement to arbitrate.[182] Domestic courts, especially Common law courts by the application of the doctrine of separability,[183] have been reluctant to invalidate the underlying contract between the foreign investor and the host state due to public policy factors. The especially problematic aspect of the ICSID convention, from a European perspective, is that it does not accept *ordre public* exceptions, and nor does it care for the legality of a measure.[184]

5.6.1 When Two Imperatives Meet

The ICSID Convention in particular, as Tietje and Wackernagel observe, is problematic from a European perspective.[185] It is well known that ICSID Awards, with their legal proceedings entirely contained within the ICSDI Convention lacking any

2013). See *Achmea C-284/16* (2018) and, analogically, *Joined cases c-402/05 p and c 415/05 p Kadi* (2008).

179 Douglas (2014).

180 Douglas (2014), p. 2. See also *World Duty Free Award* (2006); *Fraport AG Award* (2007), paras 396–401; *Phoenix v Czech Republic Award* (2009) paras 101–5; *Hamester GmbH v Ghana Award* (2010), para 127; *Ambiente v Argentine, decision on Jurisdiction and Admissibility* (2013), para 517.

181 Roe (2016) and Douglas (2014). See, for example, *Beijingjianlong v Golden Ocean Group* (2013).

182 Recently, there has been debate about the scope of the court's discretion regarding competing policy 'imperatives where a claimant which has done wrong has nonetheless been wronged': *Hounga v Allen and Another* (2014); see also *Micula UK2* (2017).

183 Separability, which is recognised by many legal systems, is a legal doctrine that allows an arbitration agreement to be considered entirely separately from the underlying contract in which it is contained. This is important where there are questions about the enforceability of the underlying agreement. For Swiss and UK law, see *Aeroflot v Berezovsky* (2013), para. 84 and for EU law, see *C-269/95 – Benincasa v Dentalkit* (1997) and *World Duty Free Award* (2006).

184 Tietje and Wackernagel (2015), p. 210.

185 Tietje and Wackernagel (2015), p. 210.

domestic court review or interference, are considered automatically recognised and enforced within the 150 contracting parties.[186]

Articles 53 and 54 of the ICSID Convention unequivocally entail unconditional enforcement of ICSID Awards while Article 107 TFEU unequivocally entails that no state aid is to be paid.[187] Therefore, peaceful coexistence between the ICSID Convention and EU state aid law is not possible without both sides adopting a reasonably straightforward exercise in accommodation.[188] Harmony between these two post-*Achmea*, however, appears to be beyond reach based on international investment tribunals' assessment of the impact of *Achmea* and their stern response to it.[189]

Indeed, as was discussed in Sect. 4.4.3 Chap. 4, several issues between the EU and international investment law are highlighted by the application of the VTCL by investment tribunals in their practice. In particular, Articles 30 and 31 VCLT have been subject to findings that stand in stark contrast to each other, especially on the following subjects:

- whether these disputes should be interpreted in light of EU law[190]
- whether EU law is national or international law
- the hierarchy of legal orders[191]
- the order of succession.

Besides the dilemmas on interpretation and the order of procedure, which Sects. 5.4.2 and 5.4.3 above discussed, a severe failure regarding state aid issues is that the VCLT does not deal with the relations of IGO's or a State with an IGO such as the EU.[192] Explicitly, if EU law is understood to be public international or national law, this complex situation exhibits itself, for example, in the intra-EU–ECT practice. Under it, the tribunals have perceived EU law to be: (1) national law in *Achmea BV Final Award* (2012) and *Achmea v Slovak Republic* (2008); (2) international law in *Electrabel Award* (2015) and *Vattenfall II (Decision on the Achmea issue) (2018)*; and (3) a matter of fact in *AES v Hungary (III) Award* (2010).

Essentially, if EU law is deemed to be public international law, Articles 30(2) and 30(4) VCLT rules on succession are applicable.[193] Under this scenario, the

[186] Tietje and Wackernagel (2015) and Lavranos (2018a, b). However, this self-contained regime is only procedural, not factual. Investment tribunals need to be able to preserve its legitimacy for domestic courts that the tribunals rely upon for enforcement and democratic constituencies—which, as has happened in the EU, may doubt and reject the whole ISDS regime.

[187] Tietje and Wackernagel (2015), p. 207.

[188] Bermann (2012), p. 425; Tietje and Wackernagel (2015), p. 443.

[189] *Vattenfall II (Decision on the Achmea issue)* (2018).

[190] As discussed in Sect. 4.4.3 in Chap. 4.

[191] As discussed in Sect. 4.4.2 in Chap. 4.

[192] As discussed in Sect. 4.3.3 in Chap. 4.

[193] Other rules of conflict do not apply to the relationship of the ICSID convention and the EU. First, as there is no identity of the parties concerned for the ICSID Convention, Article 59 requiring 'all the parties to [a treaty] conclude a later treaty relating to the same subject matter' is not applicable.

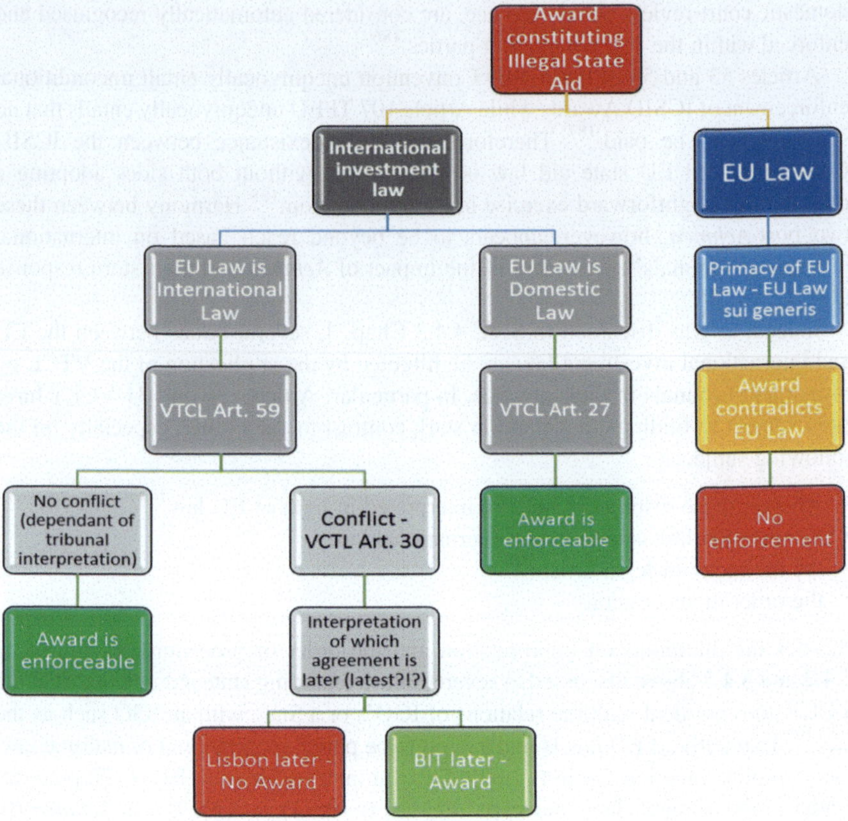

Fig. 5.3 Interpretation of Awards constituting illegal state aid—international investment tribunals and the CJEU

Lisbon Treaty is more recent than the ICSID Convention.[194] However, if EU law is deemed to be internal law by an investment tribunal, a Member State cannot invoke provisions of EU law as justification for its failure to breach IIA

Suspension of the ICSID Convention under Article 58 and modification under Article 41 both require at least that the other ICSID members be notified. No such notification having been filed (Tietje and Wackernagel 2015, pp. 217–218), the *Vattenfall II* tribunal denied the EU's *sui generis* character: *Vattenfall II (Decision on the Achmea Issue)* (2018), paras 145–147; see also Hepburn (2018).

[194]The Lisbon treaty is also more recent than the ECT, the source for several intra-EU and extra-EU claims. However, in *Vattenfall II (Decision on the Achmea issue)* (2018) on the effect of the *Achmea C-284/16* (2018) case, the tribunal deemed the ECT Article 16 *lex specialis and lex superior*, and thus as prevailing (paras 192–196 and 227). Further, due to the same provisions having existed in previous versions of the EU treaties that were dated prior to the ECT, the tribunal deemed the status as *lex posterior* unclear (paras 216–218). See also Hepburn (2018).

provisions.[195] For interpretation of Awards constituting illegal state aid in relation to international investment tribunals and CJEU, see Fig. 5.3.

Under this scenario, the EU legislation's character as *sui generis*, according to Tietje and Wackernagel, means that for intra-EU ISDS claims, Article 27 VCLT[196] cannot be applied directly. Otherwise, the Member States have no other option but to disregard their international obligations, without taking into consideration whether a domestic or European (EU) public authority is the source preventing their compliance.[197] A Member State in this situation could, of course, invoke Article 50 TEU and leave the European Union, constituting a unilateral act. Under the status quo, indiscriminate application of Article 27 VCLT is not justified, theoretically leading to a leaving of the EU to regain 'full' sovereignty, to be able to comply with the ICSID Convention.

Therefore, Article 27 VCLT use only makes sense in areas of a Member State's public authority under the status quo. Any application of the Article beyond that would cause a mix-up between rules of international responsibility and international rules of conflict. As noted by Tietje and Wackernagel, it is possible that the ICSID Member States, under the ICSID Convention, incurred international responsibility when becoming EU Member States—although it would be quite a surprise if the ICSID drafters intended to prevent sovereign states from entering into future regional integration agreements.[198] Because of these contradictions, especially within an ICSID setting, the crossfire between investor protection and EU state aid law has emerged as the foremost example of issues related to the right to regulate.[199]

This jurisdictional feud is intensified by the fact that ICSID arbitration's seat is always in Washington, DC, far from the internal market, and the ICSID tribunals consistently keep on denying the relevance of EU law and any authority of the CJEU over ICSID arbitrations. A *jurispathic* approach from investment tribunal is likely to evoke a similar response from the EU,[200] as emphasised by the case study on *Micula* in Chap. 4.

[195] This is what happened in the *Micula* case.

[196] Article 27 VCLT sets that, 'A party may not invoke the provisions of its internal law as justification for its failure to perform a treaty.'

[197] Tietje and Wackernagel (2015), p. 231.

[198] Tietje and Wackernagel (2015), p. 232.

[199] The Commission faced massive opposition to ISDS in a public consultation on the EU's approach to investment protection. See the Commission's media release regarding the online consultation on investment protection and investor-to-state dispute settlement in the TTIP (European Commission (EC) 2015c). In the aftermath of these online public consultations, the Commission also noted that disputes involving state aid regarding ISDS have been especially problematic: European Commission (EC) (2015d).

[200] A jurispathic response, according to Paul Schiff Berman, is to 'kill off all competing laws by declaring that one set of norms – and only one – shall prevail': Berman (2013) and Matei and Ciurtin (2016).

The *Micula* case, which was 'the first time if not the first case' in which the EU Commission has dealt with the exclusive competence in the area intra-EU BITs,[201] acted as a wake-up call for the EU institutions on the disturbance BITS and TIPs including ISDS can cause in the internal market.[202] Indeed, notwithstanding arguments that *Micula* was an anomaly, it was not the first clash of state aid law and BITs,[203] nor was it the last.

5.6.2 Awards As State Aid

Similar cases to the *Micula* case have surfaced both in the past[204] and in the present. In particular, the photovoltaic[205] energy sector, which received generous tariff schemes and subsidy schemes for solar energy from several Member States (including the Czech Republic, Spain, Italy and Bulgaria), and then changed its policy due to the 2008 economic crisis, has initiated similar cases under the Energy Charter Treaty.[206] Of these four countries, Spain faces the overwhelming majority, with as many as 48 claims, of which most are pending.[207]

Of the decided cases, *Eiser Infrastructure Ltd and another v Spain,*[208] *Novenergia v Spain,*[209] *Masdar v Spain*[210] and *Antin Infrastructure and Others v*

[201] Rovetta and Gambardella (2015), p. 1.

[202] See European Commission's press release, EU and Japan reach agreement in principle on Economic Partnership Agreement (European Commission (EC) 2017e). See also Commission documents 'Investment in TTIP and beyond – the path for reform' (EC 2015a) and 'A new EU trade agreement with Japan' (EC 2017a), p. 6. See also the European Parliament resolution of 8 July 2015 containing the European Parliament's recommendations to the European Commission on the negotiations for the Transatlantic Trade and Investment Partnership (TTIP) (Parliament 2015), paras (xiv)–(xv) and the case of the CJE (*Achmea C-284/16*, 2018).

[203] See, for example, *C-284/16 Achmea (AG Opinion)* (2017); Tietje and Wackernagel (2015); Matei (2015a).

[204] Due to different reasons—either by the claimant withdrawing the case (*AES v Hungary (III) Award*, 2010) or the tribunal siding with the state for other reasons (*Electrabel Decision on Jurisdiction*, 2012). In general, for liability for damages that have illegal origins, see *C-346/03 – Atzeni and Others* (2006).

[205] 'Photovoltaic sector' precludes electricity from sunlight.

[206] Ortolani (2015), p. 126; Cross and Kube (2018).

[207] See Investment Dispute Settlement Navigator, Investment Policy Hub (UNCTAD 2017) at https://investmentpolicy.unctad.org/investment-dispute-settlement/country/197/spain.

[208] *Eiser Award* (2017). The investor was awarded €128 million by an ICSID tribunal.

[209] *Novenergia II v Spain Award* (2018). The tribunal granted €53.3 million award to the investor. (Cruz Pena 2018).

[210] *Masdar v Spain Award* (2018). The ICSID tribunal awarded €64.5 million plus interest to Masdar (technically a Dutch investor but indirectly owned by the government of Abu Dhabi).

Spain Award[211] resulted in Awards for the investors while *Isolux v Spain*[212] and *Charanne*[213] were decided in favour of the state. However, following a request by Spain, the Swedish Court of Appeals stayed the enforcement of the Award for *Novenergia v Spain*. The *Spain v Novoenergia*[214] case is now awaiting a decision at the Swedish Court of Appeals about whether it can make a ruling on the matter by applying *acte clair* doctrine[215] or abide by Spain's request to send the case for a preliminary ruling from the CJEU regarding the status of intra-EU BITs litigated under the ECT.

In *Eiser Infrastructure Ltd and Another v Spain, Isolux v Spain, Charanne* and *Masdar v Spain*, the Commission intervened in a similar fashion to the earlier *Micula Award*. By its decision in the *Spanish Renewable Energy Schemes*,[216] the Commission prohibited Spain from proceeding with paying the Awards stemming from the new and un-notified state aid. Accordingly, these energy schemes were deemed unlawful state aid.[217] Hence Awards reinstituting this unlawful state aid would be subject to notification obligation[218] and would thus be reliant on Commission authorisation.

In the *Spanish Renewable Energy Schemes,* the Commission addressed investment tribunals directly, making it clear that tribunals lacked the competence to grant

---

[211] *Antin Infrastructure and others v Spain Award* (2018). The arbitrators awarded €112 million and additional pre-award interest and partial costs for denial of FET. The tribunal refused to reopen its proceedings to consider the possible impact of *Achmea C-284/16* (2018).

[212] *Isolux Award* (2016).

[213] *Charanne Final Award* (2016).

[214] T 4658-18 *Spanien v Novenergia II* – Suspension of Enforcement (2018). Before appealing for the suspension and the referral from the Swedish Court, Spain had unsuccessfully tried to set aside the Award at the Swedish chamber of Commerce (Charlotin 2018).

[215] The *acte clair* doctrine was first developed by the CJEU in *C-283/81 – CILFIT v Ministero della Sanità* (1982). The *acte clair* doctrine establishes an exemption to Article 267 TFEU, which otherwise requires that a national court against whose judgment there is no higher instance to appeal to must refer a question to the CJEU where a question regarding the interpretation of EU law arises. However, if the answer is 'so obvious as to leave no scope for any reasonable doubt as to the manner in which the question raised to be resolved', a request for a referral to the CJEU is not mandatory: *C-283/81 – CILFIT v Ministero della Sanità* (1982), para 16.

[216] *State aid SA.40348* (2015). This declares several Awards from investment tribunals to be unlawful state aid. See *Eiser Award* (2017); *Isolux Award* (2016); *Charanne Final Award* (2016).

[217] *State Aid SA.40348 (2015/NN)* (2017), para 89. Some energy schemes, which Spain had notified in June 2014 before implementing the measures, were deemed lawful and internal market-compatible state aid. *State Aid SA.40348 (2015/NN)* (2017), paras 90–153. These schemes fell under the Energy and Environmental State Aid Guidelines (EEAG) and contributed to the common interest: *State Aid SA.40348 (2015/NN)* (2017) paras 91–99. The aid was also necessary and appropriate (para 104) and proportional (paras 113–118). The aid granted through the post-June 2014 schemes had been implemented after a non-discriminatory competitive bidding process had been carried out in line with point (69) EEAG (paras 125–131). Therefore, in line with EEAG, the aid had only limited effects on competition and trade (paras 132–135).

[218] *State Aid SA.40348 (2015/NN)* (2017) para 165. The Commission provides as an example the *Eiser Award* (2017), and other similar Awards as belonging to this category.

state aid.[219] Furthermore, the investors were deemed not to have any 'right to State aid'.[220] It is a Member State's prerogative to either withdraw an aid scheme or not to grant aid.[221] As a final note, the Commission pinpointed that its *Spanish Renewable Energy Schemes* decision was part of EU law, and thus effectively binding on arbitration tribunals where they apply EU law. This means that the validity of this decision can only be challenged in the European Courts.[222] Additionally, the Commission's decision provided Spain with some time to freeze the enforcement of payments until Spain, *post* the CJEU's decision in *Achmea*, could raise objections that the tribunals lacked jurisdiction over intra-EU disputes in the Swedish Svea Court of Appeals.[223]

The Czech Republic has faced at least seven claims. So far, the decisions have been in favour of the state—for example, Czechia won the *Wirtgen & JSW Solar* case[224] and the *Antaris v the Czech Republic*[225] case. Five other claims are still pending.[226] Meanwhile, Italy has been sued twelve times by investors. Of the four

---

[219] *State Aid SA.40348 (2015/NN)* (2017), para 165.

[220] *State Aid SA.40348 (2015/NN)* (2017), paras 154–158, referring to the words of Advocate General Wahl in *C-526/14 – Kotnik and Others* (2016), para 79: 'under EU State aid rules, no undertaking can claim a right to receive State aid; or, to put it differently, no Member State can be considered obliged, as a matter of EU law, to grant State aid to a company' and to the Order in *T-670/14 – Milchindustrie-Verband and Deutscher Raiffeisenverband v Commission* (2015) para 29. Clearly, the commission wishes to draw the line for competence/competence issues that are constantly under challenge by ISDS Awards. According to Righini (2018), some of these cases, in contrast to the *Micula* case, would consist of pure compensation for damages. However, the proper authority to challenge the Commission's state aid decision is the CJEU, not an arbitration tribunal based on an intra-EU BIT provision. Notably, both Micula and Electrabel eventually took their claims to the CJEU, with the difference that Electrabel did not go on a parallel court shopping spree.

[221] *State Aid SA.40348 (2015/NN)* (2017), para 155.

[222] *State Aid SA.40348 (2015/NN)* (2017), para 166.

[223] The Svea Court of Appeals has also stayed of enforcement of an award under the BLEU–Poland BIT in *PL Holdings v Poland Final Award* (2017), due to Poland's application for a stay.

[224] *Wirtgen & JSW Solar* (2017).

[225] The *Antaris Award* (2018) claim was bought under both the ECT and the Germany-Czechoslovakia BIT. The EU Commission chose not to intervene as *amicus curiae* (para 39) as the tribunal made the Commission's intervention conditional on paying 'in full the reasonable costs of both parties resulting from the submissions' (para 38.6). The same situation has taken place for the *Eiser Award* (2017) and *Natland and Others v Czech Republic Partial Award* (2017) cases. Thus the tribunal did not examine the validity of the intra-EU BITs. However, for the *Antaris Award* (2018), the tribunal's majority relied on a Commission state aid decision that the Solar Levy was neither retroactive nor in breach of the principle of legitimate expectations. See the Commission's *State Aid Decision SA.40171 Czechia Promotion of electricity production from renewable energy sources* (28 November 2016, para 150) and the *Antaris Award* (2018) para 430.

[226] See UNCTAD's database Investment Policy Hub at http://investmentpolicyhub.unctad.org/ISDS/CountryCases/197?partyRole=2.

decided cases so far, two cases, *Blusun v Italy*[227] and *Belenergia v Italy,*[228] found in favour of the state. Bulgaria has four claims pending.[229]

Still, in December 2021, the investment tribunals presiding over the claims against the Member States in the intra-EU BIT context have not paid heed to the Commission's *Spanish Renewable Energy Schemes* decision or deemed the CJEU's *Achmea* judgment applicable to any ongoing arbitration claims.[230] Even the Declaration of the Member States on the legal consequences of *Achmea* and the Intra-EU BIT Termination Agreement has had little effect. From a common sense perspective, this is baffling. One might wonder what gain the investment tribunals see in the use of continuous unsuccessful evasion tactics *vis-à-vis* EU law and continuing to hand down evidently unenforceable Awards. As the enforcement of investment tribunals verdicts is entirely dependent upon the disposition of the national courts to enforce these, Tietje and Wackernagel observe that the tribunals are 'institutions wielding neither the purse nor the sword',[231] which depend on their own legitimacy as a shield against defiance.[232] A failure to pay proper heed to EU law will surely continue to undermine the legitimacy of investment tribunals in EU relations.[233]

As identified above,[234] unlawful or internal market-incompatible state aid cannot be merited as compensation for invertor's claims, as this would in itself constitute unlawful state aid.[235] As observed by some authors, the prohibition of state aid could easily be circumvented.[236] Hence an Award introducing a reinstalment of an unlawful or incompatible measure does not redeem the measure from its origins. Otherwise, the rationality behind the recovery of state aid that has already been paid out with the potential effect of distorting the internal market would be made redundant.

---

227 *Blusun v Italy* (2016).

228 *Belenergia v Italy* (2019).

229 See UNCTAD's database Investment Policy Hub at http://investmentpolicyhub.unctad.org/ISDS/CountryCases/197?partyRole=2.

230 See especially *Vattenfall II (Decision on the Achmea Issue)* (2018).

231 Leonhardsen (2011), p. 5. The term 'legitimacy' in this context means, as explained by Bodansky (2012), p. 326, 'the justification and acceptance' of the authority exercised by arbitration tribunals by virtue of an international investment treaty between states'.

232 Tietje and Wackernagel (2015), p. 207.

233 Some authors, like Tietje and Wackernagel, who have adopted a positive attitude towards ISDS, were so disillusioned about the *Micula* tribunal's decision that they even discussed the possibility of personal liability of the arbitrators. Accordingly, tribunals 'consciously rendering an unenforceable award and thereby effectively preventing the dispute from being settled could go beyond' may be facing issues of civil liability: Tietje and Wackernagel (2015), pp. 236, 240. Notably, since July 2018, some lawyers have started avoiding participation in intra-EU BIT arbitration panels which are tasked with examining the implications of the *Achmea* decision: Peterson (2018a) and Ross (2018).

234 See also Chap. 3 and Sect. 4.4.1 of this thesis.

235 With the exception being the enforcement of state aid law conflicts with the EU law itself. For a better picture of how Awards will constitute as illegal state aid, see Fig. 5.3 earlier in this chapter.

236 Tietje and Wackernagel (2015), p. 222, referring to *C-346/03 – Atzeni and Others* (2006) as an example of the CJEU's handling of this type of scenario. See also Ortolani (2015), p. 125 et seq and the *Micula* case in Chap. 4.

Nevertheless, some authors hold that generally Awards, ICSID or other, and the enforcement of those, do not constitute illegal state aid.[237] A BIT or a TIP would be compatible with state aid law by itself unless it were part of a state aid scheme that itself established illegal state aid. The application of the provisions of a BIT or a TIP by a tribunal may lead to a breach of state aid law, as revealed by, *inter alia, Micula, Eiser v Spain*[238] and *Isolux.*[239]

By now, post-*Micula* and *Achmea*, intra-EU Investment Awards that establish illegal state aid are unenforceable in the EU, just as the Commission has consistently upheld.[240] Therefore, it is of interest that Ortolani and Tietje have perceived the enforcement of intra-EU Investment Awards as unavoidable international obligations. Both scholars argue, by utilising the doctrine of imputability,[241] that only voluntarily adopted measures fall within the scope of application of Article 107 TFEU.[242]

5.6.3 *Imputability*

One of the most persuasive arguments put forward by academia about there being no general conflict with the enforcement of intra-EU BIT awards and state aid has been the imputability argument.[243] Ortolani and Tietje, perceive the enforcement dilemma of intra-EU Investment Awards in general as inevitable international obligations. Hence, both scholars argue that, by utilising the doctrine of imputability,[244] only voluntarily adopted measures are within the scope of application of Article 107 TFEU.[245]

---

[237] Ortolani (2015), p. 121 et seq; Tietje and Wackernagel (2015) et seq. By referring to *T-62/08 – ThyssenKrupp Acciai Speciali Terni v Commission (2010)*; *Joined Cases C-448/10 p to C-450/10 p – ThyssenKrupp Acciai Speciali Terni and Others v Commission* (2011) para 101 and *C-61/79 – Denkavit* (1980) para 31.

[238] *State aid SA.40348 (2015/NN)* (2017), para 165.

[239] *Isolux Award* (2016).

[240] See the German Federal Supreme Court of Justice, Bundesgerichtshof decision, *Beschluss des I. Zivilsenats vom 31.10.2018 – I ZB 2/15* to set aside the €22 million Award for the Dutch insurer Achmea *'Bundesgerichtshof beschluss- I ZB 2/15 – (Achmea)* (2018).

[241] See Bacon (2017), pp. 67–70; Rose and Bailey (2013), pp. 1285–1286.

[242] Ortolani (2015) and Tietje and Wackernagel (2014).

[243] Ortolani (2015), p. 121 et seq; Tietje and Wackernagel (2014), p. 3 et seq. By referring to *T-384/08 – Elliniki* (2011), *T-62/08 – ThyssenKrupp Acciai Speciali Terni v Commission* (2010), *Joined Cases C-448/10 P to C-450/10 P – ThyssenKrupp Acciai Speciali Terni and Others v Commission* (2011), para 101 and *C-61/79 – Denkavit* (1980), para. 31. The basis for arguments used is from *T-351/02 – Deutsche Bahn v Commission* (2006), para 31: 'for advantages to be capable of being categorised as aid within the meaning of Article 87(1) EC, they must, inter alia, be imputable to the State'.

[244] See Bacon (2017), pp. 67–70; Rose and Bailey (2013), pp. 1285–1286.

[245] Ortolani (2015) and Tietje and Wackernagel (2014).

In other words, due to a state having no autonomy in either implementing EU law nor recognition or enforcement of Awards, the EU's case law deems that involuntary reimbursements of damages caused by the state do not constitute state aid.[246] Notably, the cases cited involve Member State obligations to solely EU law; thus, due to the primacy of EU law, one cannot automatically apply the same logic to other international law.

The imputability arguments rely on two main arguments: first, that there is no general conflict between EU state aid law and BITs/Awards originating from BITs; and second, that in case of conflict, EU treaties and investor-state arbitration conventions have the same status under the Vienna Convention for the Member States.

Tietje and Ortolani[247] draw a parallel to ICSID awards and EU law as international legal orders under conflict rules of the Vienna Convention, observing that there is no general conflict with EU law.[248] According to them, there is also no general conflict of EU state aid law and BITs, and even if there were, EU treaties do not specify superiority over investment treaty arbitration conventions. Kende,[249] however, questions the doctrine of imputability as appropriate in the context of intra-EU BITs. Accordingly, the decisions of arbitration tribunals are no more or less imputable to the Member States than the decisions of their national courts, since the Member States have agreed voluntarily to the rules on the selection of arbitrators and the ISDS procedures.[250]

The Commission rejects the imputability arguments[251] in a state aid context and argues against the applicability of *Asteris*[252]—that is, that compensation merely for damages as such does not substitute as an economic advantage.[253] Instead, the Commission offers as an alternative the *Atzori* case,[254] which regards indemnification clauses for the recovery of state aid as itself constituting state aid.

[246] On payment of damages, they cite *Joined Cases 97 and 193/86 Asteris* (1988).

[247] Struckmann et al. (2016), pp. 264–265 also support this conclusion.

[248] The same logic is also analogously applicable to Awards other than ICSID; however, CJEU's decision in *Achmea* might contradict this reasoning: *C-284/16 Achmea (AG Opinion)* (2017).

[249] Kende (2015).

[250] Kende (2015), pp. 41–43. This opinion is seconded by Rösch (2017).

[251] See *Micula II (EU)* (2014), paras 117–120. The basis for arguments used is from *T-351/02 – Deutsche Bahn v Commission* (2006), para 31: 'for advantages to be capable of being categorised as aid within the meaning of Article 87(1) EC, they must, *inter alia*, be imputable to the State'.

[252] *Joined Cases 97 and 193/86 Asteris* (1988).

[253] *Joined Cases 97 and 193/86 Asteris* (1988), para 23.

[254] Since AG Ruiz-Jarabo Colomer in *AG Opinion in Joined Cases C-346/03 and C-529/03 Atzori* (2005), para 198 established that the awarding of damages equalling the sum of unlawful aid granted would reinstitute that unlawful aid, the CJEU(GC) has maintained this notion in its ruling in *T-384/08 – Elliniki* (2011).

Arguments regarding the doctrine of imputability do not, however, cut to the core of cases like *Micula*—something on which most legal scholars agree.[255] If other, external, international legal obligations can exceed EU law, to the extent of potentially legitimising illegalities,[256] the prohibition of state aid would easily be evaded. The Commission's use of state aid arguments in the *Micula* case is based on real and relevant legal concerns. There is more at stake here than competition neutrality for investors. Within this context, the crossfire between investor protection and EU state aid law will continue as long as the investment tribunals decline the right to arbitrate these claims.[257]

5.7 Summary and Analysis

Since 2006, the collisions of state aid law and investment protection have provided quite a spectacle regarding the complexity of the paradigm of peaceful coexistence in international investment law. These collisions between arbitration tribunals and the EU law occur where these two supranational legal orders overlap an individual and their perspectives on this overlap are opposing. Because the relevant Treaties (the Europe Agreements,[258] the Accession Treaties[259] and the Treaty of Lisbon)[260] lack explicit expression in the relevant area in the matter, the legal uncertainty has provided rich ground for these opposing perspectives to flourish. This situation is demonstrated by the judiciary conflicts around intra-EU BITs, entirely founded on the perspective adopted by different tribunals/courts on matters relating to these BITs (e.g. the discriminatory nature, arbitrability and termination).

As shown in Sects. 5.2 and 5.3 above, the tribunal's expansion of the scope of investment protection through their practice has collided head-on with the CJEU's case law, equally extending its public policy scope. From the EU's perspective, protecting the right to regulate public policy objectives, such as state aid control, is

[255] Ortolani (2015), Tietje and Wackernagel (2014), Kleinheisterkamp (2011, 2012b) and Matei (2015c, 2016). State aid practitioners also adopt this viewpoint: Casteleiro (2015), Lamadrid de Pablo (2015) and Rovetta and Gambardella (2015). Some, however—especially legal practitioners who are active in arbitration cases—raise a dissenting voice. See Fietta (2015), Lavranos (2015, 2016) and Struckmann et al. (2016).

[256] This can be seen in *C-346/03 – Atzeni and Others* (2006). Tietje and Wackernagel (2015), p. 22 agree that this is indeed the case.

[257] The Commission (EC 2015a) recognises that disputes involving state aid have raised specific problems regarding ISDS.

[258] See EC (2016) for information on the Europe agreements. Full texts available from the Commissions database at http://ec.europa.eu/world/agreements/default.home.do.

[259] For the Accession Treaties, see the EUR-Lex at http://eur-lex.europa.eu/collection/eu-law/treaties/treaties-accession.html.

[260] Treaty of Lisbon amending the Treaty on European Union and the Treaty establishing the European Community (EU 2007).

essential to the autonomy and legitimacy of the EU.[261] The literature notes that the autonomy of the EU law functions as a basis for its legitimacy.[262] One way to understand this conflict is to observe how the hierarchy of sources of law differs between the courts involved. The international sources of law used by the arbitration courts are, in order of precedence: (1) international treaties; (2) general customary international law; and (3) general principles of law.[263] At the same time, the EU courts' sources of law are those of the EU legal order, in order of precedence: (1) EU primary legislation;[264] (2) general principles of law; (3) the EU's international agreements; (4) EU secondary legislation;[265] (5) conventions between the Member States.[266] EU law, although based on treaties (TEU and TFEU) and the Charter of Fundamental Rights (Charter), is hard law rather than soft law. It is integrated and included in the Member States' national legislation and enforceable through national courts as an extension of the EU's organs. Under EU law, the legal instance that has the final word in interpreting EU law is the CJEU. As the guardian of the EU treaties, the CJEU also protects the autonomy of the EU's legal order and judicial system against intrusive external influences that contradict EU law.

However, the investment tribunals explicitly, by their practice, both denounce the EU's autonomy and disregard the unenforceability of Awards that are discrepant with EU law (see Sect. 5.4). Their efforts to categorise EU law as either international or domestic law have been seen as detrimental—as trying to fit a square peg into a round hole.[267] Consequently, with the increasing use of ISDS, there have been increasing numbers of collisions in areas where the BIT regime and the EU exercise international rules of conflict of laws regarding party autonomy and the right to regulate.

Especially challenging in these intersections has been the crossfire of 'investment incentives' and competition law and policy, as shown in Sect. 5.5.1 above. Since the role of competition policy is to hinder anticompetitive practices, it must be neutral in its application. Therefore, neither domestic nor foreign companies should be perceiving special treatment. Hence the EU legislates and practises state aid control.

---

[261] European Parliament in Resolution on the Future European International Investment Policy, para 23, Conclusions on a comprehensive European international investment policy (Council of the European Union 2010); Towards a Comprehensive European International Investment Policy (European Commission (EC) 2010), p. 9; Trade for All (EC 2015b), p. 14. See also Sect. 5.3 for the CJEU's Opinions and case law regarding this subject.

[262] *Achmea C-284/16* (2018) paras 33 and 34; Eckes (2016), pp. 10, 31; Gallo and Nicola (2015); Bermann (2012), p. 431.

[263] According to the Statute of the International Court of Justice (ICJ), Article 38 §1.

[264] Treaty on European Union (TEU), Treaty on the Functioning of the European Union (TFEU) and the Charter of Fundamental Rights (Charter)—General Principles of Law.

[265] Legislative Acts: Regulations, Directives & Decisions; Non-legislative acts; Delegated Acts and Implementing acts; Other Acts—i.e. Recommendations and opinions et al.

[266] Committee of Permanent Representatives in the European Union (COREPER) Decisions—International agreements.

[267] See also Sect. 5.6.1 above.

Many Member State government actions result in a benefit to an enterprise. Thus national initiatives to attract foreign direct investment may easily classify as a state aid measure.[268]

The EU institutions' concerns around this situation are escalated in parallel with the tempo of ISDS proceeding inside the EU, as highlighted by Sect. 5.5. Cases like *Micula* and *Spanish Renewable Energy Schemes*[269] have established that Member States implementing EU law or correcting national practices, or laws discrepant with EU law, which conflict with those states' international obligations to foreign investors under BITs, may become subject to claims and substantial liabilities.[270] The *Micula* case created an institutional distrust, leading up to the European Parliament disavowing the ISDS clause. The chair of the International Trade (INTA) Committee, Bernd Lange, declared the arbitrational tribunals obsolete on 8 July 2015.[271]

Since then, the Commission has moved to end intra-EU BITs,[272] to limit the scope of investment protection and to end investor-state arbitration in all the EU's international agreements, to prevent similar situations from arising in other settings.[273] For procedural matters of ISDS in intra-EU settings, a final nail in the coffin was supposed to be, in principle, the CJEU's rejection of it in *Achmea*. The Member States[274] finally yielded to several years of pressure from the Commission after the CJEU ruling in *Achmea C-284/16*, declaring intra-EU BITs incompatible

---

[268] Particularly investment subsidies for cross-border merges and acquisitions. See American Bar Association publication regarding competition as public policy: ABA (2010), Ch 6.

[269] *State aid SA.40348 (2015/NN)* (2017). This Commission declares several Awards from investment tribunals to be unlawful state aid. See *Eiser Award* (2017); *Isolux Award* (2016); *Charanne Final Award* (2016).

[270] See also *Achmea B.V Final Award* (2012); *Achmea v Slovak Republic* (2008) previously *Eureko* (2010); *Eastern Sugar – Final Award* (2007); *Eastern Sugar – Partial Award* (2007); *AES v Hungary (III) Award* (2010); *EDF v Hungary* (2014); *Electrabel Decision on Jurisdiction* (2012); *Electrabel Award* (2015); *Binder v Czech Republic Award* (2007); *Oostergetel v Slovak Republic* (2010); *Charanne Final Award* (2016); *RREEF Infrastructure* (2016); *Isolux Award* (2016); *WNC Award* (2017); *Anglia Auto Accessories Final Award* (2017); *US Steel v Slovakia* (2013); *Saluka* (2006).

[271] Euronews (2015).

[272] By publishing the Communication, Protection of Intra-EU Investment (EC 2018a).

[273] As stated in Sect. 1.2 in Chap. 1, these situations can arise in any setting that involves the EU or one or more of its Member States because their IIA relations with non-EU countries operate on an international scale in different forms. EU Member States have signed around 1400 IIAs, of which 190 are intra-EU BITS (European Commission 2015a). The EU has 55 TIPs in force and more under negotiation (UNCTAD 2016). There is also the Energy Charter Treaty that has been the basis on several intra and extra BIT claims. According to the Commission, the ECT contains an 'implicit disconnection clause'. See, for example, *Charanne Final Award* (2016); *RREEF Infrastructure* (2016) para 51; Charlotin (2018). Nonetheless, investment tribunals have rejected this argument, with the exception of *Electrabel Decision on Jurisdiction* (2012). See, for example, *RREEF Infrastructure* (2016), para 82; *Blusun v Italy* (2016), para 66. See also Cross and Kube (2018), pp. 6–8; and Tietje (2008), p. 10.

[274] The Declaration of the Member States on the legal consequences of *Achmea DG ((FISMA)* (2019a, b, c).

with EU law. By denying ISDS in these agreements, the CJEU provided the incitement for the Member States to mutually terminate these BITs, thus returning the arbitrability of investment disputes to the domestic courts.

Achmea firmly set the position adopted by the EU regarding ISDS automatically affecting awards related to these proceeding, at least in the context of intra-EU BITS.[275] By revisiting and reiterating the *Opinion 2/13* constitutional message in *Achmea,* the CJEU opened the possibility that this incompatibility between ISDS and EU law may have much wider application. Hence, some voices noted that the debate on the legality of extra EU-BITs and the EU's TIPs should be revisited.[276] However, authors with deep insight into the arbitration circles and the arbitration circles themselves have both flagged that the issue between investment protection, ISDS and EU law is far from settled.[277]

First, while *Achmea* applies to ISDS in general, and therefore also covers ISDS proceedings and Awards stemming from unlawful or internal market-incompatible aid, this ruling does not address the substantial matters related particularly to state aid control. As explained earlier in this book (Chap. 3) and demonstrated by the case study on *Micula* in Chap. 4, state aid law has specific characteristics that set it apart from other areas of EU law.

Second, the CJEU chose not to address the question from the German court about the possibly discriminatory nature of the BITs. Instead of pondering this substantial issue, the CJEU chose to apply a procedural approach, namely the ISDS system and its effects on the autonomy of EU law,[278] which removed the need to address the follow-up questions. Similarly, the CJEU did not address the discriminatory topic in the much-awaited *Micula* ruling. It is likely that this issue will not be addressed directly after the Member States chose to terminate all intra-EU BITs. However, the Declaration of the Member States on the legal consequences of Achmea notes that they cannot derogate from the general principles of EU law, such as the general principle of non-discrimination.[279] It therefore supports the notion that the BITs are discriminatory.

Third, it is essential to remedy the silence regarding ISDS in the current (perhaps by additional protocol that terminates the BITs at accession or at ratification of an accession Agreement) and future accession process and agreements. The EU candidate countries currently have more than 100 bilateral investment treaties with EU Member States in force.[280]

---

[275] Lavranos (2018a, b), Szilágyi (2018) and Hess (2018).

[276] Lavranos (2018a, b) and Szilágyi (2018).

[277] Lavranos (2018a, b) and Hindelang (2018). See also Pinsolle and Michou (2018) for an investment arbitrator's perspective.

[278] Dimopoulos (2018).

[279] *DG ((FISMA)* (2019c), p. 2.

[280] UNCTAD's Investment Policy Hub at https://investmentpolicy.unctad.org/country-navigator.

Fourth, as highlighted by Lavranos and Dimopoulos, the CJEU specifically addresses only ISDS under BITs, which provide that applicable law includes the law in force at the host state.[281] Explicitly, the CJEU did not draw any distinction between ICSID and non-ICSID proceedings.[282] As explained in Sect. 5.6.1 above, ICSID covers both a self-contained regime and automatically recognisable and enforceable awards in all 150 signatory states to the ICSID Convention. Thus, any review or interference by domestic courts regarding ICSID awards is absent. The handling of the intra-EU BITs ICSID disputes is, however, not provided with any guidance from the CJEU.[283] Nonetheless, the Intra-EU BIT Termination Agreement specifies that it also applies to the ICSID Convention.[284]

Fifth, neither did the CJEU address situations with courts and investment tribunals having a seat outside the EU. These courts/tribunals do not necessarily care about CJEU decisions or EU law.[285] In the aftermath of the Commission state aid decision in *Micula II EU*,[286] it was up to ISDS practitioners to recommend that future disputes on the relevant subject be held outside the EU.[287] In contrast to tribunals seated inside the EU, those seated outside the EU may casually reject the Commission's arguments over intra-EU claims while these BITs remain in force. If enforcement of Awards stemming from these is pursued outside the EU, those tribunals may not pay heed to *Achmea*.[288]

To hinder this from occurring, Kende suggests that the EU could hypothetically conclude international agreements or issue internal rules to block the international enforceability of intra-EU BITs, as the United States did by adopting the American Service – Members' Protection Act.[289] The EU can also use its economic clout and policy to convince third countries to not to enforce Awards based on intra-EU BITs. While such a move may not be well received by third countries, the global criticism of ISDS by many nations might make these nations more sympathetic to these policies and less likely to harm the EU's international relations.

Sixth, even though *Achmea* hints at wider applicability of incompatibility of ISDS in TIPs, the compatibility of ISDS with EU law in this setting remained uncertain until the CJEU's startling *Opinion 1/17*. In this Opinion, the ECJ refined

---

[281] Such as the Netherlands-Slovakia BIT that was the relevant BIT for the *Achmea C-284/16* (2018) ISDS proceedings: Lavranos (2018a, b) and Dimopoulos (2018).

[282] Lavranos (2018a, b).

[283] Lavranos (2018a, b).

[284] See the Intra-EU BIT Termination Agreement preamble at p. 2, SN/4656/2019/INIT, OJ L 169, 29.5.2020, p. 1–41.

[285] Hindelang (2018) and Lavranos (2018a, b).

[286] *Micula II (EU)* (2014).

[287] For example, see Wehland (2016) and Lavranos (2015).

[288] Notably, though, as shown in Sect. 4.2.4 in Chap. 4, the US Court of Appeals in *Micula IV USA* (2017) chose not to enforce the Award before the judgment of the CJEU CG.

[289] Kende (2015), p. 55. This act contained prohibitions on the United States providing military aid to countries that had ratified the treaty, establishing the International Criminal Court relating to the application of the decisions of the International Criminal Court to its military service personnel.

the concept of the EU's external autonomy. According to the ECJ, ICS in CETA guarantees that the autonomy of the EU judicial system is not compromised; hence, it can coexist with ICS under public international law. These guarantees are procedural (a CETA tribunal cannot interpret and apply EU law, decide on the legality of a measure under EU law or domestic law and order the EU to pay damages to an investor) and normative (say, guaranteeing the effectiveness of EU law, such as competition law and particularly state aid law). Nevertheless, *Opinion 1/17* raises some serious questions. Although the ECJ appeared reassured that CETA's police power exception provisions guaranteed its signatory parties the ability to regulate legitimate policy objectives, one cannot help but wonder how watertight these guarantees are. Because the CETA provisions disable the domestic courts of the EU, the review decisions made by CETA tribunals and these tribunals also cannot ask the CJEU for a referral, so there are no guarantees that these do not (wrongly) interpret EU law at least indirectly. Although CETA has no direct effect and the EU itself is safe from being held liable for damages, the Member States are not. Indeed, when complying with EU law, they can still be subject to claims initiated by Canadian investors. Therefore, their conflicting obligations, except for state aid measures, remain unsolved (see Chaps. 2 and 4 and Sect. 5.6 above). Indeed, for ICS under CETA, the CJEU seems to have compromised the principles it has jealously guarded in the past, giving control to an external tribunal.

However, the ECJ notes that national courts may send referrals to the CJEU about CETA,[290] which suggests that the ECJ has not abandoned its control to ICS under CETA after all. Because the ECJ does not close this option, the possibility remains for the EU or a Member State to enforce limits on the damage awards ordered by ISDS bodies. A refusal to pay the award would lead to a challenge in court by the winning party, which from a purely technical perspective is not an ISDS decision review in itself.[291] This argument would align with CJEU's *Joined cases c-402/05 p and c-415/05 p Kadi* (2008) decision, in which it only ruled on the application of the UN Security Council's measure within the EU legal order, rather than on the measure itself.

Opinion 1/17 also has an ambiguous relationship with the CJEU's *Achmea C-284/16* case. First, the CJEU implicitly disassociated *Achmea C-284/16* from CETA. However, the ECJ then elaborated on an investment tribunal test which, while generic, could well be applicable for the CETA Tribunal as well. If such a tribunal would be subject to the Achmea test under *Opinion 1/17*, it might be found to be incompatible with the autonomy of the EU's legal system.[292] Nevertheless, it seems that in *Opinion 1/17* the CJEU had to adjust to extreme political pressure from the Member States. The CJEU's rejection of ICS in CETA might have rung the death knell for all ISDS in the EU's trade deals. Consequently, and evidently, external autonomy differs from internal autonomy, at least when the EU's investment policy is on the line.

---

[290] *Opinion 1/17* (2019), para 117.

[291] Peers (2019).

[292] Peers (2019).

Seventh, neither *Achmea C-284/16* or *Opinion 1/17* provided any definite answer about whether ISDS can still be utilised for extra-EU BITs or these should be renegotiated in line with Article 321 2) and the Grandfathering Regulation.[293]

Eighth, the temporal effect applies,[294] meaning that *Achmea* cast doubt on the validity and enforceability of the ongoing intra-EU BITs disputes and Awards from successful ISDS claims before *Achmea*.[295] Preliminary rulings by the CJEU have *ex tunc* (from the outset) temporal effects. Several authors have noted that it might be tempting for the Member States to try to annul these *res judicata*. Indeed, both Spain and Hungary have attempted to stay arbitration proceedings[296] and overturn unfavourable Awards. The Declaration of the Member States on the legal consequences of *Achmea* clarified this situation. Accordingly, ongoing intra-EU BITs disputes 'that can no longer be annulled or set aside and were voluntarily complied with or definitively enforced' pre-*Achmea* would remain valid.[297]

Consequently, Member States will hardly be able to recover money that has already been paid out to compensate the investors for breaches of intra-EU BITs. It seems that the Member States are merely applying the general principle of legitimate expectations—which, as noted by Lavranos, should protect most investors who have ongoing litigation that has started before *Achmea* and for those who have already collected their awards.[298] However, the situation for state aid disputes might be an exception because investors do not enjoy such protection in this context. State aid rules already have an inbuilt system for recovering money that has been paid out under dubious circumstances, combined with extremely narrow applicability of the principle of legitimate expectations. Therefore, it is highly likely that an investor who has received an Award based on illegal state aid will escape retroactive recovery before the time limit of 10 years, set by Article 17.1 of the Procedural Regulation, has passed.

As expected, several arbitrators have adopted an extremely narrow reading of the very broad wording on the CJEU's ruling in *Achmea,* as exhibited in several cases. It is very likely that they will do the same regarding *Opinion 1/17*. Paradoxically, many arbitrators deemed *Achmea* not applicable for ICSID Awards due to the preliminary ruling in *Achmea* not specifically addressing ISDS procedures under the ICSID Convention.[299] Further, as *Achmea* did not stem from a breach of the ECT, but from a breach of a BIT, the Stockholm Chamber of Commerce refused to stay the

---

[293]Regulation (EU) 1219/2012European Parliament (EP); Council (2010).

[294]Murauskas (2013), pp. 80–81. According to Murauskas (2013), p. 84, the CJEU applies temporality in line with the theory of instrumentalism that was founded by the legal pragmatist J. Dewey (1914).

[295]The temporal effect of the *Achmea* ruling, as the CJEU did not attach any temporal limitations to its judgment or include any transitional period, was brought up by Lavranos (2018a, b).

[296]*Masdar v Spain Award* (2018).

[297]The Declaration of the Member States on the Legal Consequences of *Achmea*, para 7.

[298]Lavranos (2018a, b).

[299]As can be seen in *Masdar v. Spain Award* (2018); *Novenergia II v Spain Award* (2018); *Gavrilovic DOO v Croatia Award* (2018). See also Pinsolle and Michou (2018).

Novoenergia Award on Spain's appeal. In August 2018, the investment tribunal for *Vattenfall v Federal Republic of Germany (Decision on the Achmea issue)*[300] adopted a stark stance on the possible overlap of the subject matter of the EU Treaties and the ECT.

According to the tribunal, Article 16 ECT would prohibit the EU treaties from being formed 'so as to derogate from an Investor's right to dispute resolution under Article 26 ECT'.[301] This type of tactic hints at the investment tribunals' eagerness to end this particular conflict by putting an end to the Commission's and the CJEU's claims to be a *sui generis* system that has to be paid heed to in international investment law. Further, the *Vattenfall II* tribunal's decision, meticulously rejecting the significance of EU law and any implications of the *Achmea* case *vis-à-vis* the multilateral ECT, potentially hardens other international tribunals' approaches to the matter.

However, due to the nature of preliminary rulings, in the end it is the national court that sets the parameters for the rulings. Different from rulings based on infringement proceedings (Article 258 TFEU), judgments based on Article 267 TFEU are deemed case by case, responding to the parameters (i.e. the questions) set by the referral, so are incredibly narrow in scope. Indeed, as the ISDS proceeding for *Achmea* took place under the New York Convention, the CJEU did not get an opportunity to offer its opinion on the ICSID proceedings directly. However, experts in EU law, understanding how the CJEU works, are aware that the court has a way of communicating its standpoint indirectly. This expert insight builds upon an intimate understanding of the way the CJEU expresses itself and the case law to which it refers. In *Achmea,* the CJEU was very clear that ISDS could be a threat to the EU's legal autonomy. The arbitration rules applicable were not relevant to this finding. The same principle applies regarding *Opinion 1/17*. Future ICSID proceedings will have to abide by the test developed by the ECJ in *Opinion 1/17* (see Sect. 5.3 above). Hence, it is redundant to think that ICSID providing a more significant threat on the right to regulate would be acceptable. Intra-EU BITs within the scope of the Energy Charter Treaty are also still intra-EU, so should not necessarily be treated as something else.

Even if the process of abolishing ISDS in the EU context is slow, the wheels of change have been set in motion. In Poland, an investor withdrew their claim in the belief that continuing it would no longer lead to an enforceable Award, post the *Achmea* ruling.[302] Spain, which has found itself a respondent in a series of claims after its withdrawal from the renewable energy scheme, to avoid further collapse of its economy in the wake of the recession of 2008, finally succeeded in staying the

[300] *Vattenfall II (Decision on the Achmea issue)* (2018).

[301] Para. 195.

[302] Pinsolle and Michou (2018); *Vattenfall II (Decision on the Achmea issue)* (2018).

Novoenergia Award at the Swedish Svea Court of Appeals.[303] For the EU's investment policy, the slow transformation of ISDS to ICS seems to be certain.

Cases

Accession by the Communities to the Convention for the Protection of Human Rights and Fundamental Freedoms, Opinion 2/94, ECLI:EU:C:1996:140 (European Court of Justice, 1996)

Achmea B.V. (formerly known as Eureko B.V.) v Slovak Republic Final Award, PCA Case No 2008-13) (UNCITRAL, 2012)

Achmea B.V. (formerly known as Eureko B.V.) v Slovak Republic Award on Jurisdiction, Arbitrability and Suspension PCA Case No 2008-13 (Permanent Court of Arbitration, 2008)

Advocate General's Opinion in Avis 1/17, ECLI:EU:C:2019:72 (Advocate General Bot, 2019)

Aeroflot-Russian Airlines v. Berezovsky & Ors EWCA Civ 784 (UK Court of Appeal, 2013)

AES Summit Generation Limited and AES-Tisza Erömü Kft v The Republic of Hungary, ICSID Award, ICSID No. ARB/07/22, Italaw (International Centre for Settlement of Investment Disputes, 2010)

AES Summit Generation Limited and AES Tisza Eromu Kft v Republic of Hungary (Application for Annulment), No. ICSID Case No ARB/07/22 (ad hoc, 2012)

Alcoa Trasformazioni Srl v European Commission Case T-177/10, ECLI:EU: T:2014:897, T-177/10 (Court of Justice of European Union (GC), 2014)

Alex Genin, Eastern Credit Limited, Inc. and A.S. Baltoil v The Republic of Estonia, ICSID Case No. ARB/99/2 (ICSID ad hoc, 2001)

Ambiente Ufficio SpA and others v Argentine Republic, decision on Jurisdiction and Admissibility ICSID Case No ARB/08/9 (ICSID ad hoc, 2013)

Amministrazione delle finanze dello Stato v Denkavit italiana Srl, case 61/79, ECLI: EU:C:1980:100 (European Court of Justice, 1980)

Amministrazione delle finanze dello Stato v Denkavit italiana Srl, case 61/79, ECLI: EU:C:1980:100 (European Court of Justice, 1980)

Amministrazione delle Finanze dello Stato v Simmenthal SpA., case 106/77, ECLI: EU:C:1978:49 (European Court of Justice, 1978)

Anglia Auto Accessories Limited v Czech Republic Final Award, SCC Case V 2014/181 (Stockholm Chamber of Commerce, 2017)

[303] Unfortunately, it rejected Spain's request to send a referral to the CJEU, as requested by Spain, regarding intra-EU ISDS under the ECT. See Swedish Svea Court of Appeals, question about request for a preliminary ruling from the Court of Justice of the European Union on 25.4.2019 (*T 4658-18 – Spanien v Novenergia II,* 2019). Legal uncertainty on this therefore remains.

Annunziata Matteucci v Communauté française of Belgium and Commissariat général aux relations internationales of the Communauté françaisc of Belgium, case 235/87, ECLI:EU:C:1988:460 (European Court of Justice, 1988)
Antaris Solar GmbH and Dr Michael Göde v Czech Republic, No. PCA Case No. 2014-01 (Permanent Court of Arbitration (PCA), 2018)
Antin Infrastructure services Luxembourg S.à.r.l. and ANTIN Energia Termosolar B.V. v The Kingdom of Spain Award, ICSID case No. ARB/13/31 (ICSID ad hoc, 2018)
Asteris AE and others and Hellenic Republic v Commission of the European Communities, joined cases 97, 193, 99 and 215/86, ECLI:EU:C:1988:199 (European Court of Justice, 1988)
Beijingjianlong Heavy Industry Group v Golden Ocean Group Ltd, EWHC 1063 (Comm) (High Court of England and Wales, 2013)
Belenergia S.A. v Italian Republic, ICSID Case No. ARB/15/40 (ICSID ad hoc, 2019)
Blusun S.A., Jean-Pierre Lecorcier and Michael Stein v Italian Republic, ICSID Case No. ARB/14/3 (ICSID (International Centre for Settlement of Investment Disputes) ad hoc, 2016)
Bundesgerichtshof Beschluss des I. Zivilsenats vom 31.10.2018 – I ZB 2/15 (Bundesgerichtshof, 2018)
Charanne B.V. and Construction Investments S.à.r.l. v Kingdom of Spain Final Award, SCC Case No. 062/2012 (Stockholm Chamber of Commerce, 2016)
Commission of the European Communities v Federal Republic of Germany, case C-5/89, ECLI:EU:C:1990:320 (EuropeanCourt of Justice, 1990)
Commission of the European Communities v Ireland, case C-459/03, ECLI:EU:C:2006:345 (European Court of Justice, 2006)
Commission of the European Economic Community v Italian Republic, case 10/61, ECLI:EU:C:1962:2 (European Court of Justice, 1962)
Commission's state aid decision SA.40171 (2015/NN) – Czech Republic (Promotion of electricity production from renewable energy sources) (2016)
Deutsche Bahn AG v Commission of the European Communities, T-351/02, ECLI:EU:T:2006:104 (Court of Justice of the European Union (GC), 2006)
Eastern Sugar B.V. (Netherlands) v The Czech Republic, SCC Case No. 088/2004 – Final Award (UNCITRAL ad hoc arbitration tribunal, 2007)
Eastern Sugar B.V. (Netherlands) v The Czech Republic, Partial Award SCC Case No. 088/2004- Partial award, Italaw (Stockholm Chamber of Commerce (SCC), 2007)
Eco Swiss China Time Ltd v Benetton International NV, case C-126/97, ECLI:EU:C:1999:269 (European Court of Justice, 1999)
EDF (Services) Limited v Romania, Award, No. ICSID Case No. ARB/05/13 (ad hoc, 2009)
EDF International S.A. v Republic of Hungary, Swiss, No. 4A_34/2015 (Tribunal federal, 2015)

Eiser Infrastructure Limited and Energía Solar Luxembourg S.à.r.l. v Kingdom of Spain Award, ICSID Case No ARB/13/36 (International Centre for Settlement of Investment Disputes ad hoc, 2017)

Eiser Infrastructure Limited and Energia Solar Luxembourg S.A.R.L. v. Kingdom of Spain – Petition to Enforce Arbitral Award No. Case 1:18-cv-01686 (United States District Court for Columbia, pending)

Electrabel S.A. v Hungary Award, ICSID Case No ARB/07/19 (International Centre for Settlement of Investment Disputes, 2015)

Electrabel S.A. v. The Republic of Hungary Decision on Jurisdiction, Applicable Law and Liability, ICSID Case No. ARB/07/19 Italaw (ICSID, 2012)

Electricite de France (EDF) International S.A. v Republic of Hungary (PCA (Permanent Court of Arbitration), 2014)

Elliniki Nafpigokataskevastiki AE Chartofylakeiou, Howaldtswerke-Deutsche Werft GmbH and ThyssenKrupp Marine Systems AG v European Commission, T-384/08 . ECLI:EU:T:2011:650 (Court of Justice of the European Union (GC) 2011)

Eureko B.V. v. The Slovak Republic, Award on Jurisdiction, Arbitrability and Suspension, PCA Case No. 2008-13, Italaw (Permanent Court of Arbitration, 2010)

European American Investment Bank AG v Slovak Republic Award on Jurisdiction, PCA Case No. 2010-17 (UNCITRAL, 2012)

European Community, represented by the Commission of the European Communities v First NV and Franex NV, case C-275/00, ECLI:EU:C:2002:711 (European Court of Justice, 2002)

Exportur SA v LOR SA and Confiserie du Tech SA, case C-3/91, ECLI:EU:C:1992:420 (European Court of Justice, 1992)

Flaminio Costa v E.N.E.L, case 6-64 No. 61964J0006, ECLI:EU:C:1964:66, Eurlex (European Court of Justice (ECJ), 1964)

Francesco Benincasa v Dentalkit Srl., case C-269/95, ECLI:EU:C:1997:337 (European Court of Justice, 1997)

Françoise-Eléonor Hanssens-Ensch v European Community, case C-377/09, ECLI:EU:C:2010:459 (European Court of Justice, 2010)

Fraport AG Frankfurt Airport Services Worldwide v Republic of the Philippines Award, ICSID Case No. ARB/03/25 (ICSID ad hoc, 2007)

French Republic (T-427/04) and France Télécom SA (T-17/05) v Commission of the European Communities, joined cases T-427/04 and T-17/05, ECLI:EU:T:2009:474 (Court of Justice of the European Union (CFI), 2009)

G.I.H.G. Limited, Natland Group Limited, Natland Investment Group NV, and Radiance Energy Holding S.A.R.L. v. The Czech Republic, (PCA Case No. 2013-35) (Permanent Court of Arbitration (PCA), 2017)

Giuseppe Atzeni and Others (C-346/03), Marco Scalas and Renato Lilliu (C-529/03) v Regione autonoma della Sardegna, joined cases C-346/03 and C-529/03, ECLI:EU:C:2006:130 (European Court of Justice, 2006)

Gustav FW Hamester GmbH & Co KG v Republic of Ghana Award, ICSID Case No ARB/07/24 (ICSID ad hoc, 2010)

HGA Srl and Others (C-630/11 P), Regione autonoma della Sardegna (C-631/11 P), Timsas srl (C-632/11 P) and Grand Hotel Abi d'Oru SpA (C-633/11 P) v European Commission, No. ECLI:EU:C:2013:387, Joined Cases C-630/11 P to C-633/11 P (European Court of Justice, 2013)

Hounga v Allen & Anor UKSC 47 (UK Supreme Court, 2014)

Industrie-en Handelsonderneming Vreugdenhil BV v Commission of the European Communities, case C-282/90, ECLI:EU:C:1992:124 (European Court of Justice, 1992)

Ioan Micula, Viorel Micula, S.C. European Food S.A, S.C. Starmill S.R.L. and S.C. Multipack S.R.L. v. Romania, No. WL 4643180, at *1 No. 15 MISC. 107, 2015 (Southern District of New York, 2015)

Ioan Micula, Viorel Micula, S.C. European Food S.A, S.C. Starmill S.R.L. and S.C. Multipack S.R.L. v. Romania, Brief for Amicus Curiae the Commission of the European Union in Support of Defendant-Appellant before the US Court of Appeals, No. 15-3109-cv (United States Court of Appeals Second Circuit, 2016)

Isolux Infrastructure Netherlands B.V.v Kingdom of Spain Award, SCC Case V 2013/153 (Stockholm Chamber of Commerce, 2016)

Jan Oostergetel & Theodora Laurentius v Slovak Republic Decision on Jurisdiction (UNCITRAL ad hoc, 2010)

Joined cases C-402/05 P & C-415/05 P Yassin Abdullah Kadi v Council and Commission of the European Communities, ECLI:EU:C:2008:11 (AG opinion Poiares Maduro, 2008)

Jürgen Wirtgen, Stefan Wirtgen, Gisela Wirtgen and JSW Solar (zwei) GmbH & Co. KG v Czech Republic, Final Award, No. PCA Case No. 2014-03 (PCA ad hoc arbitration, 2017)

Kingdom of Spain v Commission of the European Communities, case C-169/95, ECLI:EU:C:1997:10 (European Court of Justice, 1997)

Kingdom of the Netherlands v European Parliament and Council of the European Union, case C-377/98, ECLI:EU:C:2001:523 (European Court of Justice, 2001)

Konungariket Spanien v Novenergia II – Energy & Enviroment (SCA), SICAR, B 124550, inhibition Mål nr T 4658-18 (Svea hovrätt, 2018)

Land Rheinland-Pfalz v Alcan Deutschland GmbH, case C-24/95, ECLI:EU:C:1997:163 (European Court of Justice, 1997)

LG&E Energy Corp., LG&E Capital Corp., and LG&E International, Inc. v Argentine Republic, Decision on Liability, ICSID Case No. ARB/02/1 (ad hoc, 2006)

Masdar Solar & Wind Cooperatief U.A. v. Kingdom of Spain- Petition to Enforce Arbitral Award, Case No. 1:18-cv-02254 Masdar Solar & Wind Cooperatief U.A. v Kingdom of Spain (United States District Court for Columbia, pending)

Masdar Solar & Wind Cooperatief U.A. v. Kingdom of Spain Award, ICSID Case No. ARB/14/1 (ad hoc, 2018)

Mathias Kruck and others v. Kingdom of Spain and others v Spain case, Decision on the Proposal to Disqualify Mr Gary B. Born, ICSID Case No. ARB/15/23 (ICSID ad hoc, 2018)

Micula and Others v Romania [2017] EWHC 1430 (Comm), [2017] BUS LR 1147 (England and Wales High Court (Commercial Court), 2017)

Micula v. Gov't of Romania, 15-3109-cv (2d Cir. 2017) summary order, 15-3109-cv (Court of Appeals for the Second Circuit, 2017)

Milchindustrie-Verband eV and Deutscher Raiffeisenverband eV v European Commission, case T-670/14, ECLI:EU:T:2015:906 (European Court of Justice, 2015)

Novenergia II – Energy & Environment (SCA), Société d'Investissement à Capital Risque v The Kingdom of Spain – Petition to confirm foreign arbital Award, No. Case 1:18-cv-01148 (United States District Court for Columbia, pending)

Novenergia II – Energy & Environment (SCA)SICAR v Spain, Award, SCC Case No. 063/2015 (SCC (Stockholm Chamber of Commerce), 2018)

NV Algemene Transport – en Expeditie Onderneming van Gend & Loos v Netherlands Inland Revenue Administration, English special edition 1963 00001, Case 26-62 (European Court of Justice (ECJ), 1963)

NV Algemene Transport – en Expeditie Onderneming van Gend & Loos v Netherlands Inland Revenue, case 26-62, ECLI:EU:C:1963:1, Eur-Lex (European Court of Justice, 1963)

Opinion 1/00 on the draft of a convention between the European Community and third countries about the establishment of a European Common Aviation Area, ECLI:EU:C:2002:231 (European Court of Justice, 2002)

Opinion 1/09 of the Court (Full Court), EU:C:2011:123 (European Court of Justice, 2011)

Opinion 1/17 of the Court (Full Court), ECLI:EU:C:2019:341 (European Court of Justice (Full Court), 2019)

Opinion 2/13 of the Court (Full Court), ECLI:EU:C:2014:2454, Opinion 2/13 (European Court of Justice (Full Court), 2014)

Opinion 2/15 of the Court (Full Court), ECLI:EU:C:2017:376, Opinion 2/15 (European Court of Justice (Full Court), 2017)

Opinion delivered pursuant to the second subparagraph of Article 228 (1) of the Treaty – Draft agreement between the Community, on the one hand, and the countries of the European Free Trade Association, on the other, relating to the creation of the European Economic Area, ECLI:EU:C:1991:490 (European Court of Justice, 1991)

Opinion of Mr Advocate General Ruiz-Jarabo Colomer Giuseppe Atzeni and Others (C-346/03), Marco Scalas and Renato Lilliu (C-529/03) v Regione autonoma della Sardegna, ECLI:EU:C:2005:256 (Adocate General opinion, 2005)

Phoenix Action Ltd v Czech Republic Award, ICSID Case No ARB/06/5 (ICSID ad hoc, 2009)

PL Holdings S.a.r.l. v. Poland (SCC Case No. 2014/163) (Stockholm Chamber of Commerce, 2017)

Producteurs de légumes de France v European Commission, case T-328/09, ECLI: EU:T:2012:498 (Court of Justice of the European Union (GC), 2009)

The Queen, on the application of International Association of Independent Tanker Owners (Intertanko) and Others v Secretary of State for Transport, case-308/06, EU:C:2008:312 (European Court of Justice (Grand Chamber), 2008)

Ravil SARL v Bellon import SARL and Biraghi SpA, case C-469/00, ECLI:EU: C:2003:295 (European Court of Justice, 2003)

RREEF Infrastructure (G.P.) Limited and RREEF Pan-European Infrastructure Two Lux S.à.r.l. v Kingdom of Spain Decision on Jurisdiction, ICSID Case No ARB/13/30 (ICSID, 2016)
Rupert Joseph Binder v Czech Republic Award on Jurisdiction of 6 June 2007 (UNCITRAL ad hoc, 2007)
Sabine von Colson and Elisabeth Kamann v Land Nordrhein-Westfalen, case 14/83, ECLI:EU:C:1984:153 (European Court of Justice, 1984)
Saluka Investments B.V. v The Czech Republic partial Award (Permanent Court of Arbitration (PCA), 2006)
Slowakische Republik (Slovak Republic) v Achmea BV Case C-284/16, ECLI:EU:C:2018:158 (European Court of Justice (Grand Chamber), 2018)
Slowakische Republik v Achmea BV, case C-284/16 Opinion of Advocate General Wathelet, ECLI:EU:C:2017:699 (Advocate General Wathelet, 2017)
Srl CILFIT and Lanificio di Gavardo SpA v Ministry of Health, case 283/81, ECLI:EU:C:1982:335 (European Court of Justice, 1982)
State aid SA.38517(2014/C) Romania Implementation of Arbitral award Micula v Romania of 11 December 2013, No. (ex 2014/NN), C(2014) 6848 final, Italaw (European Commission, 2014)
State aid SA.40348 (2015/NN) – Spain support for electricity generation from renewable energy sources, cogeneration and waste, C(2017) 7384 final (European Commission, 2017)
T-Mobile Netherlands BV v Raad van beestuur van de Nederlandse Mededingingsautoriteit, ECLI:EU:C:2009:343 (European Court of Justice, 2009)
Tadej Kotnik and Others v Državni zbor Republike Slovenije, case C-526/14 (Grand Chamber), ECLI:EU:C:2016:102 (AG Opinion, 2016)
Técnicas Medioambientales Tecmed, S.A. v The United Mexican States Award, ICSID Case No. ARB(AF)/00/2 (ad hoc, 2003)
ThyssenKrupp Acciai Speciali Terni SpA (C-448/10 P), Cementir Italia Srl (C-449/10 P) and Nuova Terni Industrie Chimiche SpA (C-450/10 P) v European Commission, ECLI:EU:C:2011:642, Joined cases C-448/10 P to C-450/10 P (European Court of Justice, 2011)
ThyssenKrupp Acciai Speciali Terni SpA v European Commission, case T-62/08, ECLI:EU:T:2010:268 (Court of Justice of the European Union (GC), 2010)
U.S. Steel Global Holdings I B.V. v The Slovak Republic, No. PCA Case No. 2013-6 (Permanent Court of Arbitration, 2013)
U.S. Steel Global Holdings I.B.V. v The Slovak Republic, UNCITRAL Procedural Order No. 6 (Stipulated Termination Order) No. PCA Case No. 2013-6 (2014)
Vattenfall AB, Vattenfall Europe AG, Vattenfall Europe Generation AG v Federal Republic of Germany, ICSID Case No. ARB/09/6 (ICSID Tribunal, 2011)
Vattenfall AB; Vattenfall GMBH; Vattenfall Europe Nuclear Energy GMBH; Kernkraftwerk Krummel GMBH & Co. OHG; Kernkraftwerk Brunsbuttel GMBH & CO. OHG v Federal Republic of Germany (Decision on the Achmea Issue), No. ICSID Case No. ARB/12/12 (ICSID ad hoc, 2018)
Vincenzo Manfredi v Lloyd Adriatico Assicurazioni SpA (C-295/04), Antonio Cannito v Fondiaria Sai SpA (C-296/04) and Nicolò Tricarico (C-297/04) and

Pasqualina Murgolo (C-298/04) v Assitalia SpA., ECLI:EU:C:2006:461 (European Court of Justice, 2006)

WNC Factoring Ltd v Czech Republic Award PCA Case No 2014-34 (Permanent Court of Arbitration, 2017)

World Duty Free Company Ltd v. The Republic of Kenya, Award, ICSID Case No. ARB/00/7 (ICSID ad hoc, 2006)

Yassin Abdullah Kadi and Al Barakaat International Foundation v Council of the European Union and Commission of the European Communities, joined cases c-402/05 p and c-415/05, ECLI:EU:C:2008:461, 2008 I-06351 Eurlex (ECJ (Grand Chamber), 2008)

Zuckerfabrik Bedburg AG and others v Council and Commission of the European Communities, case 281/84, ECLI:EU:C:1987:3 (European Court of Justice, 1987)

References

Alter KA (2008) Agents or trustees? International courts in their political context. Eur J Int Relat 14(1):33–63

Amerasinghe CF (2005) Principles of the institutional law of international organizations. Cambridge University Press, Cambridge

American Bar Association (ABA) (2010) Competition as public policy. ABA, Chicago

Anderer CE (2010) Bilateral investment treaties and the EU legal order: implications of the Lisbon Treaty. Brooklyn J Int Law 35(3):851–882

Andersen TT, Hindelang S (2016) The day after: alternatives to intra-EU BITs. J World Invest Trade 17(6):984–1014

Ankersmit L (2016) The compatibility of investment arbitration in trade agreements with the judicial system. J Eur Environ Plan Law 13(1):46–63

Bacon K (2017) European Union law of state aid, 3rd edn. Oxford University Press, Oxford

Basener (2017) Investment protection in the European Union: considering EU law in investment arbitrations arising from intra-EU and extra-EU bilateral investment agreements. (PhD Dissertation). Universität Köln

Berman PS (2013) Jurisgenerative constitutionalism: procedural principles for managing global legal pluralism. Indiana J Global Leg Stud 20(2):665–695

Bermann GA (2012) Navigating EU law and the law of international arbitration. Arbitr Int 28(3): 397–446

Bizikova L (2018) The CJEU in Slovakia v Achmea, or is justice best served cold? http://arbitrationblog.kluwerarbitration.com/2018/03/11/cjeu-slovakia-v-achmea-justice-best-served-cold

Bodansky D (2012) Legitimacy in international law and international relations. In: Dunoff JL, Pollack MA (eds) Interdisciplinary perspectives on international law and international relations: the state of the art. Cambridge University Press, Cambridge

Broude T (2013) Keep calm and carry on: Martti Koskenniemi and the fragmentation of international law. Temple Int Comp Law J 27(2):279–292

Brower CNBS (2014) What's in a meme? The truth about investor-state arbitration: why it need not, and must not, be repossessed by states. Columbia J Transnatl Law 52(1):689–777

Brower CN, Schill SW (2008) Is arbitration a threat or a boon to the legitimacy of international investment law? Chic J Int Law 9(2):471–498

Brown JG (2013) International investment agreements: regulatory chill in the face of litigious heat. WJ Leg Stud 3(1):i
Buergenthal T (2006) The proliferation of disputes, dispute settlement procedures and respect for the rule of law. Arbitr Int 22(4):495–500
Bungenberg M, Titi C (2019) CETA opinion – setting conditions for the future of ISDS. https://www.ejiltalk.org/ceta-opinion-setting-conditions-for-the-future-of-isds
Burgstaller M, Hindelang S, Pernice I (2013) How 'new' EU Member States should approach investment claims by EU investors. European Perspectives on Foreign Investment (EPFI), Berlin Occasional Law and Policy Papers. https://www.academia.edu/6913434/European_Perspectives_on_Foreign_Investment_EPFI_Berlin_Occasional_Law_and_Policy_Papers_1_2013_How_new_EU_Member_States_should_approach_investment_claims_by_EU_investors
Businesseurope (2015) EU state aid control in the context of global competition. Paper presented at the ERA annual conference on European state aid law 2015. https://www.businesseurope.eu/publications/eu-state-aid-control-context-global-competition-address-morten-qvist-fog-era-annual
Casteleiro AD (2015) Four cases for 2015 (III): Case T-646/14, Micula v Commission – State aids and International Dispute Settlement Systems. Retrieved from https://delilawblog.wordpress.com/2015/02/06/andres-delgado-casteleiro-four-cases-for-2015-iii-case-t-64614-micula-v-commission-state-aids-and-international-dispute-settlement-systems
Charlotin D (2018) With an apparent eye on set-aside, Spain unsuccessfully asks Novenergia tribunal for clarification on ECT–EU law relationship. IAReporter, 10 April. https://www.iareporter.com/articles/with-an-apparent-eye-on-set-aside-spain-unsuccessfully-asks-novenergia-tribunal-for-clarification-on-ect-eu-law-relationship
Clarke JL (2003) Competition policy and foreign direct investment. Paper presented at the fifth meeting of the European Trade Study Group, September
Cole T, Bantekas I, Ferretti F et al (2014) Legal instruments and practice of arbitration in the EU. http://www.europarl.europa.eu/studies
Council of the European Union (1988) Council Directive of 24 June 1988 for the implementation of Article 67 of the Treaty. Publications Office of the European Communities, Brussels
Council of the European Union (2010) Conclusions on a comprehensive European international investment policy (Vol. 3041st FOREIGN AFFAIRS). Publications office of the European Union, Luxembourg
Coyne CJ, Moberg L (2015) The political economy of state-provided targeted benefits. Rev Austrian Econ 28(3):337–356
Craig P, de Búrca G (2011) EU law: text, cases and materials, 5th edn. Oxford University Press, New York
Cremona M, Thies A (eds) (2014) The European Court of Justice and external relations law: constitutional challenges. Hart, Oxford
Croisant G (2019) Opinion 1/17 – The CJEU confirms that CETA's investment court system is compatible with EU law. http://arbitrationblog.kluwerarbitration.com/2019/04/30/opinion-117-the-cjeu-confirms-that-cetas-investment-court-system-is-compatible-with-eu-law
Cross C, Kube DV (2018) Is the arbitration clause of the Energy Charter Treaty compatible with EU law in its application between EU Member States? https://www.bilaterals.org/IMG/pdf/180226_gutachten_english_b.pdf
Cruz Pena J (2018) España pierde su segundo arbitraje internacional por el recorte a las renovables. El Confidencial. https://www.elconfidencial.com/economia/2018-02-19/espana-pierde-su-segundo-arbitraje-internacional-por-el-recorte-a-las-renovables_1523687
Dani M, Akhtar-Khavari A (2016) The uncertainty of legal doctrine in indirect expropriation cases and the legitimacy problems of investment arbitration. Widener Law Rev 22(1):1–32
De Búrca G (2010) The European Court of Justice and the international legal order after Kadi. Harv Int Law J 51(1):1–52
De Cecco F (2012) State aid and the European economic constitution. Hart, Oxford

Dimopoulos A (2014) The involvement of the eu in investor-state dispute settlement: a question of responsibilities. Common Mark Law Rev 51(6):1671–1720
Dimopoulos A (2018) Achmea: the principle of autonomy and its implications for intra and extra-EU BITs. https://www.ejiltalk.org/achmea-the-principle-of-autonomy-and-its-implications-for-intra-and-extra-eu-bits
Djajić S (2017) Searching for purpose: critical assessment of teleological interpretation of treaties in investment arbitration. Int Rev Law 3:1–28
Douglas Z (2014) The plea of illegality in investment treaty arbitration. ICSID Rev 29(1):155–186
Duarte FDA (2019) Autonomy and Opinion 1/17 – a matter of coherence? https://europeanlawblog.eu/2019/05/31/autonomy-and-opinion-1-17-a-matter-of-coherence
EC (2010) Communication from the Commission to the Council, the European Parliament, the European Economic and Social Committee and the Committee of the Regions: towards a comprehensive European international investment policy (Vol. COM(2010)343 final pp. 12). European Union, Brussels
Eckes (2016) International rulings and the EU legal order: autonomy as legitimacy? CLEER Papers 2:31. Centre for the Law of EU External Relations, The Hague
Eckes C (2018) Don't lead with your chin! If Member States continue with the ratification of CETA, they violate European Union law. https://europeanlawblog.eu/2018/03/13/dont-lead-with-your-chin-if-member-states-continue-with-the-ratification-of-ceta-they-violate-european-union-law
ECOFIN (2006) 2006 EFC Report to the Commission and the Council on the Movement of Capital and the Freedom of Payments. http://register.consilium.europa.eu/doc/srv?l=EN&f=ST%205044%202007%20INIT
Euronews (2015) MEPs seek investor dispute compromise in trade deal row. https://www.euronews.com/2015/07/08/meps-seek-investor-dispute-compromise-in-trade-deal-row
European Commission (EC) (2012) Commission staff working document – capital movements and investment in the EU Commission Services paper on market monitoring. https://www.eumonitor.nl/9353000/1/j9vvik7m1c3gyxp/vix38eqezrwa
European Commission (EC) (2015a) Get the facts: intra-EU bilateral investment treaties. https://ec.europa.eu/newsroom/fisma/item-detail.cfm?item_id=24581&newsletter_id=166&utm_source=fisma_newsletter&utm_medium=email&utm_campaign=Finance%20&utm_content=Get%20the%20facts%20Intra-EU%20bilateral%20investment%20treaties%20&lang=en
European Commission (EC) (2015b) Investment in TTIP and beyond – the path for reform. http://trade.ec.europa.eu/doclib/docs/2015/may/tradoc_153408.PDF
European Commission (EC) (2015c) Online public consultation on investment protection and investor-to-state dispute settlement (ISDS) in the Transatlantic Trade and Investment Partnership Agreement (TTIP). http://trade.ec.europa.eu/doclib/docs/2015/january/tradoc_153044.pdf
European Commission (EC) (2015d) Report on the online consultation on investment protection and investor-to-state dispute settlement in the Transatlantic Trade and Investment Partnership Agreement. http://europa.eu/rapid/press-release_MEMO-15-3202_en.htm
European Commission (EC) (2016) European neighbourhood policy and enlargement negotiations. https://ec.europa.eu/neighbourhood-enlargement/policy/glossary/terms/europe-agreement_en
European Commission (EC) (2017a) Agreements – Trade – European Commission. http://ec.europa.eu/trade/policy/countries-and-regions/agreements
European Commission (EC) (2017b) Commission staff working document on the movement of capital and the freedom of payments. http://europeanmemoranda.cabinetoffice.gov.uk/files/2017/02/ST-6606-2017-INIT-EN.pdf
European Commission (EC) (2017c) Treaty of Lisbon enters into force – Implications for the EU's trade policy. http://trade.ec.europa.eu/doclib/press/index.cfm?id=493
European Commission (EC) (2017d) TTIP – The EU–US trade deal. http://ec.europa.eu/trade/policy/in-focus/ttip/index_en.htm.
European Commission (EC) (2017e) EU and Japan reach agreement in principle on Economic Partnership Agreement. http://europa.eu/rapid/press-release_IP-17-1902_en.htm

European Commission (EC) (2018a) A new EU trade agreement with Japan. http://trade.ec.europa.eu/doclib/docs/2017/july/tradoc_155684.PDF

European Commission (EC) (2018b) Communication from the Commission to the European Parliament and the Council, Protection of intra-EU investment. https://eur-lex.europa.eu/legal-content/EN/TXT/?uri=COM%3A2018%3A547%3AFIN

European Parliament (2014) Investor-state dispute settlement (ISDS) provisions in the EU's international investment agreements. http://www.europarl.europa.eu/thinktank/en/document.html?reference=EXPO_STU(2014)534979

European Parliament (2015) European Parliament resolution of 8 July 2015 containing the European Parliament's recommendations to the European Commission on the negotiations for the Transatlantic Trade and Investment Partnership (TTIP). https://www.europarl.europa.eu/doceo/document/TA-8-2015-0252_EN.html

European Union (2007) Treaty of Lisbon amending the Treaty on European Union and the Treaty establishing the European Community

European Union and Canada (2016) EU–Canada Comprehensive Economic and Trade Agreement. European Union, Brussels

European Union and Singapore (2017) EU–Singapore Free Trade Agreement. European Union, Brussels

Fietta V (2015) Further attempts by the European Commission to eradicate intra-EU BITs. http://www.volterrafietta.com/further-attempts-by-the-european-commission-to-eradicate-intra-eu-bits

Finckenberg-Broman P (2019) State aid prohibition as an instrument in the gender war: promoting work for women in the European Union? In: Rimmer SH, Ogg K (eds) Research handbook on feminist engagement with international law. Edward Elgar, Cheltenham

Fleming J (2014) ISDS clause: a gateway to future trade deals. http://www.euractiv.com/section/trade-society/news/isds-clause-a-gateway-to-future-trade-deals

Fouchard C, Krestin M (2018) The judgment of the CJEU in Slovak Republic v Achmea – a loud clap of thunder on the intra-EU BIT sky! http://arbitrationblog.kluwerarbitration.com/2018/03/07/the-judgment-of-the-cjeu-in-slovak-republic-v-achmea

Gaffney JP (2018) Slovak Republic v. Achmea: a disproportionate judgement? http://arbitrationblog.kluwerarbitration.com/2018/09/14/slovak-republic-v-achmea-a-disproportionate-judgment

Gallo D, Nicola FG (2015) The external dimension of EU investment law: jurisdictional clashes and transformative adjudication. Fordham Int Law J 39(5):1081–1152

Gaukrodger D (2017) Addressing the balance of interests in investment treaties: the limitation of fair and equitable treatment provisions to the minimum standard of treatment under customary international law. OECD, Geneva

Giorgetti C (2013) Who decides who decides in international investment arbitration? Univ Pa J Int Law 35(2):431–485

Griller S, Obwexer W, Vranes E (eds) (2017) Mega-regional trade agreements: CETA, TTIP, and TiSA – new orientations for EU external economic relations. Oxford University Press, Oxford

Guillaume G (2000) The proliferation of international judicial bodies: the outlook for the international legal order. Speech by His Excellency Judge Gilbert Guillaume, President of the International Court of Justice, to the Sixth Committee of the General Assembly of the United Nations

Happ R, Tietje C (2013) EU, investment treaties, and investment treaty arbitration: current developments and challenges. Transnatl Dispute Manag 10(2). https://www.transnational-dispute-management.com/article.asp?key=1937

Hartley TC (2004) European Union law in a global context: text, cases and materials. Cambridge University Press, Cambridge

Hazzaa H, Kumpf SN (2015) Egypt's ban on public interest litigation in government contracts: a case study of 'judicial chill'. Stanford J Int Law 51(2):147–171

Hepburn J (2018) Vattenfall Tribunal issues decision rejecting Germany's post-Achmea jurisdictional objection. https://www.iareporter.com/articles/vattenfall-tribunal-issues-decision-rejecting-germanys-post-achmea-jurisdictional-objection
Hess B (2018) The fate of investment dispute resolution after the Achmea decision of the European Court of Justice. Revista Eletrônica de Direito Processual 19(3):114–137
Hindelang S (2012a) Circumventing primacy of EU law and the CJEU's judicial monopoly by resorting to dispute resolution mechanisms provided for in inter-se treaties: the case of intra-EU investment arbitration. Leg Issues Econ Integr 39(2):179–206
Hindelang S (2012b) Member State BITs – there's still (some) life in the old dog yet. Incompatibility of existing Member State BITs with EU law and possible remedies. In: Sauvant KP (ed) Yearbook on international investment law & policy. Oxford University Press, Oxford
Hindelang S (2018) The limited immediate effects of CJEU's Achmea judgement. https://verfassungsblog.de/the-limited-immediate-effects-of-cjeus-achmea-judgement
Hindelang S (2019) Conceptualisation and application of the principle of autonomy of EU law: the CJEU's judgment in Achmea put in perspective. Eur Law Rev 44(3):383–400
Jennings MB (2016) The international investment regime and investor–state dispute settlement: states bear the primary responsibility for legitimacy. Bus Law Int 17(2):127–151
Jestaedt T, Derenne J, Ottervanger T (2006) Study on the enforcement of state aid law at national level. http://ec.europa.eu/competition/state_aid/studies_reports/study_part_1.pdf
Johnson L, Volkov O (2014) Investor-state contracts, host-state 'commitments' and the myth of stability in international law. Am Rev Int Arbitr 24(3):361
Juillard P (2001) Bilateral investment treaties in the context of investment law. Paper presented at Investment Compact Regional Roundtable on Bilateral Investment Treaties for the Protection and Promotion of Foreign Investment in South East Europe
Kende T (2015) Arbitral awards classified as state aid under European Union law. ELTE Law J 1: 37–56
Keohane RO, Moravcsik A, Slaughter AM (2000) Legalized dispute resolution: interstate and transnational. Int Organ 54(3):457–488
Kleinheisterkamp J (2011) The next 10 year ECT investment arbitration: a vision for the future – from a European law perspective. London School of Economics, London
Kleinheisterkamp J (2012a) European policy space in international investment law. ICSID Rev – Foreign Invest Law J 27(2):416–431
Kleinheisterkamp J (2012b) Investment protection and EU law: the intra- and extra-EU dimension of the Energy Charter Treaty. J Int Econ Law 15(1):85–109
Kleinheisterkamp J (2015) Investment treaty law and the fear for sovereignty: transnational challenges and solutions. Mod Law Rev 78(5):793–825
Kochenov D (2015) EU law without the rule of law: is the veneration of autonomy worth it? Yearb Eur Law 34(1):74–96
Kokott J, Sobotta C (2012) The Kadi case: constitutional core values and international law – finding the balance? Eur J Int Law 23(4):1015–1024
Konttinen J, Teivainen A (2013) Professor: Finland's legislative power may be in jeopardy. http://www.helsinkitimes.fi/finland/finland-news/domestic/8717-professor-finland-s-legislative-power-may-be-in-jeopardy.html
Koutrakos P (2016) The relevance of EU law for arbitral tribunals: (Not) managing the lingering tension. J World Invest Trade 17(6):873–894
Krajewski M (2019) Is CETA the 'golden standard'? ECJ considers CETA court to be in compliance with European Union law. https://verfassungsblog.de/ist-ceta-der-golden-standard-eugh-haelt-ceta-gericht-fuer-unionsrechtskonform
Lamadrid de Pablo A (2015) State aid and investment arbitration: an improbably (and fascinating) conflict. https://chillingcompetition.com/2015/02/05/state-aid-and-investment-arbitration-an-improbable-and-fascinating-conflict
Langford M, Behn D, Lie R (2017) The ethics and empirics of double hatting. ESIL Reflect 6(7): 1–12

Latif A (2017) Landmark cases on European Union Law. http://www.eulaws.eu/?p=171
Lavranos N (2015) Micula vs. (Brussels) Dracula. http://www.globalinvestmentprotection.com/index.php/micula-vs-brussels-dracula
Lavranos N (2016) The lack of any legal conflict between EU law and intra-EU BITs/ECT disputes. https://efilablog.org/2016/02/25/the-lack-of-any-legal-conflict-between-eu-law-and-intra-eu-bitsect-disputes
Lavranos N (2018a) Black Tuesday: the end of intra-EU BITs. http://arbitrationblog.practicallaw.com/black-tuesday-the-end-of-intra-eu-bits
Lavranos N (2018b) Insight: the end of intra-EU BITs – what next? https://www.borderlex.eu/comment-end-of-intra-eu-bits-what-next/
Lavranos N (2019) Court of Justice of the EU approves CETA investment court system. http://arbitrationblog.practicallaw.com/court-of-justice-of-the-eu-approves-ceta-investment-court-system
Lenk H, Rönnelid L, Dahlquist J (2016) The infringement proceedings over intra-EU investment treaties: an analysis of the case against Sweden. Swedish Institute for European Policy Studies, Stockholm
Leonhardsen EM (2011) Looking for legitimacy: exploring proportionality analysis in investment treaty arbitration. J Int Dispute Settlement 3(1):95–136
Mackenzie R, Sands P (2003) International courts and tribunals and the independence of the international judge. Harv Int Law J 44(1):271
Maduro MP (2007) Interpreting European law: judicial adjudication in a context of constitutional pluralism. Eur J Leg Stud 1(2):137
Matei E (2015a) A European approach to BITs, MITs and ISDS. https://www.slideshare.net/EmanuelaMatei/eu-approach-to-bit-autosaved
Matei E (2015b) Hemispheres of European investment law: in search of lost certainty. https://www.linkedin.com/pulse/autistic-link-unites-two-hemispheres-european-investment-matei
Matei E (2015c) Putting the cart before the horse: a doomed constitutional strategy for negotiating the T-TIP. http://eulawanalysis.blogspot.com/2015/08/putting-cart-before-horse-doomed.html
Matei E (2015d) The chamber of secrets: the repudiation of the ISDS. Revista Română de Dept European 4:1–19
Matei E (2016) SA.38517 - Commission Decision of 30 March 2015 on State Aid Granted by Romania to Micula. Eur State Aid Law Q 15(1):134
Matei E, Ciurtin H (2016) Turning enemies into adversaries: TTIP negotiations and the quest for a new Westphalia momentum. Turkish Commer Law Rev 2(1):27–76
Murauskas (2013) Temporal limitations by the Court of Justice of the EU: dealing with the consequences. Eur J Legal Stud 6:100
Niemelä P (2017) The relationship of EU law and bilateral investment treaties of EU Member States. Unpublished doctoral dissertation, University of Helsinki
Nikitin P (2018) The CJEU's Achmea judgment: getting through the five stages of grief. http://arbitrationblog.kluwerarbitration.com/2018/04/10/cjeus-achmea-judgment-getting-five-stages-grief
OECD (2005) International investment law: a changing landscape. OECD, Paris
Olivet C, Eberhardt P (2012) Profiting from injustice: how law firms, arbitrators and financiers are fuelling an investment arbitration boom. http://corporateeurope.org/sites/default/files/publications/profiting-from-injustice.pdf
Ortolani P (2015) Intra-EU arbitral awards vis-à-vis Article 107 TFEU: state aid law as a limit to compliance. J Int Dispute Settlement 6(1):118–135
Papadopoulos T (2019) The importance of European company law for intra-EU investments after Achmea. Bus Law Rev 40(1):7–9
Peers S (2019) 'We *aren't* the world': the CJEU reconciles EU law with international (investment) law. http://eulawanalysis.blogspot.com/2019/05/we-arent-world-cjeu-reconciles-eu-law.html

Perera SM (2012) Equity-based decision-making and the fair and equitable treatment standard: lessons from the Argentine investment disputes–part I. J World Invest Trade 13(2):210–255
Peterson L (2018a) Analysis: in a striking new award, ICSID tribunal rules that Achmea judgment does not cast shadow over ICSID-based arbitration; but efforts to empanel ad-hoc committees to review such intra-EU BIT awards keep getting harder. https://www.iareporter.com/articles/analysis-in-a-striking-new-award-icsid-tribunal-rules-that-achmea-judgment-does-not-cast-shadow-over-icsid-based-arbitration-but-efforts-to-empanel-ad-hoc-committees-to-review-such-intra-eu-bit-awa
Peterson L (2018b) Reasons for dismissal of recent attempt to disqualify arbitrator Gary Born come to light. https://www.iareporter.com/articles/reasons-for-dismissal-of-recent-attempt-to-disqualify-arbitrator-gary-born-come-to-light
Picker CB (2008) International law's mixed heritage: a common/civil law jurisdiction. Vanderbilt J Transnatl Law 41:1083–1138
Pinsolle and Michou (2018) The Achmea v Slovakia Judgment of the CJEU, is it really the end of Intra-EU Investment Treaties? Two leading arbitration practitioners say not necessarily. Quinn Emanuel Firm News. Retrieved from https://www.quinnemanuel.com/the-firm/news-events/the-achmea-v-slovakia-judgment-of-the-cjeu-is-it-really-the-end-of-intra-eu-investment-treaties/
Pinto CS (2016) The narrow meaning of the legitimate expectation principle in state aid law versus the foreign investor's legitimage expectations. Eur State Aid Law Q 15(2):270–285
Puig S (2016) Blinding international justice. Va J Int Law 56(3):647–700
Reinisch A (2013) EU on the investment path: Quo vadis Europe – the future of EU BITs and other investment agreements. Santa Clara J Int Law 12(1):111–157
Righini E (2018) The European Court of Justice, international arbitrations and the exercise of (an unsatisfactory) state aid control. https://www.womenatcompetitionblog.com/single-post/2018/08/09/The-European-Court-of-Justice-International-Arbitrations-and-the-exercise-of-an-unsatisfactory-State-aid-control
Roberts A (2010) Power and persuasion in investment treaty interpretation: the dual role of states. Am J Int Law 104(2):179–225
Roberts A (2013) Subsequent agreements and practice: the battle over interpretive power. In: Roberts A (ed) Treaties and aubsequent practice. Oxford University Press, Oxford
Roe T (2016) Illegality and jurisdiction in investment arbitration. Turk Com Law Rev 2:17
Rösch KÖ (2017) May the European Court of Justice tame intra-EU investment tribunals. Lund Student EU Law Rev 1(1):25
Rose V, Bailey D (eds) (2013) Bellamy & Child European Union law of competition, vol 2. Oxford University Press, Oxford
Ross A (2018) Three Crowns partners resign from panels considering Achmea. https://globalarbitrationreview.com/article/1172997/three-crowns-partners-resign-from-panels-considering-achmea
Rovetta AD, Gambardella AM (2015) Intra-EU BITs and EU law: what to learn from the Micula battle. Glob Trade Cust J 10(6):194–197
Sands P (2011) Conflict and conflicts in investment treaty arbitration: ethical standards for counsel. In: Brown C (ed) Evolution in investment treaty law and arbitration. Cambridge University Press, Cambridge
Sands P (2015) Final lecture – developments in geopolitics: the end(s) of judicialization? Paper presented at the ESIL Annual Conference 2015: The Judicialization of International Law – A Mixed Blessing?, Oslo. http://www.jus.uio.no/pluricourts/english/news-and-events/events/2015/esil-2015-en/video-and-streaming/final-lecture.html
Sauter W (2013) Proportionality in EU law: a balancing act? TILEC Discussion Paper No. 2013-003. https://papers.ssrn.com/sol3/papers.cfm?abstract_id=2208467
Schill SW (2007) Do investment treaties chill unilateral state regulation to mitigate climate change. J Int Arbitr 24(5):469–477

Schilling T (1996) The autonomy of the community legal order: an analysis of possible foundations. Harv Int Law J 37:389–411

Schneiderman D (2016) On suffering and societal constitutionalism: at the border of international investment arbitration and human rights. In: Tsvi K, Scolnicov A (eds) Boundaries of state, boundaries of rights: human rights, private actors, and positive obligations. Cambridge University Press, Cambridge

Schreuer C, Kriebaum U (2011) From individual to community interest in international investment law. In: Fastenrath U, Geiger R, Khan D, Paulus A, von Schorlemer S, Vedder C (eds) From bilateralism to community interest: essays in honour of Bruno Simma. Oxford University Press, Oxford

Shelkoplyas N (2003) The application of EC law in arbitration proceedings. Unpublished doctoral thesis, Tilburg University

Simma B (2009) Universality of international law from the perspective of a practitioner. Eur J Int Law 20(2):265–297

Simmons BA (2014) Bargaining over BITs, arbitrating awards: the regime for protection and promotion of international investment. World Polit 66(1):12–46

Struckmann K, Forwood G, Kadri A (2016) Investor-state arbitrations and EU state aid rules: conflict or co-existence. Eur State Aid Law Q 15(2):258–269

Sykes AO (2005) Public versus private enforcement of international economic law: standing and remedy. J Leg Stud 34(2):631–666

Szilágyi SG (2018) The CJEU strikes again in Achmea: is this the end of investor-state arbitration under intra-EU BITs? http://worldtradelaw.typepad.com/ielpblog/2018/03/guest-post-the-cjeu-strikes-again-in-achmea-is-this-the-end-of-investor-state-arbitration-under-intr.html

Tavares-Lehmann AT, Toledano P, Johnson L, Sachs L (eds) (2016) Rethinking investment incentives: trends and policy options. Columbia University Press, New York

Tetley W (1999) Mixed jurisdictions: common law v civil law (codified and uncodified). La Law Rev 60:677

The Organisation for Economic Co-operation and Development (OECD) (2003) Checklist for Foreign Direct Investment Incentive Policies. Retrieved from Paris: https://www.oecd.org/daf/inv/investment-policy/2506900.pdf

Tienhaara K (2010) Regulatory chill and the threat of arbitration: a view from political science. In: Brown C (ed) Evolution in investment treaty law and arbitration. Cambridge University Press, Cambridge

Tienhaara K, Downie C (2018) Risky business? The Energy Charter Treaty, renewable energy, and investor-state disputes. Glob Gov: Rev Multilateralism Int Organ 24(3):451–471

Tietje C (2008) The Applicability of the Energy Charter Treaty in ICSID Arbitration of EU Nationals vs EU Member States. Transnatl Dispute Manag 1. https://www.transnational-dispute-management.com/article.asp?key=1428

Tietje C (2013) Bilateral investment treaties between EU Member States (intra-EU-BITs): challenges in the multilevel system of law. Transnatl Dispute Manag 10(2). https://www.transnational-dispute-management.com/article.asp?key=1945

Tietje C, Baetens F (2014) The impact of investor-state dispute settlement (ISDS) in the Transatlantic Trade and Investment Partnership. https://www.rijksoverheid.nl/documenten/rapporten/2014/06/24/the-impact-of-investor-state-dispute-settlement-isds-in-the-ttip

Tietje C, Wackernagel C (2014) Outlawing compliance? The reinforcement of intra-EU investment awards and EU state aid law. Transnatl Dispute Manag 3. https://www.transnational-dispute-management.com/article.asp?key=2116

Tietje C, Wackernagel C (2015) Enforcement of intra-EU ICSID awards. J World Invest Trade 16(2):205–247

Tietje C, Sipiorski E, Töpfer G (2012) Responsibility in investor-state-arbitration in the EU: managing financial responsibility linked to investor-state dispute settlement tribunals established by EU's International Investment Agreements. European Union, Brussels

UNCTAD (2016) International Investment Agreements Navigator. http://investmentpolicyhub.unctad.org/IIA

UNCTAD (2017) Special update on Investor-state dispute settlement: facts and figures. http://unctad.org/en/PublicationsLibrary/diaepcb2017d7_en.pdf

UNICTRAL (2019) Report of Working Group III (Investor-State Dispute Settlement Reform) on the work of its thirty-seventh session, New York, 1–5 April. https://uncitral.un.org/en/working_groups/3/investor-state

United Nations Commission on International Trade Law (UNICTRAL) (2018) Possible reform of investor-state dispute settlement (ISDS). https://uncitral.un.org/en/working_groups/3/investor-state

Van Harten G (2013) Sovereign choices and sovereign constraints: judicial restraint in investment treaty arbitration. Oxford University Press, Oxford

Van Harten G (2015) A parade of reforms: The European Commission's latest proposal for ISDS. Osgoode Leg Stud Res Pap 21:1–15

van Os R, Knottnerus R (2011) Dutch bilateral investment treaties: a gateway to 'treaty shopping' for investment protection by multinational companies. Stichting Onderzoek Multinatonale Ondernemingen, Amsterdam

Vandevelde KJ (2010) A unified theory of fair and equitable treatment. N Y Univ J Int Law Polit 43(1):43–106

Wehland H (2016) The enforcement of intra-EU BIT awards: Micula v Romania and beyond. J World Invest Trade 17(6):942–963

Weiler JH, Haltern UR (1996) The autonomy of the community legal order-through the looking glass. Harv Int Law J 37:411

Working Group on the Relationship between Trade and Investment (1998) The relationship between foreign investment and competition policy. https://docs.wto.org/dol2fe/Pages/FE_Search/FE_S_S005.aspx

Ziegler KS (2013) The relationship between EU law and international law. University of Leicester, Leicester

Chapter 6
Proving the Point: The Point Proved

6.1 Overview

This chapter aims to provide an insight into how the EU uses trade instruments for regulatory export of state aid law and how this practice interacts with the EU's IAAs (including both bilateral investment agreements and investment chapters in trade agreements). While the first five chapters of this book set up the background for the arguments of the monograph, and explained the implications in law and fact of the collisions between the international investment regime and the state aid regime, this chapter demonstrates how EU state aid law translates into the international dimensions by showing how EU's trade instruments are utilised to insert EU state aid legislation either into the governing norms for trade relations or into the trading party's legislation.

The EU has adopted an active approach in negotiating, entering and concluding international agreements from the beginning. These agreements come in various forms, such as plurilateral regional agreements, preferential trade agreements, cooperation agreements with trade components and political cooperation agreements.[1] Under the EU's Common Commercial Policy, these agreements can cover a wide range of trade-related measures, and often go beyond the traditional areas covered by the WTO.[2]

Provisions on competition policy and subsidies control have often been included.[3] In this way, trade agreements have become an essential element in the EU's overall strategy to employ its state aid rules in third countries. For that reason, besides managing to commit third countries to respect state aid-type rules stricter

[1] The legal basis for these agreements is Article 207 TFEU (former Article 133 EC Treaty). Only Association agreements are based on Article 217 TFEU.

[2] See Horn et al. (2010).

[3] Polityka (2018).

P. Finckenberg-Broman, *Weaponizing EU State Aid Law to Impact the Future of EU Investment Policy in the Global Context*, Studies in European Economic Law and Regulation 23, https://doi.org/10.1007/978-3-031-10108-3_6

than the WTO's subsidies control, the EU also established the means for regulatory transfer of these rules on the plurilateral and bilateral levels. Besides negotiating and concluding trade and political cooperation agreements, the EU influences and supports other multilateral, regional and national initiatives in numerous forms, including the development of competition rules and subsidies control.[4]

The EU's competence to conclude international agreements containing FDI did not exist before the Lisbon Treaty entered into force in 2009.[5] Before the Lisbon Treaty, investment provisions incorporated in the EU's international agreements merely had the purpose of encouraging investment flows between the EU and its trading partners without any specific procedural commitments. Therefore, questions about the compatibility of ISA with EU law *vis-à-vis* external relations did not arise pre-Lisbon Treaty.

Hence, this chapter explicitly discusses the first argument of this book on how the EU incorporates provisions of fair competition and state aid policy in international trade agreements to guarantee that these agreements in general, and investment chapters in particular, will not conflict with EU state aid law.[6] Fundamentally, EU investment policy must be in line with the primary law of the EU[7] to ensure the following:

- guarding the autonomy of EU law[8] (as explained in Chaps. 2 and 5)
- protecting 'fairness' in the competition (to protect the competitiveness of EU firms from being severely impaired by state aid-enhanced third country firms[9]
  - in the internal market (state aid as a shield, as shown in Chap. 3).
  - globally (state aid as a sword, as explained in Chap. 3)
- protecting the capacity of the Commission to implement policy objectives in line with changing EU policy priorities[10] (as explained in Sects. 2.2, 2.5, 3.4 and 3.5).
- guarding the CJEU's ability to use state aid law to maintain a frictionless internal market (as explained in Chap. 3).

For that reason, provisions on subsidies and investment in EU trade instruments—every bilateral and plurilateral trade agreement with countries or trading blocs in

---

[4]Some of the countries with which the EU has Association Agreements (AA), as well as other regional trade blocs such as the West African Economic and Monetary Union (WAEMU also called as UEMOA), have also implemented rules on state aid as part of their competition policies: OECD (2011), pp. 9–10. It should be noted that these rules are not yet effectively implemented and enforced.

[5]See former Article 133 EC Treaty and compare with Article 207 TFEU.

[6]See Sect. 1.4 in Chap. 1 for this thesis argument.

[7]*Case 6-64 – Costa v ENEL* (1964). See also *Opinion 2/13 of the Court (Full Court)* (2014).

[8]Some authors, such as Eckes (2018), believe that in light of *Achmea C-284/16* (2018), the ICS probably violates EU law.

[9]As argued by Kleinheisterkamp (2012a); see also Eckes (2016), pp. 10, 31.

[10]Koenig (2014), p. 611argues that state aid has developed from a simple prohibition into 'an all-purpose tool to camouflage policy making'.

force or under negotiation by the EU—have been systematically searched and collected (see Appendices 1 and 2 for these data). Subsequently, the data collected has been sifted and analysed. This process has provided an insight into how the EU systematically includes subsidies/state aid provisions in its trade instruments:

(a) as self-standing provisions to guarantee that these agreements, in general, are in line with EU law
(b) as incorporated provisions to substantially reduce investors' ability to invoke claims on the grounds of breach of investment protection clauses (state aid as a shield).

While both findings confirm the first argument of this book, the findings in (b) are self-explanatory contrary to the findings in (a), which require some clarification corresponding to the indirect effect these may have on the EU's investment policy. Because this effect depends on the extent to which these state aid provisions require the third countries to employ state aid rules, this chapter also explores the different types of trade and policy instruments employed by the EU through a state aid lens. Especially, it elaborates on how the scope of the EU's extraterritorial state aid policy materialises, namely the type of control applied, the level of success and the effect on the third country, depending on the specific type of instrument employed. For this purpose, relating to these specific benchmarks, this monograph divides the EU's international agreements into four distinct categories, with a short case study on a selection of countries in some of the categories. These categories are the global, the European Neighbourhood Policy, the accession and candidate countries, and the EEA/EFTA model. These categories are also distinguishable through the geographical location of the country in relation to the location of the EU.[11]

This chapter does not particularly study or elaborate upon multilateral trade instruments, as they are not the focus of this book. Nevertheless, they are so entangled with the subject matter of this book that these trade instruments cannot be overlooked entirely. Previous chapters of this monograph (particularly in Chaps. 2 and 3) have discussed these types of trade instruments. Therefore, this chapter merely mentions them briefly. From an IIA aspect, the chapter provides a short overview of the situation regarding the ECT using a state aid lens.

Besides data collected from EU's trade instruments and case studies conducted on the impact of these agreements to the EU's trading partners under the four categories of agreements, this chapter draws from the CJEU's case law, the Commission's policy documents, relevant works of literature and different type of documents from international organisations active in this specific area. In particular, the Commission's reports on the European Neighbourhood Policy and Enlargement Negotiations, as well as different types of trade-related policy documents and fact sheets, have been relied on. The chapter does not provide a specific review of works of literature as it echoes the review provided in Sect. 3.4 in Chap. 3.

---

[11]Corresponding to the 'domino theory' of regionalism, was provided by Baldwin (1993) for enlargement of Europe's economic integration.

While this chapter adopts a top-up view in the discussion and analysis conducted here, it does so by asking the question:

How is EU State aid law going (from regional) international (to global)?

This chapter concludes that state aid provisions in the EU's trade instruments act as a sword and a shield for IIAs. Including self-standing state aid provisions into these agreements guarantees that they are generally in line with EU law. Besides the obvious—the protection of European enterprises from disadvantages in global competition compared with third-country firms who may benefit from state aid—these provisions also protect the internal market competition (the shield) from 'unfair foreign subsidies' effects. The provisions may also act as a vessel for regulatory export (the sword). As some trade agreements require the implementation of state aid into national laws, the ability of enterprises to acquire investment through subsidies is substantially reduced, which in due course aligns the investment policy of these countries to be compatible with EU state aid laws. State aid provisions also act as a shield, explicitly *vis-à-vis* jurisdictional conflict, when they are incorporated into investment protection clauses in such a way that it substantially reduces investors' ability to invoke claims on the grounds of breach of investment protection. Some of the proposals made by this book are shown to have already taken place in practice. This book further finds that the scope of the EU's extraterritorial state aid policy emerges from the type of control applied, the level of its success and the effect on the third country, depending on the specific type of instrument employed.

This chapter is divided into six parts. The next section explains and categorises the EU's strategies to employ state aid rules in third countries. This is followed by some insights into the workings of the EU's plurilateral regional agreements from a state aid perspective and a case study of Switzerland to show how third-country national laws may be affected by the EU's state aid policy. The chapter then discusses how the different types of EU bilateral agreements entered into depending on the relationship the third country has with the EU. The type of bilateral agreement varies in relation to these countries' possible aspiration to accede into the EU, as well as the EU's influence and geographical nearness to these nations. This is followed by an elaboration of how investment provisions, from a state aid perspective, have been revised to remedy these dilemmas. The final part of the chapter summarises the effect of the collisions between the international investment regime and state aid regime on the future of EU's global trade.

6.2 The EU's Strategies to Employ State Aid Rules on Third Countries

In contrast to foreign investment policy, competition policy, of which state aid is a part, has had time to settle into established practice for over 60 years since the Treaty of Rome.[12] Hence, the EU's competition policy, including state aid control, has had plenty of time to evolve supranationally. Certainly, the EU's administration of state aid is one of the most sophisticated control systems of subsidies on the supranational level, which includes both regional and global application.

Some authors regard competition policy as the first supranational policy on both the regional[13] and extraterritorial[14] levels. In the wake of time, the EU has adopted a holistic trade strategy, which includes several strategies to employ state aid rules to third countries. Therefore, this type of regulatory transfer takes place on both the multilateral and the bilateral levels. Besides negotiating and concluding trade and political cooperation agreements, the EU supports other national and regional policy initiatives in numerous forms, including the development of competition rules and subsidies control.[15]

State aid provisions can often be found in older trade agreements (at least from the 1990s), but Blanca Rodriguez Galindo, the Head of the EU's International Relations Unit of DG Competition, informs us that a systematic inclusion of state aid provisions in FTAs was not negotiated before 2006.[16] This timeline matches with the launch of EU's Global Europe strategy[17] and the speech of the EU's former competition commissioner, Neelie Kroes, in 2007 emphasising the fundamental importance of state aid control in the context of global competition.[18] Her speech demonstrated the conclusions the Commission had reached in its overall review of EC trade policy, launched the year before, to turn it into an external competitiveness tool.[19]

A closer examination of the EU's existing trade agreements, such as the EU–Singapore FTA and the EEA Agreement, utilised to observe how this plays out in practice,[20] reveals two main types of state aid control being provided for: (1) parallel state aid systems—either multilateral or domestic; or (2) 'WTO plus' systems, which take the WTO anti-subsidy rules as a starting point and add further substantive and

[12] See Chap. 2.

[13] McGowan and Wilks (1995).

[14] Papadopoulos (2010).

[15] Bilal (2004).

[16] Galindo (2015).

[17] In 2006. See the Commission's Communication 'Global Europe: Competing in the World' COM (2006) 567 final.

[18] Kroes (2007), p. 2.

[19] Kroes (2007), p. 4.

[20] For the EU's existing trade agreements, see https://ec.europa.eu/trade/policy/countries-and-regions/negotiations-and-agreements.

procedural disciplines.[21] The type of control applied, and the level of success,[22] vary according to the following four distinct categories of international agreements.[23] The type of agreement seems to correlate with how significant trade and cooperation with the EU is for the third country/countries, the geographical nearness to the EU and whether the other party to the agreement is a nation or a trading bloc:

1. the *global*, with three sub-categories:
   a. *megaregional bilateralism* (such as CETA, JEEPA, EUSFTA), which utilises the 'WTO plus' system for state aid control.
   b. *megaregional plurilateralism* with regional trade blocs (such as Cariforum, Mercosur, ASEAN), which has the weakest subsidies and competition provisions in general, at times only incorporating provisions to review or continue negotiations on competition policies in the future
   c. *supranational subsidies control* through multilateral instruments (WTO, UNCTAD)
2. the European Neighbourhood Policy, which has bilaterals with two sub-categories of countries:[24]
   a. Eastern nations—Armenia, Azerbaijan, Belarus, Georgia, Moldova and Ukraine; these trade agreements mainly deploy a gradual transition to domestic parallel state aid systems
   b. Southern nations—Algeria, Egypt, Israel, Jordan, Lebanon, Libya, Morocco, Palestine, Syria and Tunisia; these trade agreements have also aimed to implement domestic parallel state aid systems.

---

[21] Schonberg (2017), p. 52. Notably, some authors find these provisions lacking, as most of these have no legally enforceable obligations: Horn et al. (2010), p. 1580.

[22] Lavenex and Schimmelfennig (2009) argue that the success of regulatory transfer also depends on the specific instruments of regulatory transfer. Blauberger and Krämer (2012) identify three major groups of countries—which consist of category 3 and 4 discussed and studied by this thesis—where this has been successful.

[23] These four categories have been identified and individually or partially assessed (concerning EU eastward enlargement) by Sedelmeier (2011). In his contribution on the international dimension of EU competition law, Papadopoulos (2010) also divides the EU's international agreements, which are devoted to competition or include competition provision in four distinct categories. These match only partially with the categories of this thesis. A major difference is that his first category, bilateral enforcement cooperation agreements (ICN), does not cover state aid control globally, so is irrelevant to this thesis. Also, the multilateral competition regime, which is covered by his fourth category, is not the focus of this dissertation. Hence, this type of agreement is not dealt with in depth. Papadopoulos's second category (bilateral trade agreements) and his third category (plurilateral-regional agreements), with the difference of being limited to plurilateral-regional agreements to which the EU is a signatory, are essential for this dissertation. For the purposes of this thesis, these are divided into four, instead of two, parts to reflect the degree of equilibrium achieved in state aid control.

[24] See Commission's website at https://ec.europa.eu/neighbourhood-enlargement/neighbourhood/countries_en.

3. accession and candidate countries through bilateral agreements with three sub-categories of countries, which must implement domestic parallel state aid systems that are fully harmonised with the EU's state aid regime, including accepting the interpretive methods of the CJEU before accession:
   a. accession
   b. candidate
   c. Stabilisation and Association Agreements (SAAs) for Western Balkans: Albania, Macedonia, Montenegro, Serbia, Kosovo and Bosnia[25]
4. the EEA/EFTA model—a plurilateral regional agreement:
   a. EEA implements EU State aid rules fully
   b. EFTA introduces a parallel multilateral state aid system
   c. Switzerland—being in EFTA but not part of the EEA, is not part of the multilateral system but instead has introduced domestic laws on subsidies control.

Importantly, for countries that are not Member States of the EU or the EEA, the state aid rules of the TFEU or the EEA Agreement are not applicable, except where such countries have agreed on their application.[26] This does not mean that individual undertakings of third countries that do business inside the EU or have business directed to the EU are exempted from EU state aid rules if receiving EU internal market incompatible state aid; however, depending on the location of the undertaking and its nationality, enforcement such as a claw-back procedure can be difficult or impossible to execute in the absence of state aid control provisions in international competition, cooperation and enforcement agreements. In these situations, besides diplomacy, the EU may try to rely on multilateral state aid control in the form of subsidies control.

6.2.1 *Multilateral State Aid Control*

Outside of the EU's internal market, and where there are no bilateral agreements in which countries have agreed on an application of state aid control, this control is replaced by multilateral subsidies control.[27] Therefore, the EU is an active proponent of multilateral control on competition-related activities[28] such as OECD, UNCTAD

[25] Lavenex and Schimmelfennig (2009) discuss EU eastward enlargement in the context of European 'external governance'.

[26] ((INTERACT) & (ETC) 2015), p. 16. Some countries in process of accession (IPA countries) have agreed to an application of state aid rules. IPAs constitute EU candidate countries and potential candidate countries.

[27] For more on this subject, see Sect. 3.3.1 in Chap. 3.

[28] See http://ec.europa.eu/competition/international/multilateral/index.html.

and subsidies control under the WTO[29] in line with Articles 206 and 207 TFEU—the EU's CCP. The aim is to promote cross-jurisdictional recognition and merging of practices and control instruments for state aid/subsidies to facilitate enforcement in other jurisdictions. The goal is to achieve this cooperation via an exchange of views on enforcement issues and the related broadening of policy between the respective competition authorities.[30]

Several multilateral international global organisations promote state aid/subsidies control. Notably, these IGOs (other than the EU) do not have legislative powers as such and lack an executive power over sovereign states. Instead, as nations have not signed over their competence to decide over their laws in this specific area, the subsidies control functions are dependent on the extent of a nation's willingness to abide by these multilateral norms.

In a non-European context, the principal promoters of subsidies control are the WTO, UNCTAD, OECD and the World Bank. Of these four, the WTO provides the sole multilateral core for global rules governing subsidies control. The WTO's legal framework includes subsidies control provisions incorporated in GATT Article XVI and the automatic applicability of the Subsidies Agreement to all the WTO members.[31] As explained in Sect. 3.3.1, these rules cover many forms of government actions similar to the EU's state aid rules.[32] Apart from the WTO's legal framework, promotion for subsidies control mainly occurs in the form of soft law instruments as guidelines and recommendations.

UNCTAD works on competition policies to ensure that partner countries enjoy the benefits of increased competition.[33] For that purpose, UNCTAD has implemented a multilateral instrument on competition policy, 'the Set of Multilaterally Agreed Equitable Principles and Rules for the Control of Restrictive Business Practices' (the UN Set).[34] However, the UN Set, which was adopted in December 1980 by UNGA Resolution 35/63, was still the only multilateral instrument on competition policy in 2018.[35] Furthermore, the UN Set does not cover subsidies. UNCTAD's other Competition instruments, the Model Law on Competition, which

[29] EC (2017).

[30] EC (2017). GATS Article XV recognises the potential of subsidies to services having distortive effects on trade. While this article imposes WTO members to enter future negotiations to extend GATS to include subsidies, at the beginning of 2019 there was still no agreement.

[31] The Uruguay Round Agreement, summary of provisions.

[32] Ehlermann and Goyette (2006), Rubini (2010) and Schön (2004).

[33] United Nations Conference on Trade and Development (UNCTAD), Competition Law and Consumer Protection Policy, https://unctad.org/en/Pages/DITC/CompetitionLaw/Competition-Law-and-Policy.aspx.

[34] UNCTAD, The United Nations Set of Principles on Competition (The UN Set), https://unctad.org/en/Pages/DITC/CompetitionLaw/The-United-Nations-Set-of-Principles-on-Competition.aspx.

[35] The most recent Model Law on Competition was revised in 2018: UNCTAD (2018).

is revised every year[36] and the Handbook on Competition Legislation,[37] also lack provisions on subsidies.

UNCTAD's subsidies policy, like the subsidies policies of the OECD and the World Bank, focuses on reports and sector-specific recommendations. Mainly, UNCTAD has published statements and roadmaps towards phasing out sector-specific subsidies.[38] Occasionally, UNCTAD's Intergovernmental Group of Experts (IGE) on Competition Law and Policy peer reviews sector-specific and economy-wide competition and consumer policies and suggests possible subsidy reforms.[39]

The OECD[40] and the World Bank[41] both have also released several publications that call for comprehensive subsidy reforms. The motivation for these requests is the fact that in modern times subsidies, being among the most potent public policy instruments in use, are innately linked with global harmful consequences and a waste of economic resources. However, owing to national political economy considerations, these necessary reforms are rarely implemented. Driven by the need to reach more tangible results for subsidies control, the EU has systematically been negotiating to include provisions on subsidies control in international agreements to which the EU is a party. Since the mandates of competition authorities and their basis for action are given by the domestic competition law and not by the trade agreement, another critical aspect of subsidies provisions in trade agreements and IIAs is the creation of a coherent policy environment for foreign and domestic companies alike.[42] These agreements come in the form of bilateral agreements, where the EU is one part and a third country is the other part, or a plurilateral regional agreement, which is concluded between the EU and another regional trading bloc.

6.3 Plurilateral Regional Agreements

Plurilateral regional agreements are international agreements that are negotiated by representatives from these regional blocs on behalf of their member states. Papadopoulos observes that these agreements should be examined as a distinct category.[43] Nevertheless, competition rules in plurilateral regional agreements

[36] The most recent Model Law on Competition was revised in 2018: UNCTAD (2018).

[37] Handbook on Competition Legislation, Vol. 2 (2013–14), at https://unctad.org/en/PublicationsLibrary/ditcclp2012_handbook_en.pdf.

[38] UNCTAD (2016).

[39] See, for example, the Report of the Intergovernmental Group of Experts on Competition Law and Policy on its seventh session Annex I, paras 2–6 (IGE 2007).

[40] The OECD has published almost 200 different type of contributions on subsidies, which can be found at https://www.oecd-ilibrary.org.

[41] The substantial amount of publications relating to subsidies can be found on the World Bank web page at http://www.worldbank.org/en/research.

[42] Miroudot and Bartók (2008), p. 2.

[43] Papadopoulos (2010), p. 154.

remain under-researched. A distinct feature in this category of Agreements that was found by the research undertaken for this monograph (see Appendix 2) is the general lack of substantive provisions covering competition regimes, especially regarding subsidies control. This discovery also reflects Papadopoulos adopted approach that plurilateral regional blocs consistently reject the possible adoption of a multilateral agreement on competition under the patronage of the WTO.[44] Indeed, when examining the outcomes of the negotiation rounds for an EU-Mercosur trade agreement, one of the roadblocks to conclude the negotiations has been the difficulties to find a mutually agreed scope for subsidies provisions.[45]

6.3.1 The EEA Agreement and EFTA

Of plurilateral regional agreements other than the EU, the EFTA countries (apart from Switzerland) are unique, due to being subject to state aid rules, which mainly mirror those of the EU.[46] In 1972, all EFTA countries concluded identical bilateral agreements with the EU.[47] Twenty years later, to achieve further integration of the EU, three of the EFTA countries—Norway, Iceland and Lichtenstein[48]—created the multilateral EEA Agreement to create a new free trade area. Switzerland was the only EFTA country that decided to stand outside the EEA.

The EEA Agreement has strong links with EU law and is based on the Treaty of Rome as a template.[49] Fundamentally, the EEA Agreement seeks to reconcile two conflicting objectives regarding the adoption of the acquis: the legislative autonomy of the signatory states and the homogeneity of EEA law. For the sake of homogeneity, the EEA Agreement provides for two separate legal systems to be applied in parallel in the EEA without conflicts.[50] It is achieved by the EEA system being based

[44] Papadopoulos (2010), pp. 154–155. This standpoint is also confirmed by the OECD (2011).

[45] As an example, see the reports from the 30th, the 32nd, the 34th and the 35th rounds of negotiations of the Trade Part of the Association Agreement between the European Union and Mercosur at https://ec.europa.eu/trade/policy/countries-and-regions/negotiations-and-agreements.

[46] Rosenthal and Nicolaides (1997) and Rydelski (2004).

[47] At the start of 1972, there were nine EFTA states: Austria, Finland, Denmark, Norway, Portugal, Sweden, Switzerland, Iceland and the United Kingdom. However, in 1972, Denmark and the United Kingdom left EFTA for the European Economic Community (EEC), which is now the EU. Portugal followed in 1985. Instead of joining the EEA, Austria, Finland and Sweden decided to join the EU in 1995: EFTA (2014).

[48] The EEA Agreement was signed in Porto on 2 May 1992 and entered into force in 1994. At the time, Liechtenstein—which joined in 1995—was not one of the signatory states: European Free Trade Association (EFTA) (2018).

[49] Article 3, 'Agreement between the EFTA States on the Establishment of a Surveillance Authority and a Court of Justice' (1992) (Surveillance and Court Agreement). See also Rydelski (2004), p. 189.

[50] See Commission decision of 30 October 2002 relating to a proceeding pursuant to Article 81 of the EC Treaty and Article 53 of the EEA Agreement (COMP/35.587 PO Video Games, COMP/35.706 PO Nintendo Distribution and COMP/36.321 Omega-Nintendo), 2003/675/EC (*2003/675/*

on two pillars, the EU and the EFTA pillar, which mostly contain common regulation. In some cases, however, reference may be made either to the EU's or EEA's internal rules.[51]

The EEA has its own a supranational executive body, the EFTA Surveillance Authority (ESA), in charge of rule enforcement, closely modelled on the Commission. The ESA, with its own decision-making autonomy, cooperates closely with the Commission,[52] and is also located in Brussels.[53] The EFTA Court in the EEA has the same function as the CJEU in the EU.[54] In support of the EEA Agreement's objective of establishing a dynamic and homogeneous EEA and ensuring a fair and efficient market following the EEA Agreement,[55] it contains competition rules applicable throughout the EEA.

As a dynamic agreement, the protocols and supplementary appendices of the EEA Agreement are continuously adapted to EU legislation to incorporate the EU competition *acquis* for the EFTA countries that are members of the EEA. The EEA agreement covering state aid rules can be found in Part IV competition and other common rules, Chapter 2 Articles 61 to 64. These provisions mirror those of the Lisbon Treaty.[56] In particular, Article 61 of the EEA Agreement has the same content as article 107 TFEU, with EEA adaptations.[57] More rules on state aid are also contained in Annex XV and Protocols 26 and 27 of the EEA Agreement. Annex XV covers all EU *acquis* relevant to state aid, including secondary legislation, and jurisprudence by the CJEU and the Commission's decisions up to August 1991.

The EEA Agreement applies to two types of situations. Namely where trade between one or more EFTA states (which have ratified the EEA Agreement) and one or more EU Member States is affected, or when trade between the EFTA states themselves is affected (Article 56.1a). EU law is applicable when trade between the EU Member States is affected. Finally, there are some non-binding competition acts such as guidelines and announcements, intended to disclose how the regulations should be interpreted as given by the EFTA Surveillance Authority (ESA).[58]

EC Commission Decision Nintendo and Others, 2002). See also Rosenthal and Nicolaides (1997), Rydelski (2004), Bourgeois et al. (2007) and EC (2008).

[51] See the EEA Agreement Articles 89–93 and the EFTA (2018) web page.

[52] Rydelski (2004), pp. 193–194.

[53] EFTA (2014).

[54] EFTA (2014); EFTA Court (Court 2018).

[55] On homogeneity, see the EEA Agreement Part VII, Ch 3, Section 1. See also Rydelski (2004), p. 190.

[56] Available at http://ec.europa.eu/competition/international/multilateral/eea_agreemt_comp.pdf. See also EFTA web page for protocols 26 and 27 concerning state aid at https://www.efta.int/eea/eea-agreement. See also Commission's web page at http://ec.europa.eu/competition/international/multilateral/eea.html.

[57] The adaptations are specified in Annex XV of the EEA Agreement.

[58] Hettne and Fritz (1994), pp. 31–32. For more on ESA see http://www.eftasurv.int/about-the-authority/mission-and-values.

Rules relating to case law are contained in Article 6 of the EEA Agreement and Article 2 of the Surveillance and Court Agreement, which claims that provisions corresponding to EU regulations should be interpreted according to relevant cases in EU case law announced before the date of signing of the EEA Agreement. The ESA and the EFTA Court are also expected to take due account of the CJEU's case law after the signing of the EEA Agreement pursuant to Article 3.2 of the Surveillance and Court Agreement.

The functioning of the judicial process regarding state aid measures within the EEA corresponds with that of the EU. The ESA has the authority to make decisions on state aid, as does the Commission in the EU, that can be appealed to the EFTA Court. Rydelski shows that the EFTA Court has closely followed the jurisprudence of the CJEU.[59] Recent case law, such as *Case E-25/15 EFTA Surveillance Authority v Iceland* (2016) on infringement proceeding against Iceland for failure to recover unlawful state aid, shows that the EFTA Court continues to do so.[60]

In summary, when compared in parallel, the EEA and EU systems are virtually the same. The structure of the systems and the way rules are applicable through these systems follow a similar logic. Even the competence and authority of the governing bodies that apply the rules of these two systems have an identical structure as the EEA Agreement is based on the internal EU *acquis*. Where a cross-border effect between EU and EFTA countries occurs, the Commission and ESA cooperate in a similar manner as the local authorities cooperate with the EU (EU) and ESA within EFTA. Hence, the outcome of the strive for homogeneity of state aid control between the EEA and the EU has been highly successful, and the parallel application of the entire state aid regime seems to work painlessly.

---

[59] Rydelski (2004), p. 199. He specifically refers to two cases from the EFTA Court, the *Husbanken* case, ESA decision No. 177/97/COL (*ESA – Husbanken*, 1997) and *Case E-4/97 – Norwegian Bankers' Association v EFTA Surveillance Authority* (1998), p. 40, and the *Differentiated Social Security Contributions* case. In the *Husbanken* case, the EFTA court uses case law of the CJEU, namely *C-225/91 Matra SA v Commission* (1993) para 18; *Case 323/82 – Intermills* (1984) para 16; *C-198/91 Cook v Commission* (1991); *C-266/96 Corsica Ferries France SA v Gruppo* (1998) para 45; and *C-179/90 Merci convenzionali porto di Genova Spa* (1991) para 27. The CJEU cases cited by the EFTA Court in the *Differentiated Social Security Contributions* case were *C-202/88 France v Commission* (1991); *C-159/94 Commission v France* (1997); and *T-106/95 Fédération française des sociétés d'assurances* (1997).

[60] The EFTA Court refers to, *inter alia*, the CJEU's decisions from the twenty-first century: *C-209/00 Commission v Germany* (2002), paras 34 and 35; *Case C-454/09 Commission v Italy* (2011), para 37; and *T-62/08 – ThyssenKrupp Acciai Speciali Terni v Commission* (2010), para 234.

6.3.2 *The Curious Case of the Effect of State Aid in Switzerland*

Switzerland is part of the EFTA and therefore has had a bilateral Free Trade Agreement with the EU (then the European communities) since December 1972.[61] Of the four EFTA countries, Switzerland decided to stand outside the 1992 EEA agreement. Because the parties of the EEA discontinued the cooperation towards a fully harmonised system before the EU–Switzerland 1972 trade agreement was fully developed and updated, several inconsistencies remain in this regard.[62] In contrast to the well-developed and advanced EEA system, the entire EU–Swiss bilateral trade system stands on the primary agreement, which contains some provisions on competition regulation.

Contrary to the EEA, the EU–Swiss bilateral has no secondary acts regarding state aid. In particular, Switzerland does not have to abide by the prohibition of state aid in Article 107 TFEU.[63] However, Article 1(b) of the EU–Swiss FTA states that the purpose of the agreement is to create fair competition conditions for trade between the contracting parties. The applicable provision for state aid/subsidies control in Article 23(1)(iii) is identical to the general prohibition in Article 107.1 TFEU. Nevertheless, Article 23(1) (iii) of the Swiss–EU FTA did not introduce legislation on state aid control in Switzerland.[64] According to Hoffet, this is a consequence of the inherent problem of Article 23(1)(iii) provision of the Swiss–EU FTA. Namely, while Article 23(1)(iii) fails to define the consequences of a violation of the rule, the Swiss Federal Supreme Court interpreted the Swiss–EU FTA very restrictively in its early case law.[65]

Further, neither organised cooperation nor exchange of information between the competition authorities of the EU and Switzerland exists. Because of the bilateral agreement between the EU and Switzerland lacks both jointly coordinated surveillance and an obligation to impose measures on state aid control, each party acts autonomously within its respective jurisdiction. The implementation and monitoring of Article 23(1)(iii) are done individually and separately by the relevant authorities of the contracting states. Explicitly, Article 23 of the Swiss–EU FTA restricts the competence of each party's Competition Authority to cover only its jurisdiction. That is, the European Commission has competence only in the EU, and the Swiss Competition Commissions (COMCOs) has competence only in Switzerland. A joint

---

[61] Agreement between the Member States of the European Coal and Steel Community and Swiss Confederation – final Act (1972) entered into force 1.1.1974.

[62] Raymond H.C. Luja (2007). See also the letter from the President of the Swiss Confederation to the President of the Council of the European Union, Application Letter for Accession to the EU (Switzerland), Berne, 20 May 1992, at http://trade.ec.europa.eu/doclib/cfm/doclib_section.cfm?sec=140.

[63] Obrist (2013), p. 246.

[64] Hoffet (2016), p. 1.

[65] Hoffet (2016) and Dietrich et al. (2019).

committee, which has the task of keeping the parties informed of protective trade measures adopted by one of the parties, also provides a consultation mechanism in order to achieve mutually acceptable solutions regarding the adopted measures.

In 2018, Switzerland still had no specific legislation regarding state aid. Hence, it was evident that the harmonised monitoring, enforcement and control of state aid measures that exists between the EU and the EEA partners does not take place between the EU and Switzerland. However, unlike the EU–Swiss FTA, the 1999 bilateral agreement between the EC and Switzerland on air transport (ATA) introduced sector-specific state aid control in Switzerland by way of an international treaty.[66] The ATA includes provisions drafted to reflect articles 107–109 TFEU but with a narrower scope restricted to cover measures relating to goods only.[67] The ATA also empowers the Swiss Competition Commission to enforce state aid rules within Switzerland at a national level.[68]

However, the absence of comparable national legislation in the field of state aid law does not mean that measures constituting state aid can be granted at discretion.[69] The European Commission's state aid decision on Swiss company tax regimes provides a striking example of the limitations faced by Switzerland and its cantons in granting subsidies.[70] In the *Swiss Company Tax Regimes* case in 2007, despite the European Commission not having jurisdiction over Switzerland in EU state aid cases, the European Commission claimed that cantonal tax regimes were incompatible with the EU–Swiss FTA regarding EU State aid law.[71]

The background to this decision dates back a few years. After receiving complaints from the Member States, Members of the European Parliament and businesses, the Commission had decided to review some of the Swiss cantonal tax regimes to assess their compatibility with the State aid provision in Article 23(1) of the EU FTA.[72] This investigation led to the European Commission finding that the Swiss cantonal tax regimes constituted state aid in the form of unfair tax advantages to multinational companies.[73]

---

[66] Hoffet (2016), p. 1. The ATA negotiations took place after a Swiss referendum had rejected the ratification of the EEA Agreement. By the ATA, Switzerland and the EU could uphold the Swiss policy in line with the European integrations at least sectorally: van Zebinsky (1996), p. 99.

[67] Zurkinden and Scholten (2004), p. 217.

[68] Dietrich et al. (2019).

[69] Hoffet (2016), p. 1.

[70] Decision of the Commission of the European Communities of 13 February 2007 regarding the incompatibility of certain Swiss company tax regimes with the Agreement between the European Economic Community and the Swiss Confederation of 22 July 1972 C (2007) 411 Final (*Commission Decision of Certain Swiss Company Tax Regimes C (2007) 411 Final*, 2007).

[71] *Commission Decision of Certain Swiss Company Tax Regimes C (2007) 411 Final* (2007). See also Commissions press release – 'EU–Switzerland: State aid decision on company tax regimes', 13 February 2007 (European Commission (EC) 2007) at https://europa.eu/rapid/press-release_IP-07-176_en.htm.

[72] European Commission (EC) (2007).

[73] *Commission Decision of Certain Swiss Company Tax Regimes C (2007) 411 Final* (2007).

The Commission based its decision on the following. First, the Swiss cantons could, under Swiss law, exempt multinational companies that were established in Switzerland from profits generated abroad.[74] This exercise proved to be such a powerful incentive over the years that all Swiss Cantons have made use of this favourable Swiss tax provision. To minimise their tax liabilities, many of the multinationals that were most active in the EU market based their headquarters, coordination and distribution centres in Switzerland instead of in Member State of the EU. In other words, Swiss cantons provided state aid to multinational companies that in fact were established in the EU. Consequently, these subsidy schemes affected the trade between the EU and Switzerland.

The 'cause and effect' logic behind *Commission Decision of Certain Swiss Company Tax Regimes C (2007) 411 Final* (2007) is well described by the words of the EU's external relations commissioner, Benita Ferrero-Waldner: 'Switzerland enjoys the benefits of privileged access to the internal market and must accept the responsibilities that go along with this. The decision the Commission has taken is not about tax competition but about state aid undermining the level playing field necessary for our partnership and the trade relations between Switzerland and the EU.'[75]

After the Swiss response, which was to reject the Commission's state aid decision as unfounded, and six years of political pressure by the EU to end these tax schemes, 'the Swiss Federal Council adopted a mandate to find a solution with the EU on the challenged corporate tax features'.[76] After 11 more years, a new Swiss corporate tax proposal, intended to abolish the current cantonal tax privileges, is expected to enter into force in January 2020.[77] This case illustrates the Commission's approach towards state aid measures originating from a third country, which is a crucial trading partner in its geographical vicinity. Visibly, the Commission does not view favourably subsidy races that negatively affect the EU's internal market.

6.4 State Aid in the EU's Bilateral Agreements

In 2007, the EU competition commissioner, Neelie Kroes, emphasised the fundamental importance of State aid control in the context of global competition.[78] Her speech demonstrated the conclusions the Commission had reached in its overall review of EC trade policy, launched in 2006, to turn it into an external competitiveness tool.[79] Indeed, the EU has systematically included competition provisions,

[74] This is a subsidy in form of tax relief.

[75] European Commission (EC) (2007).

[76] Obrist (2013), p. 649.

[77] PwC (2019).

[78] Kroes (2007), p. 2.

[79] Kroes (2007), p. 4. In line with the EU's Global Europe policy and the SAAP.

including those of state aid in bilateral FTAs or PTAs since 2006 (around 36 FTAs)[80] in order to ensure that trade and investment liberalisation are not circumvented through anticompetitive conduct by enterprises and public authorities.

As established in Chaps. 2 and 3, the approach adopted by free-market theories regarding subsidies is that these may invalidate the benefits of trade liberalisation gained by the decrease in customs tariffs. The EU has therefore established EU state aid rules that are unique due to their scope and that apply to every sector of the economy, with the world's strictest enforcement system in place. Because other multilateral international norms are more lenient with regard to subsidising practices, by entering bilateral agreements with third countries, the EU is attempting to fight unfair foreign subsidies.

As stated earlier in this chapter, bilateral agreements vary depending on a third country's possible aspiration to accede into the EU, the EU's influence and its geographical nearness to these nations. By these specific benchmarks, EU's international agreements can be divided into four distinct categories: the global, the European Neighbourhood Policy, the accession and candidate countries, and the EEA/EFTA model (see Sect. 6.3 above). Some bilateral agreements require the third country to implement state aid laws into national laws as part of the integration process, eventually aligning these nations' state aid policy with that of the EU.

6.4.1 Candidate Countries and Potential Candidate Countries

Bilateral agreements in the form of either Association agreements or Europe Agreements regulate the relations of candidate[81] and potential candidate[82] countries. These countries must coordinate with the arrangement in place within the internal market and hence are obliged to adopt, implement and enforce all current EU *acquis*. Above all, they may not implement countervailing measures against the other contracting party upon accession to the EU.[83] Hence, to help to prepare these candidate countries for the transition to the EU, the EU concludes bilateral agreements with them. These agreements emphasise that the state aid rules will apply where intraregional trade is affected.

Moreover, from the very beginning of accession negotiations, candidate countries' existing state aid schemes fall under the Commission's 'magnifying glass' to

---

[80] Galindo (2015).

[81] Albania, the Republic of North Macedonia, Montenegro, Serbia and Turkey are candidate countries. In April 2018, three of these countries—Montenegro, Serbia and Turkey—were in the negotiations for accession in progress. For European Neighbourhood Policy and Enlargement Negotiations (EC 2016), see the Commission's web page at http://ec.europa.eu/environment/enlarg/candidates.htm.

[82] Kosovo, and Bosnia and Herzegovina are potential candidate countries (EC 2016).

[83] See Papadopoulos (2010), p. 118.

review details on their state aid measures,[84] with the Commission monitoring the process of regulatory alignment of accession countries' competition laws.[85] Each year, a detailed assessment of the state of play in each candidate country and a potential candidate is included in the Commission's 'Enlargement Package'.[86] These reports include following up the implementation of state aid law, as well as notification obligations and the requirement for a monitoring system. State aid schemes incompatible with the Customs Union are also identified, as the EU requires those to be abolished by the time of accession.

The state aid provisions of almost all these agreements follow the same pattern. The core provision in these agreements echoes article 107 TFEU, declaring all intervening public measures favouring certain enterprises, which distort or threaten to distort competition between the Member States, thus omitting their purpose, to be incompatible with the proper functioning of the state aid rules.[87] These agreements also make it clear that the basis for any legal assessment of relevant cases is EU law.[88] Besides being obliged to adopt and implement the EU's state aid rules, the EU accession countries must also ensure the enforcement of these rules by establishing a national enforcement authority which is tasked to do so. The inclusion of obligations to have and enforce state aid rules, in the context of competition legislation, consequently means that a candidate country's subsidies become regulated by state aid provisions.[89] Further, the agreements guarantee transparency around state aid scheme application between the parties, as well as a commitment to provide, upon request from the other party, information on the same and individual state aids.

In an attempt to ease the accession process, which can be taxing to some accession countries, they are given five years of leniency regarding state aid rules, correlating to exemptions provided by Article 107(3)(a)) TFEU.[90] Therefore, although the Europe[91] and Association agreements failure to clarify how state aid provisions should be applied appropriately, which has caused some practical

[84] The notification obligations inherent in these agreements ensure this in practice: Cremona (2003), p. 280.

[85] European Neighbourhood Policy and Enlargement Negotiations, Strategy and Reports at https://ec.europa.eu/neighbourhood-enlargement/countries/package_en.

[86] European Neighbourhood Policy and Enlargement Negotiations, Strategy and Reports at https://ec.europa.eu/neighbourhood-enlargement/countries/package_en.

[87] See Sect. 3.2 in Chap. 3 for Article 107 TFEU.

[88] See Appendix 1.

[89] See Papadopoulos (2010), pp. 118–119.

[90] These exemptions apply to EU areas suffering from serious under-employment and abnormally low standards of living to support them in adjusting their economies. See EU–Bulgaria agreement, Art. 64.4.a; EU–Croatia agreement, Art. 70.7.a; and EU–Romania agreement, Art 64.4.a. See also Papadopoulos (2010), p. 118.

[91] The Europe agreements are 'association agreements between the EU and its Member States and the Central and Eastern European countries that joined the EU in 2004/2007. They formed the legal framework for the accession process of these countries to the EU.' See Commission's website at https://ec.europa.eu/neighbourhood-enlargement/policy/glossary/terms/europe-agreement_en.

problems,[92] overall the regulatory transfer of state aid rules into the candidate, and potential candidate, countries has been very successful.

6.4.2 Stabilisation and Association Agreements Countries and State Aid

Some of the candidate countries are also part of the Stabilisation and Association Agreements (SAAs) launched in 1999.[93] The purpose of SAAs was to aid the Western Balkan countries that might become future accession candidates to meet the essential criteria for accession. Therefore, SAAs cover multi-faceted cooperation.[94] SAAs cover the Western Balkan countries: Kosovo, Macedonia, Albania, Croatia, Montenegro and Bosnia Herzegovina. By the requirement for these countries to establish a domestic regulatory framework for state aid harmonised with the EU rules, and authority for monitoring and enforcing these rules, the EU has successfully exported state aid rules indirectly to the SAAs.[95]

6.4.3 European Neighbourhood Policy

Another method to export EU rules to nations geographically located close to the EU is the European Neighbourhood Policy. This consists of 'partner countries' with which the EU shares many joint objectives. The European Neighbourhood Policy includes different types of bilateral agreements with two sub-categories, the Eastern Partnership (EaP) and the Southern Neighbourhood Countries.[96] European Neighbourhood Countries partially overlap with associate countries, as some of these have signed Association Agreements with the EU, including Deep and Comprehensive Free Trade Areas (DCFTA). By inclusion of provisions on state aid (in some cases, expressly state aid; in others, subsidies provisions WTO *mutatis mutandis*) and a requirement that these countries to set up state aid policies with the necessary regulatory framework nationally to support them, the EU has also succeeded in regulatory export of state aid policy in its geographical neighbourhood.

---

[92] Cremona (2003), pp. 267–269.

[93] European Commission, Communication on the stabilisation and association process for countries of South-Eastern Europe - Bosnia and Herzegovina, Croatia, Federal Republic of Yugoslavia, former Yugoslav Republic of Macedonia and Albania, COM/99/0235 final.

[94] Doyle amd Martinez (2017), p. 6.

[95] Popović and Caka (2017), p. 333.

[96] EC (2016).

Southern Neighbourhood Countries

The Southern Neighbourhood Countries are Algeria, Egypt, Israel, Jordan, Lebanon, Libya, Morocco, the Palestinian Authority, Syria and Tunisia.[97] Apart from Algeria, they have entered bilateral agreements that include subsidies provisions with the EU. Most of the Southern Neighbourhood Countries, apart from Lebanon and the Palestinian Authority, have implemented national competition laws.[98] These national laws apprehend three types of practices: they prohibit restrictive agreements and abuse of a dominant position, and they regulate mergers.[99] The enforcement of these laws varies; however, because these countries are not bound by their bilateral agreements with the EU to implement competition law that is compatible with EU law, none of them has yet introduced state aid legislation.

The EaP countries are Armenia, Azerbaijan, Belarus, Georgia, Moldova and Ukraine. These five countries have two different types of relations with the EU. The EU has signed associate agreements together with three EaP countries: Georgia, the Republic of Moldova and Ukraine, established Deep and Comprehensive Free Trade Areas.[100] These DCFTA states, like the Balkan states, aspire to full EU membership; therefore, they have made commitments to comply with EU regulations and standards.[101]

---

[97] See Commission's web page at https://ec.europa.eu/neighbourhood-enlargement/neighbourhood/southern-neighbourhood_en.

[98] Israel – Restrictive Practices Trade Law, 5748 – 1988 (26 July 1988, Amended 2000 and 2010). The Israeli competition regime (which also includes block exemptions) is enforced by an independent and active Antitrust Authority, which resembles that of the EU's competition regime regarding firms: Geradin (2004), p. 51. Tunisia–Tunisian Competition Act n° 2015-36 of 15 September 2015, Tunisian Official Gazette, at http://www.legislation.tn/sites/default/files/fraction-journal-officiel/2015/2015G/078/Tg2015361.pdf. Tunisia entered negotiations for a Deep and Comprehensive Free Trade Area with the EU on 13 October 2015. The intention is to substantially revamp the existing FTA between these two parties. The proposed text already includes harmonisation of competition rules by referring to EU competition law (both primary and secondary) and to the CJEU's case law. Notably, Tunisia would be obliged to establish both national state aid rules in line with those of the EU, and an independent executive authority in charge of state control (Gani 2015). See Commission's web page at http://trade.ec.europa.eu/doclib/press/index.cfm?id=1490. Marocco – the Price Liberalisation and Free Competition Act of July 2000, renewed by introducing a series of competition laws in June 2014. Law No. 104-12 of 30 June 2014 (Dahir No. 1-14-116) on free pricing and competition (the Competition Law) and its enforcement decree No. 2-14-652 of 1 December 2014 (the Decree) and in Law No. 20-13 relating to the Competition Council of 30 June 2014 (Dahir No. 1-14-117) and its enforcement Decree No. 2-15-109 of 4 June 2015. Jordan – The Competition Law no. 49 for Year 2002 (15 August 2002). Algeria – Law no. 2000–03 (5 August 2000) Egypt – Egyptian Competition Law No. 3 of 2005. Implemented Common Market for Southern and Eastern Africa (COMESA) competition rules in 2013. Syria – 2008 Competition and Anti-Trust Law.

[99] See the UN's Economic and Social Commission for Western Asia (ESCWA) report, *Competition and Regulation in the Arab Region* (Sumpf and Waked 2015).

[100] See the Commission's web page at https://ec.europa.eu/trade/policy/countries-and-regions/negotiations-and-agreements.

[101] Emerson and Noutcheva (2018), p. 17.

A particularly distinctive feature in the typical instruments of the economic policy of the DCFTA program is the strong regulatory and institutional character of competition policy, including state aid control.[102] The implementation of these rules is meant to adjust national rules to comply with those of the EU and to prepare the national institutions on how to handle the future competition. A recent example of exportation of state aid rules through these agreements is the 'Deep and Comprehensive Free Trade Agreement which is part of the Association Agreement' between the EU and Ukraine.

A Short Case Study of an EaP Country with a DCFTA: State Aid in Ukraine

Ukraine has previously been part of several international agreements that include state aid (EU–Ukraine Partnership and Cooperation Agreement, 1994) or subsidies control (the WTO Agreements, 2008 and the Energy Community Treaty, 2011). The EU–Ukraine Association Agreement includes state aid regulation by requiring Ukraine to implement state aid laws in alignment with the EU *acquis*.[103] However, before the signing of the EU–Ukraine Deep and Comprehensive Free Trade Agreement and Association Agreement, the control of subsidies/state aid was rendered a paper tiger in the absence of proper monitoring and enforcement.[104]

Implementation and enforcement of state aid rules in Ukraine have picked up since August 2017, when the new state aid law, the Law of Ukraine on State Aid to Undertakings No. 1555-VII of 1 July 2014 (State Aid Law), based on the Association Agreement itself, took effect.[105] The Association Agreement also obligates Ukraine to interpret the agreement's provisions, as well as its state aid legislation, using criteria set out in EU law and practice.[106]

The Antimonopoly Committee (AMC), the authorized body on state aid issues following Article 8 of the Law of Ukraine 'On the State Aid to the Business Entities', made its first decision on the compatibility of state aid on 17 April 2018. It deals with a new, notified aid measure, under review by the municipality of Chernihiv city. This measure was for the city's cultural centre to help cover utility and wage costs. The AMC did find it to be state aid; however, it had a limited effect on competition and was otherwise compatible due to its promotion of culture and conservation of heritage.[107] In spring 2018, Ukraine adjusted its state aid laws to be limited to the 'effect on trade on the EU'.

---

[102] Movchan and Giucci (2011), pp. 6–7.

[103] Svechkar and Glushchenko (2016).

[104] Svechkar and Glushchenko (2016, 2018).

[105] The Ukrainian state aid law can be found on the Ukrainian government website at http://pdd.amc.gov.ua.

[106] Svechkar and Glushchenko (2016).

[107] See Ukrainian government website at http://pdd.amc.gov.ua.

State Aid in the United Kingdom After Brexit

Due to Brexit, the United Kingdom has become a third country. The Commission has insisted that a trade agreement between the UK and the EU include substantial rules for state aid/subsidies control. This has been partially successful. The draft Trade and Cooperation Agreement between the European Union and the European Atomic Energy Community, of one part, and the United Kingdom of Great Britain and Northern Ireland, of the other part (EU–UK Trade Agreement)[108] has substantial rules on subsidies control. These can be found in Title XI Chapter 3.

Title XI Chapter 3 reintroduces many of the EU state aid rules and the WTO Subsidies Agreement in an interesting hybrid version. The chapter covers transfers of capital, goods and services (Article 3.1), upholds clawback procedures (Article 3.11) and demands both parties to have proper independent authorities (Article 3.9) and courts (Article 3.10) to enforce these rules. The transparency provision in Article 3.7 maintains that all granted subsidies must be made public so that the other party may scrutinise that it follows the rules. A dispute settlement mechanisms and remedial measures are introduced in Article 3.12 to guarantee that subsidies control is upheld and enforced by both parties. Should the United Kingdom decide to be non-compliant with these rules, the EU can launch antidumping and countervailing measures against it.

While the text imitates the EU's definition of subsidy and the core content of 107 TFEU it also introduces several concepts found in the EU secondary legislation and the Commission's Notice on the notion of aid while fully avoiding EU terminology.[109] Moreover, there are no references to the relevant EU Treaty articles or other EU acquis. Instead, the EU–UK Trade Agreement uses the WTO term subsidies and introduces new terminology to replace key EU terminology. While the definition of some of these new terms are copied from the existing terms some of the new terms, such as 'material effect' and temporary subsidies' are not properly defined. There are also several notable variations from the EU's State aid regime. Notably the agreement does not require an ex-ante control of subsidies and the threshold for granting aid is set higher than the EUs. As such, it provides possibilities for the United Kingdom to diverge from the EU state aid rules.

However, any major changes in state aid control in the post-Brexit United Kingdom are unlikely to take place despite the government led by Boris Johnson has made press statements arguing the contrary.[110] As noted by the UK House of Lords, the British 'competition regime' is underpinned by domestic statutes modelled on EU law and includes provisions to ensure consistent interpretation

[108] The draft of the EU–UK Trade Agreement can be found at https://ec.europa.eu/info/sites/info/files/draft_eu-uk_trade_and_cooperation_agreement.pdf.

[109] Such as *de minimis* and GBER. See Chap. 3 for these Regulations.

[110] See Peretz and Bacon (2016), Peretz (2016) and Peretz et al. (2017).

with European legislation'.[111] Nonetheless the United Kingdom can now create their own parallel system of subsidies control as the Post Brexit UK domestic competition policy regime is no longer interconnected as closely as it was while the United Kingdom was part of the EU.[112]

The role of the Commission has transferred to the United Kingdom's Competition and Markets Authority (CMA) and the UK Courts, no longer bound to follow the rulings of the CJEU, have replaced the EU courts on state aid matters.[113] From that point on, it is likely that the United Kingdom's state aid jurisprudence will start separating itself from that of the CJEU. This development will be enhanced if the post-Brexit United Kingdom applies the common law approach to its cases, while the approach of the CJEU on state aid practice is civil law based.[114]

It should be noted however that traditionally the United Kingdom is a country that has embraced the rationale of free trade and competition.[115] In the past, the United Kingdom has acted as a strong proponent of a market economy[116] and applied exceptions to state aid rules that allow public aid to the economy restrictively.[117] Also, the British public bodies are mindful of the risk of creating intra-UK subsidy races, due to a lack of domestic subsidies control.[118] The WTO's Subsidies Agreement does not tackle this issue and therefore cannot stop this type of development from taking place.

However, corresponding to the two-level game theory on state aid/subsidies policy actions in the global political economy,[119] the United Kingdom's transformation from an insider to an outsider might be caught in a Prisoner's Dilemma. Namely, the UK's ability to raise state aid breach cases by EU countries or the United Kingdom's grant of state aid nationally would be subject to possible retaliation by the EU or its Member States. Indeed, as was established in Chap. 2,

[111] House of Lords, European Union Committee 12th Report of Session 2017–19 2017 Brexit: Competition and State Aid HL Paper 67, published 2 February 2018 (House of Lords 2018), p. 72.

[112] House of Lords (2018).

[113] Griffits (2018).

[114] According to McDermott (2018), the common law approach, being less flexible than civil law, will negatively impact UK-based companies.

[115] See Schonberg (2017), p. 51. On the role of the United Kingdom in the development of EU state aid rules, see Sierra (2016), p. 331. For the rationales of free trade and competition, see Chap. 2 of this thesis.

[116] See Sect. 3.4 in Chap. 3.

[117] See state aid scoreboard for 2017 Figure 1 on State aid expenditure by Member State in 2016 http://ec.europa.eu/competition/state_aid/scoreboard/index_en.html and State aid scoreboard 2016: Results, trends and observations regarding EU28 State Aid expenditure reports for 2015, European Commission (EC) COMP.A3, DG Comp, Brussels, 16 November 2016 Annex 1 on State aid expenditure by Member State in 2015 at http://ec.europa.eu/competition/state_aid/scoreboard/technical_note_en.pdf. According to Crafts (2017), this is related to British politics, based on unsuccessful subsidy policies in the past, rather than constraints imposed by the EU.

[118] House of Lords (2018), p. 4.

[119] See Sect. 3.3 in Chap. 3 and, analogously, Sect. 2.3.1 in Chap. 2.

subsidising may lead to a vicious cycle of retaliation, which does not benefit any nation in the long run.

6.4.4 *Other Third Countries: State Aid, WTO or Something in Between?*

To avoid unnecessary conflicts regarding different subsidising practices, even the EU's megaregional bilateral agreements, such as CETA, JEEPA, EUSFTA and EU–Mexico, utilise the 'WTO plus' system for state aid control.[120]

For example, the EU–Mexico Association Agreement has the broadest subsidies provisions. After defining the scope of subsidies to cover both goods and services,[121] subsidies article x.7.3 clarifies that, apart from agricultural products, it applies to 'all enterprises pursuing an economic activity'.[122] It is likely that the threat of NAFTA's undoing occurring parallel to the negotiations of the EU–Mexico association agreement[123] contributed to a speedy negotiation and conclusions of the EU–Mexico Association Agreement, which incorporates many EU policy objectives, such as strict subsidies control.

In contrast, in a period when international trade was more stable, US trade policies were more lenient and the EU's importance as a trade partner was less critical to North American nations, the EU and Canada (which is also part of NAFTA) negotiated the CETA from May 2009 until September 2014.[124] Besides a much more extended negotiations period, the subsidies provisions in CETA Chapter 7 cover goods only.

---

[120] See Appendices 1 and 2 of this thesis for the data collected on all the EU's trade agreements.

[121] Chapter Competition, Section B Subsidies article 7.1.

[122] Chapter Competition, Section B Subsidies article 7.3. The text for the EU–Mexico Association Agreement can be found at the Commission's web page at http://trade.ec.europa.eu/doclib/press/index.cfm?id=1833.

[123] Since 2017, US President Donald Trump had been threatening to exit NAFTA unless it could be renegotiated. For example see *New York Times* article, Trump's Tough Talk on NAFTA Raises Prospects of Pact's Demise (Swanson, 2017) at https://www.nytimes.com/2017/10/11/business/economy/nafta-trump.html. For the timeline of NAFTA renegotiations to become United States–Mexico–Canada Agreement (USMCA), see Congressional Research Service, NAFTA Renegotiation and the Proposed United States–Mexico–Canada Agreement (USMCA) (Villarreal and Fergusson, 2019). The EU–Mexico trade negotiations started in May 2016 and were completed in two years.

[124] For the timeline of negotiations for the EU's trade agreements, see European Parliament (EP 2019) website at http://www.europarl.europa.eu/legislative-train/theme-a-balanced-and-progressive-trade-policy-to-harness-globalisation.

JEEPA negotiations between the EU and Japan from April 2013 until July 2017,[125] chapter 12 on subsidies, lands somewhere between that of the CETA and the EU–Mexico association agreements subsidies provisions. CETA's control of subsidies covers all goods apart from agricultural products and fisheries, as well as several services sectors.

Earlier trade agreements negotiated by the EU, such as the EU–Republic of Korea free trade agreement (FTA), which was ratified by the parties in December 2015, mostly cover goods only.[126] Nevertheless, the EU–Republic of Korea Ch.11 section B Article 11.15 on subsidies comes with a commitment to include services at a later date. The EUSFTA (EU–Singapore) subsidies chapter is similar to that of the EU–Mexico association agreements. In 2016, the EU was Singapore's second most significant trading partner in goods and first in services.[127] Then again, the EU–Mercosur Association Agreement, while including strong competition provisions for goods,[128] referring to EU primary law and even addressing controlling anti-competitive practices for services,[129] has (so far) a weak subsidies provision.[130]

This provision, under title Subsidies, looks to be still incomplete as it only recognises that certain subsidies are harmful to 'the proper functioning of markets'. So far, the chapter Trade Defense and Global Safeguards, which refers to the Subsidies Agreement, sets the level of subsidies control at the WTO level.[131] In Brussels, the EU Commission and China, on 2 June 2017, signed a Memorandum of Understanding to start a dialogue on state aid control.[132]

Indeed, observations made from these trade agreement subsidy provisions imply that the more pluses there are—that is, the more similarities to state aid rules, the more they will vary depending on the stability of global trade in general and on the economic strength of the third country, its interdependence of trade with the EU or both in particular.

[125] For the timeline of negotiations for the EU's trade agreements see European Parliament (EP) (2019) website at http://www.europarl.europa.eu/legislative-train/theme-a-balanced-and-progressive-trade-policy-to-harness-globalisation.

[126] At the time of negotiations, the EU was not such an important trading partner to South Korea as it was in 2018. For goods, see Eurostat (2019) and for services, see the Commission's web page at http://trade.ec.europa.eu/doclib/press/index.cfm?id=1825.

[127] See Commission's web page at http://trade.ec.europa.eu/doclib/press/index.cfm?id=1825.

[128] Title Competition.

[129] Chapter –Trade in Services and Establishment, Article 27.

[130] The Commission emphasises that the text is as yet incomplete and may undergo further revisions as the negotiations to legal texts are still ongoing. For the texts of the Agreement, see the Commission's web page at http://trade.ec.europa.eu/doclib/press/index.cfm?id=2048.

[131] Chapter – Trade defense and global safeguards Article 1.

[132] EC (2017).

6.5 State Aid Provisions As a Limit of Investment Protection

Self-standing subsidy provisions, however, are not sufficient enough to secure that the EU's IIAs, as interpreted by international investment tribunals, would not interfere with the EU's investment policy, of which state aid law is intrinsically part. After some self-reflection, caused by severe criticism from several sources within the EU of ISDS[133] and increasing intra-EU ISDS,[134] the Commission realised it had to create better guarantees to avoid such issues in the future.[135] For this purpose, the Commission initiated the modernisation of international investment law, and particularly ISDS. One of the subjects for modernisation was to ensure the combability of the EU's international investment agreements with state aid rules.[136] To achieve this goal, the Commission swapped ISDS provisions in its investment protection provisions with ICS, the EU's version of investor-state arbitration.

ICS, which was intended to protect, *inter alia*, the EU's right to regulate in matters such as state aid measures, was endorsed by the CJEU in *Opinion 1/17 of the Court* (2017).[137] As a further precaution, the Commission started to incorporate state aid provisions in investment protection provisions that substantially reduced investors' ability to invoke claims on the grounds of breach of investment protection clauses. These clauses particularly address subsidies. Primarily, any subsidies issues renewed or maintained by the signatory party do not constitute a breach of investment protection. The modern EU's international investment agreements, in any form, and investment protection agreements include such state aid carve-out provisions.

6.5.1 *State Aid Provisions in Bilateral IIAs*

Recent EU investment protection provisions in its international agreements such as EU–Singapore, CETA, EU–Vietnam, JEEPA and EU–Mexico include these state aid carve-out provisions.[138] For example, CETA Section D – Investment protection Article 8.9 stipulates:

---

[133] See Sect. 2.4.5 in Chap. 2.

[134] See Chap. 4.

[135] See Sect. 2.4.5 and Chap. 4.

[136] The Commission recognises that disputes involving state aid have raised specific problems regarding ISDS: EC (2015), p. 5. One reason why Commission no longer trusts in ITA is its negative experience with the *Micula* case: EC (2015).

[137] For other subjects necessary to protect, such as the autonomy of EU law, see Chap. 5. For the reasons why the CJEU endorsed ICS, see Sect. 2.4.5 in Chap. 2 and Sect. 5.6 in Chap. 5.

[138] This notion was already brought up by the Commission in its concept paper, 'Investment in TTIP and Beyond: The Path for Reform' (EC 2015), p. 5. As can be seen in CETA (EU & Canada 2016),

3. For greater certainty, a Party's decision not to issue, renew or maintain a subsidy:

(a) in the absence of any specific commitment under law or contract to issue, renew, or maintain that subsidy; or

(b) in accordance with any terms or conditions attached to the issuance, renewal or maintenance of the subsidy, does not constitute a breach of the provisions of this Section.

4. For greater certainty, nothing in this Section shall be construed as preventing a Party from discontinuing the granting of a subsidy[139] or requesting its reimbursement where such measure is necessary in order to comply with international obligations between the Parties or has been ordered by a competent court, administrative tribunal or other competent authority,[140] or requiring that Party to compensate the investor therefor.

This means foreign investors can no longer use these agreements with the EU to raise claims against the Member States in contradiction of EU state aid law. Enforcement of illegal state aid in a third country may become less complicated as some trade agreements oblige the signatory part to recover this type of aid. To ensure that their investments are substantially covered, foreign investors thus need to include in their due diligence progress the advice that incentives received from a Member State heed EU law. In this way, state aid carve-out provisions permanently fuse the notions of 'the legality of the investment and the legality of the aid offered to include such an investment'.[141] By doing this, the Commission is using state aid law as a shield.

6.5.2 *State Aid Provisions in Multilateral IIAs*

Energy Charter Treaty

One particularly impactful international investment agreement of which the EU is a part is the Energy Charter Treaty, which is still missing a shield to protect it and its Member States from being sued due to the application and obeyance of EU law. The ECT is a sectoral (energy sector) multilateral investment treaty to which the EU and its Member States are signatories.[142] Hence it is considered a 'mixed agreement' under EU law. Even though it should not matter from the EU viewpoint whether or

EUSFTA (EU & Singapore 2017) and the EU–Mexico FTA (EU–Mexico Trade agreement (not finalised or ratified), 2018), Ch 17, Art 14.3) investment chapters, these provisions have systematically been included in investment chapters ever since.

[139]This footnote reads that, 'In the case of the European Union, "subsidy" includes "state aid" as defined in its law.'

[140]This footnote reads that, 'In the case of the European Union, "competent authority" is the European Commission, in accordance with Article 108 of the Treaty on the Functioning of the European Union.'

[141]These two notions should be distinguished, according to Luja (2017), p. 188.

[142]((ECT) 2016). The Final Act of the Energy Charter Conference was signed in Lisbon on 27 December 1994. The ECT is also the only multilateral treaty to which the EU is a signatory.

not an agreement is mixed,[143] the relationship between the ECT and the EU has become quite complicated.

Different provisions of the EU treaties apply to the EU–ECT relations than to the relations between EU Member States and the ECT. While Articles 3 TFEU,[144] 207 TFEU,[145] 216 TFEU[146] and 218 TFEU[147] apply to the former, Article 351 TFEU applies to the latter.[148] Because the ECT does not contain any disconnection clause regarding intra-EU disputes, from an ECT aspect the relevant provisions governing these relations are those of the ECT, consequently binding the ECT members in their relation *inter se* through Articles 16 and 26 ECT.[149] The ECT also includes a provision on competition, Article 6 ECT, which speaks for the signatory states to upkeep their laws 'to address unilateral and concerted anti-competitive conduct in Economic Activity in the Energy Sector'.

Nevertheless, apart from *Electrabel Decision on Jurisdiction, Applicable Law and Liability, 2012*,[150] tribunals assessing the relationship of state aid law and the ECT have not paid much attention to this provision.[151] This particular tribunal, after an in-depth analysis on the relationship of EU law and the Energy Charter Treaty, considered that these two treaties should, due to their strong historical connection, be interpreted as harmoniously as possible (para. 4.130).[152] Because both treaties combat anti-competitive conduct (para 4.134) and concern the essential role the EU played in the creation of the ECT, 'it would have made no sense for the European Union to promote and subscribe to the ECT if that had meant entering into obligations inconsistent with EU law' (para 4.134). Also, as 'decisions by the European Commission are legally binding on all EU Member States which are party to the

143 'The Court has already ruled that mixed agreements have the same status in the Community legal order as purely Community agreements, as these are provisions coming within the scope of Community competence': *Case C-13/00 – Commission v Ireland* (2002), para 14; *C-459/03 – Mox Plant* (2006) paras 82–84. According to the CJEU, 'mixed agreements' have the same status in EU law as purely EU agreements.

144 Providing the underlying internal competence is exclusive, that sets the implicit external competence. The other competences attributed to the EU are shared.

145 This provision, which needs to be read together with Article 3 TFEU, formulates the areas of the EU's common commercial policy.

146 This provision specifies the competences that the EU has concerning third parties.

147 Which specifies that it is the EU Treaties that are the standard for legality of any international agreement to which the EU is a party. See Chap. 5.

148 The first part of Article 351 contains a grandfathering clause, which stipulates that international agreements concluded before 1 January 1958 or by acceding states 'shall not be affected by the provisions of the Treaties'. However, where such agreements are not compatible with EU law, these must be eliminated.

149 Kleinheisterkamp (2012b).

150 *Electrabel Decision on Jurisdiction* (2012).

151 See, for example, *Masdar v Spain Award* (2018) and *Eiser Award* (2017). Notably, the tribunals of Masdar and Eiser did not even mention Article 6 ECT.

152 By referring to Weiler and Wälde (2004), pp. 4 and 35.

ECT', the tribunal held that, in case of conflict with state aid law and the ECT, EU law would prevail.[153]

Until the time of writing (December 2021), international investment tribunals acting on the basis of the ECT have consistently held that the ECT is applicable for intra-EU disputes. While international investment tribunals decisions have arrived at very different conclusions on the applicability of EU law, they have also been remarkably united in their view that the ECT does not stand in conflict with EU law. From here on, these tribunals' analysis has sharply diverged. For example, a *Vattenfall II* tribunal that was charged with examining the effect of the *Achmea* case held that ECT Article 26 ECT would prevail over EU law. Nonetheless, even though this tribunal perceived the scope of the *Achmea* decision as unclear, it declined to engage in interpreting it. Instead, this tribunal called the EU to find a legislative solution to end the conflict, in case such exists.[154]

As it stands, international treaties entered by the EU cannot violate EU law.[155] The EU does not have the mandate to conclude such agreements that do so.[156] Therefore, the ECT should be binding to the EU only to the extent that it is in line with EU law, including state aid law. Nevertheless, ECT has caused more investment disputes than any other IIA.[157] This has been particularly intense because several of these claims, from 2009 and forward, have been intra-EU and stem from the discontinuance of measures constituting state aid violations based on the ECT. Many intra-EU claims, such as that of *Masdar v Spain Award* (2018), which is officially from a Dutch investor, which is indirectly owned by the government of Abu Dhabi, are initiated by letterbox companies. Some of these claims have succeeded in securing Awards but have been less successful in enforcing these Awards within the EU territory due to national courts having stayed their enforcement.[158] In an attempt to circumvent the EU courts, Award-winning investors have therefore turned to US courts for enforcement. This type of court shopping emphasises the importance of solving and redefining the norms of the relationship between the ECT and the EU law by either a ruling from the CJEU or political cooperation. Particularly the continuous debate on the normative priority of the rules in this conflict and insistence that there is no real normative conflict is circular and does not lead to any legal certainty for either signatory states of the ECT or investors of these states.

[153] *Electrabel* (2012), paras 4.122 and 4.119.

[154] Hepburn (2018).

[155] CJEU, *Case 26/78 – Viola* (1978) para 9. The EU has primacy over other international law: *Joined Cases c-402/05 p and c-415/05 p Kadi* (2008) para 31.

[156] According to *C-459/03 – Mox Plant* (2006) para 29, the EU or its Member States, independently or jointly, cannot alter the EU Treaties by entering international agreements.

[157] In June 2019, there were 122 official corporate claims under the ECT. Energy Charter Secretariat: ECT (1994). A list of all Investment Dispute Settlement Cases is available at https://energycharter.org/what-we-do/dispute-settlement/all-investment-dispute-settlement-cases.

[158] For example, see *T 4658-18 Spanien v Novenergia II – Suspension of Enforcement* (2018).

Following the CJEU's *Achmea* decision, the status of the intra-EU applicability of the ECT has stood in doubt and has been the subject of much debate in national courts and international investment tribunals.[159] However, the CJEU assessed this relationship recently in cases *Republic of Moldova v Komstroy* (2021)[160] and *Republic of Poland v PL Holdings S.à.r.l* (2021).[161] The ECJ (Grand Chamber) found that the principles of *Achmea* also apply to intra-EU arbitration under the ECT, i.e., it is incompatible under EU law. Because Article 26 ECT does not apply to intra-EU arbitration, the Member States cannot even enter into *ad hoc* arbitration agreements with EU-based investors when these agreements are replicating the content of an intra-EU BIT.[162] Further, several other cases developing this topic are currently pending with the CJEU, such as Opinion 1/20 (pending) concerning the status of intra EU arbitration under the modernised ECT with EU law.[163]

Most Member States in the Declaration of the Member States on the legal consequences of *Achmea* doubted the compatibility of the ETC with EU law.[164] As of 15 July 2019, the Council mandated the Commission to revise the ECT.[165] According to the Council's 'Negotiating Directives for the Modernisation of the Energy Charter Treaty':

> The modernised ECT should clarify that the EU can require market participants from third countries operating within the internal market to comply with applicable Union and Member States' laws.[166]

Subject to reform are topics such as reaffirming the right to regulate legitimate public policy objectives, definitions of investments and investors covered to stop letterbox companies from initiating claims under the ECT and other topics on dispute settlement that are subject to the modernisation of UNICTRAL and ICSID rules.

Moreover, the Council stresses the need to ensure that the ECT 'investment protection provisions cannot be interpreted as a commitment by the Parties' to maintain a regulatory status quo even though the revision of laws might 'negatively

---

[159] For example, see Sect. 5.2 in Chap. 5. Notably, AG Saugmandsgaard Øe in *Joined Cases C-798/18 and C-799/18*, fn 55 held that Article 26 ECT should not apply to intra-EU disputes.

[160] On 8 October 2019, a Parisian Court of Appeal (France) lodged a request for a preliminary ruling regarding the combability of extra-EU ECT arbitration, *C-741/19 – Republic of Moldova v Komstroy* (2021).

[161] Judgment of the Court (Grand Chamber), *Case C-109/20, Republiken Polen (Republic of Poland) v PL Holdings S.à.r.l.*, ECLI:EU:C:2021:875, 26 October 2021.

[162] *Republic of Poland v PL Holdings S.à.r.l* (2021) paras 54–55.

[163] Kingdom of Belgium requested for an opinion from the CJEU on 3 December 2020.

[164] FISMA (2019).

[165] See media release by the European Council and the Council of the European Union, 'Council Adopts Negotiation Directives for Modernisation of Energy Charter Treaty' (Council, 15.07.2019) at https://www.consilium.europa.eu/en/press/press-releases/2019/07/15/council-adopts-negotiation-directives-for-modernisation-of-energy-charter-treaty.

[166] Negotiating Directives for the Modernisation of the Energy Charter Treaty (European Council 2019), p. 3.

affect the investor's expectations of profits.'[167] Notably, it should contain state aid provisions corresponding to existing EU agreements.[168] Indeed, the modernisation process of the ECT might provide an opportunity to address some of these matters, and deal with a concern relating to violations of state aid law by, for example, introducing a state aid carve-out provision to the ECT. If the ECT fails to modernise, the EU may withdraw from it according to the requests from a cross-party coalition of European Parliamentarians.[169]

6.6 Summary and Conclusions

This chapter has found that the scope of EU's extraterritorial state aid policy has emerged from the type of control applied, the level of its success and the effect on the third country, depending on the specific type of instrument employed. Relating to these specific benchmarks, the EU's international agreements can be divided into four distinct categories: global (Sect. 6.4.4), the European Neighbourhood Policy (Sect. 6.4.3), the accession and candidate countries (Sects. 6.4.1 and 6.4.2) and the EEA/EFTA model (Sect. 6.3). These categories are also distinguishable through the geographical location of the country in relation to the location of the EU.

On a global scale, EU state aid law is best described as ripples on a pond. The inner ripples are explicit and well defined, then they become slowly vaguer until they cannot be seen (see Fig. 6.1). As well as state aid control weakening depending on how far away countries are located from the EU, another deciding factor with regard to the level of state aid control is the negotiation partners' economic strength. Surprisingly, some regional 'islands of state aid control' can be found in Africa, mainly the WAEMU.

Some proposals made by this book are shown to have already taken place in practice. In particular, empirical observations of the EU's international trade agreement conducted by the author of this book (see Appendix 2) confirm that these agreements contain elements of competition policy, particularly state aid regulation. This empirical evidence also shows that post *Micula*, state aid clauses that substantially limit investment protection provisions, so that any subsidies issues, renewed or maintained by the signatory party do not constitute a breach of investment protection, have been inserted into the EU's international investment agreements, trade

[167] European Council (2019), pp. 4–5.

[168] European Council (2019), p. 4.

[169] Statement on the modernisation of the Energy Charter Treaty available at Statement-on-Energy-Charter-Treaty-ENG_080920.pdf (euractiv.com). In its response to the Parliament, the Commission prefers to renew the ECT to avoid triggering the 20 year sunset clause. However, the Commission confirmed that if the modernisation of the ECT is 'not attained within a reasonable timeframe' the EU withdrawing from the ECT is possible. See answer given by Executive Vice-President Dombrovski on behalf of the European Commission (2.12.2020) P-005555/2020 at P-9-2020-005555-ASW_EN.pdf (europa.eu).

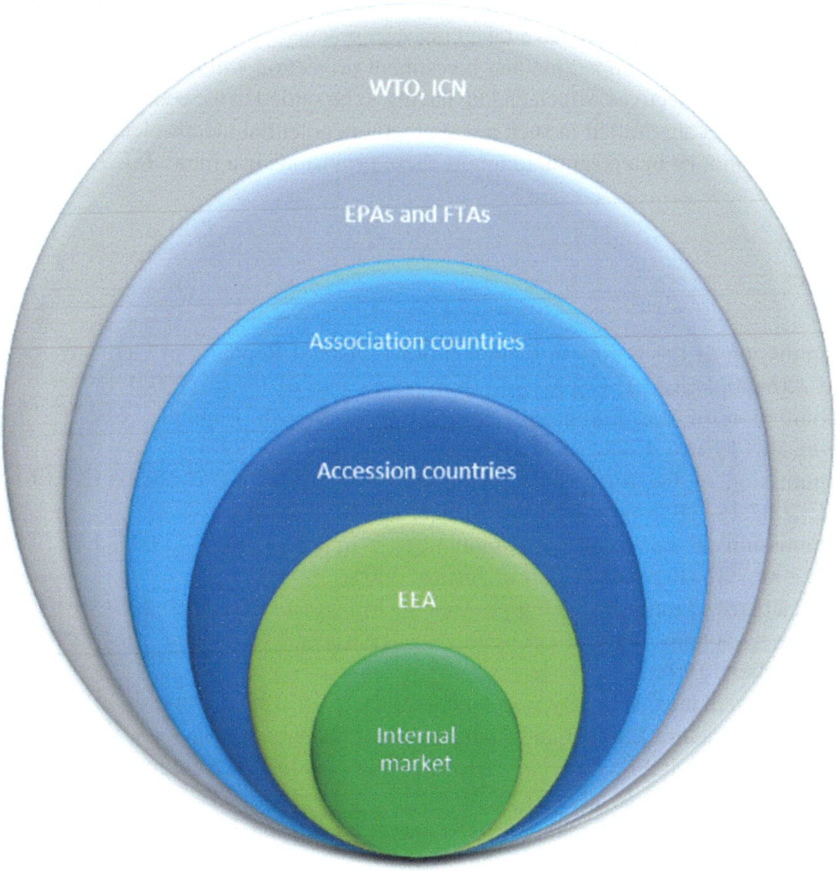

Fig. 6.1 The 'ripple' effect of EU state aid law

agreements with investment provisions and investment protection agreements (see Sect. 6.5).

State aid provisions in the EU's trade instruments act as a sword and a shield for IIAs. Including self-standing state aid provisions in these agreements guarantees that these are generally in line with EU law. Apart from the protection of European enterprises from disadvantages in global competition compared with third-country firms that may benefit from state aid, these provisions also protect competition from 'unfair foreign subsidies' within the internal market (the shield), and may act as a vessel for regulatory export (the sword). As some trade agreements require the implementation of state aid into national laws, the ability for enterprises to acquire investment through subsidies is substantially reduced, eventually aligning the investment policy of these countries so it is compatible with EU state aid laws. State aid provisions also act as a shield when these are incorporated in investment protection clauses in such a way that substantially reduces investors' ability to invoke claims on the grounds of breach investment protection. Some proposals made by this monograph are shown to already have taken place in practice.

In this way, fair competition and investment protection will hopefully no longer be conflicting objectives, which end up having to be settled in the courts. These post-*Micula* treaties are drafted in such a way, that any potential independent arbitration tribunal cannot be in a position to ignore these provisions in a future ISDS situation.

Cases

Commission of the European Communities v Federal Republic of Germany, case C-209/00, ECLI:EU:C:2002:747 (European Court of Justice, 2002)

Commission of the European Communities v French Republic, case C-159/94, ECLI:EU:C:1997:501 (European Court of Justice, 1997)

Commission of the European Communities v Ireland, case C-13/00, ECLI:EU:C:2002:184 (European Court of Justice, 2002)

Commission of the European Communities v Ireland, case C-459/03, ECLI:EU:C:2006:345 (European Court of Justice, 2006)

Corsica Ferries France SA v Gruppo Antichi Ormeggiatori del porto di Genova Coo, case C-266/96, ECLI:EU:C:1998:306 (European Court of Justice (Fifth Chamber), 1998)

EFTA Surveillance Authority v Iceland, case E-25/15 (EFTA Court 2016)

Eiser Infrastructure Limited and Energía Solar Luxembourg S.à.r.l. v Kingdom of Spain Award, ICSID Case No ARB/13/36 (International Centre for Settlement of Investment Disputes ad hoc, 2017)

Electrabel S.A. v. The Republic of Hungary Decision on Jurisdiction, Applicable Law and Liability, ICSID Case No. ARB/07/19 Italaw (ICSID 2012)

European Commission v Italian Republic, case C-454/09, ECLI:EU:C:2011:650 (European Court of Justice 2011)

Fédération française des sociétés d'assurances (FFSA), Union des sociétés étrangères d'assurances (USEA), Groupe des assurances mutuelles agricoles (Groupama), Fédération nationale des syndicats d'agents généraux d'assurances (FNSAGA), Fédération française des courtiers d'assurances et de réassurances (FCA) and Bureau international des producteurs d'assurances et de réassurances (BIPAR) v Commission of the European Communities, case T-106/95, ECLI:EU:T:1997:23 (Court of Justice of the European Union(CIF), 1997)

Federazione nazionale delle imprese elettrotecniche ed elettroniche (Anie) and Others (C-798/18), Athesia Energy Srl and Others (C-799/18) v Ministero dello Sviluppo Economico, Gestore dei servizi energetici (GSE) SpA, ECLI:EU:C:2020:876 (AG Opinion, 2020)

Flaminio Costa v E.N.E.L, case 6-64 No. 61964J0006, ECLI:EU:C:1964:66, Eurlex (European Court of Justice (ECJ), 1964)

Foresight Luxembourg Solar 1 S. Á.R1. et al. v Kingdom of Spain, SCC Case No. 2015/150 Decision of Svea Court of Appeal (Swedish), Mål nr T 1626-19 (Svea Hovrätt, 2020)

French Republic v Commission of the European Communities, case C-202/88, ECLI:EU:C:1991:120 (European Court of Justice, 1991)

Institut national d'assurance maladie-invalidité and Union nationale des fédérations mutualistes neutres v Antonio Viola, case 26/78, ECLI:EU:C:1978:172 (European Court of Justice, 1978)

Konungariket Spanien v Novenergia II – Energy & Enviroment (SCA), SICAR, B 124550, inhibition Mål nr T 4658-18 (Svea hovrätt, 2018)

Masdar Solar & Wind Cooperatief U.A. v Kingdom of Spain Award, ICSID Case No. ARB/14/1 (ad hoc, 2018)

Matra SA v Commission of the European Communities, case C-225/91, ECLI:EU:C:1993:239 (European Court of Justice, 1993)

Merci convenzionali porto di Genova SpA v Siderurgica Gabrielli SpA, case C-179/90, ECLI:EU:C:1991:464 (European Court of Justice, 1991)

Novenergia II – Energy & Environment (SCA)SICAR v Spain, Award, SCC Case No. 063/2015 (Stockholm Chamber of Commerce, 2018)

Opinion 2/13 of the Court (Full Court) ECLI:EU:C:2014:2454, Opinion 2/13 (European Court of Justice (Full Court), 2014)

Opinion 1/20 of the Court (pending)

Republic of Moldova v Komstroy, a company the successor in law to the company Energoalians, case C-741/19, ECLI:EU:C:2021:655 (European Court of Justice (Grand Chamber), 2021)

Republiken Polen (Republic of Poland) v PL Holdings S.à.r.l., Case C-109/20, ECLI:EU:C:2021:875, (European Court of Justice (Grand Chamber), 2021).

SA Intermills v Commission of the European Communities, Case 323/82, ECLI:EU:C:1984:345 (European Court of Justice, 1984)

Slowakische Republik (Slovak Republic) v Achmea BV Case C-284/16, ECLI:EU:C:2018:158 (European Court of Justice (Grand Chamber), 2018)

ThyssenKrupp Acciai Speciali Terni SpA v European Commission, case T-62/08, ECLI:EU:T:2010:268 (Court of Justice of the European Union (GC), 2010)

Wiliam Cook plc v Commission of the European Communities, case C-198/91, ECLI:EU:C:1993:197 (European Court of Justice, 1991)

Yassin Abdullah Kadi and Al Barakaat International Foundation v Council of the European Union and Commission of the European Communities, joined cases c-402/05 p and c-415/05, ECLI:EU:C:2008:461, 2008 I-06351 Eurlex (ECJ (Grand Chamber), 2008)

The consolidated version of the 1994 Energy Charter Treaty and related documents (ECT), (2016).

(INTERACT), I. P., & (ETC), E. T. C. p. (2015). State aid and ETC Questions and Answers final. In. Bratislava, Slovakia.

References

Baldwin R (1993) A domino theory of regionalism. In: Baldwin R, Haarapanta P, Kiander J (eds) Expanding membership of the EU. Cambridge University Press, Cambridge

Bilal S (2004) Can the EU be a model and a driving force for regional integration in developing countries? Paper presented at the Globalisation Studies Network (GSN) Second International Conference on Globalisation: Ovcercoming Exclusion, Strengthening Inclusion. Dakar, Senegal, 29–31 August

Blauberger M, Krämer RU (2012) European competition vs. global competitiveness: transferring EU rules on state aid and public procurement beyond Europe. J Ind Compet Trade 13(1): 171–186

Bourgeois J, Dawar K, Evenett SJ (2007) A comparative analysis of selected provisions in free trade agreements. http://sro.sussex.ac.uk/id/eprint/59639

Court E (2018) Introduction to the EFTA Court. https://eftacourt.int/the-court/introduction

Crafts N (2017) Brexit and state aid. Oxford Rev Econ Policy 33(1):S105–S112

Cremona M (2003) State aid control: substance and procedure in the Europe agreements and the stabilisation and association agreements. Eur Law J 9:265

Department for Exiting the European Union (2018) The future relationship between the United Kingdom and the European Union. https://assets.publishing.service.gov.uk/government/uploads/system/uploads/attachment_data/file/786626/The_Future_Relationship_between_the_United_Kingdom_and_the_European_Union_120319.pdf

Dietrich, Hoffet, Burger (2019) State Aid 2019 - Switzerland. Global competition Review GCR Know-how

Doyle, Martinez (2017) Political impacts of the stabilisation and association agreements: a comparative study (Policy Report No. 05/2017)

Draft Trade and Cooperation Agreement between the European Union and the European Atomic Energy Community, of one part, and the United Kingdom of Great Britain and Northern Ireland, of the other part (EU-UK Trade Agreement) (2020) (EU–UK Trade Agreement)

Eckes C (2016) International rulings and the EU legal order: autonomy as legitimacy? CLEER Papers 2016/2. Centre for the Law of EU External Relations, The Hague

Eckes C (2018) Don't lead with your chin! If Member States continue with the ratification of CETA, they violate European Union law. https://europeanlawblog.eu/2018/03/13/dont-lead-with-your-chin-if-member-states-continue-with-the-ratification-of-ceta-they-violate-european-union-law

Ehlermann CD, Goyette M (2006) The iInterface between EU state aid control and the WTO disciplines on subsidies. Eur State Aid Law 5(4):695–718

Emerson M, Noutcheva G (2018) Political and economic governance in the Balkans and Eastern Europe compared. https://www.ceps.eu/content/gergana-noutcheva

EU–Mexico Trade agreement (not finalised or ratified). (2018). European Union, Brussels

European Commission (EC) (2007) EU–Switzerland: state aid decision on company tax regimes', 13 February 2007 (EC, 2007) at https://europa.eu/rapid/press-release_IP-07-176_en.htm

European Commission (EC) (2008) Provisions on international relations in EU competition policy: situation as of 1 January 2008. https://publications.europa.eu/en/publication-detail/-/publication/50fd3279-5b8b-4f81-b534-b00fbedbff85/language-en

European Commission (EC) (2015) Investment in TTIP and beyond – the path for reform. http://trade.ec.europa.eu/doclib/docs/2015/may/tradoc_153408.PDF

European Commission (EC) (2016) European neighbourhood policy and enlargement negotiations. https://ec.europa.eu/neighbourhood-enlargement/policy/glossary/terms/europe-agreement_en

European Commission (EC) (2017) State aid: Commission and China start dialogue on state aid control. http://europa.eu/rapid/press-release_IP-17-1520_en.htm

European Free Trade Association (2014) EEA institutions. http://www.efta.int/eea/eea-institutions

European Free Trade Association (2018) About EFTA. http://www.eftasurv.int/internal-market-affairs/the-internal-market

European Union and Canada (2016) EU–Canada Comprehensive Economic and Trade Agreement. European Union, Brussels

European Union and Singapore (2017) EU–Singapore Free Trade Agreement. European Union, Brussels

Financial Stability, Financial Services and Capital Markets Union (FISMA) (2019) Declaration of the representative of the Governments of the Member States of 15 January 2019 on the legal consequences of the judgment of the Court of Justice in Achmea and on investment protection in the European Union. Publications Office of the European Union, Brussels, p 7

Galindo BR (2015) State aid control in the context of globalisation. https://www.era-comm.eu/stream/Free_e-presentations/Rodriguez_215R09/index.html

Gani W (2015) The Tunisian administration adopts a new reform of the Tunisian Competition Act. e-Competitions. https://www.researchgate.net/publication/345177707_The_Tunisian_Administration_adopts_a_new_reform_of_the_Tunisian_Competition_Act/link/5fa0243092851c14bcfc9d23/download

Geradin D (2004) Competition law and regional economic integration: an analysis of the southern Mediterranean countries. World Bank, Washington, DC

Griffits A (2018) Letter by MP Andrew Griffits to the Lord Witty, Chair, EU Internal Market Sub-Committee House of Lords, London

Hepburn J (2018) Vattenfall Tribunal issues decision rejecting Germany's post-Achmea jurisdictional objection. https://www.iareporter.com/articles/vattenfall-tribunal-issues-decision-rejecting-germanys-post-achmea-jurisdictional-objection

Hettne J, Fritz M (1994) Sverige möter EG-rätten: EES-avtalet ch dess införlivande med svensk rätt. Nerenius & Santérus förlag, Lund

Hoffet FM (2016) State Aid 2016 – Switzerland. http://www.homburger.ch/fileadmin/publications/GCRCH_State_Aid_2016.pdf

Horn H, Mavroidis PC, Sapir A (2010) Beyond the WTO? An anatomy of EU and US preferential trade agreements. World Econ 33(11):1565–1588

House of Lords European Union Committee (2018) Brexit: competition and state aid. https://publications.parliament.uk/pa/ld201719/ldselect/ldeucom/67/6702.htm

Intergovernmental Group of Experts on Competition Law and Policy (2007) Report of the Intergovernmental Group of Experts on Competition Law and Policy on its seventh session. IGECLP, Geneva

Kingdom of Belgium Foreign Affairs, Foreign Trade and Development Cooperation (2020) Belgium requests an opinion on the intra-European application of the arbitration provisions of the future modernised Energy Charter Treaty. https://diplomatie.belgium.be/en/newsroom/news/2020/belgium_requests_opinion_intra_european_application_arbitration_provisions

Kleinheisterkamp J (2012a) European policy space in international investment law. ICSID Rev – Foreign Invest Law J 27(2):416–431

Kleinheisterkamp J (2012b) Investment protection and EU law: the intra- and extra-EU dimension of the Energy Charter Treaty. J Int Econ Law 15(1):85

Koenig C (2014) Where is state aid law heading to? Heinemann, New York

Kroes N (2007) State aid and globalization – the competition perspective. Speech presented to the Informal Competitive Council on, Würzburg, 28 April

Lavenex S, Schimmelfennig F (2009) EU rules beyond EU borders: theorizing external governance in European politics. J Eur Public Policy 16(6):791–812

Luja R (2007) Should fiscal state aid go global? EC Tax Rev 16(5):231–235

Luja R (2017) State aid recovery & investor protection for non-EU taxpayers. In: Weber D (ed) GREIT Conference Series, 10th edn. IBFD, Amsterdam

McDermott P (2018) UK set to keep state aid law. https://www.trowers.com/uploads/Files/UK_set_to_keep_State_Aid_law.pdf

McGowan L, Wilks S (1995) The first supranational policy in the European Union: competition policy. Eur J Polit Res 28(2):141–169

Miroudot S, Bartók C (2008) The interaction amongst trade, investment and competition policies. https://www.oecd-ilibrary.org/trade/oecd-trade-policy-working-papers_18166873

Movchan, Giucci (2011) Quantitative assessment of Ukraine's regional integration options: DCFTA with European Union vs. Customs Union with Russia, Belarus and Kazakhstan (Vol.

Policy Paper PP/05/2011 (November). pp 15). German Advisory Group Institute for Economic Research and Policy Consulting, Berlin/Kyiv

Obrist T (2013) The end of Switzerland's cantonal tax regimes is near: what's next? https://www.mondaq.com/capital-gains-tax/263184/the-end-of-switzerlands-cantonal-tax-regimes-is-near-whats-next

OECD (2011) Roundtable on Competition, State Aids and Subsisdies. http://www.oecd.org/competition/sectors/48070736.pdf

Papadopoulos AS (2010) The international dimension of EU competition law and policy. Cambridge University Press, Cambridge

Peretz G (2016) A star is torn: Brexit and state aid. Eur State Aid Law Q 15(3):334–337

Peretz G, Bacon K (2016) Post-Brexit options for state aid. http://uksala.org/paper-on-post-brexit-options-for-state-aid

Peretz G, Bacon K, Taylor I (2017) Bringing state aid home: could an effective domestic staid aid regime be devised for the UK? http://uksala.org/bringing-state-aid-home-could-an-effective-domestic-state-aid-regime-be-devised-for-the-uk/#_ftn1

Polityka (2018) Airbus wycofał się z arbitrażu z Polską ws. Caracali. Jako przyczynę podano wyrok TSUE ws. Achmea. https://wpolityce.pl/polityka/394909-airbus-wycofal-sie-z-arbitrazu-z-polska-ws-caracali-jako-przyczyne-podano-wyrok-tsue-ws-achmea

Popović DV, Caka F (2017) State aid control in South-east Europe: waiting for a wake-up call. Eur Bus Organ Law Rev 18(2):333–349

PricewaterhouseCoopers PwC (2019) Switzerland Corporate - Significant developments. Retrieved from http://taxsummaries.pwc.com/ID/Switzerland-Corporate-Significant-developments

Rosenthal DE, Nicolaides P (1997) Harmonizing antitrust: the less effective way to promote international competition. In: Richardson JD, Graham EM (eds) Global competition policy. PIIE, Washington, DC

Rubini L (2010) The definition of subsidy and state aid: WTO and EC law in comparative perspective. Oxford University Press, New York

Rydelski MS (2004) The EEA state aid regime. In: Biondi A, Eeckhout P, Flynn J (eds) The law of state aid in the European Union. Oxford University Press, Oxford

Schön W (2004) World Trade Organization law and tax law. Bull Int Fisc Doc 58(7):283–296

Schonberg M (2017) Continuity or change? State aid control in a post-Brexit United Kingdom. Compet Law J 16(1):47–58

Sedelmeier (2011) Europeanisation in new member and candidate states. Living Rev Eur Gov 6(1)

Sierra JLB (2016) Brexit, a stress test for state aid control. Eur State Aid Law Q 15(3):331–333

Sumpf D, Waked DI (2015) Competition and regulation in the Arab region. https://www.unescwa.org/sites/www.unescwa.org/files/publications/files/economic-governance-series-2015.pdf

Svechkar, Glushchenko (2016) Getting the Deal Through. – State Aid 2016. – p 68–71, Asters

Svechkar I, Glushchenko S (2018) State aid: Ukraine. https://globalcompetitionreview.com/insight/know-how/state-aid/report/ukraine

United Nations Conference on Trade and Development, Food and Agriculture Organization of the United Nations (2016) Regulating fisheries subsidies must be an integral part of the implementation of the 2030 sustainable development agenda. Statement presented at the fourteenth session of the United Nations Conference on Trade and Development, Nairobi, Kenya, 17–20 July

United Nations Conference on Trade and Development, Food and Agriculture Organization of the United Nations (2018) Model Law on Competition. Statement. Review conducted at the seventeenth session of the United Nations Conference on Trade and Development, Geneva, 11–13 July 2018

van Zebinsky (1996) European Union external competence and external relations in air transport. Kluwer Law International BV

Weiler T, Wälde T (2004) Investment arbitration under the Energy Charter Treaty in the light of new NAFTA precedents: towards a global code of conduct for economic regulation. Transnatl Dispute Manag 1:35

Zurkinden, Scholten (2004) State Aids in Switzerland: the air transport agreement between the EU and Switzerland. Eur. St. Aid LQ, 217

Chapter 7
Extra-EU BITS: Adjusting to a New Reality or Being Phased Out

7.1 Overview

Chapters 2 and 6 explained the reasons for the EU's state aid control and how, being primary law, public policy and an inherent part of the EU's investment policy, it has affected the EU's internal and external investment policy. Hence, the final aspect of closing this specific subject is to study the extra-EU BITs that the EU's Member States have entered into with third countries.[1]

Therefore, this chapter discusses and analyses how the Lisbon Treaty and the situation of intra-EU BITs have affected and will affect the extra EU BITs of the EU's Member States and third countries in the future. It also examines the scope of Article 351 TFEU, which oversees the relationship between EU law and pre-accession international agreements entered into by the Member States with third countries, and protection of these agreements from EU law.[2] Then the reform of the Member States' model BITs is analysed by assessing the ongoing reform of these, and the enforceability of extra EU-BIT claims and Awards stemming from illegal state aid is scrutinised to identify which judicial forum would be optimal for disputes between investors and states in claims of which the EU or an EU Member State is part.

Hence, this chapter explicitly discusses the third argument of this book: that there should not exist any extra-EU BITs, leaving this area within the scope of EU Investment Treaties concluded between the EU and third countries. For this discussion and analysis, the chapter applies a bird's-eye view perspective to the discussion

[1] For a list of these agreements see EUR-Lex at https://eur-lex.europa.eu/legal-content/EN/TXT/?qid=1556809379390&uri=CELEX:52017XC0511(04).

[2] The first part of Article 351 contains a grandfathering clause, which stipulates that international agreements concluded before 1 January 1958 or by acceding states 'shall not be affected by the provisions of the Treaties'. However, where such agreements are not compatible with EU law, these must be eliminated.

P. Finckenberg-Broman, *Weaponizing EU State Aid Law to Impact the Future of EU Investment Policy in the Global Context*, Studies in European Economic Law and Regulation 23, https://doi.org/10.1007/978-3-031-10108-3_7

and analysis. It also asks the questions: Are these really a problem? If yes, can this problem be solved? Within this context, this chapter will elaborate upon:

- whether the extra BITs cannot threaten the autonomy of EU law
- whether the lack of state aid provisions can lead to ISDS, leading to a collision of IIL and EU law
- in the case of the former occurring, the best way to fix these issues, adjust existing BITs or replace them with the EU's international agreements
- when a Member State has breached the terms of an extra-EU BIT, which court an investor should bring their claims to.

The discussion and analysis of this chapter build mainly on the EU's primary case law as interpreted by the CJEU, the EU's secondary law (notably the Grandfathering Regulation,[3] and the Commission's and the Member States' publications). To some extent, this book also draws from scholarly works on the subject of extra-EU BITs. These focus mainly on the scope of immunity provided by Article 351 TFEU and the Grandfathering Regulation for pre-accession extra-EU BITs.[4] For a practical example of how the remaining extra-EU BIT can be adapted to remove the abovementioned risks, this chapter provides a short case study showing how the Netherlands has modernised its extra-EU BITs.

[3]Regulation (EU) No 1219/2012 of the European Parliament and of the Council of 12 December 2012 establishing transitional arrangements for bilateral investment agreements between Member States and third countries (Grandfathering Regulation).

[4]Authors such as Kleinheisterkamp (2011, 2012a, b), Lavranos (2013) and Niemelä (2017) have discussed extra EU BITs. Kleinheisterkamp discusses the internal power struggle that went on during the negotiations for the Grandfathering Regulation. He examines extra-EU BITs in light of the autonomy of EU law, the scope of Article 351 TFEU (which is a standstill provision for pre-accession extra-EU BITs) and Article 4(3) TEU (which stands for loyalty and the general duty to cooperate with the EU) and finds several issues regarding extra-EU BITs and the EU's legal order, concluding that the incompabilities must be renogotiated. Niemelä (2017) explains the current status of extra-EU BITs, namely protected by article 351 TFEU and the Grandfathering Regulations, but under conditionality. He also pinpoints 'that the discrimination and autonomy concerns are equally relevant in respect of extra-EU and intra-EU BITs'. However, despite the Commission having the competence to pressure the member states to renegotiate these BITs (by initiating infringement proceedings), he finds it unlikely that the Commission will do so for a number of reasons. Lavranos (2013) rejects any issues concerning extra-EU BITs and adopts a highly critical perspective on the Grandfathering Regulation. According to him, it is a purely EU internal political paper meant to 'power grab' all competences from the Member States regarding their existing extra-EU BITs—namely, wrongly attempting to replicate the de facto succession of the Member States by the E(E)C with regard to the old GATT 1947. Lavranos argues that while Article 351 TFEU remains 'the only correct route to follow', it also applies by analogy to the Member States' existing BITs. Indeed, Lavranos's view of the immunity of extra-EU BITs from EU law is broader than that of the other authors. However, he concludes that the final version of Grandfathring Regulation establishes the method categorising pre-accession and other existing extra-EU BITs as well as their eventual replacement, which he sees as being due to the Council (representing the Member States) being forced to compromise as the European Parliament adopted an extremely cautious approach on IDSD, which was 'allied' with the Commission exploring the extent of the EU's CPP being extended to include FDI.

This chapter finds that the ISDS provisions as applied in many extra-EU BITs risk Member States becoming liable for disregarding either state aid law or IIL because state aid provisions as a limit to investment protection are absent from these BITs. Hence, international arbitration tribunals, called to decide on a possible breach of an extra-EU BIT FET standard when a Member State adjusts investment incentives to changes in the EU's investment and state aid policy, are likely to continue to disregard state aid law. Consequently, these BITs must be replaced speedily with the EU's trade agreements or promptly altered to include these type of provisions the international arbitration tribunals. The current extra-EU BITs lacking provisions for state aid and restrictions on investment protection should be the first ones to be dealt with.

7.1.1 Within Long-Lasting Transition

Indeed, there is an ongoing process in the EU to replace the existing extra-EU BITs, which originate (mostly) from the time before the EU's external commercial policy was extended to include FDI by the Lisbon Treaty in 2009,[5] with the EU's trade agreements. Explicitly the EU can now choose to conduct the IIA itself.[6] Behind this transition period, with no set deadline, is the fact that most Member States declined the renunciation of their extra-EU BITs by other means.[7] However, the Member States are held instead in a standstill situation, with their existing extra-EU BITs remaining conditionally in force.[8] They can also only conclude an extra-EU BIT with the distinct permission of the Commission,[9] indicating that this form of a bilateral agreement is only acceptable in cases where the EU has no interest in

[5]For more details on this, see Sect. 2.4.5 in Chap. 2. See Regulation (EU) No 1219/2012 of the European Parliament and of the Council of 12 December 2012 establishing transitional arrangements for bilateral investment agreements between Member States and third countries (Grandfathering Regulation), OJ 2015 C135, p. 1 (EP and Council 2010, Article 3).

[6]To mention a few, TTIP information available at Commission (EC 2017); EU–Canada Comprehensive Economic and Trade Agreement (CETA) text available at EU and Canada (2016) and EU–Singapore Free Trade Agreement (EUSFTA) text available at EU and Singapore (2017). For a list of all EU existing trade agreements and those under negotiation, see the Commission's web page at https://ec.europa.eu/trade/policy/countries-and-regions/negotiations-and-agreements.

[7]Proposal for a Regulation of the European Parliament and of the Council establishing transitional arrangements for bilateral investment agreements between Member States and third countries COM (2010), 344 final: Kleinheisterkamp (2012a), p. 9. In the Commission's original draft, these BITs would have been terminated unless expressly authorised by the Commission, under certain conditions.

[8]Grandfathering Regulation Articles 2–6. For extra-EU BITs in force post-Lisbon treaty see Articles 2–6. For extra-EU BITs signed from December 2009 until the entry into force of the Grandfathering Regulation on 9 January 2013, see Articles 12–15.

[9]European Commission (2017) and the Grandfathering Regulation Articles 7–11: EP and Council (2010).

concluding a similar agreement. Therefore, since the EU's renewal of its investment policy in 2017, the extra-EU BITS entered by the Member States under the Commission's scrutiny and approval should avoid the issues of the past.[10]

7.2 No State Aid Provisions in Extra EU BITs = Repeating Intra-EU BIT Issues

7.2.1 Lack of State Aid Provisions Leading to ISDS (Which Is Against EU Law)

However, this does not mean that extra-EU BITs negotiated before 2017 will not cause an open conflict between state aid law and IIL. Extra-EU BITs, corresponding to the problems of intra-EU BITs and state aid law (namely the principle of legitimate expectations versus legitimacy and autonomy), are affected because extra-EU BITs typically focus on investment protection at the cost of public interests.[11] Among other things, this means that these BITs often lack provisions on public policy and state aid measures.[12] Therefore, the legal practice by the international investment tribunals in general, which holds that these BITs supersede EU law while the CJEU holds the opposite view, duplicates the issues inherent in intra-EU BITs.[13]

Notably, the legal situation for extra-EU BITs is distinct. With regard to the actions of the Member States, extra-EU BITs are subject to internal market control although the actions of the third country, which is part of the agreement, will fall under other relevant public international law.[14] Therefore, for the sake of legal certainty towards third parties,[15] the standstill provision in Article 351(1) TFEU

[10]For example, see the Colombia–France BIT signed on 10 July 2014 at https://investmentpolicy.unctad.org/international-investment-agreements/countries/72/france. Compare this with the France–Mauritius BIT signed on 8 March 2010. See also Sect. 7.4 in this chapter for the new Dutch model bit compared with the old one. The other Benelux countries, Belgium and Luxembourg, are also in the process of renewing their extra-EU BITs. See the Belgian Government's report, the Voortgangsrapport 2019 inzake handelsverdragen (Volkvertegenwoordigers 2019) at https://diplomatie.belgium.be/sites/default/files/downloads/54k1806007.pdf.

[11]Titi (2013). This is because the capital-exporting countries, namely the Western Member States of the EU in the past mostly entered into IIAs with developing countries (see Sect. 2.3.3 in Chap. 2). For example, see the Dutch, German and French Model BITs at UNCTAD's Investment Policy Hub at https://investmentpolicy.unctad.org/country-navigator.

[12]Juillard (2001), p. 5 point out that this includes the 1967 OECD Draft Convention on the Protection of Foreign Property; see also von Walter (2011), p. 141.

[13]See Chaps. 4 and 5.

[14]Such as the Subsidies Agreement.

[15]The EU aims to protect the right and obligations of the Member States concerning third countries.

guarantees that awards stemming from pre-EU BITs[16] do not have to be in conformity with EU law in every situation. Hence, the scope of the protection the standstill provision offers is what decides the fate of an extra-EU-BIT.[17]

In the past, the Commission has taken pre-emptive measures, such as entering an MoU in 2003 with the United States and the acceding states from Central and Eastern Europe and with the US government obliging the acceding nations to renegotiate their BITs, to hinder these types of issues from occurring.[18] Also, to avoid future clashes between intra-EU BITs and EU law, the Commission has launched a series of infringement proceedings in the past obliging the Member States to eliminate incompatibilities between their international and EU law obligations in favour of the latter. For example, at the time when Denmark, Sweden, Finland and Austria acceded to the EU, their refusal to renegotiate their BITs in accordance with Articles 351 TFEU and 4(3) TEU resulted in the Commission initiating infringement proceedings against these nations.[19] After the CJEU had judged in favour of the Commission in *C-249/06 – Commission v Sweden* (2009), *C-205/06 – Commission v Austria* (2009) and '*C-118/07 – Commission v Finland* (2009), these Member States conceded.

Especially the extra-EU BIT case *C-126/97 – Eco Swiss* (1999),[20] which demonstrated the CJEU's perspective regarding collisions of extra-EU BITs with state aid law. In the *Eco Swiss* case, the Benetton Group licensed Eco Swiss, a Hong Kong company, to produce watches. This licensing agreement, however, included clauses that breached the EU's competition law.[21] As a result, Eco Swiss successfully initiated international commercial arbitration against Benetton for damages under Dutch Law.[22] However, Eco Swiss never got to realise the Award ordered by the tribunal in this case. The CJEU annulled the enforcement of this Award because it infringed the EU's competition law.

Consequently, a Member State cannot offer state aid to foreign investors without notifying the Commission *ex-ante* or being preapproved by other relevant EU law provisions.[23] As Kleinheisterkamp puts it, the Commissions would most likely initiate 'infringement procedures under Article 258 TFEU against a Member State

---

[16]Meaning BITs concluded by a Member State, before accession to the EU, with a third country.

[17]See Sect. 7.3 below for *C-264/09 – Commission v Slovakia* (2011a) and *AG Opinion Jääskeläinen* in *C-264/09 – Commission v Slovakia (AG)* (2011) para 10.

[18]MoU EC & US on Certain BITs.

[19]Other such measures were, for example, infringement proceedings against Romania, Sweden, Austria, the Netherlands and the Slovak Republic in 2015 (EC 2015).

[20]*Eco Swiss China Time Ltd v Benetton International NV.92, C-126/97.*

[21]Eco Swiss was prohibited from selling these watches, marked as 'Benetton by Bulova', in Italy. Benetton also failed to notify the Commission ex-ante about these measures: Bermann (2012), p. 411.

[22]Bermann (2012), pp. 411–412.

[23]As established in Sect. 3.5.1 in Chap. 3. See also cases such as *C-8/08-T-Mobile Netherlands BV v Raad van beestuur van de Nederlandse Mededingingsautoriteit* (2009) and *C-295/04-Manfredi* (2006).

that breaches its duty of loyal co-operation under Article 4(3) TEU by refusing to re-negotiate a BIT that, in the Commission's view, is an obstacle to a policy of the Union'.[24] Indeed, there is no reason—especially after the CJEU's judgment in *Achmea C-284/16* (2018) and *Opinion 1/17*—that other principles would apply for extra-EU BITs.[25] In both these instances, the ECJ highlighted the constitutional character of the EU and the importance of its capacity to act autonomously within its *sui generis* legal framework to protect public interests that have been established by the EU's primary law and the general principles of EU law. State aid control is part of the EU's public policy. Hence, the scope of these decisions should cover state aid measures implemented by the Member States and ISDS awards reinstituting unlawful state aid.

7.2.2 *ISDS in Extra-EU BITs: Infringing the Autonomy of EU Law?*

One could argue that, in principle, any ISDS award that deals with the application and interpretation of EU law is incompatible with EU law due to the extensive arguments of autonomy, uniformity and effectiveness the CJEU brings up in *Achmea C-284/16* and *Opinion 1/17*.

Given that the outcome of these two rulings which scrutinised the autonomy of EU law concerning ISDS was a method for its reform in order for these two to coexist, *Achmea C-284/16* and the *Opinion 1/17* most likely set the new standard for all EU related IIAs, including extra-EU BITs. By renegotiating their existing extra-EU BITs, the Member States could avoid these BITs from falling into conflict with EU law where the scope of these two overlaps. Replacing ISDS with ICS (CETA's) would enable the Member states to fulfil their obligation under articles 351(2) and 4(3) TEU, namely to address incompatibilities with EU law.[26] During the transition period from extra-EU BIT reign to a full EU investment reign, it would be practical and in line with EU law to utilise the process set by the Grandfathering Regulation.[27] It provides that the review of extra-EU BITs, both current and future ones, can be made following criteria developed by the CJEUs jurisprudence. Indeed, the EU

[24] Kleinheisterkamp (2012a), p. 11. European Commissioner for Trade Karel De Gucht noted that 'Articles 5 and 6 would still leave the Commission the power to review investment agreements and withdraw authorisation in case these agreements create major problems': Gucht (2011).

[25] *Opinion 1/17* (2019).

[26] See ('*C-264/09 - Commission v Slovakia*') for a IIA between Slovakia and Switzerland.

[27] The Grandfathering Regulation (European Parliament (EP) & (Council) 2010), Arts 7–13.

Member States used this process to update their bilateral aviation treaties with third countries.[28]

For an investor to raise claims on a breach of an extra-EU bit but based on EU law, as can be read from *Achmea C-284/16* and the *Opinion 1/17*, an ICS type of solution should not be the answer. For measures that fall within the scope of EU law, the right Court for an investor to turn to is the CJEU.[29]

7.2.3 Which Tribunal/Court to Turn to for Extra-EU BIT Claims

Given that extra-EU BITs simultaneously belong to two different international legal spheres, IIL and EU law, an investor can hence turn to an international investment tribunal or the CJEU or both. Article 263 TFEU, which enables individuals (natural or legal persons) bring proceedings against the EU legal acts and its bodies if the act was addressed to that individual 'or which is of direct and individual concern to them… and does not entail implementing measures.'[30]

A compelling case which demonstrates an excellent way to raise claims based on extra EU BITs is the *Banco Popolar* case.[31] The bank was resolved consistent with an EU regulation[32] once its liquidity fell under a required minimum. It was the Single Resolution Board Executive Committee that made this decision,[33] and the Commission supported it.[34] Notably, the group of Mexican investors who raised claims under the Spain–Mexico BIT against Spain for resolving Banco Popular in

---

[28] See e.g. Commission press release Air transport: Infringements concerning bilateral aviation agreements with Russia available at https://europa.eu/rapid/press-release_MEMO-11-167_en.htm (EC 2011).

[29] See Chap. 5 above.

[30] Article 263(4) TFEU. The CJEU has clarified what type of EU measures can be challenged in, for example, Judgment of the Court (Grand Chamber), 3 October 2013, Inuit Tapiriit Kanatami and Others v European Parliament and Council of the European Union Case (*C-583/11 P Inuit*, 2013); (*C-274/12 P – Telefónica v Commission*, 2013), para.27; (*C-456/13 P - T & L Sugars v Commission*, 2015), para 31.

[31] GBM Global, Sociedad Anònima de Capital Variable, Fondo de Inversiòn de Renta Variable, et al., *Claimants vs. Kingdom of Spain*, ICSID Case 1:18, para 120.

[32] Regulation (EU) No 806/2014 of the European Parliament and of the Council of 15 July 2014 establishing uniform rules and uniform procedure for the resolution of credit institutions and certain investment firms in the framework of a Single Resolution Mechanism and a Single Resolution Fund and amending Regulation (EU) No 1093/2010 (SRM Regulation), 15 July 2014, Official Journal of the European Union (EP and Council 2014).

[33] Decision to take resolution action in respect of Banco Popular Español, SA (2017/C 222/05) on 7 June 2017 (SRB 2017).

[34] *Commission Decision (EU) 2017/1246 of 7 June 2017 endorsing the resolution scheme for Banco Popular Español S.A.*

2017[35] chose not to challenge the EU resolution decision under ISDS proceedings.[36] Instead, the investors initiated ISDS proceedings against Spain only, based on their inaction to stop the insolvency. The investors took separate challenges against the Single Resolution Board Executive Committee decision the Commission decision and the European Central Bank to the CJEU.[37] This approach, chosen by the claimant's lawyers, shows an understanding of EU law—that is, the choice to raise claims at the tribunal that has the competence to make a judgment about the case.[38]

7.3 Can the Extra-EU BITS Be Redeemed?

Regarding the non-modernised pre-accession extra-EU BITs, Article 351(1) TFEU and the Grandfathering Regulation uphold their continued existence.[39] However, these agreements must be compatible with EU law. Article 351(2) TFEU distinctly requires Member States to take the necessary steps to eliminate incompatibilities with the EU Treaties. Article 351(1) TFEU and the Grandfathering Regulation are, however, not applicable for the founding Member States of the European Communities as these do not protect international agreements signed before the

[35] '*RFA-ICSID 1:18* (2018), para 5.

[36] Exhibit A, GBM Global, Sociedad Anònima de Capital Variable, Fondo de Inversiòn de Renta Variable, et al., ICSID Case 1:18, Para 120; and Exhibit B GBM Global, Sociedad Anònima de Capital Variable, Fondo de Inversiòn de Renta Variable, et al., *Claimants v Kingdom of Spain*, UNICTRAL Case 1:18, para 120. These claims were initiated under both the ICSID and UNICTRAL conventions because some of the investors were dual citizens (ICSID does not accept claims from dual citizens).

[37] In June 2019, 87 individual cases had been initiated following the resolution of *Banco Popular Español SA*. Mostly, these cases—such as *T-484/17 Fidesban and Others v SRB* (pending) and *T-512/17 OCU and Others v SRB* (pending), ask for annulment of the Decisions of the SRB Decision or the Commission, or both. Some cases, such as *T-515/17 – Sánchez Valverde e Hijos v SRB* (pending) and *T-482/17 Comercial Vascongada Recalde v Commission and SRB* (pending), also include a request for compensation of damages. For a full list of these cases, see European Banking Institute, The Banking Union and Union Courts overview of cases as at 14 June 2019 (EBI 2019) at https://ebi-europa.eu/publications/eu-cases-or-jurisprudence.

[38] This type of arrangement would also be appropriate for the many intra-EU BITs proceedings under the ECT. See Sect. 6.5.2 in Chap. 6 and Chap. 5.

[39] The Grandfathering Regulation shares the logic of Article 351 TFEU. It emphasises that FDI is now of exclusive competence of the EU, and hence, according to Article 2(1) TFEU, the Member States can no longer 'legislate and adopt legally binding acts' unless authorised by the EU. It also upholds pre-accession extra-EU BITs under certain conditions. See the Preamble of the Grandfathering Regulation and Sect. 7.2.2 above. The analogous applicability of Article 351 TFEU post-accession agreements, before the exercise of EU powers in the area covered by those agreements, has not been examined by the CJEU. Only AG Kokott in *C-188/07 – Commune de Mesquer v Total France (AG)* (2008) paras 94 et seq. and some scholarly literature, such as Lavranos (2013) and Pantaleo (2014), have toyed with this notion. Lavranos (2013) finds support for analogous applicability of Article 351 TFEU while Pantaleo (2014) and Kokott and Sobotta (2016) arrive at the opposite conclusion.

establishment of the European Economic Community on January 1958. Paradoxically, most extra-EU BITs are signed by these founding Member States.

Hypothetically, this means that the extra-EU BITs that substantially conflict with EU law, namely by breaching the autonomy of the EU's legal order (ISDS clauses) or state aid law, or both, need to either be renegotiated or terminated.[40] Given the nature of extra-EU BITs with long sunset clauses, for the Member States renegotiating these BITs is a viable option until replaced by an EU IIA with the third country.

Indeed, Article 351(1) TFEU and the Grandfathering Regulation create a temporary safe harbour for the Member States to obey their international agreements concluded before they transferred this competence to the EU. Hence the scope of Article 351 TFEU is twofold. On the one hand, it protects the Member States domestically from EU institutions during the transition period, as any violation of EU law is not something for which they can be held responsible.[41] On the other hand, it assures that the Member States do not become responsible for relationships with third countries.[42]

After all, an extra-EU BIT that conflicts with EU law does not hinder the third country party from requiring compliance under the BIT, by the Member State, to its obligations. Article 351(1) TFEU and the Grandfathering Regulation are not in themselves any form of legal shield for those BITs. The BITs Regulation is a transitional tool to provide legal certainty during the national to EU IIAs transition, by providing a detailed rule set.[43] This provisional basis for short-term protection of Member States' existing agreements follows the spirit of Article 351 TFEU in providing temporary legal safeguards. It is important to note that Article 351 TFEU does not propose to 'guarantee the continued existence of prior contractual obligations'.[44] Therefore, while the Member States may be able to hold on to their extra-EU BITs for quite some time by modernising those to be in line with EU law, including state aid law, ultimately it is the EU's actions and decisions that steer the duration of the transition period.

[40] *C-203/03 – Commission v Austria* (2005) para 61. See also Kleinheisterkamp (2012b).

[41] Pantaleo (2014), p. 312; Niemelä (2017), pp. 29–30; Kleinheisterkamp (2012a), pp. 11–13.

[42] Pantaleo (2014), p. 312; Niemelä (2017), pp. 29–30; Kleinheisterkamp (2012a), pp. 11–13.

[43] Pantaleo (2014), p. 312; Niemelä (2017), pp. 29–30; Kleinheisterkamp (2012a), pp. 11–13.

[44] Van Rossem (2009), p. 16.

7.4 Modernisation of Dutch Extra-EU BITs: Avoiding Future Collisions

State aid provisions were mainly extinct in extra-EU BITs until 2018. Nonetheless, state aid rules still apply for extra EU BITs due to the primacy of EU law.[45] Indeed, the extra-BIT regime is not immune to the controversies regarding the clashes of the international investment regime and EU law discussed earlier in this monograph.

This situation is reflected by the attempt of the Netherlands to revamp its existing 79 extra-EU BITs through a renegotiation process.[46] The objective of the remodelling of these BITs is to establish better-balanced rights and obligations of states and investors. Despite the former Dutch BIT model from 2004 including (Article 6) police powers regarding 'measures taken in the public interest and under due process of law', this has not hindered tribunals to Award investors for breaches of EU law. Therefore, this clause safeguards the 'right to regulate'. Indeed, the new BIT model, adopted on 19 October 2018 has some likeness with the EU's International Investment Agreements—especially ICS in CETA.

Besides narrowing the definition of an investor, to limit claims by letterbox companies,[47] which constitute 87 per cent of claims that supposedly stem from Dutch investors,[48] the Dutch new BIT Article 2.2 sets a 'right to regulate'. Accordingly, a state party's regulation that interferes with an investment or harms investors' expectations does not necessarily equate a breach of the BIT. This feature potentially redeems the BIT from future breaches with EU law and IIL.

---

[45] For primacy of EU law in agreements concluded by EC Member States, see *Ravil*, C-469-00, EU: C:2003:295, para 37.

[46] Both the old and the new model BIT can be found on the Netherlands government website at https://www.rijksoverheid.nl/ministeries/ministerie-van-buitenlandse-zaken/documenten/publicaties/2019/03/22/nieuwe-modeltekst-investeringsakkoorden.

[47] Dutch new BIT Article 1(b)(ii) sets that only legal persons with 'substantial business activities' in the Netherlands (or is a subsidiary which is controlled by a Dutch company with substantial business activities in the Netherlands) are protected under the BIT. A letterbox company, which has no substantial commercial or operational presence in the country in which it is officially established, is established to avoid stricter legal, social and fiscal obligations in countries where the company is commercially active.

[48] Treaty-based ISDS cases brought under Dutch IIAs: An overview study by UNCTAD/DIAE, commissioned by the DG Foreign Economic Relations, Ministry of Foreign Affairs, the Netherlands: UNCTAD (2014); Roos van Os and Knottnerus (2011). According the IMF, the Netherlands is the world's leading country in terms of inward-bound FDI and the world's second biggest in terms of outward-bound FDI investment. See IMF database at http://data.imf.org/?sk=40313609-F037-48C1-84B1-E1F1CE54D6D5&sId=1482247616261. According to Knottnerus et al. (2018) only 13 per cent of these investors are Dutch. Indeed, the Centre for Research on Multinational Corporations (SOMO) report found that the Netherlands had been the home base for ISA claims amounting to US$100 billion.

In particular, a revolutionary aspect of the new Dutch BIT model is that it introduces several obligations to investors.[49] *Inter alia*, it seeks to limit both MFN and NT protections and to restrict foreign investors from awaking frivolous claims (Article 8.3). Moreover, if an investor breaches these liabilities in respect of the investment, the New BIT Article 7(4) enables the host state to initiate claims for damages against the investor in its home state. Article 9 of the new BIT seeks to limit claims of FET breaches by the introduction of a CETA-type illustrative list, which establishes the measures constituting breaches of the obligations of a state.[50] However, the draft BIT leaves broad discretion to international investment tribunals to interpret what counts as a legitimate expectation regarding the investors. Notably, the draft BIT attempts to prevent court shopping by investors (Article 8.3) and arbitrators double hatting (Article 20), triggering partiality and bias. Instead of party-appointed arbitrators, an appointing authority will select these.

Above all, the new BIT, in contrast to the old BIT, includes competition policy provisions, which means that it protects the Member States from being torn between obliging state aid law and international investment law. These state aid provisions entail the possibility of state parties either introducing or maintaining competition measures (Article 2.3), including the discontinuation of or recovery of subsidies. The limitation(s) are that the measure(s) must comply with the state parties' international obligations or where/when a competent court or authority has ordered them. Hence, the new Dutch BIT seeks to ensure existing and future investment incentives do not run afoul of state aid control and contribute to a comprehensive EU investment policy, hopefully devoid of contradicting legal obligations.

7.5 Summary and Conclusions

Indeed, the scope of the EU's external competences is still in flux, which means the extra-EU BITs status will also continue to evolve. Regarding the question this chapter asks, are the Extra-EU BITs really a problem? The answer is that these BITs have multiple issues. While extra-EU BITs continue their long-lasting transition (Sect. 7.1.1), the ISDS provisions as applied in many extra-EU BITs risk Member States to become liable of disregarding either state aid law or IIL because state aid provisions as a limit to investment protection are absent from these BITs (Sect. 7.2.1). Also, these BITs likely infringe the autonomy of EU law (Sect. 7.2.2). Hence, international arbitration tribunals, called to decide on a possible breach of an extra-EU BIT FET standards when a Member State adjusts investment incentives to changes in the EU's investment and state aid policy, are likely to continue to

[49] Such as Article 5, Protection Against Business-related Human Rights Abuse, and Article 7, Corporate Environmental and Social Responsibility Regarding the Investment.

[50] This list is not exhaustive.

disregard state aid law. The right court to turn to on matters regarding EU law is the CJEU (Sect. 7.2.3).

As for the second question, if the problems related to extra-EU BITs may be solved, this chapter proposes the following. By using the process of the Grandfathering Regulation, these BITs must be as speedily as possible replaced with the EU's trade agreements or promptly altered to include provisions that transfer traditional ISDS to ICS as in CETA and the new Dutch BIT. Unfortunately, however, signing and renegotiating a new treaty is a slow process and can take many years. Similarly, provisions guaranteeing that the EU can, unhindered, apply state aid control must be introduced to these BITs. The current extra-EU BITs lacking provisions for state aid and restrictions on investment protection should be the first ones to be dealt with.

Cases

Commercial Vascongada Recalde v Commission and SRB, case T-482/17 (Court of Justice of the European Union, pending)

Commission of the European Communities v Kingdom of Sweden, ECLI:EU:C:2009:119 (European Court of Justice (Grand Chamber), 2009)

Commission of the European Communities v Republic of Austria C-205/06, ECLI:EU:C:2009:118 (European Court of Justice (Grand Chamber), 2009)

Commission of the European Communities v Republic of Austria, case C-203/03, EU:C:2005:76 (European Court of Justice (Grand Chamber), 2005)

Commission of the European Communities v Republic of Finland, ECLI:EU:C:2009:715 (European Court of Justice, 2009)

Commune de Mesquer v Total France SA and Total International Ltd., case C-188/07 (AG Kokott), ECLI:EU:C:2008:174 (AG Opinion, 2008)

Eco Swiss China Time Ltd v Benetton International NV, case C-126/97, ECLI:EU:C:1999:269 (European Court of Justice, 1999)

European Commission Decision (EU) 2017/1246 endorsing the resolution scheme for Banco Popular Español S.A. notified under document C (2017) 4038 (Vol. OJ 11.17.2017 L178/15)

European Commission v Slovak Republic, case 264/09, ECLI:EU:C:2011:580 (European Court of Justice, 2011)

European Commission v Slovak Republic, case C-264/09. Opinion AG Jääskeläinen, ECLI:EU:C:2011:150 (2011)

Fidesban and Others v SRB, case T-484/17 (Court of Justice of the European Union, pending)

GBM Global, Sociedad An'onima de Capital Variable, Fondo de Inversi'on de Renta Variable et al. v Kingdom of Spain (Request for Arbitration), Case 1:18 (ICSID ad hoc, 2018).

Inuit Tapiriit Kanatami and Others v European Parliament and Council of the European Union, case C-583/11 P, No. ECLI:EU:C:2013:625 (European Court of Justice (Grand Chamber), 2013)

OCU and Others v SRB, case T-512/17 (Court of Justice of the European Union, pending)

Opinion 1/17 of the Court (Full Court) No. ECLI:EU:C:2019:341 (European Court of Justice (Full Court), 2019)

Sánchez Valverde e Hijos v SRB, case T-515/17 (Court of Justice of the European Union, pending)

Slowakische Republik (Slovak Republic) v Achmea BV Case C-284/16, ECLI:EU:C:2018:158 (European Court of Justice (Grand Chamber), 2018)

T-Mobile Netherlands BV v Raad van beestuur van de Nederlandse Mededingingsautoriteit, ECLI:EU:C:2009:343 (European Court of Justice, 2009)

T & L Sugars and Sidul Açúcares v European Commission, case C-456/13 P, EU:C:2015:284 (European Court of Justice (Grand Chamber), 2015)

Telefónica SA v European Commission, case C-274/12 P, EU:C:2013:852 (European Court of Justice, 2013)

Vincenzo Manfredi v Lloyd Adriatico Assicurazioni SpA (C-295/04), Antonio Cannito v Fondiaria Sai SpA (C-296/04) and Nicolò Tricarico (C-297/04) and Pasqualina Murgolo (C-298/04) v Assitalia SpA, ECLI:EU:C:2006:461 (European Court of Justice, 2006)

References

Bermann GA (2012) Navigating EU law and the law of international arbitration. Arbitr Int 28(3): 397–446

European Banking Institute (2019) The Banking Union and Union Courts: overview of cases as at 14 June 2019. https://ebi-europa.eu/publications/eu-cases-or-jurisprudence

European Commission (EC) (2011) Air transport: infringements concerning bilateral aviation agreements with Russia. https://europa.eu/rapid/press-release_MEMO-11-167_en.htm

European Commission (EC) (2015) Commission asks Member States to terminate their intra-EU bilateral investment treaties. http://europa.eu/rapid/press-release_IP-15-5198_en.htm

European Commission (EC) (2017) TTIP – the EU–US trade deal. http://ec.europa.eu/trade/policy/in-focus/ttip/index_en.htm

European Parliament and Council (2010) Regulation (EU) No 1219/2012 of the European Parliament and of the Council of 12 December 2012 establishing transitional arrangements for bilateral investment agreements between Member States and third countries. European Union, Brussels

European Parliament and Council (2014) Regulation (EU) No 806/2014 of the European Parliament and of the Council of 15 July 2014 establishing uniform rules and uniform procedure for the resolution of credit institutions and certain investment firms in the framework of a single resolution mechanism and a aingle eesolution dund and amending Regulation (EU) No 1093/2010. European Union, Brussels

European Union and Canada (2016) EU–Canada Comprehensive Economic and Trade Agreement. European Union, Brussels

European Union and Singapore (2017) EU–Singapore Free Trade Agreement. European Union, Brussels

Gucht KD (2011) Remarks to the European Parliament on transitional arrangements for bilateral investment agreements between Member States and third countries. European Union, Strasbourg

Juillard P (2001) Bilateral investment treaties in the context of investment law. Paper presented to Investment Compact Regional Roundtable on Bilateral Investment Treaties for the Protection and Promotion of Foreign Investment in South East Europe, OECD, Croatia, 28–29 May

Kleinheisterkamp J (2011) The next 10-year ECT investment arbitration: a vision for the future – from a European law perspective. London School of Economics and Political Science, London

Kleinheisterkamp J (2012a) European policy space in international investment law. ICSID Rev – Foreign Invest Law J 27(2):416–431

Kleinheisterkamp J (2012b) Investment protection and EU law: the intra- and extra-EU dimension of the Energy Charter Treaty. J Int Econ Law 15(1):85

Knottnerus R, Van Os R, Verbeek BJ et al (2018) 50 jaar ISDSE- en mondiaal machtsmiddel voor multinationals gecreëerd en groot gemaakt door Nederland. https://www.somo.nl/nl/50-jaar-isds-een-mondiaal-machtmiddel-voor-multinationals

Kokott J, Sobotta C (2016) Investment arbitration and EU law. In: Armstrong K (ed) Cambridge yearbook of European legal studies. Cambridge University Press, Cambridge

Lavranos N (2013) In defence of Member States' BITs gold standard: The Regulation 1219/2012 Establishing a Transitional Regime for Existing Extra-EU BITs – a Member State's perspective. Transnatl Dispute Manag (TDM) 10(2). https://papers.ssrn.com/sol3/papers.cfm?abstract_id=2226979

Niemelä P (2017) The relationship of EU law and bilateral investment treaties of EU Member States: treaty conflict, harmonious coexistence and the critique of the investment arbitration. Unpublished doctoral thesis, University of Helsinki

Pantaleo L (2014) Member States prior agreements and newly EU attributed competence: what lesson from foreign investment. Eur Foreign Aff Rev 19(2):307–324

SRB (2017) Decision to take resolution action in respect of Banco Popular Español, S.A. (2017/C 222/05) (Vol. 11.7.2017). European Union, Brussels

Titi C (2013) EU investment agreements and the search for a new balance: a paradigm shift from laissez-faire liberalism toward embedded liberalism? https://academiccommons.columbia.edu/doi/10.7916/D85Q54F6

UNCTAD (2014) Treaty-based ISDS cases brought under Dutch IIAs: an overview. https://investmentpolicy.unctad.org/publications/135/treaty-based-isds-cases-brought-under-dutch-iias-an-overview#

van Os R, Knottnerus R (2011) Dutch bilateral investment treaties: a gateway to 'treaty shopping' for investment protection by multinational corporations. https://www.somo.nl/dutch-bilateral-investment-treaties

Van Rossem JW (2009) Interaction between EU law and international law in the light of Intertanko and Kadi: the dilemma of norms binding the Member States but not the community. Neth Yearb Int Law 40(1):183–227

Volkvertegenwoordigers, BKv (2019) The Voortgangsrapport 2019 inzake handelsverdragen van de vice-eersteminister en minister van Buitenlandse Zaken en Europese Zaken, belast met beliris en de Federale Culturele Instellingen. https://diplomatie.belgium.be/sites/default/files/downloads/54k1806007.pdf

von Walter A (2011) Balancing investors' and host atates' eights: what alternatives for treaty-makers? In: Bungenberg M, Griebel J, Hindelang S (eds) International investment law and EU law. Springer, Berlin

Chapter 8
Summary, Analysis and Conclusions: The Effect of EU State Aid Law on EU Investment Policy

8.1 Overview

Since the Commission's rejection of ISDS for the EU and its Member States in conjunction with JEEPA negotiations, the EU has undertaken a massive overhaul of its investment policy. Indeed, since 2015, trade agreements under negotiation have replaced the ISDS with the EU's own investor treaty arbitration system, ICS. ICS is designed to be permanent, unbiased, ultra-transparent and fully compatible with EU law. The EU's trade agreements with investment chapters or investment protections agreements that include ICS also contain an extensive subsidies provision.

Multiple factors have contributed towards this process, such as increased, mainly state aid-related, litigation on intra-EU BITs from 2006, in addition to years of debate within political, academic and legal circles regarding the conflict generated by international investment agreements for the EU's legal order. Most importantly, however, has been the necessity to protect 'the autonomy of the EU legal order' and the right to regulate public policy objectives, as well as to avoid jurisdictional conflicts.[1]

This book has investigated how EU State aid law affects the EU's investment policy and demonstrates how the EU's internal rules and conflicts with other international law might reverberate around the rest of the globe. This conclusions chapter will first provide a summary of the discussion of the previous chapters, after which it will reinstate the book statements and provide an overall analysis and conclusion on the subject in the light of the three arguments presented by this monograph.

---

[1] As shown by Kleinheisterkamp (2014, 2015); Eckes (2016); Gallo and Nicola (2015). See also Chap. 4.

P. Finckenberg-Broman, *Weaponizing EU State Aid Law to Impact the Future of EU Investment Policy in the Global Context*, Studies in European Economic Law and Regulation 23, https://doi.org/10.1007/978-3-031-10108-3_8

8.2 Summary of Discussions

8.2.1 State Aid Near and Far Correlating to Investment Policy

As the discussion in Chaps. 2 to 5 has shown, EU state aid law is a public policy area[2] where investor protection and the right to regulate collide as state aids/subsidies are a built-in feature of states' investment policy. These issues are substantial (Chaps. 2 to 4) and procedural (Chap. 5). Indeed, state aid/subsidies in the form of long-term investment support programs, explicitly investment incentives, is a common method for attracting FDI. However, economic evidence shows that investment incentives are harmful to competition and ultimately risk nullifying the benefits a nation can derive from FDI. The problem is that there is no comprehensive international normative system that restricts all type of investment incentives.

Studying the global economic order reveals a fascinating picture of how nation-states selectively implement liberal trade policies. In the case of liberal trade policies, FDI and competition policy are linked through trade since both these concepts eliminate barriers to international trade and investment by hindering governments anti-competitive behaviour. Nevertheless, while many nations agree on the harmful effect of too many subsidies, the same nations apply these if not hindered by international norms. Therefore, combatting anti-competitive behaviour has led to the WTO rules and originally even BITs. However, the Subsidies Agreement only catches investment incentives related to goods. Also, international rules governing trade and subsidies are codified under a single institution, the WTO, with IIAs implemented as a network of BITs (see Chaps. 2 and 3).[3]

8.2.2 EU State Aid Regime and Its Multiple Purposes

The EU is an exception. EU competition rules cover all types of anti-competitive state interventions—they apply similarly to goods, services and capital. Since the role of competition policy is to hinder anticompetitive practices, it must be neutral in its application, so neither domestic nor foreign companies should be receiving special treatment. Hence the EU legislates and practises state aid control. Many Member State government actions result in a benefit to an enterprise, so national

---

[2]State aid policy is part of the EU's public policy: *C-126/97 – Eco Swiss* (1999) para 39; *C-295/04 – Manfredi* (2006) para 31; *T-Mobile Netherlands BV v Raad van beestuur van de Nederlandse Mededingingsautoriteit* (2009) para 49.

[3]This may be subject to change, as the EU is promoting the modernisation of the WTO rules to enhance subsidies control and to establish rules that cover FDI. See European Commission (2018), p. 5.

initiatives to attract foreign direct investment may easily classify as a state aid measure (see Chaps. 2 and 3).

State aid law stems from the EU treaties, Articles 107–109 TFEU. Accordingly, Member States cannot implement measures that benefit certain firms in such a way that it risks distorting the competition in the internal market competition. Exceptions to this rule are narrow and codified by State aid law (see Chap. 3). State aid control is one of the fundamental cornerstones of EU law and a critical component of the European economic constitution. The EU's state aid regime has developed into its own unique system, which continuously keeps on adapting in order to protect the internal market by implementing new trade defences targeting subsidies. Moreover, all international agreements entered by the EU and its Member States must be compatible with EU primary law. Since the EU gained competence to conclude international investment agreements in 2009, it has become critical for the EU's investment policy and the IIAs previously negotiated by its Member States to be comprehensively aligned with EU law, particularly with EU state aid policy (Chaps. 2, 3 and 5).

State aid law and policy function both as a sword and a shield. As a shield, state aid law and policy defend the EU's internal market from EU internal and external harmful subsidy wars. This effect even covers IIAs and is about to be expanded to bring all types of harmful subsidies granted by third countries, which typically fall outside the scope of the EU state aid regime, under the EU's unilateral control.[4] As a sword, state aid law and policy are a tool for further integration and European governance (Chaps. 2, 3 and 6). Above all, the state aid policy has served as an essential tool for the constitutionalisation of European values and the deepening integration of the internal market. Besides that, the rationale for state aid control aims for economic efficiency combined with redistributive justice (Chaps. 3 and 6).

Behind the dynamic evolution of the EU's state aid policy is the Commission's application of state aid provisions and the judgments by the CJEU. Through this evolution, state aid policy has come to cover even the EU's external relations, to protect the EU internal market from subsidising practices by third nations. For successful exportation of state aid control policies, the EU uses trade instruments and collaborates with its trading partners. The extraterritorial dimension of the EU's state aid policy consists of the WTO's subsidies control and the EU's plurilateral—such as the EFTA—or bilateral—such as the JEEPA—trade instruments. The exportation of key EU rules, including state aid control, is also driven by the EU's *acquis communautaire* (Chaps. 3 and 6).

Within the internal market, Member States must notify intended measures to the Commission *ex-ante* under Article 108(3) TFEU to confirm that these are internal market compatible. A failure to abide by this procedure makes the measure illegal and subject to claw-back procedures. These cover both norms and enforcement, leading to suspension or discontinuation of the measure and potential recovery of the

[4] As proposed by the White Paper on Foreign Subsidies in 2021. This would include subsidising services and FDI.

allocated aid from its beneficiary. Indeed, the enforcement of claw-back procedures can trigger a collision of regimes between the EU state aid regime and international investment regimes (Chaps. 3 to 5).

8.2.3 *Intra-EU BITs and State Aid Law*

As state aid law imposes measures on EU Member States—such as claw-back—which conflict with those states' international obligations to foreign investors under BITs, these states become subject to claims and substantial liabilities. This scenario played out in the *Micula* case, which revealed a back door, exploitable only by foreign investors to circumvent state aid law. This back door emerges where foreign investors invoke FET provisions under a BIT against a Member State implementing clawback procedures because international investment arbitrators usually uphold the BIT over EU law.[5]

As happened in *Micula*, the consequence of this conflict may be ISDS legitimising illegalities.[6] Hence, the case study of *Micula* uncovered an unresolved conflict between a Member State applying these EU laws while also being a signatory of a BIT.[7] In *Micula*, a Member State (Romania) became trapped between choosing EU law or international investment law and facing sanctions whichever option it chose. This situation created an EU institutional distrust, leading up to the European Parliament disavowing the ISDS clause (Chap. 4). Although the *Micula* proceedings are based on an intra-EU BIT, similar disputes may arise from any IIA covering the international relations of an EU Member State, or perhaps even the EU itself with a non-EU country. Hence, the *Micula* case alerted the Commission to the need for it to protect the EU's state aid regime against future challenges based on IIAs and TIPs. Since then, the Commission has moved to end intra-EU BITs,[8] to limit the scope of investment protection and to end traditional ISDS in all the EU's

---

[5] According to the International Court of Justice (ICJ), Article 38 §1, the international sources of law used by arbitration courts are, in order of precedence, (1) international treaties; (2) general customary international law; and (3) general principles of law. At the same time, the EU courts' sources of law are, in order of precedence, (1) EU primary legislation; (2) general principles of law; (3) the EU's international agreements; (4) EU secondary legislation; and (5) conventions between the Member States.

[6] This can be seen in *C-346/03 – Atzeni and Others* (2006).

[7] See also *Achmea BV Final Award* (2012); *Achmea v Slovak Republic* (2008), previously *Eureko* (2010); *Eastern Sugar – Final Award* (2007); *Eastern Sugar – Partial Award* (2007); *AES v Hungary (III) Award* (2010); ('*EDF v. Hungary*,' 2014); ('*Electrabel Decision on Jurisdiction*,' 2012); ('*Electrabel Award*,' 2015); *Binder v Czech Republic Award* (2007); *Oostergetel v Slovak Republic* (2010); *Charanne Final Award* (2016); *RREEF Infrastructure* (2016); *Isolux Award* (2016); *WNC Award* (2017); *Anglia Auto Accessories Final Award* (2017); *US Steel v Slovakia* (2013); and *Saluka* (2006).

[8] By publishing the Communication, Protection of intra-EU investment: EC (2018). See also the Intra-EU BIT Termination Agreement.

international agreements, to prevent similar situations from arising in other settings (Chaps. 4 to 6).[9]

8.2.4 *The Autonomy of the EU Legal Order and ISDS*

The EU's *sui generis* legal order investment protection, especially ISDS, also creates serious procedural issues regarding the EU's autonomy and state aid proceedings. The escalation of these issues has been accelerated by the jurisprudence of both international investment tribunals, expanding the scope of investment protection and the CJEU extending the public policy scope of EU law. From the EU's perspective, protecting the right to regulate public policy objectives such as state aid control is essential to the autonomy and legitimacy of the EU (Chap. 5).

EU law is public international hard law, based on treaties (TEU and TFEU) and the Charter.[10] These are integrated and included in the Member States' national legislation and enforceable through national courts as an extension of the EU's organs. The legal instance that has the final word in interpreting EU law under Articles 19 TEU and 267 TFEU is the CJEU, which also protects the autonomy of the EU's legal order and judicial system against intrusive external influences that are incompatible with EU law. The CJEU holds EU law as *lex superior* in relation to the EU's international agreements.[11] The arbitration tribunals hold that the BITs, as *lex specialis,* supersedes EU law. Hence the evaluation of current intra-EU and extra-EU BITs comes with built-in conflict (Chaps. 4 and 5).

ISDS imposes a risk to an erosion of the autonomy of EU law as it enables external courts to decide on the legitimacy of EU law while incapacitating the EU courts from reviewing the external tribunal's decisions for conformity with EU law. However, the legitimacy of EU law, including state aid measures, can only be ascertained under the EU law itself. International investment tribunals' rejection of the CJEU's exclusivity as the final interpreter of EU law and their disregard of state aid procedures, which are a requirement for legitimacy, put these two in the situation where they cannot peacefully coexist (Chaps. 4 and 5). Their efforts to categorise EU law as either international or domestic law have been confusing and inconsistent. Combined with foreign investors increasingly utilising ISDS, the numbers of collisions in areas where the BIT regime and the EU exercise international rules of conflict of laws regarding party autonomy and on the right to regulate have increased (Chaps. 2, 4 and 5).

[9]The EU Member States have signed around 1400 IIAs, of which 190 are intra-EU BITS (EC 2015). The EU has 55 TIPs in force and more under negotiation (UNCTAD 2016). There is also the Energy Charter Treaty, which has been the basis of several intra and extra BIT claims.

[10]These constitute the EU's primary legislation.

[11]See *Case 6-64 – Costa v ENEL* (1964); *Opinion 2/94* (1996); *Joined Cases c-402/05 p and c-415/05 p Kadi* (2008); *Opinion 2/13 of the Court (Full Court)* (2014); *Achmea C-284/16* (2018); and *Opinion 1/17* (2019).

Intra-EU ISDS is particularly harmful to the EU's autonomy according to the CJEU. The CJEU arrived at this conclusion by a joint reading of Articles 267 TFEU, Article 344 TFEU and Article 19.1(2) TEU in *Achmea C-284/16.* Intra-EU ISDS also erodes general principles of EU law, such as the principles of effectiveness and mutual trust. In principle, the CJEU's rejection of it in *Achmea C-284/16* should have ended ISDS in intra-EU settings; however, this did not happen. Indeed, many intra-EU BIT ISDS proceeding, particularly under the ECT, are still ongoing and several arbitrators have adopted an extremely narrow reading of the very broad wording on the CJEU's ruling in *Achmea* (Chap. 5).[12]

After this ruling, the Member States denounced their intra-EU BITs.[13] According to EU law, arbitral tribunals are without jurisdiction to entertain foreign investors' claims in intra-EU BIT arbitration. Subsequently, any awards from investment tribunals, deriving from claims related to EU law within the EU, can no longer be legally enforced within the EU. The Declaration of the Member States on the legal consequences of *Achmea*, however, enables some exceptions to this situation. Accordingly, ongoing intra-EU BITs disputes 'that can no longer be annulled or set aside and were voluntarily complied with[14] or definitively enforced'[15] pre-*Achmea* would remain valid.[16] This situation should also apply to Awards originating from unlawful/incompatible state aid.

By revisiting and reiterating *Opinion 2/13*'s constitutional message in *Achmea,* even the CJEU opened the possibility that this incompatibility between ISDS and EU law may have much wider application. In theory, the *Achmea* judgment could have rendered arbitration clauses in extra-EU BITs and the EU's TIPs inapplicable. However, by *Opinion 1/17* the CJEU redeemed investor-state arbitration for the EU's TIPs on the condition that these covered certain criteria.

Opinion 1/17 built on *Opinion 2/15 of the Court (Full Court)* (2017) and distinguished the notion of the EU's external autonomy. In *Opinion 1/17*, the ECJ clarified that the EU's external autonomy permits international courts that arbitrate international agreements to which the EU is a party under certain conditions[17]—namely, if these tribunals:

[12] For example, by deeming *Achmea* not applicable for ICSID Awards, because it did not specifically address ISDS procedures under the ICSID Convention and the ECT, as it originated from a breach of a BIT instead of the ECT. See *Masdar v. Spain Award* (2018); *Novenergia II v Spain Award* (2018); *Gavrilovic DOO v Croatia Award* (2018) and *Vattenfall II (Decision on the Achmea issue)* (2018). See also Pinsolle and Michou (2018).

[13] FISMA (2019a, b, c).

[14] Hence being imputable by the state (see Sect. 5.6.3 in Chap. 5).

[15] Meaning that these have become *res judicata.*

[16] The Declaration of the Member States on the legal consequences of *Achmea*, para 7.

[17] The ECJ confirmed that the CETA tribunals are not 'part of the judicial system of either of the Parties.' See *Opinion 1/17 (2019)*, para 114.

- are authorised only to interpret and apply the provisions of that distinct international agreement according to international law[18]
- are not able to issue awards that prevent the EU institutions from operating consistent with the EU constitutional framework.[19]

The CJEU found that ICS in CETA fulfilled these conditions. However, ICS in CETA, even though approved by the CJEU as compatible with EU law, is not free of problems. While investment protection has no direct effect and protects the EU from frivolous claims and liability for damages for regulatory changes, the Member States are still left vulnerable to these claims. However, ICS in CETA does protect the Member States implementing EU state aid law from investors' claims.

8.2.5 *Extra EU-BITs and State Aid Law*

The formulation of most extra-EU BITs still in force lack such guarantees as ICS does in CETA and are therefore problematic from an EU perspective. However, these BITs will continue to evolve, corresponding to the fluctuation of the EU's external competences (Chaps. 5 to 7). During their transition to be aligned with EU law or replaced by the EU agreements, investment protection provisions in extra-EU BITs risk Member States becoming liable for disregarding either state aid law or the BIT. Hence, ISDS procedures initiated on the basis of a breach of an extra-EU BIT FET standard, where a Member State aligns its investment incentives to match the EU's state aid policy, are likely to continue to disregard state aid law.

8.3 Original Contribution

The main original contribution of this book to legal science is to provide a single work that examines the interplay of state aid rules and EU investment policy both internally and externally, covering both the EU and global levels. It also provides empirical evidence to identify and show the effect/possible effect that state aid law has had, and will continue to have in the future, on the EU's investment policy in a global context. Specifically, it addresses how the policy of EU state aid practice collaborates with the EU investment regime within the internal market, and from there reflects on the external trade relations of both the Member States and the EU through this practice. So far, contributions by legal authors have only studied and

[18] See *Opinion 1/17 (2019)*, para 118: 'since those Tribunals stand outside the EU judicial system, they cannot have the power to interpret or apply provisions of EU law other than those of the CETA or to make awards that might have the effect of preventing the EU institutions from operating in accordance with the EU constitutional framework.'

[19] *Opinion 1/17 (2019)*, paras 106–161.

discussed these aspects separately. Further, this monograph discusses other aspects that have received little attention from legal academia. It elaborates on the interlinkage of subsidies policy, trade and international investment policy jointly on a global level and provides a comparison of how this interlinkage functions and is governed by the EU's legal framework. Finally, the book discusses the extraterritoriality of state aid policy and of state aid more broadly.

Balancing investor protection with the right to regulate has been much debated in recent years. In the EU, this topic has been particularly relevant regarding state aid law. Subsidies/state aids in for of investment incentives are a built-in feature of investment policy. EU state aid law, which enjoys public policy status, regulates and restricts the Member States from granting investment incentives in order to preserve fair competition within the internal market. This defence mechanism is applied broadly and catches even non-EU investors that operate within the internal market through different corporate arrangements. This type of interlinkage is unique to the EU as other jurisdictions do not regulate investment incentives in a similar manner. Uneven management of state aid norms internationally is therefore a significant dilemma for international investors operating within the EU, states, supranational organisations and national and international courts and arbitration tribunals. Yet the interlinkage of subsidies policy, trade and international investment policy jointly on a global level have received little attention from legal academia. Therefore, this book contributes to widening the understanding in this area by elaborating on this interlinkage and provides a comparison of how this interlinkage functions and is governed by the EU's legal framework.

Further, the EU has developed an extensive extraterritorial state aid policy which has had a significant role in shaping its investment regime. This book discusses the extraterritoriality of state aid policy and of state aid broadly. It reveals a rich extraterritorial dimension that has been under-researched in legal literature due to its focus on the internal market. To protect state aid policy in the internal market from erosion of external distortions and actors, the export of state aid has taken place in diverse forms. This extraterritorial dimension encompasses the development of multilateral international cooperation on subsidies regulation, the development of international competition norms and on the bilateral plain—through the EU's accession, associate, economic partnership and FTAs.

After the Lisbon Treaty added FDI to the EU's Common Commercial Policy, international investment agreements also fell within the scope of EU law, with the consequence that these agreements had to be compatible with EU primary law. Explicitly, from then on, all international agreements entered by the EU, its Member States or both, including investment incentives, had to comply with state aid provisions of TFEU. Yet there is no single substantial legal scholarly work that covers the interplay of state aid rules and EU investment policy both internally and externally, covering both the EU and global levels. So far, contributions by legal authors have only studied and discussed these aspects separately. Therefore, the main original contribution of this book to legal science is to fill this gap in the existing literature.

It has done so by using a doctrinal analysis—namely by studying, discussing and analysing the impact of EU state aid law on the EU Member States' BITs and EU Trade Agreements through the different forms in which EU state aid law appears. These are dependent on the EU investment policy aspect utilised as a platform for analysis, from the global dimension of economic partnership agreements, FTAs and EU bilateral treaties with third countries, to extra-EU BITs and the internal market intra-EU BITs.

As the struggle between the EU law and IIL, particularly State aid law and investment protection has played out in Courts and on the political plane (trough trade negotiations and reforms of international agreements governing investment protection) this monograph elaborates on 'who gets to decide on state aid policy now and in the future'. Will it be the EU that sets the borders and the status of State aid law and policy law regarding investment protection or shall the international investment tribunals dominate this matter by their legal practice? Hence, this book offers a glimpse of a conceivable future of EU investment policy in a global context. The relevance of this book's central research question, 'How is the European Union (EU) state aid law affecting the future of EU investment policy in a global context?' is demonstrated by the findings of this book.

An analysis of the relevant literature, and observation of recent policy changes on its subject matter, as reflected in the Commission's policy documents, the EU's international agreements and declarations by the Member States, shows that this effect has occurred in many ways. The intra-EU BITs are about to become extinct. The EU has also learned from conflicts of investment protection and state aid regarding intra-EU BITs and applied these lessons learned on a global scale. By incorporating fair competition and state aid policy in international trade the EU is reasserting that it is the EU that decides on State aid law and policy law regarding investment protection. Thus, state aid law affects and will continue to affect the future of EU investment policy in a global context.

8.4 The Purpose and Statements of This Monograph

The purpose of this book was to investigate how the EU's state aid law affects the EU's investment policy globally and how these rules, when in conflict with other public international law, may reverberate from EU internal to EU external relations. Indeed, this book has argued that EU state aid law is affecting the future of EU investment policy in a global context.[20] This is occurring in three ways, discussed below.

---

[20] See Sect. 1.4 in Chap. 1.

8.4.1 The First Argument: Incorporation of State Aid Clauses in Trade Agreements

This book has argued that EU state aid law is affecting the future of EU investment policy via the EU's incorporation of clauses promoting state aid policy in international trade agreements, hence ensuring that these agreements in general, and investment chapters in particular, will not conflict with EU competition law. This precautionary action is a necessary component of ensuring that EU bodies are not in direct violation of EU primary law, of which state aid law is an integral part when they apply, practise and enforce EU state aid policy. Hence EU investment policy must be consistent with the primary law of the EU;[21] otherwise:

- the autonomy of the EU would be destabilised[22]
- the Commission's ability to govern would be compromised (regarding the prevention of discrimination between firms within the internal market and when implementing policy objectives in line with changing EU policy priorities)
- the CJEU's ability to utilise state aid law as a tool for internal market integration would also be compromised.

8.4.2 The Second Argument: Ending Intra-EU BITs

This book argued that intra-EU BITs (apart from not being compatible with Articles 344 and 267 TFEU) are inherently discriminatory and hence must be terminated. This termination took place in May 2020.[23] However, the CJEU's *Achmea* decision nullifying ISDS provisions in intra-EU BITs[24] was not about state aid law, nor did the CJEU engage in discussion about whether the intra-EU BITs are inherently discriminatory.

Until all intra-EU dispute resolution is aligned with EU law arbitration, tribunals can continue to disrespect EU state aid law, and some foreign investors will continue to receive favourable treatment over other investors in the internal market.[25] Therefore, as can be seen in *Micula*,[26] substantial legal issues regarding state aid remain unsolved. An intra-EU BIT should not legally distort competition on the internal

[21] *Case 6-64 – Costa v ENEL* (1964). See also *Opinion 2/13 of the Court (Full Court)* (2014).

[22] *Achmea C-284/16* (2018); *Opinion 2/13 of the Court (Full Court)* (2014).

[23] By 23 Member States signing the intra-EU BIT Termination Agreement. The Member States that did not sign and had intra-EU BITs in force are doing it bilaterally or are under infringement procedures.

[24] The Declaration of the Member States on the legal consequences of *Achmea*, p. 1.

[25] For example, by enabling foreign investors to successfully initiate ISDS to reclaim investment incentives such as tax breaks granted in breach of state aid rules to foreign investors.

[26] *Micula Award* (2013).

market, hence any existing and new dispute-resolution mechanism protecting cross-border intra-EU investments must ensure that these cannot ignore EU state aid law.[27] In that way, disputes such as the *Micula* proceeding,[28] used as a case study for this book, will no longer emerge to create tension and conflict within the EU's legal order.

8.4.3 *The Third Argument: Replacing Extra-EU BITs with EU FTAs*

The Lisbon Treaty extended the EU's CCP to include investment treaties in 2009. Therefore, this book argued that from an EU law perspective there should not exist any intra-EU BITs nor any extra-EU BITs, leaving this area within the scope of EU investment treaties concluded between the EU and third states.

However, currently many extra-EU BITs remain in force, potentially causing *Micula*-type cases that conflict with state aid law.[29] Therefore, the existing extra-EU BITs should be replaced with the EU's trade agreements, which align with EU legislation, prioritising extra-EU BITs that do not have provisions for competition policy and state aid as a counterbalance to investment protection. Other extra-EU BITs must be altered promptly to include provisions that transfer traditional ISDS to ICS, as in CETA and the new Dutch BIT.

8.5 Main Findings

This monograph has demonstrated that the three arguments it has put forward have legal standing. A conflict situation that originated from legal conflicts within the EU has found expression on a global scale. This effect is observable in the formulation of trade agreements to which the EU is a party and has activated the EU to take the initiative to propose and support a revamping of several international conventions that relate to international investment agreements.

After studying EU state aid law and the case law of the CJEU and the international investment tribunals, this book has illustrated why and how the EU 'project' is and can be affected negatively by IIAs. Indeed, the EU is not immune to external influence that challenges its very foundations, legitimacy and autonomy, as well as

[27] See the Declaration of the Member States on the legal consequences of *Achmea*, p. 3 for the possible creation of new dispute-resolution mechanism for the protection of cross-border intra-EU investments.

[28] *Micula Award* (2013).

[29] On the subject of the primacy of legal sources and jurisdictions, CJEU/national courts/arbitration tribunals.

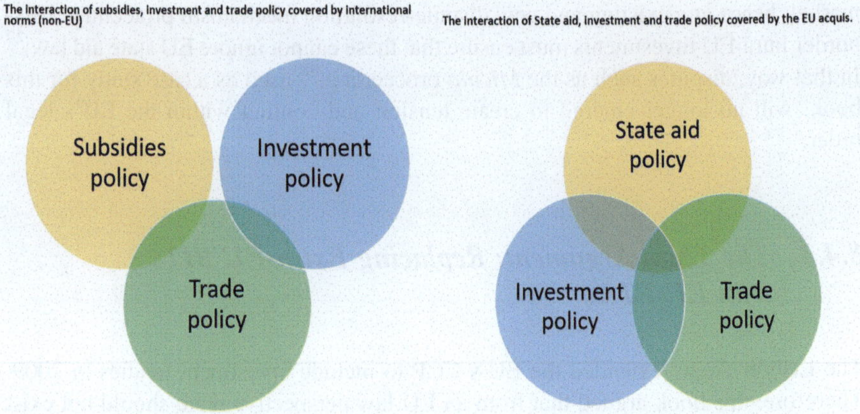

Fig. 8.1 How global international norms on subsidies, investment and trade differ from the EU acquis

disrupting the evolution of the internal market. Therefore, while global trade and investment policy are interlinked with subsidies policies, the correlation and coverage of international norms (other than that of the EU) differ from those of the EU, as can be seen in Fig. 8.1. Hence, state aid policy, the EU's investment policy and trade must overlap within the internal market as compelled by EU's *acquis communautaire*'s influence on EU's external dimension, which is governed by its CCP.

Further, while state aid policy, FDI and the regime of IIL share economic objectives and support the notion of free global trade and trading, at the same time these notions collide because state aid policy also strives for European integration and upholding European governance.[30]

ISDS obstructs the Commission's and the CJEU's work towards these goals because the regime of IIL focuses on guaranteeing foreign investors' rights from regulatory changes. Given that state aid law and investment protection both regulate investment incentives, but from an opposing perspective, these easily collide.[31] Namely, state aid law restricts the granting of investment incentives while the international investment regime endorses them.

Moreover, ISDS also undermines the autonomy of the EU legal order, which carries the risk of weakening the legitimacy of the EU and the authority of its bodies. Because intra-EU ISDS is particularly harmful to the EU's legal order, the intra-EU BITs, which are discriminatory and in breach of EU law in several aspects, had to

[30] See the second argument of this thesis.

[31] *Micula Award* (2013). This started a lengthy procedure of appeals and cases. See *Micula I (EU)* (2014); *Micula II (EU)* (2014); *Micula III (EU)* (2016); *Micula V (EU)* (2019). See also *Micula I (USA)* (2015a); *Micula I (USA)* (2015b); *Micula III (USA)* (2016).

go.[32] However, many of these disputes are still ongoing, particularly intra-EU claims originating from the ECT. FET clauses combined with ISDS are bound to collide with state aid law and threaten the autonomy of EU law unless investment protection chapters, such as the ICS in CETA, provide enough guarantees that EU law will not be breached. One of these guarantees is that IIAs that the EU or its Member States are part of cannot be used to initiate claims that negate the EU from employing its state aid law.

Empirical observations of the Member States' BITs and the EU's TIPs and investment protection agreements in Appendixes 1 and 2 reveal that state aid policy has a substantial effect on the EU's investment policy. It has even influenced global norms regarding subsidies control. In fact, the scope of the EU's extraterritorial state aid policy is much more extensive than generally recognised by legal authors. This is remarkable, as the exportation of state aid rules has taken place in plain sight. On the other side of the coin, with the relations—both political and social—between business, state and citizens being reflected in competition policy and legislation, it is interesting to notice the huge difference in the application and enforcement of antitrust rules compared with state aid control on a global scale.

The four distinct categories: presented in the introduction of this book—(1) global, (2) the European Neighbourhood Policy, (3) the accession and candidate countries, and (4) the EEA/EFTA model—clearly relate to the type of control applied, the level of its success and the effect on the third country, depending on the specific type of instrument employed. Indeed, the effect of EU state aid law appears much as ripples in a pond, where the distinct inner ripples gradually fade as they move outwards (see Fig. 6.1). Besides state aid control weakening the further the countries are located from the EU, another deciding factor regarding the level of state aid control is the negotiation partners' economic strength.

Some proposals made by this book are shown to have already taken place in practice. The EU's international trade agreements in Appendixes 1 and 2 confirm that these agreements contain:

- elements of competition policy, particularly state aid regulation.
- post-*Micula*, state aid clauses that substantially limit investment protection provisions.

Given that most, if not all, IIAs with investment protection provisions entered into before the Lisbon Treaty by the Member States include elements that are problematic from an EU legal perspective, it will be a massive task to redeem these provisions and neutralise the negative effects caused by ISDS as practised by international investment tribunals. Meanwhile, international investment arbitration will continue its usual business. Until the roots of these issues are dealt with, ISDS will continue to collide with EU law. Therefore, the renegotiating of treaties and convention that

[32] By overriding EU law (on subsidies in the form of investment incentives) where foreign investors are covered by an intra-EU BIT, these investors receive preferential status over other investors that are not covered by these. See the second argument of this thesis.

govern traditional ISDS, so it pays better heed to legitimate public policy objectives such as state aid rules (and several other issues), is crucial. This is particularly urgent for the ECT because the very nature of intra-EU BIT arbitration clashes with the EU's legal autonomy. Also, the extra EU-BITs that have no such provisions taming investment protection should be promptly renegotiated to alter traditional ISDS to ICS, as in CETA or the new Dutch BIT.[33] As from July 2019, the EU has also undertaken the task of revising the ECT. Indeed, the future of international treaties involving the EU is already being applied in the present.

8.6 Conclusions: State Aid to Tame Investment Protection Now and in the Future

The research question put forward by this monograph was, 'How is the European Union (EU) State aid law affecting the future of EU investment policy in a global context?' A short answer is—in several ways. Much has changed in the EU's investment policy over the last five years, and many predictions of the future have become the present. Above all, the EU organs have absorbed the lessons from the EU experience of intra-EU BITs and acted by restructuring all aspects of FDI policy to better align with EU law, particularly in order to contain sufficient elements of state aid regulation to tame investment protection so fair competition and investment protection can peacefully coexist. ICS in CETA, when read together with the CJEU's *Opinion 1/17* and *Achmea*, also aims to assure that the arbitration tribunal cannot ignore these provisions. The CJEU did leave a back door open for it to get involved if a CETA Tribunal were to apply EU law incorrectly in the future.

Moreover, the EU is not only reactive but also proactive in its dealings with the issues caused to the EU's legal system by investment protection and ISDS. Because the regulatory exportation of the EU core values interacts with the norms governing globalisation in the ever-expanding network of global/international law, the EU is actively working towards enhanced multilateral control of subsidies as well as modernising international investment law towards more transparency and improved respect of public policy objectives. The EU's internal market is not immune to the influence of international investment relations and law, and nor are these immune to the EU's internal policy.

Hence the state aid policy also affects non-EU countries indirectly. When countries agree on common norms, as a spillover effect, internal measures are adopted to maintain those norms. Thus, state aid and subsidies may indirectly find their way to national courts. Also, as a considerable economic power, the EU can pressure other nations to align their domestic laws even when outside the scope of a free or preferential trade agreement.

[33] See the third thesis argument.

This book maintains that the instruments of the EU's extraterritorial state aid policy can be used to tame investment protection. This 'taming process' emerges in different forms depending on what type of legal instrument is employed to implement it, as the impact of the EU's law depends on the type of control applied, the level of success and the effect on the third country. In a broad sense, state aid is a tool for European governance (internal and external) to align its own, its Member States and even its trading partners' investment policy in such a manner that the autonomy of the EU legal order and the right to regulate on public policy objectives are protected and unnecessary future jurisdictional conflicts may be avoided.

This book finds that state aid provision in the EU's trade instruments acts both as a sword and a shield for IIAs. Including self-standing state aid provisions in these agreements guarantees that, in general, they are in line with EU law. Besides the obvious—the protection of European enterprises from disadvantages in global competition compared to third-country firms which may benefit from state aid—these provisions also protect competition from 'unfair foreign subsidies' within the internal market (the shield) and they may also act as a vessel for regulatory export (the sword). As some trade agreements require the implementation of state aid into national laws, the ability of enterprises to acquire investment through subsidies is substantially reduced, in due course aligning the investment policy of these countries to be compatible with EU state aid laws. State aid provisions also act as a shield when these are incorporated in investment protection clauses in such a way that substantially reduces investors' ability to invoke claims on the grounds of breach investment protection.

In this way state aid, as it is or *mutatis mutandis*, will keep on changing as a form of Europeanising of values, laws or at least behaviour of third countries. As Sands put it, 'the ends of judicialization here essentially become a story of survival, a tale of one institution protecting itself from the activity of another'.[34] Indeed, the transformation of ISDS to ICS in EU investment policy, accentuated by state aid policy, seems to be certain.

8.7 Future Challenges

While the adoption of ICS, as in CETA, with state aid provisions does fix many issues relating to investment protection and state aid law, some future challenges remain. This monograph identifies the following, and calls for further research on:

- reducing/negating the current and forthcoming legal disputes on IIAs v state aid law eroding the EU's public policy of governance[35]

[34] Charlotin (2018).

[35] Analogically FISMA (2019b), p. 3, paras 1–4.

- adopting the unilateral rules proposed by the commissions Draft Regulation on foreign subsidies to control foreign subsidies in form of capital flows that distort the competition within the internal market and may lead to ISDS under existing IIAs
- improving the coordination and preplanning by the EU and the Member States to negate future treaty collisions of investment protection and state aid law in any setting.[36] This includes ensuring that the extra-EU BITs do not collide with EU law and modernising the ECT to ensure that it does not apply to intra-EU disputes. The current and future accession agreements must also be amended to include the termination of the BITs at either accession or at ratification.
- after the traditional intra-EU ISDS is gone, ensuring that investors in the EU receive fair and equal treatment in every Member State[37]
- hindering the multinational corporations and arbitration industry from continuing practices in breach of EU law by proceedings and enforcement of Awards taking place in courts outside the EU.[38]

Indeed, the EU has adopted several approaches to solving these issues and will continue to do so. On a purely judicial plane, the CJEU's jurisprudence is refining the EU's legal hold on the relationship between IIA's and EU law. Also, as *amicus curiae*, the Commission is involving itself in judicial proceedings that take place outside the EU's judicial system to convince the deciding courts to pay heed to EU law. Depending on the degree of success of these attempts, the EU could, after the Intra-EU BIT Termination Agreement, issue internal rules to block the international enforceability of intra-EU BITs.[39]

From a political perspective, the EU is attempting to solve these issues through bilateral trade negotiations and by driving multilateral initiatives to modernise relevant international instruments, such as the WTO rules, and international enforcement rules, such as those administered by ICSID and UNICTRAL. Since several nations have already raised concerns about ISDS, the later approach in particular has been met with positive reactions from both nations and IGOs such as UNICTRAL. However, the lessons of the past show that multilateral action on a global scale is hard to achieve and can be a very slow process. Meanwhile, the EU may use its economic power to convince third countries to reject the enforcement of Awards based on intra-EU BITs. Because the more radical approaches, such as the adoption of internal rules with extraterritorial reach and utilising economic power, may not be well received by third countries, it remains important for the EU to find a balanced approach where other nations feel that they reciprocally gain from these policies. In this way, good international relations can be preserved.

[36] Analogically, FISMA (2019b), p. 3, paras 1 and 2.

[37] Analogically, *DG (FISMA)* (2019b) p. 4 para 6. This was also the motive behind (AFFGN 2016).

[38] Analogically, *DG (FISMA)* (2019b) p. 3 para 2.

[39] See Sect. 5.7 in Chap. 5.

Cases

Electricite de France (EDF) International S.A. v Republic of Hungary (PCA (Permanent Court of Arbitration), 2014)

Accession by the Communities to the Convention for the Protection of Human Rights and Fundamental Freedoms, Opinion 2/94, ECLI:EU:C:1996:140 (European Court of Justice, 1996)

Achmea B.V. (formerly known as Eureko B.V.) v Slovak Republic Final Award, PCA Case No 2008-13) (UNCITRAL, 2012).

Achmea B.V. (formerly known as Eureko B.V.) v Slovak Republic Award on Jurisdiction, Arbitrability and Suspension PCA Case No 2008-13 (Permanent Court of Arbitration, 2008)

Anglia Auto Accessories Limited v Czech Republic Final Award, SCC Case V 2014/181 (Stockholm Chamber of Commerce, 2017)

Charanne B.V. and Construction Investments S.à.r.l. v Kingdom of Spain Final Award, SCC Case No. 062/2012 (Stockholm Chamber of Commerce, 2016)

Eastern Sugar B.V. (Netherlands) v The Czech Republic, SCC Case No. 088/2004 – Final Award (UNCITRAL ad hoc arbitration tribunal, 2007)

Eastern Sugar B.V. (Netherlands) v. The Czech Republic, Partial Award SCC Case No. 088/2004 – Partial award, Italaw (Stockholm Chamber of Commerce, 2007)

Eco Swiss China Time Ltd v Benetton International NV, case C-126/97, ECLI:EU: C:1999:269 (European Court of Justice, 1999)

Electrabel S.A. v Hungary Award, ICSID Case No ARB/07/19 (International Centre for Settlement of Investment Disputes, 2015)

Electrabel S.A. v The Republic of Hungary Decision on Jurisdiction, Applicable Law and Liability, ICSID Case No. ARB/07/19 Italaw (ICSID, 2012)

Eureko B.V. v The Slovak Republic, Award on Jurisdiction, Arbitrability and Suspension, PCA Case No. 2008-13, Italaw (Permanent Court of Arbitration, 2010)

Flaminio Costa v E.N.E.L, case 6-64 No. 61964J0006, ECLI:EU:C:1964:66, Eurlex (European Court of Justice (ECJ), 1964)

Georg Gavrilovic and Gavrilovic d.o.o. v Republic of Croatia Award ICSID Case No. ARB/12/39 (ICSID, 2018)

Giuseppe Atzeni and Others (C-346/03), Marco Scalas and Renato Lilliu (C-529/03) v Regione autonoma della Sardegna, joined cases C-346/03 and C-529/03, No. ECLI:EU:C:2006:130 (European Court of Justice, 2006)

Ioan Micula, Viorel Micula, S.C. European Food S.A, S.C. Starmill S.R.L. and S.C. Multipack S.R.L. v Romania, No. WL 4643180, at *1 No. 15 MISC. 107, 2015 (Southern District of New York, 2015)

Ioan Micula, Viorel Micula, S.C. European Food S.A, S.C. Starmill S.R.L. and S.C. Multipack S.R.L. v Romania, ICSID Award, Case No. ARB/05/20, Italaw (ICSID ad hoc, 2013)

Ioan Micula, Viorel Micula, S.C. European Food S.A, S.C. Starmill S.R.L. and S.C. Multipack S.R.L. v Romania, Brief for Amicus Curiae the Commission of the European Union in Support of Defendant-Appellant before the US Court of Appeals, No. 15-3109-cv (United States Court of Appeals Second Circuit, 2016)

Isolux Infrastructure Netherlands B.V. v Kingdom of Spain Award, SCC Case V 2013/153 (Stockholm Chamber of Commerce, 2016)

Jan Oostergetel & Theodora Laurentius v Slovak Republic Decision on Jurisdiction (UNCITRAL ad hoc, 2010)

Joined cases C-402/05 P & C-415/05 P Yassin Abdullah Kadi v Council and Commission of the European Communities, ECLI:EU:C:2008:11 (AG opinion Poiares Maduro, 2008)

Masdar Solar & Wind Cooperatief U.A. v Kingdom of Spain Award, ICSID Case No. ARB/14/1 (ad hoc, 2018)

Micula v Commission, case T-694/15 (Court of Justice of the European Union, 2019)

Micula v Romania, 2014/NN, SA.38517 (Commission DG Comp, 2014).

Micula and Others v Commission, case T-646/14, No. ECLI:EU:T:2016:135, OJ C 136 Removal from the register (Court of Justice of the European Union (GC), 2016)

Novenergia II – Energy & Environment (SCA) SICAR v Spain, Award, SCC Case No. 063/2015 (Stockholm Chamber of Commerce, 2018)

Opinion 1/17 of the Court (Full Court), ECLI:EU:C:2019:341 (European Court of Justice (Full Court), 2019)

Opinion 2/13 of the Court (Full Court), ECLI:EU:C:2014:2454, Opinion 2/13 (European Court of Justice (Full Court), 2014)

RREEF Infrastructure (G.P.) Limited and RREEF Pan-European Infrastructure Two Lux S.à.r.l. v Kingdom of Spain Decision on Jurisdiction, ICSID Case No ARB/13/30 (ICSID, 2016)

Rupert Joseph Binder v Czech Republic Award on Jurisdiction of 6 June 2007 (UNCITRAL ad hoc, 2007)

Saluka Investments B.V v. The Czech Republic partial Award (Permanent Court of Arbitration (PCA), 2006)

Slowakische Republik (Slovak Republic) v Achmea BV Case C-284/16, ECLI:EU:C:2018:158 (European Court of Justice (Grand Chamber), 2018)

State Aid SA.38517(2014/C) Romania Implementation of Arbitral award Micula v Romania of 11 December 2013, No. (ex 2014/NN), C(2014) 6848 final, Italaw (European Commission, 2014)

T-Mobile Netherlands BV v. Raad van beestuur van de Nederlandse Mededingingsautoriteit, ECLI:EU:C:2009:343 (European Court of Justice, 2009)

US Steel Global Holdings IBV v The Slovak Republic, PCA Case No. 2013-6 (Permanent Court of Arbitration, 2013)

Vattenfall AB; Vattenfall GMBH; Vattenfall Europe Nuclear Energy GMBH; Kernkraftwerk Krummel GMBH & CO. OHG; Kernkraftwerk Brunsbuttel GMBH & CO. OHG v Federal Republic of Germany (Decision on the Achmea Iissue), No. ICSID Case No. ARB/12/12 (ICSID ad hoc, 2018)

Vincenzo Manfredi v Lloyd Adriatico Assicurazioni SpA (C-295/04), Antonio Cannito v Fondiaria Sai SpA (C-296/04) and Nicolò Tricarico (C-297/04) and

Pasqualina Murgolo (C-298/04) v Assitalia SpA, ECLI:EU:C:2006:461 (European Court of Justice, 2006)
Viorel Micula v Goverment of Romania Memorandum opinion (2015)
WNC Factoring Ltd v Czech Republic Award PCA Case No 2014-34 (Permanent Court of Arbitration, 2017)

References

AFFGN (2016) Intra-EU investment treaties - non-paper Austria, Finland, France, Germany and the Netherlands. Retrieved from http://www.s2bnetwork.org/wp-content/uploads/2016/05/Intra-EU-Bits2-18-05.pdf

Charlotin D (2018) With an apparent eye on set-aside, Spain unsuccessfully asks Novenergia tribunal for clarification on ECT–EU law relationship. https://www.iareporter.com/articles/with-an-apparent-eye-on-set-aside-spain-unsuccessfully-asks-novenergia-tribunal-for-clarification-on-ect-eu-law-relationship

Eckes C (2016) International rulings and the EU legal order: autonomy as legitimacy? CLEER PAPERS 2016(2):1–31

European Commission (2018) WTO – EU concept paper on WTO Reform, Brussels, 18 September 2018, accessed from: http://trade.ec.europa.eu/doclib/docs/2018/september/tradoc_157331.pdf

European Commission (EC) (2015) Provisions on international relations in EU competition policy. http://ec.europa.eu/competition/international/legislation/legislation.html

European Commission (EC) (2018) WTO modernisation – introduction to further EU proposals. https://www.wita.org/atp-research/eu-concept-paper-on-wto-reform

FISMA (2019a) Declaration of the representative of the Goverment of Hungary of 16 January 2019 on the legal consequences of the judgment of the Court of Justice in Achmea and on investment protection in the European Union. European Union, Brussels

FISMA (2019b) Declaration of the representative of the goverments of the Member States of 15 January 2019 on the legal consequences of the judgment of the Court of Justice in Achmea and on investment protection in the European Union. European Union, Brussels

FISMA (2019c) Declaration of the representative of the governments of the Member States of 16 January 2019 on the legal consequences of the judgment of the Court of Justice in Achmea and on investment protection in the European Union: The representatives of Goverments of Finland, Luxembourgh, Malta, Slovenia and Sweden. European Union, Brussels

Gallo D, Nicola FG (2015) The external dimension of EU investment law: jurisdictional clashes and transformative adjudication. Fordham Int Law J 39:1081–1152

Kleinheisterkamp J (2014) Who is afraid of investor-state arbitration? Or comparative law? LSE Law: Policy Briefing Paper No. 4. https://ssrn.com/abstract=2483775

Kleinheisterkamp J (2015) Investment treaty law and the fear for sovereignty: transnational challenges and solutions. Mod Law Rev 78(5):793–782

Pinsolle P, Michou I (2018) The Achmea v Slovakia judgment of the CJEU: is it really the end of intra-EU investment treaties? Two leading arbitration practitioners say not necessarily. https://www.quinnemanuel.com/the-firm/news-events/the-achmea-v-slovakia-judgment-of-the-cjeu-is-it-really-the-end-of-intra-eu-investment-treaties

United Nations Conference on Trade and Development (2016) International Investment Agreements Navigator. http://investmentpolicyhub.unctad.org/IIA

Appendix A. The EU's BITs, TIPs and IPAs with Countries (State of Play, October 2019)[1]

[1]Last update 28.10.2019. All EU's trade agreements are available at European Union Treaties Office, External Relations http://ec.europa.eu/world/agreements/default.home.dohttps://ec.europa.eu/trade/policy/countries-and-regions/negotiations-and-agreements/ and (UNCTAD, 2016a). https://ec.europa.eu/trade/policy/countries-and-regions/negotiations-and-agreements and (UNCTAD, 2016a).

P. Finckenberg-Broman, *Weaponizing EU State Aid Law to Impact the Future of EU Investment Policy in the Global Context*, Studies in European Economic Law and Regulation 23, https://doi.org/10.1007/978-3-031-10108-3

Country	type of agreement	In place or partly in place	pending	being updated or negotiated	IIA	ISDS provisions ISA or ICS	scope	subsidies caluses	scope	notes
Albania (Western Balkans)	Stabilisation and Association Agreement	In force since 2009			Art 91	No		Art 71	Mirrors Art 107 TFEU	Title VI, a two stage implementation of key EU aquis as domestic rules. Required to establish national State aid control corresponding to EU's stage one.
Algeria	Association Agreement (EUROMED)	In force since 01/09/2005			Art 57	No		Art 23	WTO, GATT & SCM Agreement.	
Andorra	Customs Union	In force since 01/01/1991	Negotiations from 2016 to participate in the internal market		Several provisions.					
Armenia(EaP)	Updated Partnership and Cooperation Agreement (CEPA) (signed 24/11/2017)	Provisionally applied since 06/2018			Section H	No		Ch 10 section C	Goods and services. Mutatis mutandis Art 107 TFEU & SCM Agreement.	Transparency & notification obligation + addittional State aid rules .
Australia	Australia Agreement		Negotiations launched 6/2018		Yes, no number yet.	No		Yes, no number yet	Goods and services. Mutatis mutandis SCM Agreement ++. Agricultural goods exempted.	Services of general economic interest, enchanced transparancy.
Azerbaijan (EaP)	Partnership and Cooperation Agreement	In force since 1999	Modernisation negotiations from 11/2017		Arts 48-60	Arts 89 & 92.		A general competition provision in Art 43.		Azerbaijan is not a WTO member

Country	type of agreement	in place or partly in place	pending	being updated or negotiated	IIA	ISDS provisions ISA or ICS	scope	subsidies caluses	scope	notes
Bosnia and Herzegovina (Western Balkans)	Stabilisation and Association Agreement	In force since 01/06/2015			Art 91	No		Title VI	Mirrors Art 107 TFEU. Title VI, a two stage implementation of key EU aquis as domestic rules. Competition laws are part of stage one.	Notification obligation. Law on state Aid System in Bosnia and Herzegovina has not been implemented yet even though antitrust laws are implemented and enforced dnationally.
Cameroon (Central Africa)	Interim Economic Partnership Agreement	Provisionally applied since 2014			Several provisions .	No		Art 24	WTO, Agriculture export subsidies.	Restricted to prohibition of export subsidies. Art 57 agrees to futher development of competition provisions for the FTA and locally in Central Africa.
Canada	Comprehensive Economic and Trade Agreement (CETA)	Signed 30 October 2016, provisionally applied since 21/09/2017			CH.8	Section D, ICS	Section D Art 8.9 clarifies that a partys decision not to issue,new or maintain a subsidy does not amount as a breach of investment protection. See also Art 3.3. subsidies	Ch.7	WTO,GATT and SCM Agreement. Enforces prohibition of agriculture export subsidies	Notification obligation for goods and services,consultations between parties on subsidies with adverse effect.
Chile	Association Agreement and Additional Protocol	In force since 01/03/2005	Modernisation negotiations started 11/2017		Art.21. text proposal Chapter II section Aincludes an IIA.	text proposal includes ICS	Section B Art 2.9 clarifies that a partys decision not to issue,new or maintain a subsidy does not amount as a breach of investment protection. See also subsidies chapter.	Art. 78. The proposed new texts (by the EU) cover both goods and services. Mutatis mutandis SCM Agreement ++.		Vaguely formulated, only reinforcing existing WTO rules.
China	EU-China investment agreement		Negotiations started 21/11/2013							

Country	type of agreement	in place or partly in place	pending	being updated or	IIA	ISDS provisions ISA or ICS	scope	subsidies caluses	scope	notes
Colombia, Ecuador and Peru	Trade Agreement	Signed 26/07/2012, provisionally applied since			Art 116	No		Art 293	Goods only. WTO, GATT and SCM Agreement.	Notification obligation
Côte d'Ivoire	Economic Partnership Agreement	signed 26/11/2008, provisionally applied since 03/09/2016			Several provisions.	No		Confirms WTO rules on competition and subsidies.		Section III, paragraph 4(c), of the WAEMU Treaty has regional supranational State aid rules rules.
Cuba	Political Dialogue and Cooperation Agreement	Provisionally applied since 1/11/2017			Art 80	No		Art 68	Confirms WTO rules on competition and subsidies.	
Egypt (EUROMED)	Association Agreement	In force since 01/06/2004			Art 46	No		Arts 23 & 34	Reinforces WTO, GATT and SCM Agreement during a 5 year transition period to Art 34 .	Art 34 1(iii) Art 107 TFEU but excludes agricultural products. Notification obligation.
Faroe Islands	Agreement	In force since 01/01/1997			No			Art 25(iii)	Mirrors Art 107 TFEU.	Art 29, notification and consultation if needed.
Fiji and Papua New Guinea)	Interim Partnership Agreement	Ratified by Papua New Guinea in May 2011. Not ratified by EU yet.			No			Ch.3, Art 24	EU to phase out export subsidies of agriculture export subsidies (WTO agriculture agreement)	
Georgia (EaP)	Association Agreement	In force since 01/07/2016			Several provisions.			Title IV Ch 10 Art 206	Mutatis mutandis SCM Agreement (covers also services). Notification obligation + enforceable through a dispute settlement	Commitment to implement EUs key aquis as national law. Georgian Law on competition 21.03.2014 No: 2159 from 31 March 2014 Ch III Art 12 mirrors EU State

Country	type of agreement	in place or partly in place	pending	being updated or	IIA	ISDS provisions ISA or ICS	scope	subsidies caluses	scope	notes
Ghana	Stepping stone Economic Partnership Agreement provisionally applied	Provisionally applied since 15/12/2016			Title IV, art 44.	No		Title IV, art 44 corporation on e.g. competito		
Iceland	Economic Area Agreement (EEA) and EFTA	In force since 1994			No. Possibly to be rewiewed in the future (Art 81).	No		Part IV, Ch.2 Art 60	Mirrors Art 107 TFEU	The EFTA surveillance authority & Commission ensure enforcement. Implementation of the full EU State aid law regime, the intreprative methods and earlier case law of the CJEU.
India	Free Trade Agreement		Negotiations started 2007, last round in 2013							
Indonesia	Free Trade Agreement		Negotiations started 01/09/2016							
Irak	Partnership and Cooperation Agreement				Section III	No.		No.		
Israel (EUROMED)	Association Agreement	In force since 01/06/2000			Several provision.	No		Title IV, Ch.3 art 36.1 (iii)	Mirrors Art 107 TFEU. Applicable to measures affecting trace between the EU and Israel.	Title IV, Ch.3 Art 36.3 - a 3 year implementation period of necessary domestic rules. Notification obligation.
Japan	Economic partnership Agreement (JEEPA)		Negotiations concluded 12/2017, awaiting signature. Texts available at http://trade.ec.europa.eu/doclib/press/index.cfm?id=1684.		Several provision.	No		Chapter 12	Goods and services (services restricted to selected areas). Agricultural products and fisheries exempted.	Mutatis mutandis SCM Agreement & Arts 106.3(SGEIs) and 107 TFEU. Notification obligation. Unlimited subsidies are prohibited.
Jordan (EUROMED)	Association Agreement	In force since 01/05/2002			Title V Art 67	No		Title IV, Ch.2 Art 53.1 (c)	Mirrors Art 107 TFEU.	Title IV, Ch.2 Art 53.3- a 5 year implementation period of necessary domestic rules.

Country	type of agreement	in place or partly in place	pending	being updated or negotiated	IIA	ISDS provisions ISA or ICS	scope	subsidies caluses	scope	notes
Macedonia, Former Yugoslav Republic of (Western Balkans)	Stabilisation and Association Agreement	In force since 01/04/2004			Art 24	No		Title VI Art.69.1 (iii). Title VI Art 68 & Art.69.3 competition rules must be adopted within 5 years.	Title VI Art.69.1 (iii) mirrors Art 107 TFEU.	Macedonia adopted the Law on State Aid in April 2003.The Law is fully harmonized with the EU State aid law regime. Enforced by the Macedonian State Aid Commission.
Malaysia	Free Trade Agreement		Negotiations started 10/2010, paused since 04/2012							
Marocco (EUROMED)	Association Agreement	In force since 01/03/2000	Updating to a Deep and Comprehensive Free Trade Area on hold since April 2014		Title V Art 50	No.		Title IV, Ch.2 Art 36.1 (c)	Mirrors Art 107 TFEU.	Title IV, Ch.2 Art 36.3- a 5 year implementation period of necessary domestic rules. Notification obligation.
Mexico	Global Agreement	In force since 01/10/2000	Modernisation of Global Agreement reached in April 2018.		Chapter XX	ICS Chapter XX, Section B	CH 1 Art. 14 clarifies that a partys decision not to issue,new or maintain a subsidy does not amount as a breach of investment protection. Clawback of illegal State aid cannot be base for claims.	Previous agreement none. 2018 Agreement Ch(xx) Section B, Art x.6	All Goods (with the exemption of fish and agriculture products) and services	Mutatis mutandis Arts 107, 106.3 TFEU & SCM Agreement. SGEIs exemtion Art X.7. 4. and transparency and notification obligation Art X.9.
Moldova (EaP)	Association Agreement	In force since 01/07/2016			Several provisions .	No. But will possibly be rewieved in the future (Art 206.2).		Title V CH. 10 section 2	Mirrors the EUs State aid provisions and binds Moldova to the jurisprudence and intrepretative methods of the CJEU.	Arts 340 & 341, commitment to implement State aid legislation as national law and to sufficiently enforce it. Domestic law (Moldovan Competition Law No 183 of 11 July 2012).

Country	type of agreement	in place or partly in place	pending	being updated or negotiated	IIA	ISDS provisions ISA or ICS	scope	subsidies caluses	scope	notes
Republic of Korea	Free Trade Agreement	In force since 01/07/2016			Several provisions .	No		Ch 11, Section B.	Art 11.15 Goods (exeption of agricultural products and fisheries).	A commitment to attempt to cover services in the future. Mutatis mutandis WTO SCM agreement with transparency and notification obligation.
Russia	Partnership and Cooperation Agreement	In force since 01/12/1997			Title VII Art 58	No		Art. 53.2.2	Export subsidies only.	A declaration of readiness to restrict subsidies further after 3 years of the agreements entry into force.
San Marino	Customs Union	In force since 01/04/2002	Negotiations from 2016 to participate in the internal market							
Serbia (Western Balkans)	Stabilisation and Association Agreement	In force since 01/09/2013						y	Mirrors Art 107 TFEU	Title VI, a two stage implementation of key EU aquis as domestic rules. Competition laws are part of stage one. Notification obligation.
Singapore	Free Trade Agreement (EUSFTA)		awaiting signature		Several provisions .	Following the ECJ Opinion 2/15, the EUSFTA was split into a FTA and an IPA.		y		
	Investment protection Agreement		awaiting signature			Ch. 3 ICS	Ch 3, Art 2.2 clarifies that a partys decision not to issue,new or maintain a subsidy does not amount as a breach of investment protection.	y		
South Africa	Trade, Development and Co-operation Agreement (TDCA)								Mirrors Art 107 TFEU	

Country	type of agreement	in place or partly in place	pending	being updated or negotiated	IIA	ISDS provisions ISA or ICS	scope	subsidies caluses	scope	notes
Switzerland (EFTA)	Free Trade Agreement (Bilateral) and Agreement between the European Community and the Swiss Confederation on Air Transport (ATA)	In force since 01/01/1973						Article 23(1)(iii) and ATA Arts 13 &14.	The bilateral FTA mirrors Art 107 TFEU and the ATA mirriors Arts 107-109 TFEU.	subsidies is restricted by a competitive neutrality principle in article 94 of the Federal Constitution & the Federal Act on the Privileges, Immunities and Facilities and the Financial Subsidies granted by Switzerland as a Host State.
Syria (EUROMED)	Cooperation Agreement	In force since 01/07/1977. Currently suspended as regards trade in some areas.	An Association Agreement negotiated in 2004 on hold.		Art 98 + several provisions .	No			The Association Agreement Art 29 was supposed to introduce WTO rules applicable to subsidies to Libya-EU relations.	Syria is not a WTO member.
Thailand	Free Trade Agreement		Negotiations started 01/03/2013, no negotiations scheduled since 2014							
Tunisia (EUROMED)	Association Agreement	In force since 01/03/1998	Updating to a Deep and Comprehensive Free Trade Area ongoing from 10/2013							
Turkey (Accession agreement + EUROMED)	Customs Union	In force since 31/12/1995						yes	Mirrors Art 107 TFEU.	Commitment to implement key EU aquis as national law. Domestic Law No. 6015 on the monitoring and control of State aid from 10/2010 mirrors primary EU State aid law but fails to implement secondary law.

Country	type of agreement	in place or partly in place	pending	being updated or negotiated	IIA	ISDS provisions ISA or ICS	scope	subsidies caluses	scope	notes
Ukraine (EaP)	Deep and Comprehensive Free Trade Agreement Association Agreement	Signed 29/05/2014, provisionally applied since 01/01/2016			Several provisions .			yes	Mirrors Art 107 TFEU. Applicable to measures affecting trace between the EU and Ukraine.	Commitment to implement key EU aquis as national law. Domestic law mirrors EU State aid law.
United States	Transatlantic Trade and Investment Partnership (TTIP)		Negotiations started 2013, paused until further notice 2016							
Vietnam	Free Trade Agreement (EVFTA)		Final text agreed upon 07/2018, expected to enter into force in 2018		Several provisions .	Following the ECJ Opinion 2/15, the EVFTA was split into a FTA and an IPA.		CH.10 Section D	Goods and servies (services restricted to selected areas). Agricultural and fisheries products exempted.	Mutatis mutandis SCM Agreement. Wider in scope. Notification obligation.
	EU-Vietnam Investment Protection Agreement (IPA).						CH 1 Art. 4(t) clarifies that a partys decision not to issue,new or maintain a subsidy does not amount as a breach of investment protection.			

Appendix B. EU's BITs, TIPs and IPAs with Trading Blocs (State of Play in October 2019)

P. Finckenberg-Broman, *Weaponizing EU State Aid Law to Impact the Future of EU Investment Policy in the Global Context*, Studies in European Economic Law and Regulation 23, https://doi.org/10.1007/978-3-031-10108-3

Trading block	Type of agreement	In place or partly in place	Pending, being updated or negotiated	IIA	ISDS provisions ISA or ICS	Scope	Subsidies caluses	Scope
ACP (Djibouti, Eritrea, Ethiopia, Sudan, Zambia) African, Caribbean and Pacific Group of States (the Cotonou Agreement)	Economic Partnership Agreement (amended).		Amendment signed 22/06/2010, not yet applied. The original was signed in 23/06/2000 but not ratified.	Art 75	No		the 1rst and 2nd amendments introduce some subsidies restrictions in Annexes	
ACP Pacific (Fiji and Papua New Guinea)	Interim Partnership Agreement (This agreement is meant to be with a trading block even though is currently only ratified by Papua and the EU.	Ratified by Papua New Guinea in May 2011. Fiji applied to join the agreement in July 2014. Samoa and the Solomon Islands have informed the European Commission of their wish to join the EPA.		No			Ch.3, Art 24	EU to phase out export subsidies of agriculture export subsidies (WTO agriculture agreement)
ANCOM-Andean Community (Bolivia, Colombia, Ecuador, Peru and Venezuela)	Political dialogue and Cooperation Agreement		Signed 15/12/2003, not ratified.	Several provisions.	No.		Art.17 promotion to establish and apply competition policy in the Andean Community.	
ASEAN-Association of South-East Asian Nations	ASEAN-EU Cooperation Agreement	In force since 01/10/1990	Negotiations for a region-to-region FTA with ASEAN were launched in 2007 and paused in 2009 to give way to bilateral FTAs.	Art 3	No.		No	

Trading block	Type of agreement	In place or partly in place	Pending, being updated or negotiated.	IIA	ISDS provisions ISA or ICS.	Scope	Subsidies caluses	Scope	Notes
CAMC - Central America (Costa Rica, El Salvador, Guatemala, Honduras, Nicaragua and Panama)	Association Agreement with a strong trade component	Signed 29/06/2012, provisionally applied since 2013		Several provisions.	No		Part IV, Title II Section D	WTO, GATT &SCM Agreement + restricted to prohibition of agriculture export subsidies.	Art 344 notification obligation for goods and services. Consultations between parties on subsidies with adverse effect.
Central Africa (Cameroon, Central African Republic, Chad, Congo (Brazzaville), Congo - Democratic Republic of (Kinshasa), Equatorial Guinea, Gabon, São Tomé & Principe).	Economic Partnership Agreement	Provisionally applied since 2014 for Cameroon only.		No			Art 24	WTO, Agriculture export subsidies.	Restricted to prohibition of export subsidies. Art 57 agrees to futher development of competition provisions for the FTA and locally in Central Africa.
CARIFORUM (Antigua, Barbuda, Bahamas, Barbados, Belize, Dominica, Dominican Republic, Grenada, Guyana, Jamaica, St Kitts and Nevis, St Lucia, St Vincent and the Grenadines, Suriname, Trinidad and Tobago + Haiti)	Economic Partnership Agreement	Provisionally applied since 2008 with the exeption of Haiti	With Haiti.	Title II	No		Arts 28 & 97	WTO,GATT and SCM Agreement. Restricted to prohibition of agriculture export subsidies and cross subsidation.	Export subsidies only.
Colombia, Ecuador and Peru	Trade Agreement	Signed 26/07/2012, provisionally applied since 2013		Art 116	No		Art 293	Goods only. WTO, GATT and SCM Agreement.	Notification obligation

Trading block	Type of agreement	In place or partly in place	Pending, being updated or negotiated.	IIA	ISDS provisions ISA or ICS.	Scope	Subsidies caluses	Scope	Notes
EAC- East African Community (Burundi, Kenya, Rwanda, Tanzania, South Sudan and Uganda)	Economic Partnership Agreement		Signed 09/2016 by Kenya and Rwanda. Ratified by Kenya. Awaiting signature and ratification of others	to conclude negotiotai ons on investmen t developm ent within 5 years of entry into force & Art	No		Art 68 restring EUs agricultural exports only.	Part I Art 3 - to conclude negotiations on Competition policy within a 5 years timeline.	
ECOWAS- Economic Community of West African States (Benin, Burkina Faso, Cabo Verde, Gambia, Ghana *, Guinea, guinea Bissau, Liberia, Mali, Niger, Nigeria, Senegal, Sierra Leone, Togo)			Negotiations concluded 06/2014. Not signed yet by Gambia, Nigeria and Mauritania. Not ratified yet.	No	No				Art 106 agreement to continue negotiations on competition policy.
The European Economic Area(EEA) Iceland, Norway and Lichtenstein	Economic Area Agreement (EEA) and EFTA	In force since 01/01/1994		No. But will possibly be rewieved in the future (Art 81).	No		Part IV, Ch.2 Art 60	Mirrors Art 107 TFEU.	The EFTA surveillance authority & Commission ensure enforcement. Implementation of the full EU State aid law regime, the intreprative methods and earlier case law of the CJEU.

Trading block	Type of agreement	In place or partly in place	Pending, being updated or negotiated.	IIA	ISDS provisions ISA or ICS.	Scope	Subsidies caluses	Scope	Notes
EFTA (Iceland, Norway, Lichtenstein and Swizerland)		In force since 01/01/1994		No			Part IV, Ch. 2	Mirrors the EU State aid law regime.	The EFTA surveillance authority & Commission ensure enforcement. Implementation of the full EU State aid law regime, the intreprative methods and earlier case law of the CJEU.
ESA- Eastern and Southern Africa (Comoros, Madagascar, Mauritius, the Seychelles and Zimbabwe)	Economic Partnership Agreement	Signed 08/2009 (Comoros 07/ 2017), provisionally applied since 14 May 2012.		Title II, Art 40	No		No		Art 53 agreement to continue negotiations on competition policy.
Mercosur (Argentina, Brazil, Paraguay and Uruguay)	Mercosur Association Agreement		Text in principle finalised on 28 June 2019.				yes	Confirms WTO rules but does not restrict to goods only. Instead aimed at subsidies that distort competition.	
Gulf Cooperation Counci (GCC) Bahrain, Oman, Kuwait, Qatar, Saudi Arabia, United Arab Emirates.	Cooperation Agreement		Negotiations for a Free Trade Agreement started 1990, but suspended since 2008.	Art 7	No		No		
SADC (Botswana, Swaziland, Mozambique, Namibia, Lesotho and South Africa)	Economic Partnership Agreement	In force since 05/02/2018		Ch. IX Art 74	No		Ch. VII Art 68	Export subsidies only.	

Appendix C. *Micula* Case Timeline

1993
Signing of the Agreement for Romania's Association to the European Union (European Agreement)
1995
February Coming in force of the EU Association Agreement (European Agreement). Article 64. 1.(iii) of these agreements prohibits state aid. Articles 69 and 71 of the EA obliged Romania to align its domestic legislation with the EU *acquis*.
June Romania presents the official application for EU membership
1998
October Romania enacts Emergency Government Ordinance 24/1998 (EGO 24)
1999
April • EGO 24, which provides a subsidies scheme for disfavoured regions in Romania, becomes effective. This law is meant to be in place for 10 years. • As required by the European Agreement, EU State aid rules are implemented into the Romanian legal framework by the Statutory Act No. 143/1999 as part of the harmonisation process necessary for acceding countries.
December The European Council decides to open accession negotiations with Romania
2000
January Statutory Act No. 143/1999 enters into force.
February Romania begins accession talks to the Union.
May The Romanian Competition authority, by its Decision No 244/2000, declared EGO 24 containing State aid for operating purposes and therefore as *contra legem* to EU law.

(continued)

P. Finckenberg-Broman, *Weaponizing EU State Aid Law to Impact the Future of EU Investment Policy in the Global Context*, Studies in European Economic Law and Regulation 23, https://doi.org/10.1007/978-3-031-10108-3

(continued)

June SC European Food SA obtains a permanent investor certificate which enables it to benefit from EGO 25.
July The Romanian Government amends EGO 24 by the amending act Emergency Government Ordinance 75/2000 ('EGO 75'). This amend disregards the changes necessary, as pointed out by Romanian Competition authority the fails to remove the operative State aid from the scheme, therefore, it remains as *contra legem* to EU law.
2001
January The Romanian Competition Council unsuccessfully challenges EGO 75 as a failure before the Bucharest Court of Appeal—that is, it does not follow the Decision No 244/2000 to implement its decision. The failure is on the grounds of the Romanian Competition Council, being an administrative authority lacks legislative powers.
2002
February The Romanian Competition Council loses (on the same grounds) its challenge regarding EGO 75 at the Romanian Supreme Court.
May
May Signing of the Romania–Sweden BIT.
June S.C. Starmill S.R.L. and S.C. Multipac obtain a permanent investor certificate for EGO 75.
2004
April
Romania–Sweden BIT enters into force.
August
Romania repeals all economic incentives (including 'EGO 75') to ensure its legislation complies with EU state aid rules. This means that EGO 75 is terminated four years earlier than the 10 years it was intended to.
April 25, 2005
February
Revocation of EGO 75 takes effect.
April
Signing of the Accession Treaty to the European Union of Romania and Bulgaria.
July
Micula and its companies raise claims against Romania for revoking EGO 24.4 years ahead of time.
1 January 2007
The Accession Treaty to the European Union of Romania enters into force
2008
September
Micula Arbitration Tribunal Decision on Jurisdiction and Admissibility
2013
December
Micula Final Award

(continued)

(continued)

2014	
February	
Miculas turns to Bucharest Court of the first instance to enforce the Final Award.	
March	
An executor is put in place to secure the payment by Romania of 80 per cent of the Award. Romania pays part of the Award (about 76 million euro) by offsetting tax debts for SC European Food SA.	
April	
Romania unsuccessfully applies for the annulment and stay of the Final Award to ICSID ad-hock annulment committee and (also unsuccessfully) asks the Bucharest Court to stay the execution of the Award.	
May	
The Commission intervenes by ordering a Suspension injunction, *Micula I (EU)*, of the payments and to annul the execution of the Award and asks for the Romanian court to send a referral for a preliminary ruling to the CJEU.	
September	
The ICSID annulment ad hoc committee lifts the stay of enforcement of the Final Awa, d and the Bucharest Court supports this. The Bucharest Court also refuses to send a referral from the CJEU on the matter.	
October	
The Commission opened a formal investigation procedure on the matter.	
Romania starts payments to the Claimants (of about 80 million EURO) without notifying the Commission.	
November	
After refusal by the Bucharest Court to stay the payment of the Final Award, Romania appeals this decision to the Bucharest Court of Appeal.	
2015	
January	
The court-appointed executor starts seizing some Romanian assets (about 2 million EURO).	
February	
Bucharest Court of Appeal lifts the Bucharest Courts decision and suspends the forced execution of the Award.	
March	
The Romanian Ministry of Finance voluntarily transfers 106,5 million EURO (the remaining amount of the Award) to an account assigned to the claimants. The account is blocked until the Commission authorises the release of the funds on it.	
EU Commission publishes its *Decision State aid SA.38517 (2014/C) (ex 2014/NN) implemented by Romania—Arbitral Award Micula v Romania of 11 December 2013* prohibiting the Implementation of the Arbitral Award.	
Miculas ask for confirmation of the Award in USA Courts, District Court for the District of Columbia in Washington DC and District Court for the Southern District of New York.	
May	
The New York Court Decides (on Claimant's Motion) to Confirm the ICSID Award.	
The US District Court for the District of Columbia holds that the *Micula Award* cannot be enforced	

(continued)

(continued)

enforcement of an ICSID award requires a plenary action
August
Opinion and Order of the US Court on Romania's Motion to Vacate and/or Stay Judgment and EU Commission's Amicus Brief Motion.
September
Opinion of the US District Court for the Southern District of New York.
November
Viorel Micula (*Micula IV (EU)*) appeals to the CJEU to reverse the Commissions State aid decision and allow the enforcement of the *Micula Award.*
2016
January
The Brussels Court of First Instance decides that the *Micula Final Award* cannot be executed by a Member State as it violates the Commission's State aid decision.
Ioan ('*Micula V (EU),* 2019) appeals to the CJEU to reverse the Commissions State aid decision and allow the enforcement of the *Micula Award.*
February
The ad hoc *Micula* tribunal declines Romania's request for annulment of the Final Award (Decision on Annulment).
2017
January
Decision of the UK High Court of Justice on Romania's Request to Set Aside the Registration of the ICSID Award (*Micula I (UK)*, 2017)
June
London High Court Rejects Applicants' Request for a Security Order
October
Court of Appeals of the Second Circuit of the USA decision rejecting enforcement of ICSID Awards against foreign states in Oct 2017.
November
Miculas seek enforcement of the Final award in the District of Columbia courts in Washington, DC, Civil Action No. 17-CV-2332
2018
July
Judgment of the English Court of Appeal - 27 Jul 2018 staying the enforcement of the *Micula Final Award* as the case is pending for the CJEU (GC).
December
The Commission refers Romania to the CJEU for failing to fulfil its Treaty obligations as it has not fully recovered unlawful State aid to Micula claimants. (about 92 million EURO)
2019
January
The Nacka District Court in Stockholm holds that the *Micula Final Award* cannot be enforced by a Member State as it violates the Commission's State aid decision.
March
Brussels Court of Appeal suspended the enforcement of the *Micula Final Award* as the case is pending for the CJEU(GC). Further, the Brussels Court of Appeal requested a referral from the CJEU on the impact of *Achmea* on the Member States' obligation to enforce arbitral awards.

(continued)

(continued)

June
The General Court of the CJEU in *Micula V (EU)* annuls the Commission State aid decision due to technical issues. According to GC, the Commission was not the correct authority to enforce the state aid rules before Romania's accession to the EU. Instead, it was within the competence of the Romanian Competition Authority. Because the Commission had not properly separated pre- and post-accession state aid, the case fell on technicalities. The GC, however, did not dispute that the Award at least partially constituted illegal State aid.
September
The Commission appeals the General Courts decision to the European Court of Justice. Application: OJ C 348 from 14.10.2019, p.14 case *C-638/19 P - Commission v European Food and Others* (2022).
The United States District Court for the District of Columbia allows the enforcement of *Micula Award* in *Ioan Micula , et al., v. Goverment of Romania, Case No. 17-cv-02332 (APM)* September 11, 2019 (*Micula VI (USA)*
2020
February
The UK Supreme Court allows the enforcement of *Micula Award* in *Micula and others v Romania* [2020] UKSC 5, 19 February 2020 (*Micula UK3*).
2022
January
The European Court of Justice (Grand Chamber) judgement case *C-638/19 P - Commission v European Food and Others* (2022) sets aside the General Courts decision *Micula V (EU)*. Contrary to the GC the ECJ held that the applicable timepoint for determining if EU law was applicable to an arbitral award is the date when the award was adopted. Because the *Micula Award* was adopted post-accession, the Commission had the competence to decide on state aid under Article 108 TFEU. Therefore, the General Court must now complete their analysis on the Commission's decision and the extent of illegal state aid received by Micula's & others.

The manufacturer's authorised representative in the EU is Springer Nature Customer Service Centre GmbH, Europaplatz 3, 69115 Heidelberg, Germany. If you have any concerns regarding our products, please contact ProductSafety@springernature.com

Printed and bound by CPI Group (UK) Ltd, Croydon, CR0 4YY
30/09/2026
02225493-0010